August 8, 20.

To Mickey

With Warmest Regards,

Terry

THE GREAT CACTUS WAR

by Terry Domico

Green Flash Books

The Great Cactus War

For information contact the publisher at: *greenflashbooks@usa.com*

Green Flash Books is an imprint of Turtleback Books Publishing, Ltd., Post Office Box 2012, Friday Harbor, Washington, 98250 USA.

Ordering Information:
Visit our webpage at **www.greenflashbooks.com**
Trade discounts are available.

Domico, Terry (1946-   )
    The Great Cactus War / Terry Domico
    Includes text notes, bibliography, and index.

ISBN-10: 1-883385-17-2
ISBN-13: 978-1-883385-17-0
Library of Congress Control Number: 2018902762

1. Botanical History. 2. History-Australia-weeds-prickly pear cactus. 3. History-United States of America-Luther Burbank-spineless cactus. 4. Invasive insects- Cactoblastis moth. 5. Biological control of prickly pear cactus. 6. Biological control of Cactoblastis. 7. History of cochineal.

Printed in the United States of America.

10 9 8 7 6 5 4 3 2 1

Other Books
by Terry Domico

WILD HARVEST

BEARS OF THE WORLD

KANGAROOS: THE MARVELOUS MOB

THE NATURE OF BORNEO

THE LAST THYLACINE

*NATURAL AREAS OF THE
SAN JUAN ISLANDS*

Dedication

To Henry and Pavel
for your unfailing
encouragement
from separate continents.

Table of Contents

Acknowledgments

Few books are entirely the work of one person and this book is no exception to that general rule. There were scores of generous people who helped me in this project, many of them unknowingly.

I would like to extend thanks to them all, especially Laura Helmuth, formerly at Smithsonian Magazine, who started me on the long path to create this book; to Amy Greenfield, whose own book, *A Perfect Red*, inspired me to investigate the rest of prickly-pear's story; to Isobel Baldwin, Anne Thorpe, Robert Baldwin and Janice Perry, relatives of Alan Dodd who freely shared their information to help me understand who he really was; to Drs. Jim Carpenter and Stephen Hight for wonderful research road trips and great conversations about the nature of life; to Dr. George Fox for your backseat company during our road trip through Argentina; to Laura Varone and Dr. Guillermo Logarzo, who welcomed me to FuEDEI; to Mike Chuk, Peter and Liz Clark, Ross McPherson and Peter Kleinsmith, who are combatants in the "new" cactus war; to John Eggleston for freely sharing your information about Jondaryan Station during the dark days of the "pear"; to Bob Hornback for discussions concerning Luther Burbank; to Dr. John Hosking for our plant-collecting field trips and for your comments on portions of the text; to Grace Lithgow and Dr. Rachel McFadyen; to Geoff Monteith for your welcome to the inner sanctums of the Queensland Museum and for sharing ever more information about Alan Dodd and John Mann; to Christopher Nicholes for sharing your father's book;

to Bruce Coward for sharing your family photos; to Gary Ryan, Jeff Ajani, Percy Picton, Walter Schroder, Peter Elverton, Thomas Foster, Barry Sinclair, Margaret Cameron, Anne Croft, Merlene Coates-Freeman, Betty Little, Malcolm Kirk, Alan and Lori Melbourne, Ian and Karen Nixon; Lynn Taylor, Libby Robertson of "Satur House," Bob Kirk, Bob and Clarence Kerr, Eric Geldard, Les Tanner, Esmé Davis, Harold Rennich, Marie Gore, E. Davis with the Chinchilla Historical Museum, Kerry Mulholland and Elizabeth Beeton, who provided photos and information about Ron Mundell, Graham Donnelly and Clarence Ulm; to Craig Walton and Bill Palmer with a special thanks; to Ian and Don Wolski, who brought the persistence of prickly-pear seeds on their farm to my attention; to Katie Lingard, journalist for the Chinchilla News; to Fern Reynolds for your help in organizing my prickly-pear talks; to Peter Gunders, ABC Radio; a most grateful thanks to the reference and research librarians diligently working at the Australian National Library in Canberra, especially Ralph Sanderson, whose "lateral thinking" saved the day, and to Shelly Grant and Jenny Higgins; to the New South Wales State Library in Sydney, and to Simon Farley of the John Oxley Library in Brisbane, who went far beyond the call of duty in helping me locate obscure images and reference materials; thanks also to the many other librarians who helped me, including those working at the San Juan Island Library and the Salamander Bay Branch of the Newcastle Library; to Shirley Gun and Chris Berg of the TNC; to Joe Bravada; Rebeca Gutierrez, Maurice Duffel, Faith Campbell, Bill Spitzer, Barron Rector, Robyn Rose and Vanessa McDonough; to Jeff Vaughan for your good humor and participation in many long road trips; a special thanks to Beth Rahe Balas for your comments on the text, and to Eleana Pawl, who helped so much with her editing and gentle guidance in shaping this book.

THE GREAT CACTUS WAR

by Terry Domico

---

*"Little incidents, are, so to speak, the foliage of great events
and are lost in the distance of history."*
... From "Les Misérables" by Victor Hugo (1862)

"CACTUS" = Meaning "ruined," "wrecked," or "spoiled."
... Australian slang

Preface

This is the true story of the greatest plant invasion in human history. Growing seemingly without limits, a type of fleshy cactus known as "prickly-pear" tested the mettle of an entire nation during the first third of the twentieth century and brought thousands of rural dwellers literally to their knees to pray for deliverance. In the process, many of them not only lost the family home to the ravages of this plant, but their farms and livelihood as well.

In 1901, the government of Australia offered a generous reward, valued at nearly three-quarters of a million dollars in today's terms, to anyone who could come up with a practical solution to this crippling plague. Six years later the reward was doubled. And yet, in spite of years of intense effort of both government workers and dedicated individuals, this great green "octopus" continued to spread across the landscape, almost unabated.

At its peak, a thick blanket of cactus averaging from four to six feet and up to thirty feet high (1.2 to 9 m), held within its spiny grip more than sixty million acres. This was a region larger than all of Great Britain or of the combined areas of the American states of New York, New Jersey, New Hampshire, Delaware, Massachusetts, Connecticut, and a large part of Pennsylvania.

For Australia, this loss represented a huge portion of its best farming and dairy land. "It has to be seen to be believed," many reporters of the day insisted. Alarmingly, the "pear" was also estimated to be spreading at a rate of over a million acres per year.

The solution to the problem, when it came, was exquisitely

simple. A small moth with the big name of *Cactoblastis cactorum* was discovered in Argentina and introduced to the prickly-pear. The moth's cactus-eating larvae did the rest, performing what seemed a miracle to nearly everyone, including the scientists who had discovered it.

By the end of World War II, the problem with the "pear" was just a memory. It had been eaten into submission. The general public of Australia, and of the world, soon forgot about the battle with cactus in the tumult of post WWII recovery. However, recent observations in Australia are indicating that the cactus war may not be completely over. Then too, *Cactoblastis* - "the little hero that saved Australia" - has moved on to new territory and might be poised to create a new natural disaster of its own.

****

The idea of doing a book about the great Australian prickly-pear war came gradually. Two developments convinced me of the need for a comprehensive work on the subject. The first was researching and writing a report in 2012 for *Smithsonian* concerning the invasion of *Cactoblastis* into the United States.

Also, back in Australia, a new kind of cactus plague was brewing on the outback landscape. I first heard about it when an ABC (Australian Broadcasting Corporation) radio news report mentioned in 2014 that the Australian Parliament had just upgraded invasive cactuses to "weeds of national significance."

A few months later, when a friend and I drove up to north-central Queensland on a five-week-long road trip to investigate a regional cactus outbreak, we were shocked by what we saw. Thick stands of cactus, apparently having been fortified by the processes of natural hybridization, were taking over the landscape and nothing seemed to be able to stop it. The story of the Great Cactus War, I now realized, was no longer just ancient history but something current and compelling.

I first encountered this notion of a war on cactus more than twenty-five years ago. At that time I was in Australia, working on a biological survey assignment that would ultimately result in the publication of my book, *Kangaroos: The Marvelous Mob*, (Facts on File, 1993) and a special report that helped to quell a United States congressional proposal to place sanctions on certain Australian imports into America until the commercial harvesting of kangaroos was stopped.

As a method to study species diversity and relative abundance over a broad region, I chose the simple expedient of using roads as transects and road-killed kangaroos for my data points. Over weeks and months of driving and stopping to examine dead kangaroos along the way, this technique eventually gave me a general idea of the "kangaroo landscape." It also brought me into nearly every little outback village in eastern Australia.

One summer day near a small hamlet located in south-central Queensland, I pulled my car off the road seeking to park it in the deep shade of a large tree. It was "stinking hot" (as the locals termed it) and I was grateful for the respite. Within a minute after shutting off the car's engine, I was asleep in a heat-induced coma. When I awoke later, somewhat refreshed, I noticed a faded sign on an unpainted wooden shed that stood nearby: "Cactoblastis Museum."

Intrigued, I got out of the car and approached the door of the shed. It was locked. At that moment a very thin old man opened the door in a neighboring residence and called out, "Won't be a minute!" After introducing himself as the museum's caretaker, he unlocked the shed door and ushered me in.

Scattered over dust and cobweb-covered shelves and tables were dozens of cardboard boxes - some open, others taped shut. Here and there leaned a rusty tool or implement of a sort that I had never seen before. Stopping at one cluttered table, I perused an open box containing letters and publications, being careful not to provoke any lurking spiders with my fingers.

One of the items that I found in that box was a 1931 annual

report from the Queensland Prickly Pear Land Commission. The report's opening sentence read, "The year just closed has witnessed the greatest advance yet made in the campaign for the eradication of prickly-pear." The paragraph went on ,". . . large areas of land formerly abandoned to the pest were now, through the work of Cactoblastis, being rapidly cleared of the pear and being made available for resettlement."

An old newspaper clipping slipped from the table to the floor. Picking it up, I saw that it was from the September 7th, 1936, *Brisbane Daily Telegraph*. Its bold headline screamed "*THE PRICKLY PEAR MENACE HAS DISAPPEARED FROM STATE: Minister Tells of Cactoblastis's Great Work.*" Fascinated, I read the entire text and then fished out another clipping that was still in the box.

I was brought up short when the old man who had been standing quietly (perhaps impatiently) in the doorway all the while suddenly announced, "If you would like to read any more of that stuff, take 'em with you!"

"You sure it's okay?" I asked. Assured that it was indeed okay, I picked up a large dust-covered envelope and proceeded to stuff it with the aforementioned report and various other papers and news tidbits that I gathered up. When I returned to my car, I had more than enough material for several evenings' reading back in my lonely outback camp. It was interesting stuff.

Nearly a year had elapsed before I chanced to go past that old shed again. I parked in the shade of the same tree, but to my surprise the shed and its dilapidated sign were gone. When I inquired at the house, I learned that the old man had died. Apparently, the need for a museum about the war against prickly-pear had died along with him. With my tattered envelope full of clippings and reports being the only tangible evidence that the shed had ever existed, I drove on down the road to complete the work on my kangaroo project.

Eventually, when I realized the historical significance of these documents, I donated them to the state library, after duly making photocopies of them all. (I still have those photocopies stuffed in the same old envelope.) I do not know what happened to the rest of the contents of the shed, including that collection of strange tools.

During the nearly five-year-long research phase of this book, I traveled over 40 thousand miles (65,300 km) and accumulated nearly 110 thousand pages of documents and photographs. I examined and photocopied hundreds of records relating to people's personal struggles with the cactus plague in Australia.

To locate this material, I frequented numerous libraries and repositories of information in both Australia and the United States. I also visited dozens of governmental offices, relevant historical locations, laboratories, searched the internet, and went into the field with research scientists in Australia and the United States. My travels also took me to Argentina - the place where *Cactoblastis* had first been discovered - where I met and accompanied a team of American scientists who were there to study this insect in its native habitat.

I also had the honor of examining the contents of fourteen boxes of historic records from the (Australian) Commonwealth Prickly Pear Board and Sherwood Laboratories. The material had been narrowly rescued from disappearing as simply "old rubbish" when the laboratory closed permanently in late 2010. (I would like to give special thanks to Craig Walton and Dr. Bill Palmer, who helped me gain access to those very important boxes!) And then, there was the matter of collecting stories from the people who had been directly affected by the great Australian cactus plague.

Information leading to these folks often came from chance encounters: people that I happened to meet on a train or even at a highway rest stop. One summer, in the very heart of the former prickly-pear region, I delivered a series of "power-point" lectures on the history and causes of the Great Cactus War from town to town. The talks were well attended and through them, I discovered several more "survivors of the cactus."

On several occasions, a member of the audience would duck out and soon return to present me with a bundle of old letters tied up with string or a shoe box full of old photos. One dear lady, after handing me one of these boxes, exclaimed, "I've been hiding this thing under my bed for years and years. I didn't know why. . . until now." Many of those letters and documents spoke of the intense but futile work of battling the pear with nothing but hand-tools and the heartbreaking loss of a way of life when entire families were forced off the land.

In total, I found more than a dozen informants who could speak about the days when the "pear" dominated the landscape. Most of them were in their late 90s; one was over 100 years old. Unfortunately, within a year of my recorded interviews with these folks, more than half of them had passed away.

****

Researching the history of prickly-pear has been remarkably complicated. Most early sources, especially newspaper reports, are anonymous and many other narratives are undated. Although I have made every effort to verify and cross-check the information presented here, it is not possible to be certain of every detail.

This project has taught me the lesson that "history" is more about interpretation than just facts. Every police detective knows that if an event happens in front of ten eyewitnesses, there will be ten different versions of that event. It is the detective's job to listen to each one of those accounts, interpret them, and write as accurate an account as possible of what had happened.

With that same goal in mind, this book attempts to focus a very complicated and often poorly documented series of interrelated events into a thematic narrative that graphically tells the story of prickly-pear and Australia's Great Cactus War.

At the moment, as I contemplate all the varied work that this project entailed, I am holding a 32 gigabyte memory stick between my thumb and forefinger. It is a commonplace item that nowadays costs less than the average lunch to purchase. However, it remains a complete marvel to me.

Stored in this small device are thousands of photographs and copies of old newspaper clippings, nearly 150 hours of voice recordings from various interviews, two 20-minute-long movies, years of correspondence from around the world, a searchable database with more than 1,200 subject headings, and the entire text of this book that you are about to read. Like my great-grandfather must have felt when he first beheld the electric light, I hadn't imagined something like this would exist in my lifetime.

****

Since this book has been produced for a varied international audience, I have included both metric and statute measurements to the text. Also the value of costs, historically expressed in pounds sterling, has been updated to its approximate modern equivalent in US dollars at the time of this book's publication based on the "Pre-decimal Inflation Calculator" of the Reserve Bank of Australia and the "Consumer Price Index" of the Federal Reserve Bank of Minneapolis.

Chapter 1 : From Whence It Came
...and the Secret of Grana

Oh, Columbus! When you came home
From your voyage on the ocean blue,
Although no record exists today,
Did you bring along the prickly-pear too?
"Never mind! Never mind!" history will say
To anyone who bothers to care,
Soon cactus grew in Spain, Germany, and China,
And in English gardens so fair.

Although some people value prickly-pear cactus greatly, it has been called the world's most noxious weed by many others. Human beings really seem to have a love/hate relationship with this plant just about wherever it is found. Unfortunately, much of Australia's experience is in the "hate" category and reads almost like science fiction. "Ugly green monsters who take root and cover the earth," was how one newspaper graphically described prickly-pear's advance across the Australian landscape during the latter 19th and early 20th centuries. Indeed, it is difficult to visualize the virtually impenetrable mass that this invasive plant eventually became.

In many districts, roads were reduced to mere trails hemmed in on either side by solid six to eight foot-high (2-2.4 m) walls of prickly-pear. At the invasion's peak in 1925, the cactus is reported to have dominated more than sixty million acres, including some of Australia's best potential farming and dairy land. Worse yet, it was

1

estimated to still be spreading at a rate of more than a million acres a year.

In the late 1800s, Joseph Maiden, one of Australia's leading early botanists, foresaw the coming crisis and set about collecting and studying the plant in its various forms. He describes one such encounter:

> With a full knowledge of the seriousness of this pest and with the exercise of every caution, I failed to get my specimens without shaking spinules [small needle-like spines] onto my clothes, and was reminded of the trip for nearly a fortnight [two weeks] in consequence. I also stepped onto one of the spines, which went completely through the boot-upper and drew blood. I mention this to show that it is a plant which can protect itself, and that it is not to be trifled with.

Being a non-native plant, just how did prickly-pear become established in Australia? And by what process did it manage to tyrannize so much of that country's rural population? To answer these questions we need to begin at the beginning: the original European discovery of the plant in its native land.

DID COLUMBUS ALSO DISCOVER PRICKLY-PEAR?

Prickly-pear is a type of cactus that is indigenous only to the "New World" (North and South America). It is found primarily in the southern United States, Mexico, South America and the islands of the Caribbean.

Before Christopher Columbus and his ambitious partisans arrived, prickly-pear (or any cactus for that matter) was a completely unknown plant in Europe. It was a very familiar sight, however, to the people who historically lived in the civilizations of the original prickly-pear habitat.

Ever since the arrival of human beings to these regions, perhaps 20,000 years ago, prickly-pear was a staple food, along with maize, beans, and agave. In most of those ancient cultures the cactus had also been used as a source of fermented drink and medicine.

The selective cultivation of some of prickly-pear's better varieties (those having sweeter fruit and fewer spines) is thought to have been practiced for thousands of years. This seems to have led to the creation of a domestic, often nearly spineless, species known as *Opuntia ficus-indica*, the "Indian fig."

Apparently, the Indian fig has been farmed for so long that its biogeographic and evolutionary origins are now obscure. From analyses of DNA sequences, it appears that the Indian fig may be a close relative of a group of wild treelike prickly-pears from central and southern Mexico. But the results of genetic research are not conclusive.

Another useful item that some of these native cactus farmers produced was a brilliant red dye extracted from certain insect parasites that live exclusively on prickly-pear. As discussed in more detail later, this scarlet coloring known as "cochineal" (after the cochineal insect) would eventually play a significant role in the histories of both the Spanish and British empires. Long before Columbus, however, cochineal dye had already become very important to the economies of the indigenous cultures.

"Like other ancient Mexicans, the Aztecs prized bright colors and for them red held special allure," writes Amy Butler Greenfield in *A Perfect Red*, her book on the history of cochineal dye. "They collected staggering amounts of the dyestuff as tribute from the chief centers of production . . . modern estimates suggest this may have amounted to over nine tons of cochineal [per year], or more than a billion insects." Further south in Peru, instead of demanding raw dyestuff, governors of the Inca Empire regularly exacted from its subjects tribute in the form of finished cloth richly dyed in cochineal and other brilliant colors.

There's little doubt that Columbus and his crew were the first Europeans to see a cactus of any kind. These plants are a conspicuous part of the vegetation of the Caribbean islands that they visited. Haiti, for instance, hosts some thirty species of cactus

3

including the bizarre "Turk's cap cactus" (*Melocactus* spp.) and even a tree-sized prickly-pear. It seems logical that plants as obvious and strange as these would have most certainly piqued the explorer's curiosity. If they did, however, no mention of it has been found.

Christopher Columbus was an Italian explorer who was essentially "hired" in 1491 by Queen Isabella of Spain (after much convincing of the Queen and her more reluctant husband, Ferdinand) to discover a westward trade route from Spain to Asia and India. Being more direct, this proposed sailing route would give the Spaniards the competitive edge for commerce in the region. At that time European traders had to sail around the horn of Africa in order to reach Asia by sea. . . a long and perilous voyage.

However, as we all know, instead of charting a new sailing route, Columbus discovered a richly endowed continent - a hitherto unknown "New World." This was an event that would eventually influence, in one way or another, nearly every species of life on earth.

Upon Columbus's return to Spain (now a national hero), he was immediately summoned to appear in Barcelona before the king and queen. Ever the showman, in his entourage Columbus brought with him six native American "Indians," who were then duly baptized in the presence of the royalty. Then he brought out a variety of gifts from the new land: gold and silver trinkets, stuffed birds and animals, live parakeets, and strange plants.

Very likely, prickly-pear was one of those "strange plants" that Columbus presented to the royal court, but we'll never know that for sure. Certainly the new plants would have been passed on to the Royal Botanic Gardens for safekeeping and propagation. But when I inquired at that venerable institution, the staff could find no records of it.

In fact, Columbus's entire original journal detailing his first voyage was lost sometime after being forwarded to the king and queen. The only accurate record of the voyage that exists today is a partly summarized, partly quoted copy written some forty years later by Fray Bartolomé de La Casas, a Dominican friar and historian.

4

(La Casas had access to Columbus's original journal, before it disappeared, but there is no mention of a cactus-like plant in his writings.) Then La Casas's own manuscript also mysteriously vanished for about 250 years, but then thankfully resurfaced in a private library.

A PRICKLY AND PROFITABLE IMMIGRANT

Following his initial voyage of discovery, Columbus sailed back to the "New World" three more times, thus paving the way for European settlement of the Americas. Much to his bitter disappointment, he never did find that shortcut to Asia. But, by the time Columbus's sailing career was over, prickly-pear cactus (whether by his hand or by others) had found its way securely into Europe.

Because of prickly-pear's bizarre appearance (when compared to most known land plants), many 16th century botanists made special mention of it in their notes. It took the scientific and scholarly writers of Europe nearly three centuries to work out just where to place this weird plant in the catalogue of living things.

During this time, prickly-pear didn't wait around for anyone's "go-ahead." It quickly became naturalized in many of the places where it had been introduced, eventually spreading throughout the southern part of the European continent and across many of the Mediterranean islands. When the Moors were expelled from Spain in the early 1600s, they took prickly-pear with them into northern Africa. Because of its sweet fruit and usefulness as a living fence, the plant was welcomed everywhere it went throughout this entire period.

Perhaps the first illustration and discussion of prickly-pear to be published in Europe appeared in 1526 in a comprehensive history of the Spanish colonies in the American "Indies." This was followed by several more 16th century publications, including the prominent *The Herball or Historie of Plants* in 1597 by English physician and gardener John Gerarde.

Intrigued by this plant's most unusual form, Gerarde described the cactus, still known only as the "Indian fig," as a "tree made of leaves without body or boughs." He also mentions that it had already been brought into Italy, Spain, England and other countries but had not yet borne fruit in England, "although I have bestowed great pains and cost in keeping it from the injury of our cold climate."

Another British publication, *The Gardener's Dictionary*, noted in 1735 that the Indian fig, ". . . had been a long time in England and is the most common sort in Europe." The book lists eleven kinds of Indian fig. More importantly, they were also observed to grow wild around Naples in great abundance. (This may be our first preview of prickly-pear's dark side as a potential pest.)

Due to their novelty, prickly-pears were first established in botanical gardens all over Europe. (For example, a 1651 catalogue of plants from the royal botanical gardens in Poland lists a prickly-pear.) From those horticultural centers, the cactuses soon found a home in the gardens of the aristocracy.

Only the wealthiest could afford to have cacti in their collections, and a few noblemen featured prickly-pear in their roof gardens. The formidable spines, gorgeous flowers, and strange forms of these plants were irresistible attractions then, and still are today.

Although cactus collecting (of all species) continued to be an expensive passion indulged in mostly by rich European plant amateurs well into the early 20th century, it wasn't long after prickly-pear's arrival into Europe that ordinary peasants were planting Indian figs in the unused corners of their farms.

In northern Europe, prickly-pears needed a hothouse and loving care to survive the winter. But in southern Europe, especially around the Mediterranean, the cactus simply thrived. It was soon flourishing in many places that have a warm climate, such as in the south of France, southern Italy, along the Struma River in Bulgaria, in southern Portugal, eastern and southern Spain, in Greece, and on the islands of Malta and Sicily.

The environment on Sicily was particularly suitable for cultivating prickly-pear. By the mid-1800s, they were being grown there on large plantations as an important fresh-fruit crop. Yields of up to twenty-two tons of fruit per hectare (about 2½ acres) were common. One visiting French agriculturist after having seen the abundance of production in 1840 wrote:

> Prickly-pear is the manna, the providence of Sicily. . .
> The peasants are fed entirely on these fruits from the
> moment at which they come to maturity, for as long
> as they remain on the plant; they consume twenty-five
> or thirty of them each day. Sicily fattens during those
> four months; when this is past, fasting begins.

In total, 20 species of prickly-pear have been naturalized and are now growing wild in Europe. Although two very hardy species can be found in the low-lying valleys of the Alps, the most widely established types are restricted to the milder Mediterranean region.

After nearly 500 years of growing on rocky hillsides and being used as dividing walls between fields, prickly-pears have become so much a part of the tradition and agriculture around the Mediterranean provinces that local people frequently believe them to be native plants. Some of these cacti are even reported to be growing next to Greek and Roman ruins (a peculiar juxtaposition to those in the know).

An enduring botanical curiosity, prickly-pear was soon spread to many other nations of the world, perhaps in large part by sailors carrying its fruit on long voyages to prevent scurvy. Prickly-pear was first recorded in China in 1625. Today in China at least 30 species of prickly-pear are cultivated, of which four have naturalized and grow wild in the southern and southwestern regions.

Several centuries ago, the Indian fig also became a permanent part of the landscape in the "Land of Israel." Hedges of these spiny plants protected fields from the unwanted attentions of wandering livestock, and their sweet fruit was eagerly eaten by their owners.

Prickly-pear is also common in other parts of the Middle East and in such north African countries as Egypt, Libya, Saudi Arabia, and Jordan.

MADAGASCAR'S CACTUS ADVENTURES

In a pattern that was to be repeated in many other places around the globe, the introduction of prickly-pear into a new country often led to direct changes in the course of that nation's history. What happened in Madagascar, the world's fourth largest island, is both unique and typical of many of these transformations.

Madagascar was not known to Europe until the year 1500 when a Portuguese ship making its way to India was blown off course. The ship's captain, Diogo Dias, became the first European to land there. However, not much outside attention would be given to this intriguing place (other than by pirates and slave traders) for nearly another century and a half.

Then in the mid-1600s, the French began to establish a line of trading posts along Madagascar's east coast. To protect their interests they also built a number of forts, but these were often attacked and destroyed by the native people.

In 1769 at the coastal fort of Fort Dauphin (now the town of Tolagnaro), the resolute defenders came up with the clever idea of establishing an impregnable barrier of cactus on the vulnerable seaside of the fort. To create this defensive wall, propagules of a rather nasty South American prickly-pear (*Opuntia monocantha*) were requisitioned and duly planted. Unlike most of its predecessors, Fort Dauphin survived until well into the next century.

By the early 1800s, prickly-pear was also protecting gardens and farms from animals and thieves all across the southern part of Madagascar. This useful cactus had been adopted and rapidly dispersed by the Malagasy natives.

One indigenous group, the formerly nomadic cattle-raising Mahafale, ultimately embraced several species of prickly-pear as

8

important elements of their culture. The women harvested the fruit for their families to eat and sold the surplus as a cash crop. The men singed the cactus's succulent pads over a fire to remove the thorns and then fed them to their cattle.

Rather than continuing to migrate in pursuit of water and pasture during the long dry season, the Mahafale had turned to the moisture-rich prickly-pear to keep their stock alive. To this day several thousand of the Mahafale still maintain cactus plantations for stock feed, and living fences of prickly-pear surround their corrals and villages.

The French eventually annexed Madagascar and declared it a colony in 1897. During the early days of colonial rule, those numerous dense stands of prickly-pear that covered considerable portions of the southern island allowed the indigenous people to hide from French authorities. . . in particular the tax collectors.

In due time, prickly-pear became a focal point in the relationship between the colonists and the native people. Many French residents became increasingly hostile towards the cactus, viewing it as an evil foe that aided native disobedience. But others argued, more reasonably, that it was a vital plant for pastoralists and their cattle.

The issue came to a head in the early 1920s when the French colonial government introduced a tiny scale insect to control the cactus. This resulted in the rapid destruction of vast groves of prickly-pear that were being used for food and fodder. As a consequence, this loss appears to have led to a severe famine that affected most of the indigenous people in the region.

Today, both that original prickly-pear and two varieties of a more-recently introduced species, *Opuntia ficus-indica* (the Indian fig), can be found in southern Madagascar and famine appears to be a thing of the past.

That small insect which was so devastating to the prickly-pear in this region was actually a species of cochineal (*Dactylopius ceylonicus*). Since cochineals are very closely linked to the history of prickly-pear, we really should get acquainted with these little bugs.

9

SO WHAT IS COCHINEAL?

Like prickly-pears, cochineals are native only to North and South America. They feed almost exclusively on prickly-pear. (*Opuntia* and *Cylindopuntia* spp.) Of the ten or eleven recognized species of cochineal insects, all are parasitic and each has a very specific range of cactus host species. (As you will see later, this "specificness" plays a very important role in prickly-pear history.)

Cochineals are in the same insect order as cicadas, whiteflies, and aphids. They are soft-bodied, oval-shaped, and usually range in size from a grain of barley to that of a dried pea depending on the species. Cochineals penetrate the prickly-pear's cuticle with their beak-like mouth parts and feed on its juices. A heavy infestation of these insects can quickly kill a cactus.

Mature males and females look very different from one another. The adult male is a small short-lived insect equipped with a pair of transparent wings and long "tail" filaments. It looks a bit like a tiny mayfly, and like the mayfly it does not feed.

The adult female, on the other hand, does not develop wings. She is sessile - permanently attached by her proboscis to a single spot on the plant. The active male is the one who "comes a-calling." Once she has "settled in," her legs shrink and become useless. Her shape becomes roly-poly. She soon secretes a fine, white, waxy protective coat that resembles a bit of wool or cotton fluff. This covering may function both as insulation during cold nights and an "entangling" deterrent to potential predators.

The eggs, laid beneath the female's body, usually hatch within a few hours into tiny six-legged "crawlers" that resemble baby ticks. During her lifetime, a female cochineal insect can produce from 300 to 400 eggs, though over 1000 have often been recorded. Through a clever reproductive process known as parthenogenesis (literally meaning "without beginning") the eggs are fertile even without her having mated.

Newly hatched male and female crawlers are at first indistinguishable from one another, but their differing behavior soon sorts them out. The male crawler moves about the plant freely as it grows, frequently inserting and withdrawing its proboscis to feed. Finally it spins an oval silky white cocoon before emerging as an adult.

The female crawler, however, usually selects a permanent position within a day or two and is fixed there for the rest of her life. Although several generations of insects can occur during the year, an individual female may occasionally live as long as six months or so.

If you were to squash one of those females between your fingers, a splash of vivid crimson (redder than red) would instantly stain your skin. This is carminic acid, a chemical produced by the insect to help protect it from predators and parasites. It is also the source of what was once considered the world's most important dye. Ironically, the zealous pursuit to possess the source of that dye eventually led to the prickly-pear's greatest advances in territory around the globe.

It is not known who were the first people to discover and make use of this bright red animal dye. Plant-based colorants have been in use for millennia - perhaps for as long as people have been wearing articles of clothing or making useful objects. A daub of pigment or a patterned combination of colors most likely enhanced the value of an article by giving it special meaning, at least to its creator or owner. Perhaps this process was the early beginnings of what we call "art."

We do know that along the arid coastal region of Peru, pre-Inca civilizations were using dyes as early as 500 BC. Dye analysis on ancient Peruvian textiles has revealed the presence of cochineal. In fact, domestication of the cochineal insect is suspected to have begun in Peru. But like the vague historical record of the domestic prickly-pear known as "Indian fig," the chronology of cochineal's past is similarly blurred. Yet, it is inextricably linked; cochineal is traditionally cultivated on Indian fig.

Though all species of cochineal are known to yield a bright red color, it is the larger domestic variety that produces the most dye in proportion to its dry weight and is of the best quality. This domesticated insect, known to scientists as *Dactylopius coccus*, is more than twice the size of its wild cousins. It is also a rather delicate creature, requiring very particular attention during its cultivation. A sudden frost or thunderstorm can quickly destroy it. Consequently, it has never been found living in the wild.

In the region of today's Mexico, dried cochineal was carried by Aztec merchants to the southern limits of that province and beyond into neighboring Guatemala. Here it was traded for items as varied as quetzal plumes, jaguar skins, and amber. It is obvious that cochineal was widely used and highly valued.

During the Spanish conquest of the New World during the early 16th century, the "conquistadors" (as they called themselves) became greatly impressed by the wonderful colors of Aztec textiles. They soon encountered Aztec artisans who used the red cochineal pigment for both dyeing and painting, and they observed huge quantities of cochineal pigment for sale in city marketplaces.

ENTER OUR MOST ROYAL RED

The Spanish called the dyestuff "grana cochinilla." *Cochinilla* is derived from the Latin word *coccinus*, meaning "scarlet-colored." The Spanish word *grana* means "seed" or "grain," which is what the dried insect material most resembles. Our English word "cochineal" was derived from *cochinilla*.

This new dyestuff generated a great deal of interest. Although it resembled kermes, (the exceedingly-expensive red dye which was still in vogue back in Europe), cochineal was even more brilliantly colored.

Scarlet or crimson fabrics could be acquired and worn only by the very wealthiest members of European society, who could afford them. A 1438-1439 accounting of King Henry VI's wardrobe testifies that his <u>cheapest</u> article of scarlet clothing cost more than £14 sterling. For that same amount of money you could have purchased nearly 6,000 pounds (2,720 kilos) of Flemish cheese or 1,100 bottles of good quality Rhine wine at the Antwerp market.

By contrast, a successful Flemish master-mason with two journeyman stonecutters in his employ would have paid nearly three full years of his wages to acquire the same item. To acquire the most expensive scarlet English woolen broadcloth from Coggeshall in Essex, this middle-class tradesman would had to have coughed up more than five and a half years of his income.

Word of this new red dyestuff soon reached Charles V, the young aspiring king of Spain who seemed perpetually desperate for new revenue sources. In 1523 Charles is reputed to have sent Hernán Cortés (now the governor of New Spain [Mexico]) a letter instructing him to see if this dyestuff could be exported back to Spain, where it might produce "a great profit for the royal purse." By the end of that year, a consignment of cochineal reached Spain.

It quickly became apparent that "grana cochineal" was far superior to kermes, which was obtained from the Mediterranean oak-tree scale insect (*Kermes vermilio*). Not only did cochineal effect a more intense color than kermes, it had ten to twelve times the dyeing power per ounce of material. Because of this new dye's potent attributes, kermes and most other Old World reds eventually fell out of favor and were seldom used again in the mainstream dye industry.

"Grana cochineal" (or simply "grana"), on the other hand, found a ready market in the dye shops of Europe. After a long-delayed entry into the Native Mexican's quaint cochineal farming industry by the Spanish colonial overlords (due in part to their assumed status as "gentlemen" who preferred to raise cattle, sheep, and traditional European crops), it wasn't long before Mexican agriculture was hard-pressed to keep up with the overseas demand for this amazing dyestuff.

". . . cochineal had become indispensable to the production of high-quality fabric," writes Amy Greenfield. "As early as 1550,

13

many fashionable Europeans were insisting that their red cloth be made with cochineal. Demand grew rapidly over the next few decades, making the dyestuff's conquest unusually swift and complete . . . The priest's red velvet chasuble, the dandy's red satin sleeves, the nobleman's red silken draperies, and the countess's red brocade skirts - all were now colored with cochineal."

Europeans soon found other uses for cochineal, too. In Elizabethan England it was used as a vivid red lipstick and all around the continent artists included it in their kit of pigment mixtures. (Unlike cochineal-dyed cloth, however, most of these paints had the unfortunate tendency to slowly fade when exposed to light.) Also during this era, cochineal found wide use as a medicine, particularly for treating disorders caused by apparent depression. It was even reported to have been added to the meals of mental patients in an attempt to calm them.

MEETING THE DEMAND FOR GRANA

Back in New Spain, the colonial administration was gearing up for the mass production of cochineal. In an uncharacteristically democratic arrangement, the Spanish rulers wisely took a "hands-off" approach to cochineal farming. They entrusted the entire production component of the industry to the indigenous farmers, who knew all the secrets for successfully raising these insects.

Although most of the finished dyestuff came from small Native holdings, large plantations of more than 50,000 cactus plants were also established. In fact, the Native farmers frequently became so preoccupied with the lucrative industry of cochineal cultivation, they often neglected growing maize and other traditional food crops. In the region of Oaxaca alone, as many as 30,000 Natives were employed in the cochineal business.

As might be expected, this disregard of edible crops in favor of rearing cochineal created a very unstable subsistence economy that occasionally resulted in famine. Higher food prices naturally followed food shortages, which in turn stimulated increased crop planting and a corresponding (but only temporary) drop in cochineal production. Like his Spanish counterparts, the profit motive apparently had a strong grip on the Native cochineal farmer.

With the Spanish, "nopal" eventually became the general term for all kinds of prickly-pear, especially the Indian fig. Cactus plantations became known as "nopalerias," and on those farms, vast numbers of the domestic variety of cochineal (*Dactylopius coccus*) were raised. Double the size of their wild cousins, these insects could reach the size of a kidney bean. They also yield a higher quality and greater amount of dye per individual, with a carminic acid concentration (the bright red stuff) between 15 and 20 percent.

The domestic cochineal takes twice as long to complete its life cycle and is less hardy than the wild variety. Instead of the fluffy protective overcoat of the wild form, it has only a fine, waxy powder for a covering. (It is thought that the wild cochineal's cotton-like insulative shroud may help explain their greater climatic tolerance.) Even in a nopaleria dedicated to the raising of grana, the entire process of growing, harvesting, and killing the cochineal insects was a labor-intensive, precise, time-consuming operation that often ended in failure.

First, the nopals had to be planted from cuttings taken from older plants. While prickly-pears can grow in nutritionally-depleted soils, they respond well to fertilizer. For this the Native cochineal farmer often used wood ash and kitchen refuse. After one and a half to three years of growth, depending on the locality, the nopals were ready for "seeding" with cochineal. From then on, the plants were pruned twice a year to promote new growth and remove damaged pads. (The insects do best on young, tender plant material.)

The extremely vulnerable domestic insect colonies also had to be protected from the elements and predators. Live shrubby hedges and mud walls offered protection from wind and dust. The hedges also helped to exclude barnyard fowl which would peck and eat the developing insects. An unseasonable frost or a heavy downpour could also result in massive losses. When frost was expected, fires were sometimes lit. To protect the insects from rainstorms, farmers often constructed temporary shelters. To shield them from the hot sun, large covers of white cloth were erected.

During the winter rainy season, sections of nopal that were well-populated with cochineal were cut away from the mother plant and stored in closed baskets under the roofs of houses. Here the newly-hatched "crawlers" would remain dormant for about three weeks. Then the baskets were opened so that the cochineal could be exposed to light and fresh air for a few months. At the end of the rainy period, they could be reintroduced to the live nopals in the plantation - thus beginning a new cycle of production. On the larger plantations, special long and narrow "over-wintering houses" were sometimes erected.

Great care was taken to harvest the cochineal at the right time. The mature insects could be collected up to three times a year, usually by painstakingly sweeping them with a handheld brush into a waiting basket. A single acre of well-tended nopals could produce up to 200 pounds (91 kilos) of grana a year. Since it takes some 70,000 of these dried bugs to produce just one pound (450 grams) of grana, the yield from one acre represents some 14 million individual insects.

There was always a great deal of variety in the quality of the finished grana. Environmental conditions, the skill of the farmer, and even the method of killing the insects all contributed to its ultimate character. Merely how the insects were killed was often enough to determine the final grade of the product.

"The simplest, and possibly the oldest, method was to spread the insects on mats in the sun," wrote Robin A. Donkin in "Spanish Red," his authoritative study of the cochineal industry. "The results were most satisfactory if the 'baking' was periodically discontinued or the mats were partially shaded, but this meant that the operation might last anything up to two weeks. Nevertheless, sun-drying was usually considered best . . " This process resulted in a product known to the cochineal trade as "grana fina" (meaning fine or excellent), which became the gold standard for the industry.

Hot plates, drying ovens, boiling water and steam were also used to kill the insects. Although these techniques were much quicker, they invariably resulted in a lower grade product. At one point Spanish authorities tried to prohibit these techniques. But these attempts quickly proved unsuccessful; the demand for grana was just too great.

The wild varieties of cochineal were also harvested for a salable but inferior grade of product called "grana silvestre" (literally "woodland cochineal"). Although these insects were much smaller than the domestic variety (and thus yielded a lot less dye for the same collecting effort), they grew completely unattended on the wild nopals (prickly-pears) and could be harvested five or six times a year.

The royal tribute system that the indigenous growers were accustomed to paying to their traditional rulers was not abolished under the Spanish. Instead, tribute became the mainstay of the colonial tax system. For many years the standard annual tribute was set at one and a half pesos (less than a week's income). However, in the cochineal rearing districts, the tribute was often paid in the form of grana. Many private landholders also found additional ways to exact cochineal from their native "subjects." Even so, a lot of the Native cochineal farmers prospered under this new regime.

Although grana in varying amounts was being produced in nearly every community of Mexico's cochineal region, the center of production eventually became focused on the Oaxaca Valley. Perhaps the reason for this is that the land there remained in the hands of a large population of Native peasantry, who were concentrated in medium-sized towns and villages.

By contrast, land in many other parts of the country was usually converted into classic haciendas [ranches] owned by Spaniards of dubious nobility and who regularly exploited the labor of the local Native workers.

Once the cochineal was harvested and processed, it was taken to weigh-stations where government inspectors determined its quality and cleanliness. These authorities also made sure that the cochineal had not been adulterated with other materials (inherently a big problem). It was their pledged duty to insure that the grana being shipped back to Spain was genuine and properly described. (For local use, the Natives formed the cochineal into small cakes or tablets that were apparently not subject to such scrutiny.)

After passing inspection, the sacks of cochineal were sealed and placed in shipping boxes, which were then nailed shut and branded with an official mark. Transported overland on the backs of mules, export-grade grana would eventually arrive in a port city (usually Veracruz) where it awaited shipment across the Atlantic to the port of Seville in Spain.

The sheer amount of grana that was shipped to Spain in the cochineal industry's heyday was mind-boggling. On ten occasions between 1760 and 1782 the cochineal production registered in Oaxaca, alone, exceeded one million pounds [520 metric tons]. The demand for this dyestuff seemed insatiable, and grana soon became the second most lucrative export item (next to silver) to leave Mexico for Europe. It was so highly valued that its current price is said to have been regularly quoted on the London and Amsterdam commodity exchanges.

Seville was a very busy port, especially when the grana convoys arrived from Mexico. The distribution of the dyestuff to other parts of Europe was often handled by merchants of many nationalities. "Foreigners resident in Seville - English, Flemish, French, and men from leading Italian cities - dealt in cochineal and helped finance operations," writes Donkin.

"The product often passed through a dozen or more hands between producer and consumer. Supplies were subject to many vicissitudes, including war and piracy, and prices varied accordingly." Much of this middleman activity ended when the king of Spain enacted laws against trading by foreigners.

A PIRATE'S PLUNDER

Particularly after the demand for cochineal began to outstrip the supply, the cochineal-laden ships that traveled from Mexico to Seville often became the target of pirates and "privateers." Privateers were often just pirates who were officially sanctioned by the government of a country that was at war with Spain. For the most part, that meant England and Holland, who had long held political and religious differences with the Spanish.

In England, after raising the necessary funds to finance a venture, a privateer commander with a stout crew and a fast ship or two was issued a document known as a "letter of marque." This was a contract authorizing the captain to seize any enemy ship in the name of the Crown.

For the English and Dutch raiders, this usually meant overpowering lightly-armed Spanish merchant vessels while avoiding the more dangerous warships which often accompanied them. A "merchantman" lagging far behind a well-guarded fleet was a typical target of these "wolves of the sea."

These maritime operations weren't always conducted by lone wolves, however. During one distinguished operation in 1597, a massive expedition of over a thousand men led by the Earl of Essex captured three Spanish ships sailing from Havana that had fallen behind their convoy.

When the ships were brought back to England a month later as "prizes," the privateers learned to their great joy that they contained more than twenty-seven tons of cochineal. This was enough "to serve this realm for many years," the Queen is said have proclaimed. In truth, it wasn't nearly enough.

Everyone involved in a successful privateering enterprise - financial backers, the Crown, and ship's crew alike - received a share of the booty (albeit a very unequal share).

Pirates, on the other hand, were more democratic and egalitarian in dividing the plunder. Pirates tended to cut out the

19

privateering middlemen, who in place of sanctioning the pirates' endeavors, became their enemies instead.

Regardless of these differences, many tons of cochineal were seized by both pirates and privateers over the years and eventually sold in the commodity market without profiting the Spanish.

UNCLOAKING GRANA'S TRUE IDENTITY

The Spanish, for their part, knew that they had the "golden goose" (that laid scarlet eggs), and they took steps to protect their supply monopoly. One way was to purposely obscure the true nature and source of cochineal. To do so was actually rather easy and resulted in one of the longest-kept industrial secrets of all time (over 200 years).

For starters, the market name for cochineal was "grana." Since this is also the Spanish word for "seed," many of the would-be saboteurs of the status-quo thought that cochineal was a seed or some other plant material. Viewed only with the naked eye it certainly looked like small kernels of some sort.

There were many erroneous guesses published over the years. Instead of being a seed, some authors thought that it was extracted from the fruit of the nopal (it, too, often has scarlet juice). Others suggested, slightly more correctly, that it might come from some sort of worm. But for a long time the seed theory held sway in most circles.

It was indeed boosted in 1685 when Englishman Robert Boyle, chemist and member of the Royal Society, asked Antoni van Leeuwenhoek (the famous Dutch naturalist and microscopist) to have a look at cochineal through his lenses.

Misinterpreting what he saw, Leeuwenhoek concluded that the cochineal granule was composed of ". . .the fruit of a tree, which carries, or produces, within itself more than one hundred tiny oval seeds. . ." (The Spanish authorities would of have had a good laugh if they learned of this news.)

20

Nearly twenty years later (only after Leeuwenhoek had taken several more close looks at grana) he correctly observed that it was composed of dried all-female insect remains. He was even able to see inside of the cochineal insect's body itself and view its unhatched eggs.

Another microscopist, Jan Swammerdam, also had a look at cochineal sometime in the mid-to-late 1600's. He, too, saw bits of little bugs but (wisely or unwisely) kept his observations to himself, which were only published long after his death.

Actually, during this era there existed several published narratives that had depicted cochineal correctly. Perhaps the earliest was written by José de Acosta in 1590 (in Spanish). But because these revelations either did not make it out to the reading public or simply because no one believed them, the cochineal controversy droned on until 1729 when the publication of Melchoir de Ruusscher's book about the natural history of cochineal clearly revealed to Europeans that it was not a seed.

Later, in 1770, Abbé Raynal's historic account of the East and West Indies finally put an end to it. The civilized world now knew the true nature of grana.

In a concerted effort to preserve their monopoly, the Spanish maintained a strict embargo on the export of live cochineal insects from New Spain. Foreign visitors to the colonies were actively discouraged. The very few that were allowed to travel there did so only with strictly-controlled passports that made it nearly impossible to see any of the cochineal producing areas. Any foreigner caught with live cochineal in his possession would be dealt with severely and quickly deported. . . if he weren't executed as a spy.

Even so, by the year 1800 there had been a number of attempts by Dutch, French and British interests at establishing a cochineal industry outside of Spain's control. The English made at least two tries during the last quarter of the 18th century, most notably in Australia and India. In the American colonies, Virginia held special promise for a while but that was canceled when the

British lost control in 1781 following America's Revolutionary War.

None of these imperial enterprises were ultimately successful, in large part due to lack of knowledge. Although they now knew that cochineal was an insect, few people outside of New Spain understood the distinction between the fragile domestic (or "true") cochineal and its various wild cousins. And no one, it seems, realized that cochineal insects would not live indiscriminately on just any kind of cactus. Each cochineal species is limited to just a few specific types of prickly-pear on which it can survive.

A FRENCH SMUGGLER IN NEW SPAIN

Shortly after America's declaration of independence in 1776, the French navy covertly financed a bold one-man attempt at obtaining "true" cochineal directly from its source in Mexico. This was the first known endeavor at explicitly breaking the Spanish embargo, and it came very close to creating a successful cochineal industry on French territory.

Thirty-seven year old Nicolas Joseph Thiery de Menonville, a botanist with studies in law and medicine, was consumed with the idea of furthering the glory of the French Empire. To effect his contribution, he offered to travel alone to forbidden Mexico, somehow secure some cochineal, and bring it back alive to French soil. If the scheme worked, it would be an amazing bit of daring-do. If it failed and he was arrested, he probably would be put to death.

After a sixty-six day voyage from France, he arrived in Saint-Domingue (now known as Haiti), the wealthy Caribbean French colony occupying the western part of the island of Hispaniola. Here he would rest up from his "tedious and fatiguing" passage, collect a large portion of the promised operations money, and begin his mission. If he were successful, it would also be the place where he wanted to establish France's first cochineal plantation. But first he had to find transportation to Mexico. Not the least of his worries, he also needed to obtain an official passport from the Spanish authorities - something that was not often granted.

He calculated that his best chance at getting such a passport might be in Havana (Cuba), another Spanish colony. But how to get even that far? Fortune seemed to smile on him as he soon "learned that a merchant . . . was about to dispatch a brigantine to Havana for the purpose of recovering the cargo of a vessel that had been wrecked in the vicinity." Thiery de Menonville instantly determined to be on that ship when she left port.

After securing a French passport from the supervisor of Saint-Domingue that designated him as "a botanist and physician" (he carried his medical diploma with him), he embarked on the 21st of January, 1777, on the *Dauphin* bound for Havana.

It proved to be a rough voyage. When the ship arrived and anchored in Havana harbor two weeks later, Thiery de Menonville's health had apparently deteriorated. At first authorities would allow no one to leave the ship. A few days later, after writing (almost begging) the governor of Havana about his situation, he was allowed to go ashore so that he could recuperate. (The rest of the ship's complement was required to remain on board.)

Once ashore, he quickly went to work. Within a month, through his intelligent flattery and courteous manner, he was not only healthy again but he had become the "foreign darling" of Havana's high-society.

Impressed by Thiery de Menonville's botanical enthusiasm, his new "best friend" the governor of Havana - seeing how no harm could come of it - did not hesitate to issue him a passport to visit Mexico.

Thiery de Menonville was totally elated. "In possession of my passport, the liveliness of my joy was proportioned to the inquietude I had felt respecting the possibility of my procuring it; folded in my pocket I kept it as the dearest treasure," he later wrote.

However, when he arrived in Mexico his luck had apparently changed. Upon meeting the governor of Veracruz, Thiery de Menonville was taken aback, ". . . his sour looks, his rough tone of voice and rude speech, predisposed one against him at once."

23

Although suspicious, the governor reluctantly allowed Thiery de Menonville to reside in Veracruz and "botanize" locally, but he withheld his passport.

Unable to travel outside of the vicinity of this port city, Thiery de Menonville had no choice but to bide his time. He made a show at botanizing every day, while continuing to make friends and watch for opportunities. "Whether in the fields or in the streets, I constantly had plants in my hand, and either employed myself in observing them through a magnifying glass or in dissecting them with nicest care," he commented.

One morning while on a walk, Thiery de Menonville found a plant that would make him locally famous. It was a vine related to the morning-glory known as "Jalap," whose large roots were used as a strong purgative. These medicinal roots had long been imported at great expense by the residents of Veracruz and now the "French doctor" was able to show them that the plant was actually common locally.

"I was looked upon as a most extraordinary character in thus being able to discover a treasure in the very custody of those who were ignorant of its value," he wrote. "I succeeded even beyond my wishes in conciliating the admiration of every rank . . . sailors and soldiers laid in wait for me to ask advice for their complaints . . ."

On another day, while visiting a merchant's home, Thiery de Menonville overheard a discussion of the merits of Oaxaca's cochineal industry. Buoyed by this information, he decided that Oaxaca was the place where he wanted to go and soon began making inquiries about obtaining a passport that would allow him to travel anywhere outside of Veracruz.

He eventually received a permission to botanize on a mountain located just beyond the district. But just two days later, as he was making preparations to leave the city, an ominous letter from the viceroy arrived at the governor's mansion: his new passport was to be confiscated and then he would be deported. He was to leave on a ship that would sail from Veracruz in three weeks time.

Apparently, the local Governor's suspicions had been shared by the highest official in New Spain.

Surprisingly, Thiery de Menonville was not placed under house arrest and remained free to wander the city. He had put on a brave face when the edict had been read to him, but the news was devastating. He could not bear the disgrace of returning to France empty-handed. "Shame, humiliation, ridicule, and contempt will be your lot on every side you turn," he brooded, while pacing back and forth in his room.

Inspired by such hopelessness, he formed a desperate plan. To cover his real objective, he would pretend to go and stay for his remaining time at the estate of a certain widow of whom he had become particularly fond. His subsequent announcement of these intentions raised no eyebrows and even seemed to be encouraged. But what he actually meant to do was to sneak out of the city, secretly travel to Oaxaca some six hundred miles (965 km) to the south, secure some cochineal, and return to Veracruz unseen.

Thiery de Menonville's plan really didn't have much going for it. Oaxaca was a long ways to walk to (and return from) in less than twenty-one days. If he were discovered without a passport along the way, he would certainly be apprehended as a spy. To top it off, he wasn't even sure of the directions on how to get there. Nevertheless, he was determined to make the attempt.

"It was about nine o'clock when, after carefully locking up all my effects, I departed, as if merely taking a walk," he recounted. "I soon reached the rampart, scaled it, and bade adieu to the city." He quickly got lost, however, and asking directions from a local, returned to the city as if nothing had happened. On the following night his next attempt was more successful and he was well on his way.

He carried few possessions: money, a broad-brimmed hat, a rosary, and essential toiletries. To account for his Frenchified Spanish language and his odd clothes, he passed himself off as a Catalan (a Spaniard from the border country with France) to the people he met along the way. He avoided towns and public inns whenever possible, preferring to eat and sleep with local farmers and ranchers.

Thiery de Menonville was traveling cross-country during the dry season and thirst often became his most urgent problem. During one afternoon in the cabin of a shepherd he desperately, ". . .drank successively a quart of water (1 liter), two quarts of milk and as many of lemonade, and devoured the wing and thigh of a turkey, with three freshly-laid eggs, before I answered the least question."

After paying his host generously and complaining of a headache [probably to avoid lengthy or prying conversation], he then threw himself down on a bed of branches and slept throughout the rest of the day. At 4:00 o'clock the next morning Thiery de Menonville continued on his journey, "without taking leave of my hosts for fear of awakening them."

There were numerous small mishaps and close-calls along the way, any of which could have spelled doom for Thiery de Menonville's mission. Even so, he took the time to observe, collect plants, and record what he saw.

One morning after a violent rainstorm during the night, he discovered that the earth was in such a parched state that it "was moistened scarcely two inches [5cm] below the surface." On this same day he also, "found oaks with leaves slightly dentated; a white amaryllis, which I brought back with me; a polyanthus, whose rasped [shaved] root is used by the Indians in lieu of soap; three large flocks of sheep, twenty coveys of partridges . . . and rabbits out of number."

All the while, Thiery de Menonville was still compelled to walk over a lot of ground, "By eleven in the morning, I had traveled eight leagues (approximately 24 miles [38 1/2 km]) without eating and without drinking anything but a little lemonade, which I procured from two Indians who were building a hut, and who were the only rational beings I met with," he noted. Eventually, after hiring horses and Indian guides, his daily travel distance nearly doubled.

Shortly after reaching Oaxaca, Thiery de Menonville visited

a nearby nopal plantation that he had seen earlier in an attempt to purchase some cochineal. In his record of that pre-dawn meeting, his mastery of duplicity is apparent.

"The Negro owner was scarcely awake," he relates. "I informed him that being a physician, I wanted for the purpose of making an ointment for the gout, a few leaves of the nopal with the cochineal upon them . . . which I begged him to sell me as the case was urgent. Telling him I was willing to pay for them whatever he might require, he permitted me to take as much as I pleased."

After filling up his two baskets, handing them over to his two Native servants, and hastily departing "like a bolt of lightening," Thiery de Menonville was thoroughly elated by his success. "My heart beat in a manner that beggers description," he recalled. "It seemed to me that I was bearing away the golden-fleece but at the same time as if the furious dragon placed over it as a guard was following close at my heels."

Arriving before dawn back at the inn where he was staying, Thiery de Menonville breathlessly slipped into his room unnoticed. Here he carefully stuffed the cochineal-infested nopal pads into two small wooden traveling cases that he had paid a local carpenter to make a few days earlier. "Thus, by five in the morning I found myself in possession of a fine cargo of cochineal, which not a soul had seen me purchase or pack."

Using a series of guides and hired horses to carry him and his precious (and ever-growing) plant collection, Thiery de Menonville managed to make his way back to Veracruz. His assemblage now included several more cochineal-covered nopals, together with vanilla vines, fruit tree starts, and various wild plants.

During this trip there were two serious incidents where Thiery de Menonville could have been forced to give up the game. In the town of Tecuacan he was obliged to open his plant cases at a local customs house. Amazingly, even though they actually saw the cochineal-laden nopals intermingled among the other plants in the boxes, the bored inspectors essentially ignored the fact after a only few casual questions. "For a remedy for gout," was becoming his standard reply.

The second incident took place at the Veracruz city gate when he arrived back there before daybreak. Although the guards wanted to send him and his plant boxes over to the customs house for inspection, that office did not open until after eight o'clock: a four hour wait. Alarmed and thinking fast, he played upon the soldiers' vanity, pointedly asking them, ". . . are you such novices? Cannot you yourselves make the requisite examination? You cannot be such geese but know your business and how to act without advice . . . look, what I bring is nothing but herbs."

As he spoke, he opened some of the boxes. He was careful, however, to display only those that did not contain cochineal. After a cursory examination of just two of the boxes, the guards let him pass. Overjoyed and greatly relieved, Thiery de Menonville was soon ensconced back in his lodgings along with his prizes.

Incredibly, both Thiery de Menonville's friends and enemies alike assumed that he had been with the dear widow, Doña de Boutilloz, during the whole time he was away. His cover story had worked to a charm, but he still had one more ordeal to overcome.

Before he could board the ship that would bear him away to comparative safety and eventually take him back to Saint-Dominque, his boxes and baggage had to be inspected at the customs house. The likely prospect of discovery at this crucial final moment filled him with dread, "and in real truth this appeared to be the decisive day."

THE FAILED SUCCESS OF DE MENONVILLE'S MISSION

Followed by a line of thirty porters carrying all of his many cases of plants and nearly everything else he possessed (including several empty boxes) Thiery de Menonville brazenly arrived at the port's quay at daybreak.

"I computed that at this hour the idle were yet asleep [and] that the soldiers and officers, tired with the night guard, would be at rest in their hammocks . . ."

Placing his boxes and baggage on the ground for inspection, he was shocked a few minutes later to see that, "soldiers, sailors, and tradespeople all rushed forward to see the plants which the French botanist was bearing away." Suddenly the center of a great deal of attention, he refused to panic and acted as if everything was normal. It worked.

"The officer of the guard complimented me on my researches and collection of herbs; the searchers admired them in stupid astonishment, but at the same time were so civil as not to sound any of the cases (some had false bottoms)," Thiery de Menonville recounted. ". . . the head of the office, satisfied with my readiness to suffer examination, told me that I might pass on." Greatly relieved, he hastily got his things aboard the ship and soon departed.

However, more trials lay ahead for him. By the time Thiery de Menonville reached Saint-Dominque, he had endured a difficult four-month-long voyage filled with hurricanes and high-seas, the threat of shipwreck, and frequent becalmings.

In spite of his unceasing care, his plant cases had been drenched by waves and now most of his prickly-pear and cochineal insects were dead. But enough of them were still alive to give him hope and make the venture a success.

The intendant (administrator) of this French colony gave Thiery de Menonville a hero's welcome and ordered payment of the rest of the operational money due him. He also gave him an appointment as Royal Botanist with a salary of a thousand crowns a year and ordered that a royal garden was to be established in Port-au-Prince.

But these glories were to quickly fade. The surviving cochineal were very slow to reproduce and frequently threatened by heavy rains that might wash them off the nopals.

Thiery de Menonville also unhappily discovered that a good portion of his cochineal stock was not even "grana fina," but a variety of "grana silvestre" similar to a wild cochineal recently discovered

29

here on the island. This less valuable native insect constantly threatened to overwhelm the more delicate domestic cochineal from Mexico.

Colonial life and the troubles with breeding the cochineal began to take a toll on his health and temper. He became known for his violent rages, which were especially vitriolic if someone dared to even hint that he had stolen the cochineal from the Spanish. In one of his rarely moderated replies to this insinuation, he once wrote:

> To have stolen the cochineal would, in my opinion, been an act of social injustice . . . an injustice I sought to avoid . . . for by buying it, I only committed a wrong against the nation from whom I bore it away: now in my position I regard myself as the prototype (the first bio-pirate) of a different nation, on whom nature has bestowed the same prerogatives . . .

But all of this was to no avail. Less than three years after returning triumphantly with cochineal in hand, Thiery de Menonville fell sick with a malignant fever and died. There was an effort by his associates to continue his work but it failed due to lack of knowledge and commitment. Thiery de Menonville's abandoned garden ran wild and without the meticulous care that was necessary, his precious "true" cochineal also soon perished.

However, the wild cochineal persisted and did so to such an extent that, for a decade or so, fairly large amounts of "grana silvestre" was harvested by Black slaves and shipped from Port-au-Prince back to France. (In a little over ten years from the day of Thiery de Menonville's death, the island's black population would revolt in a bloody slave uprising that would eventually end in the creation of a new nation: Haiti.)

As the flow of this inferior grade of grana coming from Saint-Dominque finally slowed to a trickle and then slammed to a stop because of the revolution, Spain regained its total supply monopoly of the cochineal trade. But Thiery de Menonville's notes on how to raise cochineal were published in a book after his death, and this work soon inspired the English to also "give it a go," eventually setting the stage for Australia's Great Cactus War. (See Plate 1)

Chapter 2 : Royal Red in the Land Down Under

Okay, Sir Joseph Banks,
It's time to take your historical cue,
To tell your friend, the King,
That a colony in Australia is his royal due.
Along with the many convicts and their guards
In this shining adventure so bold,
Instruct Captain Phillip to put some prickly-pear
And cochineal down in the hold.

It was June of 1820. As he lay dying in his house at Spring Grove, Joseph Banks must have seriously contemplated his distinguished career. He had experienced some amazing successes and overseen his share of dismal failures. But on the whole, his country and the world of science were still going in the direction that he had urged them for so long. And then there was that whole cochineal business: What was it about this tiny insect that made things so difficult and yet so compelling?

At the age of seventy-seven, the gout that had long plagued him - and for more than a decade confined most of his activities to a wheelchair - was at last destroying his crippled body. Even so, his bright mind remained active and inquiring to the end. For more than forty-one years, as president of England's learned Royal Society, his had been the guiding hand that shaped the development and early leadership of scientific investigations around the world.

33

He could not boast of any major scientific achievement for himself, but it was his influence through unflagging and enthusiastic correspondence with fellow scientists scattered around the planet that had helped change the course of global history.

Born in 1743 into a wealthy Lincolnshire family, Banks was both enthusiastic and a natural raconteur - essential characteristics that would serve him well throughout his life. Although his parents initially held out hopes of his becoming a local county magnate or even a member of parliament in the well-established family tradition, young Joseph chose to study botany instead.

Little did they dream that their son would go on to sail around the world on an historic voyage of discovery, gain the intimate friendship and trust of the King of England, preside over the Royal Society for more than forty years, become the "father" of one of Britain's greatest colonies, and help "lift science out of the alchemist's den and place it firmly in the laboratory." Not bad for a mere "collector of plants."

Joseph Banks was just twenty-seven when he stood with hat in hand on the beach in Botany Bay (Australia) in April of 1770 as the expedition's leader, James Cook, formally took possession of this newly discovered "Great South Land" in the name of the British Crown. Two years earlier, at his own expense, Banks and his party of naturalists and artists had joined Cook on the HMS *Endeavour* for this great exploratory voyage around the south Pacific Ocean.

The ship's original assignment had been to observe the transit of the planet Venus across the disk of the sun from the vantage point of the island of Tahiti, the best place - so British astronomers thought - that the phenomenon could be witnessed in the southern hemisphere.

Having successfully completed that task and packed away their telescopes, the ship's orders then required Cook to continue westward, where they explored and mapped the New Zealand coast, and then west again to eventually discover eastern Australia.

During the short time that they were in Botany Bay (or around Australia for that matter) Banks and his good friend,

Dr. Daniel Solander (another enthusiastic botanist), almost frantically gathered plant and animal specimens whenever possible. The collecting continued even after the ship struck a reef north of the present city of Cairns and, in danger of sinking, was subsequently beached for repairs.

When the more than three-year-long voyage was completed, Banks returned to England with an astonishing assemblage that included over 3,000 dried plant specimens, nearly 1,000 original drawings, and numerous miscellaneous curiosities. More than a thousand species in this treasure-trove were said to be unknown to European science at the time.

Joseph Banks's natural talent for telling dramatic stories about exotic wildlife (like the marvelous kangaroo), strange people who wore little or no clothes, storms and shipwrecks, combined with his incredible natural history collection - which was kept in his museum-sized house at London's Soho Square - soon made him well-known throughout London society. Many said that he was becoming even more famous than Captain Cook, himself. These comments may have led to some tension between the two men.

Even though an opportunity had been offered to him, perhaps fortuitously, he never sailed with Cook again. The official reason why Banks declined to join Cook on his second voyage, was because of a snafu with the Admiralty regarding proper shipboard accommodation for him and his naturalist friends. The real explanation, perhaps, goes unrecorded.

BANKS' SUNNY SPOT IN THE ROYAL GARDEN

A rising star among intellectuals, within a month of his return home Joseph and his friend Daniel Solander were granted a long audience with King George III to review the discoveries they had made on their voyage to the South Seas. Soon after this initial meeting, Banks and the king were discussing issues of agricultural improvement - a favorite topic for both of them - on a regular basis.

A lifelong friendship was eventually forged between them, with Banks acting as the king's scientific advisor for many years until his death. In her book on the history of cochineal, Amy Greenfield explains:

> In 1773, the king appointed him unofficial director of the Royal Botanic Gardens at Kew. Later he made Banks a baronet - leading an envious contemporary to denounce Banks as a 'mere toad eater to the King.' Yet Banks evidently had the respect not only of the royal family but of his fellow scientists. His London home at 32 Soho Square, where he installed many of his antipodean treasures, became a meeting place for natural philosophers of every description, and his well-stocked library became a resource for scientists who could afford few books of their own.

Banks's house truly was the "rendezvous of those who cultivate the sciences," as one impressed visitor wrote:

> They assemble every morning in one of the apartments of a numerous library, which consists entirely of books on Natural History and is the completest of its kind in existence. There all the journals and public papers relative to the sciences are to be found and there they communicate to each other such new discoveries as they are informed of by their respective correspondents, or which are transmitted by the learned foreigners who visit London, and who are all admitted into this society.

For nearly half a century, that house in Soho Square would be a place of inspiration for many of the young men who were contemplating a career in science. When Banks was elected president of the Royal Society in 1778 at the relatively young age of thirty-five, he soon became a generous "father-figure" to those same struggling scientists, giving support to some of them even out of his own pocket. Now in a position to oversee and influence much of the scientific "coming and goings" of the British Empire, Banks held this highly-esteemed office for the remainder of his life.

Banks was especially keen on the subject of introducing new

and useful plants at home and abroad. A few of these transplants included sugar cane and bread fruit to the West Indies (He was mastermind for the breadfruit scheme and had personally picked William Bligh to captain the *Bounty*; a project that ended disastrously in one of the world's most famous mutinies.), American cranberries to northern Europe, and the lovely arbutus trees now seen in English parks. An avid agriculturist, he also was the first to notice the value of the rubber tree and became an early advocate for the cultivation of tea in India.

To act as reservoirs for interesting tropical plants, Banks established botanical gardens in Jamaica, Saint Vincent, and Ceylon. At home, the exotic plant collection in the Royal Botanic Garden at Kew - "the King's Garden," as Banks liked to refer to it - had already become world famous. During his life nearly 7,000 new plants were introduced into England.

Banks's library in Soho Square contained a copy of Thiery de Menonville's 1787 treatise on how to raise cochineal, and he was very likely one of the first English scientists to read it. He also pain-stakingly translated it from the original French and added notes from other sources in an attempt to compound "a clear account of the two forms of cochineal" known as "grana fina" (the domestic cochineal) and "grana silvestre" (the wild cochineal).

Although Banks was laying the groundwork for raising cochineal on British-held soil in an attempt to end, at long-last, the irksome Spanish monopoly, he apparently still did not understand, like others before him, that cochineal would not live on just any prickly-pear.

ATTEMPTS FOR A NEW COCHINEAL INDUSTRY

By the late 1700's England's dye works were using some 240,000 pounds (11,000 kg) of cochineal a year, most of which had to be purchased from Spanish merchants at a very dear price. Naturally, the British government was keen to help Banks in any way it could to establish a cochineal industry somewhere in their empire.

Late in 1786, Banks received a letter from Madras, India, written by a certain Dr. James Anderson, a medical officer in the British East India Company (and an amateur botanist) who was stationed there. He claimed to have found, attached to common salt grass, a type of cochineal that was native to his district. Anderson even included a sample of the dried insects in his letter, adding that they produced a good color in wine and water. When Banks informed the directors of the East India Company of this news, it generated a great deal of enthusiasm.

"Unfortunately for all concerned, Anderson's 'Cochineal Insect' turned out to be an imposter," Greenfield notes. "In July, 1787, the Court of Directors recorded the dismal results of the analysis: finding that the Indian beetle yielded only 'a dirty stain,' a range of experts had pronounced it 'entirely useless, in the dyeing [of] any color whatsoever.'"

This disappointment appears to have only strengthened Banks's resolve, however. The following spring, at Banks's urging, the British East India Company's "Committee of Secrecy" posted a large reward for "procuring the true cochineal from Spanish America." From now on Banks's machinations to secure cochineal for Britain were to go into high gear. India, it seemed to him, was as good place as any to establish the industry. Wages were cheap there and he could rely on Dr. Anderson's continued zealous assistance.

He even sent the good doctor an annotated copy of Thiery de Menonville's treatise on how to raise cochineal, urging him to start a "nopaleria" in his garden and begin growing prickly- pear in anticipation of receiving the "true" cochineal.

The East India Company then sent sealed orders (also at Banks's bidding) to several of their most trusted sea captains with the instruction to open the orders only if they happened to land in South America. While there, they were to covertly obtain the cochineal insects and their host plants and bring them to India.

While Joseph Banks was still exchanging letters with Dr. Anderson, an extraordinary opportunity to establish cochineal in yet another part of the world arose. This undertaking was much dearer to Banks's heart, as this new place was in Australia - that wonderful land he had helped discover nearly two decades earlier. Ever since his celebrated voyage he had spoken frequently about the possibilities of it becoming a new English colony.

ENGLISH VOICES IN THE GREAT SOUTH LAND

The American revolution of 1776 had brought an end to England's most important colonial possession. The American colonies were significant for many reasons, including being a profitable "dumping ground" for England's undesirables. For more than a century and a half, large numbers of British convicts had been sent each year across the Atlantic to be sold or indentured to American plantation owners.

Ever since the colony's independence, a rising crime rate had left Britain's jails and prison hulks (moored decaying ships) dangerously overcrowded. Now there was nowhere to send these people, ostensibly to form "useful" penal settlements.

To address this growing problem, a special committee was set up in the House of Commons and Joseph Banks was invited to speak to them about Australia's potential. This he did with such passion and eloquence that he was even offered a seat in the Commons, an honor which he politely refused.

The severity of the English criminal law at the time was an object of horror and "would have put any savage nation to the blush," as author Charles White remarked. For example, it was death to rob a man of more than a shilling.

Some of the other more than 150 crimes punishable by execution included: stealing linen from bleaching grounds, concealing the birth of a bastard child, sending threatening letters, selling cottons with forged stamps, breaking down the head of a fishpond whereby fish may be lost, cutting down trees in an avenue or garden, religious sacrilege, maiming or killing cattle maliciously, servants purloining their master's goods, and shooting at another person. Little wonder that the jails were so full and the hangman kept very busy. (On the other hand, an offender who had committed a personal assault even of the most violent nature, was oftentimes simply fined or imprisoned.)

Still, eight years were to pass before the government was willing to act upon Banks's recommendation for a penal colony in Australia. The catalyst for that decision appears to have been a document written by Banks himself entitled, *Heads of the Plan for Botany Bay*, in which he detailed the requirements for settling the new colony.

Banks had no doubts that Australia was the perfect place for such an enterprise. In the opening paragraph he states the paper's aim as a "plan for effectively disposing of convicts and rendering their transportation reciprocally beneficial, both to themselves and to the state, by the establishment of a colony in New South Wales, a country . . . from whence it is hardly possible for persons to return without permission."

A resolute little naval captain by the name of Arthur Phillip was selected to organize the convict fleet and to act as the fledgling colony's first governor once they reached their destination.

However, no sooner did Captain Phillip receive his appointment than he began to run into serious difficulty. After years of foot-dragging and halfhearted interest, the government now began to rush preparations.

Apparently, the motivation behind all this haste was an ill-conceived plan to recoup the cost of the adventure by timing the voyage so that the ships could first drop the convicts, their soldier guards and any free-settlers at Botany Bay, and then sail on to China in time to pick up a cargo of fresh tea to bring back to England.

Working diligently under this intense pressure, Phillip managed to assemble a fleet of eleven ships but he had endless trouble fitting it out. He complained that there were no tools for the repair and maintenance of small arms, no surgeon's instruments, not enough razors for the men, too few gardening tools, and on and on.

When the convoy finally did put to sea in May of 1787, it was soon discovered that no clothing had been provided for the 192 women convicts - except for the rags that they were wearing. And the men who were tasked with guarding the more than 560 resentful male convicts (some of whom were quite dangerous) discovered to their horror they had no ammunition for their muskets and pistols.

They ended up simply bluffing the prisoners until the fleet put into Rio de Janeiro, where Captain Phillip was able to persuade the regional Viceroy to let him purchase 10,000 musket balls. How the women obtained more clothing is not known.

CAPTAIN PHILLIP'S SECRET MISSION

Joseph Banks and Arthur Phillip were well acquainted with each other and it is very likely that Phillip had visited Banks at his home. It was probably during this time that Banks instructed Phillip on which useful plants to collect or purchase for the new colony during his scheduled resupply stopover a Rio de Janeiro. High on the list of those useful plants was certainly prickly-pear with its associated cochineal insects.

True to his nature, Banks continued offering his advice through a regular (but necessarily slow) correspondence that he carried on with Phillip for several years after he had departed for Australia. These letters often took a year or more to reach their destination.

During the three weeks in August that the convict fleet remained in the port of Rio de Janeiro, Captain Phillip assiduously followed Banks's advice on acquiring useful plants for the new settlement. Oranges, lemons and limes, bananas, cocoa, guavas, jalap, tamarind, grapes, tobacco, and rice were all brought on board. That Phillip was able to secure cochineal can be assumed by the following entry in his account of the voyage:

41

Wine was not at this season to be had, except from retail dealers, less was therefore purchased than would otherwise have been taken. Rum, however, was laid in, and all such seeds and plants procured as were thought likely to flourish on the coast of New South Wales, particularly coffee, indigo, cotton, and the cochineal fig (prickly-pear).

The fleet's next anchorage was in Table Bay, Capetown, (South Africa) in mid-October. For the following month they again replenished their stores and livestock and brought aboard even more plants. (Phillip's cabin was described as resembling a small green-house.)

While he was still at anchor here, Phillip was visited aboard his vessel by Captain John Cox, an East India Company officer. Phillip showed Cox the various plants in his cabin, including the cochineal-infested prickly-pear. "The insect," Cox later wrote, "was fixed on the plant under a very white down and Commodore Phillip, who brought both from South America with him, did not wish that either should be in the least disturbed."

On the 18th of January, 1788, more than eight months from the beginning of their voyage, the first ship of the fleet anchored in Botany Bay. This arrival was soon followed by the rest of the convoy. But Botany Bay was not to their liking (too low and marshy) and eight days later, after some exploration, Captain Phillip decided to move north and restart the settlement at Port Jackson.

Soon after Phillip's ship had departed for the new location and was out of sight (the rest of the fleet was to follow a day or so later), the people who had stayed behind were astounded to see two French ships sailing into Botany Bay. The ships, under the command of the navigator/explorer Jean-François Conte de La Pérouse, were soon anchored and a land camp begun on a point of the north shore.

Thoroughly alarmed when he learned of this news, Phillip lost no time in staking the claim for his country's new colony in a place he dubbed "Sydney Cove." However, the French were on a scientific expedition and not interested in colonial claims of their own. In any case it was a needless concern, for soon after leaving Australia six weeks later, La Pérouse's ships were apparently wrecked during a storm and never heard from again.

Occasionally teetering on the brink of starvation during its first couple of years, the new settlement at Sydney Cove struggled for existence. Unfortunately, there wasn't a single person among the convict rabble or even the free-settlers in the colony who was knowledgeable about farming or gardening. The first lot of seeds they planted completely failed.

Dysentery and scurvy became common illnesses. Even Governor Phillip became ill, yet doggedly remained on his feet. The only person who knew anything at all about growing vegetables was Phillip's servant and somehow together they were able to coax the precious cochineal-covered prickly-pear through their first winter.

This is the last information we have concerning Australia's original cochineal experiment. We can only assume that the insects most likely perished in one of New South Wales's numerous extreme weather events and that the cactus was abandoned to its own fate.

At every opportunity during his long outbound voyage and subsequent residence in Australia, Phillip sent long letters to Banks - by way of ships returning to England - informing him of his troubled progress. At times he even dispatched boxes of plant and animal specimens to accompany the letters. Although none of Banks's replies are known to still exist, they most certainly were filled with encouraging and kindly advice.

At home in England, Banks also frequently acted on Phillip's behalf - devoting a considerable amount of his time and energy trying to obtain the government's help for the struggling colony. But the administration continually sidestepped the issue. As far as they were concerned, Australia was just a convenient dumping ground for the overflow from the prisons.

After nearly five trying years of acting as the colony's first governor, Phillip's health finally gave way and he was permitted to leave Sydney late in 1792. Returning to his home in Bath, England, he eventually regained some of his strength. For his service to the Crown, he was promoted to the rank of admiral and granted a pension for the remaining years of his life.

Although Banks and Phillip were never aware of this, they had succeeded in not only colonizing Australia with English people, but had also introduced the very first element in what later would develop into the greatest infestation of weedy plants that the world had ever seen.

FINALLY! SUCCESS IN INDIA . . . SORT OF

Banks's attempts at establishing cochineal outside of Spain's control did not stop with its failure in Australia. He encouraged Dr. Anderson to continue his efforts and in preparation to eventually receiving living cochineal, even sent him nursery stock from two different types prickly-pear growing in the Royal Botanic Gardens.

Anderson's enthusiasm was infectious and soon he had a friend in Calcutta, Colonel Robert Kyd, collaborating with him. Each of the two men eventually established considerable-sized prickly-pear plantations (nopalerias) from those specimens obtained from Banks (and another variety obtained from China) in their respective cities of Madras and Calcutta.

But the cochineal was slow in coming. Frustrated, Anderson took issue with Banks's secretiveness and strongly advocated publicly posting an open reward. He also published his instructions on the care of cochineal and is reported to have even sent a copy to a Spanish botanist in Manila. You can be sure that Banks and the East India Company's "Committee of Secrecy" weren't happy about this turn of events.

It was nearly six years after receiving Anderson's first letter that one of Banks's agents managed to collect living cochineal insects, again from Rio de Janeiro. This time the three Brazilian nopal plants covered with thousands of insects were carefully packed and sent to London, arriving in the winter of 1793.

Amazingly, they arrived in good condition and were quickly installed in a special hothouse that Banks had made ready for them at his home in Spring Grove. This culture was meant to serve as a reserve while samples from them were transported to India. But once again the effort was to no avail; the entire cochineal collection soon perished when the hothouse's heating system failed.

But fate was to take another strange turn. In his normal day-to-day dealings, Banks had once recommended a talented gardener, Christopher Smith, to be hired at the botanical gardens in Calcutta. In 1795, as Smith was preparing a shipment of plants to be sent back to England, a British officer by the name of Captain Neilson of H. M. 74th Regiment arrived at the gardens bearing two small cochineal-covered prickly-pear plants. Apparently, he had read one of Anderson's pamphlets when he had been stationed in Madras. "After an assignment elsewhere, he was posted to India once again," Greenfield notes, "And when the ship carrying him there was forced to stop at Rio de Janeiro for rations . . . Neilson realized that he 'had a good opportunity.'"

Neilson's cochineal was delivered to William Roxburgh, the superintendent of Calcutta's botanic gardens, who duly placed them under Smith's care. The gardener tried in vain to foster the insects on the three supposed host species that had been so carefully planted years before. The insects died on all of them, and quite soon the project was looking hopeless. As a last resort, Smith transferred the remaining eight or nine insects that were still alive to a weedy species of prickly-pear (*Opuntia monocantha*) that, having long been naturalized in India, "grows in the jungle and is common all over Bengal."

The transplant was a success. Within a few months, Smith's cochineal collection had grown to the point where he was now cultivating the insects on some 600 potted prickly-pear plants which he kept in a conservatory to protect them from the monsoonal rains.

Ever curious, Smith soon discovered that some of the cochineal that he had put on plants growing out in the open air had also thrived, and these insects were much larger than those he was raising indoors.

Two boxes of nopal leaves covered with cochineal were then sent to Dr. Anderson in Madras to expand the success of the insect's cultivation. Initial tests on dried samples indicated that the extracted dye was very satisfactory, supposedly yielding nearly two-thirds of that from the best Mexican "grana fina." Anderson must have been overjoyed, and for a while this news seemed to bode well for India's future cochineal industry.

But Roxburgh noted with uneasiness that the cochineal's breeding cycle only took thirty days to complete. To him, this indicated that the insect that they were raising was not the domestic cochineal ("grana fina") but its wild cousin ("grana silvestre"). Far from being difficult to cultivate, these insects were ravenously eating every Bengal prickly-pear that they encountered, and they were beginning to spread like wildfire. Soon there was a growing speculation that the insects might actually destroy their food supply and die out.

More troubling was the fact that Indian landowners seemed very reluctant to grow cochineal in favor of their more traditional crops. Even with guaranteed price support from the East India Company, the farmers still regarded cochineal suspiciously and most did not want to invest their time and money in it.

After a very shaky start, the cochineal industry finally managed to get under way in India. Several thousand acres had been planted with the Bengal prickly-pear and the insects were thriving on it. In 1797 the East India Company shipped over 4,000 pounds (1,800 kg) of cochineal back to England and nearly ten times that amount the following year.

But the industry was not as profitable as was first expected. That initial estimate of the dye's yield actually turned out to be "wildly optimistic." In truth, the yield was less than one-third of that from "grana fina." Greenfield notes that India's cochineal industry was finished almost before it had begun:

In 1807, the company directors finally accepted that cochineal was a losing proposition, costing more to

46

produce and export than it earned in the marketplace. Cutting their losses, they voted to dispose with price supports altogether, a move that put an end to the market for Neilson's cochineal. Although the insect survived in the wild, commercial production virtually ceased.

This is where Joseph Banks's attempts at producing cochineal outside of Spain's control effectively ended. For many years his great house at Soho Square continued to be the central library for naturalists from all over the world, and as president of the Royal Society, Banks continued to influence the natural sciences until the end of his life. But after his death in 1820, memory of his work seems to have simply faded out of the public mind.

His collections and great library were relegated to the British Museum and his letters and papers were eventually disposed of by auction. (Most of the buyers were autograph dealers interested only in his signature.) Banks's cochineal industry may have failed, but this did not spell the end for prickly-pear cactus's role in shaping the history of British-controlled India and opening the way to Indian independence.

A HATED TAX AND THE GIANT HEDGE

On March 12th, 1930, Mahatma Gandhi and seventy-eight of his determined followers began their 24-day-long march 240 miles (386 km) south to the sea and once there, they intended to make salt on the beach. Making salt without license, under British colonial law, was an illegal activity. However, this was to be a nonviolent protest and Gandhi's group would not resist arrest.

The goal of this demonstration was, as Gandhi explained, "to deprive the Government of its illegitimate monopoly of salt. My aim is to get the Salt Tax abolished. This is for me one step - the first step - towards full freedom."

Along the way, thousands of sympathetic Indians fell in line to trudge behind that determined little brown man. When Gandhi eventually reached the sea twenty-four days later, a huge column of humanity extended for many miles behind him. Inspired by his example, more than 80,000 people would also disregard the Salt Tax and be arrested.

Along with air and water, salt is one of the great necessities of life. This is especially true in a hot country like India where people sweat out a great deal of the salt in their bodies every day. Unfortunately, the British kept a monopoly on salt production, and its tax on the commodity was so onerous that the mass of poor and lower classes of native people simply could not afford to purchase it. Salt smuggling was so common that the British colonial administration took serious steps to stop it.

Early in the 1800's, the British East India Company's quasi-government formed the "Inland Customs Department" to oversee its so-called "Customs Line", a line that literally divided the Indian subcontinent. Anyone caught crossing that line with illegal salt in their possession would be arrested, then fined or jailed, or both.

For many years salt smuggling continued to flourish. Even though Inland Customs agents had established over 1,700 sentry-posts along the line, in the main the Customs Line was still an open frontier that stretched across the whole of India. The line's administrators reasoned that to effectively stop the flow of salt smuggling, a physical barrier of some sort had to be created.

That idea eventually took the form of an impenetrable living wall of thorny plants extending the entire length of the "Line," making it the longest man-made planting in the world. When completed, this living fence stretched from the Indus to the Mahanadi in Madras, a distance of 2,300 miles (3,800 km).

It is not entirely known when the "Customs Hedge" or "saltwall" (as it came to be known) first began to be established, but it appears to be sometime in the 1840's. In his book, *The Great Hedge of India*, author Roy Moxham quotes a Mr. G. H. Smith, Commissioner of Customs from 1834 to 1854, who wrote: "On some parts of the line, the patrols have commenced sowing a live hedge, and others have in contemplation to adopt the same plan, so that in the course of a few years we may calculate upon having an impenetrable and permanent barrier to head-load smuggling across a large portion of the northwest frontier line."

Ideally the hedge would be from ten to fourteen feet high (3-4.2 m) and over six feet thick (2 m). It was usually composed of an impenetrable mixture of closely-clipped thorny trees, shrubs, and prickly-pear cactus. In at least one region, prickly-pear nurseries were specifically established to help create the hedge. (Prickly-pear was also said to be "a formidable jail fence.")

As an illustration as to just how important this project was to the British, the great "Customs Hedge" was guarded and maintained by a contingent of around 12,000 men. "The workforce seems to have reached its peak in 1872, when it totaled 14,188," notes Moxham. "Even during its final year before the line was abandoned, there was a total staff of over 10,000."

It is "impossible to say how many people were made ill as a result of salt deprivation. . . no idea of how many died," laments Moxhan:

> Their deaths were hidden in copious statistics of death from other causes; buried in the mass of deaths report-edly caused by disease or famine. We do know that the government realized that salt consumption was severely reduced by the Salt Tax. We know that the government's own figures show a consumption way below the mini-mum considered necessary for their own soldiers in India, and well below the minimum prescribed for prisoners in English jails . . . [we] also know that British doctors working in India protested to parliament, and that for the sake of keeping an easily collectable tax, the British government ignored them.

Gandhi's protest of the Salt Tax resulted in some relaxation of Britain's total monopoly on salt production in India. People living in coastal areas were finally allowed to make, on a small scale, their own salt if they wished. But the hated tax itself wasn't repealed until 1946 when Nehru became the newly-freed nation's interim-government prime minister.

Remnants of the huge "saltwall" can still be seen south of Delhi. Originally a dense mass of very tall prickly-pear, it extended uninterrupted by any other type of growth for mile after mile.

GRANA'S ESCAPE FROM NEW SPAIN

Returning to the story of cochineal: Although Banks's attempts to establish a cochineal industry somewhere within the British Empire had failed, it wasn't long after his death in 1820 that Spain lost its own colonial grip on Mexico. The Mexican Revolution not only ended nearly three centuries of Spanish rule, and in the ensuing chaos of war, the cochineal insect was also freed from the confines of its native land.

In 1821, when the Spanish formally relinquished all control of Mexico, cochineal had already been successfully established back in Spain by concerned businessmen who had anticipated Mexico's independence. A small cochineal industry had also been formed in Guatemala.

Fierce competition would eventually develop with Mexico as Guatemala ramped up its production. By the mid-1800's Guatemalan farmers would be supplying nearly three-quarters of the grana used by the British. Cochineal production also became one of the chief industries of southern Ecuador.

Then in 1827, the Dutch managed to smuggle dozens of cochineal-covered prickly-pear plants out of Mexico and successfully establish them in Java. Twenty-two years later, Java's annual cochineal harvest would exceed 80,000 pounds (36,300 kg). Not considered to be a particularly high-grade product, most of this grana was exported to China.

The most spectacular cochineal transplant success story, however, was in the Spanish-controlled Canary Islands located off northern Africa. Although the cochineal insect had been introduced into this island archipelago sometime between the mid-1820's and 1830's, the islanders initially rejected the insects as a business opportunity. Our old friend, the Indian fig (*Opuntia ficus-indica*), was already well-established on the islands to be sure, but the local farmers preferred to grow grapes for wine and eat the sweet fruit of this prickly-pear instead.

All that changed when a pathogenic fungus destroyed the grape vines on Tenerife, the largest island in the group. Desperate families quickly took to raising cochineal, and by 1855 the annual export of cochineal from all the islands reached more than a million pounds (455,000 kg). Twenty years later the production climbed to a staggering peak of over 6 million pounds (2,730,000 kg).

In reaction to the glut of all this red dyestuff, Mexico began dropping it prices, and eventually, its entire production. In spite of this, the Canary Islanders forged ahead and soon the archipelago became the world's leader in cochineal exports. Even though the price of cochineal had fallen to a quarter of what it had been in 1820, there was still enough profit in the business to make some producers relatively rich.

TEST TUBE COLORS

The status quo was again about to radically change. In 1858, the noted German chemist, August Wilhelm Hoffman, then director of London's Royal College of Chemistry, announced in a scientific journal that he had perfected a way of creating crimson dye from coal tar. Coal tar was a waste product of the gaslight industry.

Students at his school had been experimenting with this stuff for years. One, by the name of William Henry Perkins, had even succeeded in creating a marketable purple dye from it. Eventually, a whole range of bright colors would be synthesized from this gooey black substance.

At first, the synthetic dyes were met with resistance from traditional dye users. But as these chemicals were so much cheaper to obtain and just as intense in color, they slowly began to find uses for

51

it. By 1875, the "handwriting was on the wall" for the cochineal industry; synthetic dye had captured the marketplace and eventually replaced nearly all natural dyestuffs.

The cochineal industry collapsed in response, nearly vanishing altogether. A few die-hard traditionalists kept it going, but the trade became a mere shadow of its former self. A New Orleans newspaper reported in 1911 in an article titled "Cochineal is Near End," that only a few plantations of nopal cactus now remained in Oaxaca, that once vibrant heart of cochineal country. A few years later an Australian delegation visiting the Canary Islands reported that "the lucrative banana industry is now replacing the raising of cochineal."

Today, cochineal is experiencing a comeback. Health concerns over the use of synthetic dyes as food colorants led to extensive research that consistently indicated that at least one of them - known as Red Dye #2 in the United States - was a carcinogen. This has led to a ban of its use in all foods, cosmetics, and pharmaceuticals.

Cochineal is now one of a very few red dyes approved for food products by the USDA. With no known safety issues, cochineal can be found in products as varied as beverages, candies, lipstick, sausages, cheese, cough syrup, yogurt, rouge, and as a tissue-staining agent in forensic crime labs.

The world's leading producers of cochineal, which now totals more than 2,000 tons per year, are in Peru, the Canary Islands, and Chile. Mexico is barely in the game but Spain is still a significant player, annually supplying the market with somewhere between 5 to 10% of current world production. Although Chile was a latecomer to the cochineal industry - only entering the market in 1998 - its exports have steadily grown over the years.

Despite Peru furnishing the greatest annual tonnage of cochineal, the product from the Canary Islands is still considered to be superior, and therefore usually commands a higher price. In today's international cochineal market, prices can vary widely - anywhere from $8 to $45 US per pound for dried material ($18 to $100 US per kg).

During the past thirty-five or forty years, the trend on prices for this commodity has slowly dropped. This is a far cry from when in the late 17th century, the purchase of a garment dyed scarlet with cochineal could be afforded only by nobility or the wealthiest of businessmen.

Released from the restraints of agriculture when India's dye producing industry was abandoned, the now wild cochineal effectively kept the naturalized cactus (Bengal prickly-pear) more or less in check throughout the region. In Australia, however, there was no natural herbivore to help slow the spread of the cactus.

Although there has been tentative speculation that Governor Phillip's original plants may have died out along with that first batch of cochineal, it is certain that many more introductions of prickly-pear have occurred since then. After all, they are very interesting and useful plants.

AUSTRALIA'S FIRST "PEST-PEARS"

Despite spending considerable time and resources researching this part of the story, my information on the initial spread of prickly-pear in Australia is still rather sketchy. Not a lot was written about this plant in the colony's early days. However, there are some significant "mileposts" to be seen along the way.

Just forty years after the arrival of Arthur Phillip's first convict fleet in 1788, a species of prickly-pear - probably the same kind as Governor Phillip had brought with him - was listed in the catalogue of plants growing in Sydney's Royal Botanic Garden.

A handbook on the culture of grapes in New South Wales, published in 1832 by James Busby, advocated the creation of protective prickly-pear hedges similar to those found in Spain. (I'm sure many grape-growers followed his advice.)

Barely four years afterwards, in 1836, prickly-pear was being offered for sale in a Tasmanian nursery located outside of Hobart. In 1843, the annual catalogue of plants found on William Macarthur's estate at Camden, New South Wales, included at least one species of prickly-pear in addition to seven other kinds of cactus.

A few years later that annual catalogue listed three species of prickly-pear along with nearly a thousand other kinds of plants. It is not clear if these plants were offered for sale, but it is very likely that seeds, cuttings, and roots were shared with his neighbors and interested visitors.

The earliest image of a prickly-pear in Australia that I have been able to locate is a simple pencil drawing of the cactus growing alongside a wooden fence by Emily Anne Manning in her "1836-1839" sketchbook held by the New South Wales State Library.

The next oldest image is George Angas's 1852 pen and water-color of prickly-pear at Double Bay in Sydney. (See Plate 2) The detail in this work is so fine that we can almost determine with some confidence which species of cactus it is. In 1857, another one of Angas's works depicting prickly-pear was published in *The Australian Picture Pleasure Book*. The image, portraying a large house located on the outskirts of Sydney, clearly shows the early stages of prickly-pear's spread.

CONVICT SHIPS AND THE GOOD DOCTOR

Prickly-pear's conquest of Australia would receive its biggest initial boost from two of its keenest, but misguided, supporters: a young immigrant housekeeper and her employer, Dr. William Bell Carlyle.

Born in Scotland in 1788 into a family of professionals that included the well-known author Thomas Carlyle, William was a surgeon in the British Navy. Acting as "surgeon-superintendent" on the convict ship *Asia*, he first arrived in Sydney late in 1820 but soon returned to England via the usual route that included a stopover in India. After a few months at home, he then sailed on the convict ship *Morley* bound for Hobart. Over a ten-year period, Dr. Carlyle would make six voyages from England to Australia in his role of surgeon-superintendent.

For the prisoners, life aboard these transport ships was appalling. The ships' Masters could often only be described as complete brutes. "Who, with few exceptions . . . generally treat their surgeons, as they do their apprentices and men, with rudeness and brutality," writes Charles Bateson in *The Convict Ships 1787-1868*:

> Incapable of appreciating the value of learning, and despising all knowledge beyond what they themselves possess, they avail themselves of every opportunity to insult and mortify their surgeons. Under this species of treatment, with no means of redress during a long voyage, the mind becomes paralyzed, they view their situation with disgust, and if they have the means . . . they soon become confirmed drunkards. Hence their duty is neglected, and the poor convicts become the unhappy victims of the captain's brutality . . .

"As might be expected," Bateson continues, "Surgeons found employment in the convict service unattractive. The work was exacting, the conditions unpleasant, and the pay poor . . . With rare exception, those who proffered their services were either novices fresh from the lecture-room or embittered failures in the profession." Dr. Carlyle, however, was the exception to this rule and belonged in neither one of these categories.

There were many deaths during these long voyages that could have been prevented with adequate nutrition and medical care. In an attempt to better the chances of a convict surviving the ordeal aboard these ships, a system was developed by the Transport Commission that involved a medical overseer, the so-called "surgeon-superintendent."

Detailed instructions that amounted to a contract were issued to each of the ship's surgeons and to the ship's Master and his officers. Every prisoner was to be allowed to be out in the fresh air on the open deck at least twice a day and every bed was to be kept clean. The need for cleanliness and proper ventilation below decks were strongly emphasized.

To keep the ship's crew from purloining the convict's food allotment, every cask of provisions was to be opened only in the presence of the surgeon-superintendent and he was to personally see that the pork and beef was stored under lock and key. Any person showing signs of scurvy or other disease was to receive extra rations (not less) including lemon-juice, sugar, rice, oatmeal, bread, and wine.

"Thus, not only was the status of the surgeon-superintendent established," Bateson explains, "but the various officers were told precisely the nature of their duties and responsibilities, and the convicts were aware of what was expected of them."

As a result of this intervention, the mortality rate on these voyages dropped dramatically. By 1868, when England finally stopped sending convicts to Australia, some 134,262 men and 25,256 women had successfully been transported. Only 2,382 had died along the way during this eighty-one year period. Most of these deaths occurred during the colony's earlier years.

For his committed duty, in 1823 Dr. Carlyle was awarded a land grant of 2,000 acres in the attractive rolling hills of the upper Hunter River Valley, very near a place that would later become the town of Scone. He named his lovely property "Satur" and within four years he had built a fine wooden house there. In 1830, Carlyle finally quit the medical sea-service and permanently settled in Australia. A few years later he was appointed County Magistrate.

Although he appears to have never married, somewhere along the way Carlyle acquired a daughter. Because he must have felt that she needed a nanny to look after her, the good doctor then hired a 19-year-old woman in England to come out to Australia to work as his housekeeper and to care for the girl.

Fresh-faced and excited, young Mary Anne Gilder arrived in Sydney in February of 1833 and, as soon as she was able to after her long voyage, made arrangements to travel some 200 miles (320 km) inland to Scone. She was delayed from her overland journey because the ship's passengers and crew had been quarantined for 18 days upon arrival due to an outbreak of smallpox during the voyage.

THE LAUNCHING OF THE GREEN PEST

What happened next probably changed Australia forever. During my research I found more than twenty published versions of this obscure yet historic episode - mostly as comments in old books and newspaper articles - and have received at least a dozen personal correspondences from historians concerning it. Unfortunately, few of them agree with one another and all of their comments seem to be based primarily on supposition.

So, from information backed by what little historical record that I have uncovered, I'll take my own best shot at reconstructing these seemingly innocuous but significant developments.

We know from records kept by the state archives of New South Wales that Mary Gilder was released from quarantine on March 9th, 1833. The trip to Scone - most likely by bullock cart - would have taken at least several days to accomplish. Some accounts insist (without reference to source) that, under instruction from Dr. Carlyle, she obtained a single potted prickly-pear plant from a garden in Parramatta (a suburb of Sydney) and brought it north with her.

Other versions say that Carlyle brought it with him from India. Perhaps. . . but there is also a record of Dr. Carlyle having arrived in Sydney on the coastal sailer *Westmoreland* on the 19th of May. This is less than two months after Mary most likely would have reached Carlyle's home at Satur and relieved him of his childcare duties. In those days, the trip from Satur to Sydney via the coast would have taken from 10 days to two weeks to accomplish.

During his "child-free" time in Sydney (the city often referred to by rural dwellers as the "big smoke"), Carlyle may have visited William Macarthur's estate at Camden where at least one species of prickly-pear was growing at the time. Macarthur was very keen on the subject of the growing of grapes and operated a small winery.

Two years later, after Dr. Carlyle moved his residence to the coastal community of Port Macquarie, he too established a vineyard - which he dubbed "Hamilton." Perhaps, while talking about growing grapes and wine-making with William Macarthur, Carlyle himself picked up that famous potted cactus and brought it back to Satur with him. After all, protective hedges made from prickly-pear was something that author James Busby had recommended in his recently-published grape-growing handbook.

In any event, one of Mary's duties was to nurture that prickly-pear plant: something she did with almost religious fervor. Under her tender ministrations the cactus thrived and was successfully propagated. Cuttings were given away by both Mary and Dr. Carlyle to friends and neighbors for creating cheap fencing and for use as emergency stock fodder during droughts.

But this cactus was different from the one that Arthur Phillip had brought with him, and this "innocent plant" was soon destined to become the major pest species of the region.

When Mary died near Scone in a house fire sixty-six years later at the age of eighty-nine, her obituary recounts "the thousands of pounds sterling it has cost local pastoralists to eradicate the plant never appeared to diminish her satisfaction in having been its nurse. Apart from this, she ranked as the kindest of old souls . . ." (See Plate 4)

"Unluckily for Queenslanders, Scone was on the pioneers' route to Queensland," writes Barry Sinclair, one of Mary's descendants and family historian. "And as this variety flourished in the area, Dr. Carlyle became very generous in bestowing cuttings to the travelers passing through so that they could use it for fencing on their properties." After she married, Mary's own family went overland and "took cuttings with them as they moved along the route to Bundarra (New South Wales) where they settled for several years . . ." Mary later returned to live again at Satur.

LOCATION GROUND-ZERO

During my research, I came across a settlers' map of the upper Hunter Valley, dated 1837. It clearly shows the location and topography of Dr. Carlyle's property Satur, including the major streams running through it. When I overlaid a scaled digital copy of this map onto a recent satellite image of the Scone region, taking care to match up the watercourses, I had a very good indication of just where Carlyle's former property was situated.

Over the years, most of his land had been developed into various housing blocks, a horse-race oval, and the local airstrip, but a remaining ten or fifteen-acre block seemed untouched. Zooming in to have a closer look, I saw what appeared to be a large rambling house set in a patch of trees on the eastern part of the property. Could Carlyle's home still be standing?

Intrigued, I put its coordinates into my GPS and went for a long drive north to the pleasant community of Scone to make a few inquiries. Stopping by the town's local newspaper, I was graciously given a reprint copy of an 1888 photo of "Satur House" and put in touch with its current owner.

When we went out to visit the place, the photo matched the building that we were looking at. This was indeed Dr. Carlyle's former home and its coordinates agreed with those I had seen on the satellite photo. (See Plate 3) To my amazement, I suddenly realized that I was standing on "ground zero" of Australia's great prickly-pear plague!

FURTHER REFLECTIONS ON CARLYLE'S EXPERIMENT

Dr. Carlyle passed away in 1844 at the age of fifty-six, exactly twenty-four years to the day after he first left for Australia. Who actually brought the dreaded "pest-pear" to Satur and how it even got to Australia in the first place, we may never know. But there is an intriguing account of the aftermath of Dr. Carlyle's experiment.

59

More than fifty years after his death, the August 1898 issue of the *Queensland Agricultural Journal* published the substance of a symposium on weed control. One of the speakers was the Honorable J. V. Chataway - a former property manager of the Satur estate - and the topic was about his personal experiences in eradicating prickly-pear on this holding:

> It was twenty-four years ago when he was there. And on the place was an old lady who had been a nurse girl there some sixty years before, and she told him of the care with which the original prickly-pear had been then attended to. Instructions were given her by the then owner of the place [Dr. Carlyle] to look specially after the strange plant which was going to make all their fortunes, the prickly-pear having been introduced with a view of cultivating on it the cochineal insect, although, as a matter of fact, it was discovered afterwards that the wrong kind had been obtained.

Apparently, here was yet another failed cochineal scheme!

> When he [Mr. Chataway] took charge of the estate, already more than 1,000 acres of it were absolutely ruined through prickly-pear. In some paddocks there were not even the bridle-tracks . . . [only] just enough room for a few wild pigs to get into it. Great pig-yards were erected and immense boilers purchased. Horses were very cheap at the time . . . and between 300 and 400 pigs were fed on boiled horses and prickly-pear. This, however, made very little impression on the pear and, in any event, after seven or eight month's time the pigs would eat no more of it.

Giving up on the use of prickly-pear as a pig food supplement, Chataway then tried various other methods of eradication. "The best way that he found was to take a narrow gully, log it across with timber, and throw the prickly-pear into it and as the stuff sank, keep on piling more onto it. In that way he had got rid of thousands and thousands of tons of pear and even then, when the land was cleared, the work was not really done, the little spines [kept] coming up again in millions year after year."

Eventually prickly-pear was banished from Satur estate. During my own personal visit to that last remnant of the property, I could not find a single stem of it.

THE BEGINNINGS OF A PLAGUE

On dozens of other properties across the region from the last part of the 19th century on, when the settler's prickly-pear hedges had grown to the point where they became troublesome, they were cut down and abandoned in the mistaken belief that the plants had been destroyed. As we will see later, almost any fragment of prickly-pear that touches the ground will soon root and become a new plant. So instead of killing the cactus, people were unwittingly propagating it.

Alan Dodd, a scientific researcher who was tasked in the 1920's with helping to find a way to control this pernicious plant later wrote, "Thus, the incursions of prickly-pear did not advance outward from one center, but filled up the gaps between various initial focuses." An article published in *The Sydney Mail* graphically details this process:

> A plant or two of the pear will make its appearance in a paddock, carried there in the seed by some bird or animal and if not destroyed, will grow up quite in-different as to whether it is provided with water or not. Droughts do not stop it. As it grows, the leaves or slabs drop in a circle around it. They lie on the ground. Very soon they are seen curving up at the ends. A root has started underneath that leaf, right in the center and is some inches down in the ground. There is the new plant starting. It is only a foot or two from the parent one and that is how the stuff rises up so thick and impenetrable. All around are the other leaves, each attaching itself to the earth, taking root and forming the "clump" of pear which, if left alone, in a very short time possesses the entire paddock and then, having acquired the paddock pushes out into those adjoining.

Just what is it about this weird fleshy plant that makes it so

61

formidable, so enduring, and yet so attractive? Although much of its biology has already been worked out, scientists are still scratching their collective heads over important aspects of the ecology of this vegetable enigma. As we will soon see, this plant can survive some of the most inhospitable conditions imaginable. The author of the *Sydney Mail* article just quoted claimed to have "a leaf of prickly-pear impaled on a nail in a fence for about three years" . . . and yet it still lived.

Chapter 3: What <u>is</u> Prickly-pear?

Just what is a prickly-pear?
We really need to know.
In semi-arid zones and deserts
It is wont to grow.
Its leaves are really fattened stems
Which spiny "glochids" adorn.
From orange, red, or yellow flowers
Sweet fruits are often borne.

The primary reason why prickly-pear cactus became such an intractable pest in Australia was that its opponents lacked a thorough understanding of the biology of these plants. This included both the scientific community and the so-called "man on the ground." (Lack of biological knowledge also explains why so many well-meaning attempts at establishing a cochineal industry outside of Spain's control would ultimately fail.)

Even though I have endeavored to make this mandatory section on cactus biology as non-technical as possible, you may wish to skip this part and continue the story's narrative in the next chapter. However, if you do forgo this segment, a full understanding of what really happened during this "war on cactus" might be missed. As the old admonishment instructs, it is always best "to know thy enemy."

We'll start by returning to the time when cactus made its initial appearance in medieval Europe. This was during the period when the study of plants was making its first tentative steps towards today's formal science that we call "botany." Like most first steps, botany had a rather shaky beginning.

Due to the spiny nature of these plants, the few Europeans who studied botany originally placed all cacti into the thistle family. For example, one of the earliest illustrations of a cactus, published in 1588, shows a plant called the "Melon Thistle."

The Old World did not contain flora that resembled these strange plants, so people were often at a loss for words in their attempts at describing them. Oviedo y Valdés, the Spanish author of a 1526 book about the nature and history of the American Indies, when attempting to describe a large prickly-pear could not tell whether, "this is a tree or a monster amidst trees."

A SCIENCE OF CONFUSION

Although several groups of cactus, including *Cereus* (the "torch thistles") and *Opuntia* (prickly-pears) had already been distinguished among botanists, the word "cactus" wasn't specifically assigned to this family until 1753, when Carl von Linneaus published his famous book, *Species Plantarum.* In it, he outlined a binomial system of affixing a Latin genus and a species name to every living organism, the same system of classification that we use today.

The word "cactus" originates from the Greek "*kactos,*" meaning a "prickly plant." Under this generic heading, Linnaeus listed twenty-two species of cacti, including *Cactus opuntia*, the first prickly-pear to be named under his new system.

Thus began the long history of great confusion over cactus classification and nomenclature. At present, Linnaeus's original *Cactus* genus is divided into three major subfamilies (Pereskioideae, Cactoideae, and Opuntioideae) thought to contain roughly 115 genera with some 1,600 species. However, some researchers claim that the cactus family is much larger and actually contains more than 2,500 species within some 300 genera.

Why so much difference? Although truly new species of cacti are occasionally being discovered, there is a great deal of perplexing individual variation within a given species. This is due in part to the cactus's plasticity in response to specific growing conditions, and to the existence of numerous hybrid offspring from similar species.

Also, many cactus species have been renamed time and again. Described from a plant that was collected in Virginia, Linnaeus's original prickly-pear, *Cactus opuntia*, was later renamed *Opuntia opuntia*, and then once again to *Opuntia compressa*. Some cactuses have been scientifically renamed four or five times and more. The record for the official renaming of a cactus species is currently held by *Melocactus macrocanthos*, which has received some 80 different botanical names over the years.

Adding to the confusion is the human honesty and integrity factor. One botanist is even said to have described a new species of cactus in the mountains of Bolivia from a moving train. Apparently, he never bothered to get off the train to closely examine or even collect an actual specimen!

The subfamily, Opuntioideae (which contains our prickly-pears) hasn't fared much better. Opuntias are believed have been named after a prickly herb that grew around the ancient Greek city of Opuns. However, other researchers suggest that the name actually might have been derived from the North American Papago Indian word "*opun*." At this point, most likely no one will ever know.

For some inexplicable reason - perhaps because he only knew of less than two dozen species of cactus at the time - Linneaus dropped the name "*Opuntia*" then commonly used for prickly-pear and used "*Cactus*" instead. Only after dozens more prickly-pear species came under scrutiny was the genus "*Opuntia*" reapplied.

At last count, there are between 220 and 350 species of prickly-pear cacti. Although modern cactus classifiers can use sophisticated tools, such as DNA profiling, the chaos surrounding the proper nomenclature and number of species is likely to continue for many decades.

Cacti (the plural for cactus) are succulent plants that are adapted to live in arid habitats. The world's smallest cactus species, *Blossfeldia liliputana*, with a mature size of less than half an inch (10-12 mm), can comfortably sit in a teaspoon. The largest cactus, a giant *Cereus*, can live over 150 years, grow to a height in excess of 78 feet (24 m), and store up to two tons of water in its candelabra-shaped arms.

To minimize water loss, cacti are protected by thick, impermeable cuticles. Most cactus species have lost all of their true leaves, retaining only a series of spines that are produced from specialized buds called *areoles*, a key identifying feature of these plants. In addition to spines, areoles can also generate flowers.

THE STORY OF CAM - HOW CACTUS TAKES THE HEAT AND DOES NOT DIE

In the absence of persistent leaves, it is the cactus's enlarged stem that carries out photosynthesis for the plant. Interestingly, the cactus family has developed an adaptive "wrinkle" in the photosynthetic process, termed *crassulacean acid metabolism,* or CAM for short.

Unlike most other green plants - which take in carbon dioxide and transpire water and oxygen as photosynthetic byproducts during the day through numerous tiny pores, called *stomata* - cacti keep their stomata tightly closed until night. Thus the plant completes its photosynthetic cycle in two stages.

During the day, sugars are created by the normal photosynthetic process. But the cactus's oxygen and water byproducts are only allowed to escape after dark, when it is cooler and the relative humidity is the greatest. In this way, water loss can be held at a minimum.

At night, while the stomata are open to release surplus oxygen and water, the plants also take in a new supply of carbon dioxide (CO^2). The fresh CO^2 is stored within the cells for use in the morning.

Then, with the increasing light and heat of coming day, the balance within the plant's cells is shifted. The stomata close and CO_2 is taken out of its stored form - usually in the configuration of malic acid - to be converted by the plant's sun-driven chemical machinery into energy-rich sugars.

Because of their high water-use efficiency, the productiveness and vitality of cacti (particularly prickly-pears) is said to be much greater than most other arid and semi-arid plant species. But cacti are not the only plants to have "discovered" the usefulness of CAM when they are water-stressed. Our best known edible CAM plant is the pineapple.

THE INCOMPARABLE STRUCTURE OF PRICKLY-PEAR

Opuntiods (prickly-pears and their close kin) are unique to the cactus family in at least two important ways. First, their new growth carries a set of small deciduous leaves - often resembling small fleshy tabs - that soon dry up and fall off. Second, these plants have distinctly jointed segments, often called "pads" or "joints" (botanically termed *cladodes*) that possess a second type of spine called a *glochid*.

These hair-like spinules are very small (almost invisible), extremely sharp, wickedly barbed, and easily detached. They readily penetrate human skin, even through thick clothing, and soon become extremely irritating as they work their way into your flesh. Many an afternoon I've sat plucking them out of my hands and legs with a set of tweezers. But I have never been able to get them all in a single session.

Prickly-pears (*Opuntia*) are the most widely distributed cactus genus. They have adapted to many diverse habitats and can be found as far north as the Canadian provinces of British Columbia and Alberta and southward through the United States, Mexico, the Caribbean, Central and South America, and the Galapagos Islands.

67

In colder climates, prickly-pears are usually seen as small creeping plants that can dehydrate their pads to prevent freezing during winter. The little brittle prickly-pear (*Opuntia fragilis*) found on the Canadian prairie can tolerate amazing temperature extremes, ranging from -22 to 124 degrees Fahrenheit (-30 to 51 C.).

In normally warm climates having less temperature variations, prickly-pears often grow large and treelike. Desert species can be exceptionally resilient, stubbornly retaining enough water to withstand even the longest of droughts. Some nineteen *Opuntia* species (and eight related species of *Cylindropuntia* or chollas) are currently thought to have become naturalized in Australia.

MYSTERY OF THE ANCIENT CACTUS FAMILY

The evolutionary history of the cactus family is rather sketchy at best. Surprisingly, there appears to be almost no fossil record of its earlier forms. In 1944, American paleobotanist Ralph Chaney excitedly published a detailed description of what he thought was the stem and fruit impressions of a fossil cactus in a 30 to 45 million-year-old rock found in eastern Utah.

Because it resembled a modern prickly-pear, he named his discovery "*Eopuntia*." This assessment, however, has been refuted several times by other scientists over the years and it is now thought to be only a fossil impression of the tuberous rootstock of an extinct wetland plant.

I find it problematic that there are no truly ancient fossils of cacti. Although cactus plants contain a great proportion of water in their makeup, I have examined and photographed perfectly preserved fossils of several species of jellyfish that were millions of years old. When alive these organisms contained an even higher percentage of water than any cactus ever did.

So why aren't there any fossils of cacti? Is it because they tend to live in arid environments and rarely, if ever, get trapped and preserved in a water-born sediment layer? But hold on. . . even deserts experience destructive flash-floods now and then. It's an interesting enigma.

The small amount of physical evidence we actually do have to trace the evolutionary history of cacti is comprised of just a few bits of debris that were found in ground sloth dung, some spines and seeds sequestered in ancient packrat middens - not more than ten or fifteen thousand years old at best - and from what we think is fossilized cactus pollen. Since this pollen has only been detected in deposits 25 million years old and younger, it gives us some clue, perhaps, on how long cacti have actually been around.

Unfortunately, efforts at charting the rate of cactus DNA sequence changes (the so-called molecular clock) have proved to be mostly unhelpful so far. But researchers have been able to determine the three regional centers - central Mexico, the Andean region, and Brazil - from where cactus diversity originally spread.

PROPAGATION POWER

The often strikingly large and colorful blossoms of prickly-pears have a silky sheen that, at first glance, could easily be mistaken for a well-made and expensive artificial flower. Their usual color is yellow, but according to its species or variety there are also scarlet, hot-pink, orange, purple, and white flowers. These bright blossoms are the plant's shiny beacon for attracting pollinating insects and birds. The flowers may remain open for several days but usually close during the night.

Most Opuntiod blossoms are hermaphroditic, that is they have both sexes contained within the same flower. It's a common arrangement among many flowering plants and the prickly-pear seems to have developed this reproductive strategy to an extreme. Much like the typical flower structure taught in high-school biology classes, their blossoms contain a single pistil containing an ovary capped by one or more sticky stigmas (its female parts) that is surrounded by numerous pollen-bearing stamens (the male bits).

69

But like a deluxe model car, these flowers seem to have a lot more "bells and whistles." Charles Darwin was the first to note that when prickly-pear stamens are touched with a finger or a piece of straw, they visibly and often rapidly move towards the pistil. This behavior seems to ensure that any insect visitor to the blossom is dusted with pollen and that some of it goes on to pollinate another flower. It's very intriguing to watch the stamens move.

Many Opuntiod blossoms are self-fertile as well, which means they don't really need to be cross-pollinated with other flowers. In some localities over 60% of the prickly-pears are self-pollinated. And even if a flower hasn't been pollinated, it can still produce viable seed through a process known as *apomixis*. Then again, if the flower itself happens to be knocked off the plant and fall to the ground, it will sometimes take root directly and develop into a new plant.

This ability to clone itself from nearly any piece of the "mother" plant is one of the primary reasons why these cacti gained such a strong foothold once they were established in Australia. More than one study has implicated foraging cattle and horses for breaking prickly-pear plants apart while they browse. But nearly any disturbance - strong winds, heavy downpours of rain, floods, passing kangaroos, and even perching birds - can break off pieces and carry them away.

A few days after a short but violent rainstorm along the mid-coast of New South Wales, I counted four prickly-pear pads washed up with the flotsam on just a mile-long section of beach near Port Stephens. This must happen rather frequently, as there are numerous, yet widely scattered, small cactus colonies growing on the upland shore all along the coast.

No matter how these cactus fragments are dispersed, some of them will almost always develop into new plants. So within just a few months, a thicket of "pear" may double in size. Some species of prickly-pear even create young clones that grow up from the "parent's" spreading underground roots. This method of reproduction - or "multiplication" as it may be called - serves to perpetuate hybrids

70

by maintaining the exact genetic combination of the parent plant.

Within the edible plum-sized, pear-shaped fruits that attract so many animals - including humans, rabbits, emus, cattle, ants, crows, and even African elephants - are buried numerous disk-shaped seeds covered with a protective coating, called an *aril*. This tough membrane can withstand both long-term desiccation and the digestive system of nearly any animal that eats them, including many birds. Dozens of seedlings have been seen developing from emu and wild pig droppings.

When deposited in the animal's feces, the sprouting seeds are surrounded with a healthy dose of super rich fertilizer that gives them an extra nutritive boost during their critical early development as seedlings.

Robust prickly-pear plants bearing fruit have been found in dead stumps and in the forks of living trees more than 25 feet (7.6 m) from the ground. Also, regardless of whether they contain seeds or not, the prickly-pear fruits themselves can act as vegetative propagules and develop into new plants if they happen to fall to the ground.

Prickly-pear seeds apparently can remain on and in the ground without sprouting for long periods of time. Just how long this "soil seed bank" can remain viable is a question open to debate. Few studies have been conducted on this aspect of cactus biology, yet the impermeable nature and presence of chemical germination inhibitors in the seeds' coats suggest that prickly-pear seeds may remain dormant for a considerable period of time.

"BANKING" SEEDS OF RESILIENCE

Seed dormancy is thought to be an evolutionary response to unpredictable environments. Some seeds simply wait, often for many years, until moisture and climatic conditions are favorable before they sprout. The oldest tree seed known to have grown into a viable plant was from a Judean date palm, recovered from Herod the Great's palace in Israel, that was carbon-dated to be about 2,000 years in age. Another seed, a nearly 1,300-year-old sacred lotus found in a dry lake-bed in China, was likewise successfully sprouted.

Amazingly, a team of Russian scientists reported in 2012 that they had successfully grown viable plants from *in vitro* tissue cultures of placental material taken from 30 to 33,000-year-old seeds of a small tundra flower (*Silene stenophylla*). The seeds had been collected in the northern permafrost from the ancient burrows of an Ice Age ground-squirrel.

Once deposited onto the soil, not all prickly-pear seeds will germinate at once. Some will sprout quickly, especially those that have been stimulated by passing through an animal's digestive system. Having their seed coats scratched in some mechanical way, such as tumbling during a flood or being stepped upon by a heavy animal, is another sprouting stimulus.

Other seeds will continue to wait and then germinate sequentially over a period of many years. John Mann, the author of *Cacti Naturalised in Australia and Their Control*, wrote that he had "observed seedling plants growing in places where it is certain that plants had not fruited for over 30 years." Several references cite dormant periods of at least 20 years after seed production.

In Queensland, I heard reports of cotton farmers who had observed the common pest-pear (*Opuntia stricta*) springing up from seed in their fallow fields nearly 80 years after all seed-producing plants had been eliminated from the district. When I arrived to investigate these claims, one farmer told me to have a good look around. He was sure that I would not find any pest-pear outside of his fields.

Sure enough, an extensive survey revealed to me that the common pest-pear was no longer present, having long been eliminated through the combined efforts of insect predation, chemical poisons, and the brute force of chopping and burning during the last century. The only place that I could find the cactus was in the farmers' untended fields.

However, Australia's most important prickly-pear herbivore, the *Cactoblastis* moth, was still present in the region in small numbers. Here and there, *Cactoblastis* could be found infecting a local treelike cactus, known as the Velvety tree-pear (*Opuntia tomentosa*), which can be seen growing along many of the roadways in the district and is not considered to be a serious pest.

As I examined and photographed infected plants, the truth of what was happening slowly dawned upon me. I had initially discounted the farmers' assertions that when prickly-pear appeared in their fields, the *Cactoblastis* moths would come out of the woods and destroy the seedlings *en mass* and then they would retreat back into the bush.

Now I was beginning to see that these claims were apparently true. *Cactoblastis* was using the Velvety tree-pear as a "reserve host" and maintaining a low-level population between the times when the common pest-pear sprang up. Intrigued, I left the area wondering how long the prickly-pear would continue to sprout from long-dormant seeds buried in those farmer's fields.

Although little data exists on how prickly-pear seed viability varies with time, several studies have shown that despite the high proportion of viable seeds in some *Opuntia* species, they generally have a very low germination rate. This suggests that they are adapted for a dormant existence in a soil seed bank. Some species of prickly-pear actually experience increased germination rates after being stored for a year or more.

According to information about seed longevity published by England's Royal Botanic Gardens at Kew, "orthodox seeds" are those seeds that can be dried and stored. As a general principle, (known as Harrington's rule) seed life-span doubles for every 1% reduction in moisture content and doubles again for every 5° Centigrade drop in temperature. Although most orthodox seeds react in a predictable manner, some species are inherently longer-lived than others.

To illustrate, under an artificial seed bank's typical storage conditions of minus 20° Centigrade (-4° F.), lettuce seeds might be expected to survive for more than 1,500 years. By comparison, under those same circumstances, sunflowers would probably survive for around 464 years, and cactus seeds for an estimated 2,428 years.

Given the conditions of Australia's natural "seed bank" and the adaptations the *Cactoblastis* moths have made, prickly-pears may be sprouting in those Queensland farmers' fields for quite a long time to come!

HYBRIDIZATION

Prickly-pear cacti are known to hybridize rather freely through sexual reproduction. (Hybridization is the crossbreeding of two different species of plants resulting in a new variety.) This process plays an important role in the evolution of plants and can sometimes produce new varieties that are able to colonize habitat that is very different from that of either parent species.

In the case of the prickly-pear, successful hybrids are usually maintained through asexual reproduction by fragmentation. Taken to its extreme, this process has even led to the establishment of populations of certain varieties that no longer - or very rarely - reproduce by flowering. The coral cactus (*Cylindropuntia fulgida* var. *mamillata*), brittle prickly-pear (*Opuntia fragilis*) and tiger pear (*Opuntia aurantiaca*) are good examples of this. Both the tiger pear and brittle prickly-pear have been around for so long that they are considered to be independent species. The parents of the original crosses that led to these species are yet to be discovered.

In Australia, the introduction of so many prickly-pear species across the landscape has inevitably led to the creation of hybrids. One of the first to be noted was reported in the July 5th, 1923 edition of the *Moree/Gwydir Examiner*. Referring to W. B. (Wilfred Backhouse) Alexander, then Officer in Charge of the Commonwealth Prickly Pear Investigations, the newspaper commented that "within a couple of miles of Kelly's Gully Railway Station he found a species of pear much more formidable than the common pear and, as far as he was aware, unrecorded in New South Wales."

Later, Alexander began to suspect that this "new species" had actually been a hybrid and began searching for the existence of others. He found what he thought were hybrid specimens in New South Wales near his Westwood field station and at Glenmore, and in Queensland near Rockhampton and Gogango. (He even delivered a paper to the Royal Society of Queensland on the variation and hybridization of Australia's acclimatized species of prickly-pear.)

Some of these hybrid prickly-pears were named after the districts in which they predominated. There was the "Gayndah pear," which formed huge spiny masses around Rockhampton and Gayndah in eastern Queensland. There was also the "Westwood pear" and the "cabbage pear." Further west, the nearly spineless "Hawkwood pear" dominated the landscape.

In some cases, probably because of their confusing characteristics, a few of these varieties were later thought to be distinct species by botanists and named accordingly. Their proper scientific nomenclature may still be in question for some time to come.

Although Alexander certainly suspected this but probably did not fully realize it at the time, Australia's two most widespread and troublesome prickly-pears were actually one and the same species. The common pest-pear - named *Opuntia inermis* during this era - and the spiny pest-pear (*Opuntia stricta*) were later determined to just be different varieties of *Opuntia stricta*.

The spiny variety was first noticed, growing as a hedge in Rockhampton, Queensland, in about 1870. It quickly spread across the state. Exactly how the processes of hybridization aided in the development of this new variety, we may never know for sure.

However, in South Australia recent investigations into the genetic diversity of the invasive prickly-pear known as the wheel cactus (*Opuntia robusta*) has revealed high levels of gene flow and the presence of numerous individual genotypes within the studied populations. Well adapted to arid habitats and resistant to the southern winter cold, it is thought ("highly suspected" as the researchers cautiously say) that this prickly-pear has hybridized with other species of *Opuntia*.

Prickly-pear evolution appears to be still on the move. In fact, it has never stopped and never will. Although this is a highly unlikely scenario for the near future - given the conservative nature of botanical research and regulating government agencies - it would not surprise me if someday one of these new varieties achieves traits so unique that it is eventually declared to be an endemic species exclusive to Australia.

In essence, that is precisely what some of them are in the process of becoming. For the time being, however, in our present social, political, and academic culture they are all classed as "introduced" and noxious "weeds."

THE WEEDS OF CIVILIZATION

We civilized humans are renowned for moving plants and animals around the planet. Indeed, this single factor may be our species' most enduring legacy. Wherever human colonies have been begun - even in the humblest villages - the seeds and animals of agriculture are brought along with its pioneering people.

Eventually the entire landscape and its ecology are altered as the civilizing process establishes itself. It's a familiar pattern: the pioneers stake a claim to the land and any hunter/gatherer peoples found there are soon marginalized. Forests are felled. Cattle, sheep, and horses replace indigenous grazing animals.

Native prairies are plowed and planted with monocultures of grains. Semi-arid land is irrigated as rivers and streams are dammed and diverted or, lacking natural waterways, with ancient groundwater brought to the surface by deep wells. The villages become towns and eventually cities. Rain-impervious roads extend in all directions.

Taxes are levied by governments. Armies are raised for protection. War or the threat of war becomes ever-present. We call it "progress."

Within the cultural matrix of civilization, some plants and animals eventually become not welcome. Throughout the 1800s and early 1900s, people unwittingly brought dozens of plant and animal species into Australia, which, away from their natural predators, began to run rampant.

Rabbits, introduced by Geelong grazier Thomas Austin in 1859, were literally in "plague proportions" less than a century later. Blackbirds, starlings, sparrows, and pigeons released by people who missed the birds of their European home-countries multiplied into astronomical numbers.

In 1939, cane toads were brought in to control the greyback cane beetle, a sugar cane pest. The cane toads not only failed to live up to their name, but found Australia much to their liking and spread out in a hopping plague across the continent. Unfortunately, because of their poisonous nature, these toads have also become a serious threat to native wildlife.

We call our unwanted and unappreciated plants "weeds" and we take steps to eliminate the more troublesome ones. A few, however, stubbornly resist our efforts and continue to thrive. As the weed spreads, so does our determination to conquer them. Laws banning their movement or cultivation are enacted. Government agencies are created to enforce those laws and to find ways of eliminating the pests.

Weeds are essentially a bi-product of civilization. In Australia more than 400 species of introduced plants are now considered to be serious weeds. Exotic plants currently account for nearly 10 to 15% of the flora growing on that continent. Some of them - lantana, water hyacinth, blackberry, cape-weed, salvia - have become troublesome to the point of being considered noxious. But in the historical long-run, the worst of them all is prickly-pear.

THE DEVIL HAS A LOVELY FACE

Even during the height of the fight against Australia's prickly-pear plague, when the nation's mood began to change to grim determination, the cactus continued to impart its charm on newcomers and a small circle of affectionados.

In March of 1927, Brisbane's *Daily Mail* reported that locals visiting the Japanese steamer, "*Hokkai Maru*," were bemused to find prickly-pear growing in flower pots in the ship's salon. Having recently discharged a cargo of oil at Townsville, the cactus had been "discovered at Port Alma by officers of the boat, who were so pleased with its appearance that they decided to get some roots and plant them in pots to take back to relatives in Japan."

More than any other reason, it was because of this fascinating attractiveness that prickly-pear gained such a wide foothold in Australia. Less than 50 years after the first plants arrived with Authur Phillip in 1788, prickly-pears were being sold as garden ornamentals in city nurseries.

They were highly valued for their unusual shape, exceedingly bright flowers, and tasty fruit. Some people began hedging their kitchen gardens with it, using it as a living fence to keep out animal pests. In the country districts, people planted it around their homesteads to brighten the place up.

The story of prickly-pear's initial spread across Australia's vast interior is replete with charmed meeting and friendly exchange. In 1843, Edward Gore of Yandilla Station in Queensland brought three plants with him and ordered his gardener to water them twice a day. Other settlers admired Gore's cactus and carefully broke off cuttings for their own station gardens.

In 1859, a Mr. Hook was reported to have carried several of these cactus starts in his saddle pouch for a distance of nearly 400 miles (643 km). Carefully planted in a suitable spot on his property near the upper Dawson River, the pear was reported as "looking very well" several years later. By 1863, prickly-pear had spread hundreds of miles out into the Darling Downs.

78

In 1924, the *Sydney Morning Herald* published an interview with the owner of a large property located in northern New South Wales along the Gwydir River. "Nearly a hundred years ago the first holder of his station brought a pear plant from Scone," the newspaper article recounted:

> He had seen the pear there and evidently admired it as an improvement to the scenery, or as a cheap fence for paddocks . . . The first plant brought to "Keera Station" was carefully watered, but died. Later, another owner procured another plant and this time it thrived exceedingly. It grew so hardily that the station-owner suspected danger and ordered the pear growth to be dug up and destroyed. The man who dug it up, seeking an easy way to dispose of the body, threw it into the Gwydir River. That set up the pear for life. It spread along the river flats and has laid hold of the district far and wide.

A HANDSOME VISION

During the mid-19th century, there were also renewed attempts at establishing a cochineal industry in Australia; these often initiated by citizen's groups called "acclimatization societies." The purpose of acclimatization societies was to introduce useful and "more appreciated" species of plants and animals into the developing nation.

The New South Wales Acclimatization Society, for example, stated its lofty aims as ". . . stocking our waste waters, woods and plains with choice animals, making that which was dull and lifeless become animated by creatures in full enjoyment of existence and lands before useless become fertile with rare and valuable trees and plants."

In 1863, that organization made at least two unsuccessful attempts to bring cochineal from England. A year later, Sir George Grey, the Governor of New Zealand, sent a consignment of cochineal which did arrive safely in Sydney. Then nothing more was heard about it. But along with all these failed cochineal endeavors came several more species of prickly-pear, which were indeed successful. Within a few years, most of them had become naturalized.

In his book about Australian pests, *They All Ran Wild*, author Eric Rolls notes, "Although the plant was known to be a nuisance in parts of India, a paper to the Queensland Acclimatization Society in 1877 glibly stated that 'The fault is scarcely that of the prickly-pear but rather those that permitted it to attain unmanageable dimensions and to grow where it is not required.'" (In all seriousness, I wonder how they proposed to keep it from growing "where it was not required"?)

Four years later, William Baynes, a member of Queensland's Parliament, finally managed to focus public attention on the reality of the situation. He warned that prickly-pear's inordinate spread was in reality an "environmental time-bomb."

THE DEVIL'S OTHER FACE

Of the nearly forty species of cacti that actually have become naturalized in Australia, less than a dozen have proven to be serious pests. The worst of the lot - those two varieties of *Opuntia stricta*, which became commonly known as the "*pest-pear*" or just "*pear*" - eventually became the focus of Australia's national cactus eradication effort, due to the enormous damage it caused to the nation.

The "pest-pear" that plagued Australia is native to the southeastern United States, where it is known as the "erect prickly-pear" or "southern spineless cactus." Here it grows in the sandy soils of coastal forests and dunes from southern Texas to Florida and on the jungle mounds surrounding the Everglades. It can also be found in Ecuador, Central America, and throughout much of the Caribbean.

In addition to Australia, it has been introduced and naturalized in South Africa, Morocco, Tunisia, Ethiopia, Swaziland,

Namibia, Yemen, Madagascar, India, China, Spain, the Galapagos Islands, Thailand, Pakistan, New Caledonia, and the Solomon Islands.

The stems of this plant are dull green or bluish-green in color and are divided into flattened pads up to 12 inches long (30 cm), six inches wide (15 cm) and around a half-inch thick (1-2 cm). Although it possesses few spines, its areoles are literally choked with finely-barbed irritating glochids that detach easily when touched. Its flowers are bright lemon yellow and its pear-shaped fruits - which are about two inches long (5 cm) - are reddish purple when ripe. The seeds are embedded in the fruit's carmine-colored pulp.

Both the spiny and nearly spineless varieties of pest-pear grow into bush-like clumps typically ranging from 3 to 6 feet high (1 to 2 m). The spiny form, however, is armed with a dense array of sharp yellowish spines that can be more than one and a half inches long (3.8 cm) and its growth habit tends to be more erect in posture.

Most of the pest-pear's vast Australian territory has an annual rainfall of 20 to 30 inches (51-76 cm). At the peak of its invasion in 1925, the pest-pear's main province stretched in a wide band from Mackay, Queensland south to Sydney, New South Wales, a distance of more than 1,000 miles (1,600 km). (See Plate 9)

The apparent western limit of this "pear belt" was over 400 miles (650 km) inland, although pockets of scattered growth could be found in many places well outside this region. This species also occurs in the Australian states of South Australia, Western Australia, and Victoria.

Furthermore, it was in Victoria on a property located north of Melbourne, that one man's concerted effort to tame prickly-pear "for the benefit of humanity" went astray, ultimately contributing to Australia's great cactus plague. His story, begun half a world away in sunny California, eventually gripped the attention of both the US Congress and the Australian federal parliament before it reached its sad conclusion.

Chapter 4: Promises For a New World

At first they were planted as hedges,
Useful for fodder during droughts indeed.
"My spineless cactus," said Mr. Burbank,
"Will make even the poorest farm succeed."

It was barely after sunrise on a bright June morning when I first saw them in the "plant wizard's" garden. They were located just off a path behind the old carriage house. Some of them stood over 15 feet tall (4.5 m) and bore slab-like "joints" more than two feet long (0.6 m). On close inspection, I could see that a few of the last remnants of these famous spineless cactus "creations" were still relatively prickle-free nearly 100 years after they were first planted.

Except for dotted rows of bumpy little black aerioles, their smooth skin was unblemished. Other prickly-pears nearby, however, had completely reverted back to their wild state and were now covered with an impressive armament of long stiff spines.

During the first quarter of the 20th century, the vegetable products of this quiet garden located in the city of Santa Rosa, California, had been the focus of worldwide public attention. Continuous eulogizing press-coverage had made sure of it.

But there had been good reasons for all that praise. The creator of this garden, Mr. Luther Burbank, had astounded the nation with his ingenuity in coaxing an almost endless array of amazingly colorful and more productive hybrids from common fruits, vegetables, and flowers. Catching the public's imagination, he became known far and wide as the "plant wizard."

BURBANK'S EARLY SUCCESSES

Luther Burbank's celebrated career began with his discovery of a natural genetic variant of potato. Born in 1849, Luther Burbank was the thirteenth of fifteen children of Samuel Burbank (from three marriages). Luther was barely 19 years old when his father died and he had used his small inheritance to help buy a 17-acre farm near the small town of Lunenburg, Massachusetts.

Here he decided to become a produce market gardener, and it was from one of 23 seeds that he found in a seedball on an "Early Rose" potato-plant growing in his mother's garden patch that led to perhaps the world's most widely cultivated potato.

Young Burbank had a sharp eye for anomalies, and one of the plants grown from that seedball (seed #15) had tubers like no other. With thin brownish skin and delicious white flesh, they also stored well and seemed resistant to the common potato blight. He replanted these special tubers to increase his supply.

Having decided to move to California, Burbank soon sold the rights to his new potato to a local seedsman, J. H. J. Gregory of Gregory's Honest Seeds, for just $150 for travel fare. (Burbank had originally asked for $500 but settled for $150.) However, Gregory did honor him by naming it the "Burbank Seedling."

Just thirty years later, agricultural production of this particular potato cultivar was said to have been worth more than US $50 million annually. Today, a sport (an aberrant growth that can be reproduced reliably in cultivation) of those original Burbank Seedlings - now known as the "Russet Burbank potato" - is worth more than US $1.45 billion each year in the United States alone.

Following in the wake of two or three of his brothers who had gone ahead of him, (it must have been difficult to keep track of 14 siblings) Burbank arrived on the California scene in the autumn of 1875. After a couple of years of casting about, he managed to secure four acres in Santa Rosa. Here he would live and work for nearly 50 years until his death.

As his horticultural research needs expanded, he eventually added another 18 acres to his growing business in nearby Sebastopol. Known as "Gold Ridge Experimental Farm," the Sebastopol property would serve as an important proving-ground for many of his new plant varieties.

But first he had to get his nursery and seed business off the ground. He began with the ten Burbank potatoes that he had reserved by agreement with Gregory's Honest Seeds when the rest of the stock had been sold back in Massachusetts. Planting-stock from these improved potatoes were purchased by several local farmers, and they quickly proved to be a valuable asset. A bigger break came when he received an order for 20,000 of the newly-introduced 'Agen' prune-plums from an impatient man who wanted to start a large prune ranch.

When he accepted the order, Burbank did not have anything close to that number of plum trees on hand, and it normally takes about three years to raise them in the traditional manner. This order, however, had to be filled in just nine months or not at all. Burbank daringly went to work on the problem.

It was late in the season and the only seeds of any fruit tree related to plums that would sprout reliably during this period were almonds. So Burbank planted 20,000 almonds and carefully watched them sprout. Almond seedlings grow rather quickly, and soon they were ready to receive his 'Agen' plum buds for grafting. When the time for delivery came, the grafted prune-stock was ready. The fruit grower was delighted, and Burbank's reputation grew by another notch.

Burbank's career had another boost in 1885 when he successfully imported an assortment of plums from Japan. After two of the plums became best sellers, he began to conduct serious experiments in plant breeding and was soon completely absorbed by the challenges of creating new strains of plums and other plants. Eventually, he would develop more than 800 unique plant hybrids, including 200 varieties of fruit trees.

Some of these productions, such as the Santa Rosa plum, the Shiro plum, the Shasta daisy, and of course the Burbank potato, are still widely cultivated. Back home in my own garden, I counted eight Burbank "creations" - as he liked to call them - that included two types of plum, his famous potato, and three varieties of daisies.

In 1893, Burbank began publishing a series of "announcements" - really just well-written and engaging catalogues - that contained descriptions and pictures of his most striking botanical achievements. The first in this line was titled "*New Creations in Fruit and Flowers*," and it also included numerous tributes from people expressing their high opinion of his work.

From that point on, a new announcement was published almost every year. It was a stroke of marketing genius. A year later, his nursery was advertising a stock of half-a-million fruit and nut trees.

BURBANKISM

Burbank's publications created such a profound sensation throughout the horticultural world that "Luther Burbank" soon became a household name. Newspapers and magazines, in turn, began publishing descriptive articles about his new and wonderful plant creations, such as the white blackberry, mammoth cherries, freestone peaches, stoneless plums, and the paradox walnut - a cross between native and Persian varieties that yielded valuable hardwood yet grew as rapidly as pine trees. Commenting on Burbank's skill as a promoter, it was said that Burbank "played the press like a violin."

Burbank's approach to plant breeding was both simple and practical, and it also proved to be very labor-intensive. Seeds from crossbred parents were planted *en-masse*, then from the thousands of resulting seedlings, the one or two plants that displayed some desirable characteristic were carefully selected. The remainder were ripped out of the ground and destroyed by burning them in bonfires.

Sometimes the selected plants were crossbred again, and then again and again, in this painstaking process of seed-sprouting, growth, and selection, until the results finally approached what Burbank originally had in mind.

During the course of an average workday, Burbank would oversee dozens, perhaps hundreds, of these meticulous experiments. As one of his biographers wrote, "Far too often the day with Mr. Burbank begins in care, advances in anxiety, and closes in exhaustion."

Burbank did not have a university degree nor could he boast of any formal scientific training. But he was an unusually keen observer. He had read Darwin's work on the origin of species and carefully applied Darwin's theory on the accumulative effect of slight variations to his own work. It was uncanny, people often said, how he could instantly detect tiny differences in structure or color even in a tray of seemingly identical plant seedlings.

"Burbank's sole object in making crosses was to cause variation in the seedlings," wrote University of California Professor W. L. Howard, a friend and contemporary of Burbank. "He could then improve them by selection. As a disciple of Darwin he had learned his lesson thoroughly."

To keep track of all this hybrid crossing and progeny selection, Burback developed a kind of shorthand note-keeping system that was decipherable only to himself.

That brought criticism from classically-trained scientists who wanted to understand Burbank's methodology. Burbank was undeterred. Even after he was awarded a $10,000-a-year grant from the Carnegie Institution in 1905 - no small sum in those days - he would continue to neglect his write-ups on experiments. Anticipating this, the Carnegie Institution hired a young biologist with a Ph.D., George Harrison Shull, to travel from Washington DC to observe and record his methods.

But when Shull decided that Burbank's procedure was more *art* than *science*, the grant was discontinued after just five years.

Perhaps to satisfy his critics, Burbank later published a twelve-volume treatise entitled, *Luther Burbank: His Methods and Discoveries and Their Practical Application*.

THE PRICE OF FAME

As Burbank's reputation continued to soar, so did his correspondence and the number of visitors to his home. He became friends with Thomas Edison and Henry Ford, two other self-taught geniuses who had helped to transform the civilized world. The three men were photographed sitting together on the steps leading to Burbank's garden.

Scientist after visiting scientist - people like Hugo de Vries, the Dutch geneticist who invented the term "mutation" - were stunned by the range of experiments they saw in Burbank's gardens. And, they wrote letters and articles telling of their amazement.

The accolades seemed almost unending. During its 50th anniversary in 1903, the California Academy of Sciences awarded Burbank a gold medal "for meritorious work in developing new forms of plant life." The president of Stanford University appointed him "Special Lecturer on Evolution."

Even President Theodore Roosevelt is reported to have stated, "Mr. Burbank is a man who does things that are of much benefit to mankind, and we should do all in our power to help him." (In 1940, a US postage stamp was issued posthumously in Burbank's honor.)

Visitors to his gardens were soon taking up so much of Burbank's time that it seriously interfered with his work and began to negatively impact his health. On top of this, it was estimated that he received nearly 800 letters a week. Although he tried, it was proving impossible to answer every one of them. He hired a secretary to help him and developed form-letters to deal with all but the most pressing correspondence. When even this was not enough, he wrote public appeals for people not to waste his time with unnecessary questions.

To slow the non-stop pilgrimage of uninvited visitors, he also posted all of the gates to his properties with signs that read, "Positively No Visitors Allowed." And many of the callers that he actually did receive were required to purchase a "Ticket of Admittance" before they could enter the grounds. Charge for admission was $10 an hour, $5 for half an hour, and $2.50 for a quarter-hour. . . rather steep prices in an age when journeyman carpenters often earned less than $8 a day.

Fame was clearly wearing him down, however, and Burbank began to experience increasingly serious bouts of nervous illness. He even committed himself to a sanitarium for a while. But it was the prickly-pear cactus that would prove to be his greatest nemesis.

THE FATEFUL DECISION

When Burbank was a very young boy and already beginning to show a profound interest in plants, he was given a little potted cactus. He carried that cactus fondly about, very much like a pet, until an accident suddenly destroyed it. The loss upset him greatly.

So perhaps it seems natural that, after he became an adult, he would eventually focus his attention on breeding new varieties of those interesting plants. Accordingly, with high hopes, he chose the prickly-pears for his subject, but by the time this venture was over it would almost destroy the man and his brilliant career.

Burbank began - innocently enough - by assembling a collection of various kinds of prickly-pear plants from around the world. Numerous specimens, particularly of the long-cultivated and already nearly spineless Indian fig (*Opuntia ficus-indica*), were imported from Mexico and Central and South America.

Other samples came from species that had been introduced long ago into Africa, the South Sea Islands, the Mediterranean region, Japan, and even Australia. The hope was that in their new habitats, the process of natural hybridization might have yielded some characteristics useful to his breeding program. The United States

Department of Agriculture even provided him with material from its large *Opuntia* collection in Washington DC. All the while, private cactus collectors and well-wishers sent him ever more prickly-pear varieties gathered from all over America.

PERFECTING THE SPINELESS CACTUS

From this huge array, Burbank began the most ambitious plant-breeding program that he would ever attempt. Cactus seeds were planted just a few inches apart in specially prepared beds by the tens of thousands.

"Over a period of eight to twelve years," observes Peter Dreyer in his book, *A Gardener Touched With Genius*, "The Burbank principal of mass-selection was applied - hybridizing, selecting, and hybridizing again. The aim of the breeding was twofold: forage and fruit . . . Many varieties combined both objectives, and some had beautiful flowers as well."

Burbank would eventually claim to have developed some 40 variants of spineless prickly-pear to grow for fruit or as improved forage for livestock.

As the work proceeded, some of Burbank's best varieties were planted along the white picket fence that marked the perimeter of his home and experimental gardens. Here, passersby and the daily crowd of curious onlookers could see and marvel over them.

"At last. . ." wrote Burbank biographer W. S. Harwood enthusiastically, "rose a giant cactus fully eight feet in height (2.5 m), bearing thalli or leaves (cladodes) from ten inches to a foot in length (0.25 - 0.30 m), five to eight inches in width (12 - 20 cm), nearly an inch in thickness (2.5 cm), bearing fruit of a large size, not a thorn upon it, not a spicule in all its rich meat. . ."

Some of Burbank's prickly-pear hybrids produced yellow fruit, while others bore the more familiar red fruit with crimson flesh. The fruit of these new cacti was "delicious to the taste," Harwood continues. "To some it has the flavor of a peach, to some a melon, to some a blackberry - to everyone who tastes it, a different flavor from anything before eaten. It is, indeed, a new taste for the palate of the world."

Burbank was now ready for everyone to see his new cactus creations; it was time for another "announcement." In June of 1907, he offered his latest plant wonder to the world market in a special catalogue titled "*The New Agricultural-Horticultural Opuntias: Plant Creations for Arid Regions.*"

This publication - and all similar ones that followed over the next decade - featured luscious descriptions backed by actual photographs of his new spineless cacti. Sprinkled liberally throughout their pages were convincing testimonials, impressive nutritional analyses, and predictions of amazing yields. Even today, when reading one of these old pamphlets it is difficult not to become inspired.

"The leaves are to be fed to stock at any season throughout the whole year when most needed," Burbank advises the would-be grower in his introductory section to one of these publications. "And in countries where great numbers of valuable stock are lost in times of unusual drought, will be of inestimable value. . ."

He also predicts that the cactus will become an important farm and orchard crop, "especially on barren, rocky, hill and mountainsides, and gravely river beds which are now of no use whatever."

When comparing his new thornless cactus to the wild varieties, Burbank paints a vivid word picture:

> The wild cactus is generally prepared for stock by singeing the thorns with fire, yet this never destroyed all the thorns. Those who have fed the wild cactus extensively acknowledge that cattle are often seen with blood dripping from their mouths, and that their throats and tongues at last become inflamed, very painful and hard like a piece of sole leather. How would you enjoy being fed on needles, fishhooks, toothpicks, barbed-wire fence, nettles and chestnut burrs?

The wild thorny cactus is and always must be more or less a pest. Millions of cattle, sheep, goats, hogs, ostriches, have been destroyed by it. The new thornless ones will withstand flood, drought, heat, wind, and poor soil better than the wild ones and will produce one hundred tons of good food where the average wild ones will produce ten tons of inferior food.

Burbank then discloses that, "Many of the owners of the great stock ranges have seen the necessity of some insurance against these fearful losses and are devoting certain tracts to these new cactus plants to avert this danger as well as for supplementing the usual feed."

Such insurance didn't come cheap, though. The price for owning the complete rights to one of Burbank's cactus creations ranged from one to several thousand dollars, well beyond the means of the average farmer or rancher.

But instead of selling to individuals, Burbank's marketing strategy for his newest plant wonders was aimed at professional dealers. Ideally they would buy the entire rights to one of his original creations, cultivate and multiply the plants on their own grounds, and then sell the results either wholesale or directly to the public.

"Whenever possible," notes Jane S. Smith, another Burbank historian, "He licensed or sold his plant prototypes to large, well-established companies like Burpee Seeds in Pennsylvania, Stark Brothers Nurseries in Missouri, or Child's Nurseries, whose establishment was so large it became the city of Floral Park, New York."

She reflectively adds, "This was Burbank's preferred method for disseminating his work, and both his extraordinary products and his eye-popping prices ensured huge publicity for the new spineless cactus, as it had for his other introductions in the past." (In one of his annual catalogues, he had set the price for his entire lot of Burbank Hybrid Lilies at an astounding $250,000, or more than $6.5 million today. Not surprisingly, that bundle of lilies didn't sell.)

THE AUSTRALIANS ARRIVE

As might be expected, the Australians took a keen interest in Burbank's spineless cactus and soon delegation after delegation began traveling overseas to visit him. After meeting Mr. Burbank and touring his research garden, Australia's Senator James McColl arrived back home in Victoria convinced that the spineless prickly-pear would benefit his country immensely.

In a special commonwealth parliamentary report published in 1909, McColl wrote, "Mr. Burbank contends that the use of the spineless cactus opens up a new agricultural era for the millions of useless acres now in every continent, and if he is right, it also means the same for Australia." Optimistically, he added, "It is claimed that the new thornless plants will stand all the hard and arid conditions as well as the spiny varieties and will produce ten tons of feed where the wild sort one produces one."

McColl's report quickly sparked a national debate and soon a booklet entitled, "*Australia's Opportunity: Luther Burbank and the Thornless Edible Cactus,*" was appearing on the kitchen tables of homesteads and in agricultural offices across the country.

This publication made even stronger claims for the future of spineless cactus. One excerpt reads, "Indeed the value of these cacti as a sustaining food for sheep and cattle and as a delicious fruit for domestic use can scarcely be exaggerated."

Urging immediate government action, the publication goes on to predict that, "The continual dread of unfavorable seasons, which hangs like an evil spirit about the Australian farmer, would become a thing unknown. The vast arid areas of the interior, now practically uninhabited, might be covered with [a] prosperous population."

John Matthew Rutland, a wealthy orchardist also from Victoria, had anticipated the call and quietly attempted to "steal the march" on the introduction of spineless cactus into Australia. Almost two years before Burbank had even released his first cactus catalogue,

Rutland and his family were already on their way to California. There he bought a private home in Sebastopol, located close to Burbank's farm, just so that he could be near the great man's work.

On July 13, 1905, Rutland purchased a ticket of admission to see Mr. Burbank in person. This ticket allowed him only 30 minutes to state his case, yet it must have been enough time to cut a preliminary deal. (See Plate 11) Soon after this meeting, Rutland paid Burbank US $1,000 for a single slab of his most important *Opuntia*, named the "Santa Rosa." (In today's monetary values this would be the equivalent of somewhere around US $26,500.) This purchase also included the exclusive distribution rights to introduce Burbank's spineless cactus to Australia, Africa, and the rest of the southern hemisphere.

Eventually, Rutland became a frequent visitor to the Burbank home. Even during one of Luther's bouts of illness due to overwork in which "absolute rest was recommended for a number of months," the Australian orchardist came a-calling and was duly admitted.

Rutland's planting-stock order eventually grew to include four other varieties of spineless prickly-pear, a hybrid grape, the Rutland plumcot (a hybrid between an plum and an apricot named in honor of him) and six varieties of plum, for a total of $5,800 - a large sum in those days that would have had the purchasing power of more than $152,000 (US) today. From the proceeds of this single sale, Burbank is said to have built himself a fine new two-story house.

Armed with the secure knowledge of his exclusive distribution rights, Rutland and his family eventually left California to prepare for the reception of his order in Australia. (The plants were to be shipped separately at a later date.) A few days before sailing from Vancouver, British Columbia, Canada, on the 13th of December, 1907, Rutland sent Burbank a farewell letter that contained the following tribute:

> We have had a thoroughly enjoyable trip and received
> a lot of valuable information and gained considerable
> experience. I hope that you are enjoying the very best

of health and that you will be spared for many years to carry on your great work - a work that I would like if I had the knowledge and ability. . .

It would be nearly two years before Rutland's order of Burbank planting-stock would arrive in Australia. Even so, he had barely enough time to prepare for it. First, he needed to locate some suitable land for his new orchard.

Searching through his home state of Victoria, Rutland finally found a place in the Kiewa Valley that reminded him of Santa Rosa, California. He quickly purchased a 900 acre block and began clearing the red gum and box trees from 100 acres of bottom land. This cleared land was to become his orchard, the focus of his life.

Eventually, he planned to run cattle on the remainder of the property. With good deep soils and an unfailing stream of clear water, he named his new property "Santa Rosa" after the California home of Luther Burbank. Here John Rutland would live and work for the rest of his days.

TROUBLES IN THE MARKETPLACE

Even as Rutland readied his land for the licensed sales of Burbank's "plant wonders" to the rest of Australia, Mr. Burbank was actively trying to distance himself from the increasing number of "cactus pirates" (dealers of Burbank imitations) and all the burdensome details of marketing and sales. In his very first *Opuntia* catalog, Burbank admitted that the task of selling his new cactus was beginning to overwhelm him. He despairingly wrote:

> I have no time or desire to introduce these or any other Opuntias and would gladly leave the matter to some-one else but so much has been written about them that it seems necessary to have them distributed direct from my own grounds. . . so as to avoid as much as possible any misunderstandings, exaggerations, or misstatements.

Burbank also mentions John Rutland's recent cactus purchases in that catalogue, saying that they "are now being sent to Australia for sale exclusively in the southern hemisphere."

But then he reveals in the next sentence that he is already having problems with counterfeit Burbank thornless cactus that have "been offered for sale by dishonest parties for two years or more in many of the large cities of both hemispheres." This brief note was just a preview of much bigger problems to come.

Burbank seriously wanted to be free of any business responsibility that kept him away from what he considered his real work: the creation of new plant varieties. There was no shortage of candidates, honest and otherwise, who were more than willing to cash in on the famous man's unique plant products.

One of the first of these entrepreneurs to sign a contract to relieve Burbank of his toilsome burden was Charles Welch of Los Angeles. In 1907, along with several partners, Welch formed the "Thornless Cactus Farming Company" and paid Burbank around $26,000 for the rights to grow and market seven of his new cactus varieties. Valued today at more than $690,000 (US), this was probably the largest plant sale Burbank ever made.

But things didn't go well with the new arrangement. "By spring 1908, Welch boasted the production of 1,000 new plants each week at Copa de Oro, his cactus farm in the Coachella Valley," writes Jane Smith. There were problems looming on the horizon. "The Thornless Cactus Farming Company asserted that it had taken requests for 50,000 starter slabs of spineless cactus from customers around the world, [even] before a single plant had been shipped."

Customers were assured, however, that their orders would be filled "at once." In reality, very few of those orders would be filled to anyone's satisfaction. Eventually Burbank canceled the marketing agreement and resumed his own sales.

THE LUTHER BURBANK COMPANY

This state of business affairs continued for a few more years until a corporation, called "The Luther Burbank Company" was formed in 1912 by Rollo J. Hough, an Oakland banker, and W. Garner

Smith, a young insurance salesman. The company offered to pay Burbank $300,000 ($30,000 in cash up front and the balance at $15,000 a year) for the exclusive rights to sell all of his plant products - including the spineless cactus.

Burbank was also permitted to retain a degree of oversight in the structure of the company. He had the right to name the person who would be the president and his own attorney would become a sitting member of the board of directors.

"The contract was accordingly signed, James F. Edwards, a past mayor of Santa Rosa, was named president, and Burbank received his $30,000 down," writes Peter Dreyer. "Stock sales commenced in what appeared to be a very attractive investment. Ultimately, some $375,000 in stock was to be sold to the public at par, purchasers including a number of leading San Francisco bankers, merchants, and investment brokers." (This was the equivalent of nearly $10 million in today's money.)

Now that Burbank was assured that the burden of marketing and sales was finally removed from his shoulders, he could turn his entire attention to developing new plant varieties. In particular, he wanted to perfect his spineless cactus, which he still viewed as a work in progress.

With his portrait forming part of a special seal that "guarantees a genuine Luther Burbank production" printed boldly on its cover, the first spineless cactus catalogue sponsored by The Luther Burbank Company went into circulation just a few months after the company was formed. Inside the cover, Burbank explains his reasons for the new arrangement:

> A man must confine his efforts to one occupation if he is to do it well. To be a successful creator of new forms of plant life, and a successful merchant is beyond the limit of one man. Such is my case. I must either confine myself entirely to selling my new varieties of plant life and leave the development alone; or confine my efforts to new forms and improved varieties, without

distributing them to the world and making them of practical usefulness. I prefer to devote my entire energies to production. Plant life is my one absorbing thought night and day.

In view of these circumstances, a corporation has been formed which will manage, market, and carry on exclusively the business of selling the various new forms of plant life which I have evolved. This corporation is the sole distributor of the Luther Burbank horticultural productions, and from no other source can one be positively assured of obtaining genuine Luther Burbank creations.

THAT PESKY DOCTOR GRIFFITHS

There. . . now to get on with life. Unfortunately, something had changed in Mr. Burbank. He was becoming obsessed with his quest for the perfect spineless cactus and less careful in his claims for his "creations" as he had been earlier in his career.

Perhaps he was falling prey to his own legend that all the media hype had created. Or, maybe it was the scent of so much money in the air. A letter sent to John Rutland back in Australia is indicative of his excessive praise for his hybrid Opuntias:

This season I raised from a patch of one of my new cactus plants, by the most scrupulous care in measuring and weighing, 198,627 pounds (90,285 kg) of the most delicious of all fruits per acre, on three year old plants from single leaf cuttings. This is the most astounding crop of fruit ever grown on this earth, being from ten to forty times the usual amount of fruit grown per acre.

The cactus is the most neglected but the most important fruit that ever grew upon this earth. Some of my new cacti will also produce two and three hundred tons of excellent food for stock per acre without irrigation on ordinary soil.

While this news must have buoyed Rutland's sense of purpose, these and numerous other astonishing claims made by

98

Burbank about his spineless prickly-pears were being increasingly viewed with quiet skepticism by a growing circle of people back in the USA. Chief among them was Dr. David Griffiths of the United States Department of Agriculture's Bureau of Plant Industry.

Responding to numerous inquiries by farmers and ranchers, Griffiths began conducting scientific investigations on the use of prickly-pear for emergency stock fodder in districts where the presence of cattle and wild prickly-pears overlapped - from southern California to Texas. When cattle were in need of forage in these regions, he found that the ranchers' usual method of preparing the pear was to singe the spines off the plants with fire.

At the outset, Griffiths also believed that the spineless prickly-pears could be very useful as stock fodder. Eventually, Griffiths and his colleagues established mass plantings of over 25 varieties of nearly spineless cactus which they had collected from around the world. Then they organized a huge distribution program and sent out the best of these spineless variants, free-of- charge, to over 2,000 interested growers.

In an attempt to educate those people who may have been misled by "ill advised stories of the phenomenal adaptability of this class of prickly-pears," the Bureau of Plant Industry issued bulletins about the spineless prickly-pears in 1909 and again in 1912.

In both of these publications, Griffiths informs the reader that "four spineless varieties of prickly-pear are common in Mexico and have been cultivated for so long that their origin is not known. Some of these are as spineless as any known to science today." (Over in Australia, even state botanist Joseph Maiden declared that the specimens obtained from Burbank were no different than some of the cactus which had been growing in the Sydney Botanic Gardens for many years.)

With regards to the planting-stock that he was distributing free to farmers for growing as cattle forage, Griffiths notes that:

> . . . none of them is entirely spineless, and there is <u>none</u> perfectly spineless anywhere. But in all of these, the spines are so unimportant that they can be easily

handled and stock can eat them without singeing. They have been neither bred nor selected. They have been subjected to no horticultural manipulations whatever in our hands. They are exactly as we found them. . . All that the Department of Agriculture has done is to import the stock and propagate it.

Elsewhere in his publications, Griffiths repeatedly cautions farmers that the spineless forms are not cold tolerant and should not be grown where temperatures drop below 25° F. (-3.9° C.)

He also questions any assertion that annual harvests weighing from 100 to 300 tons per acre could be grown on ordinary soil. (Burbank's rich garden soils were far from ordinary.) Twenty to 25 tons per acre seemed more in line with reality, and that was with "expert cultivation and a perfect stand of cactus." Also, he warns that these plants cannot be put out to shift for themselves; that they must be watered and protected like any other farm crop.

"Since all spineless prickly-pears are more or less spiny," he adds, ". . . it is naturally to be expected that under certain conditions they will become more so. In short, it seems from investigations thus far conducted that hard, unfavorable conditions, such as proximity to the sea, alkalinity, extreme heat, extreme drought, and possibly low temperatures, contribute to increase the spines of these nearly smooth Opuntias." (Indeed, in Australia and South Africa, the so-called "domesticated" spineless cactus actually did go wild and reproduce spiny plants from seed. These spiny cacti became pests in their own right.)

A decade later in still another publication, Griffiths seems to finally have made up his mind that for use as emergency stock feed, the wild, thorny prickly-pears were actually *preferable* to the spineless varieties. "The spineless species are much less resistant to drought than many of the spiny natives," he observes. "In southern Texas, and similar regions where prickly-pear is native and rampant, fortunately the reserve is always ready.

All that is necessary is to 'limber up' the prickly-pear torch, destroy the spiny armature of the plant which has protected it from destruction by livestock even in seasons of plenty, and the herd is saved . . . This wild crop has enabled the rancher to keep his herd intact through droughty periods ranging from three months to three years."

Although Griffiths never even alludes to Luther Burbank in any of his publications, these statements must have seemed like a slap in the face to the great "plant wizard," who dreamed of changing the arid world with his spineless cactus. In an uncharacteristically churlish manner, Burbank repeatedly attacked and belittled Griffiths publicly in his own brochures and in the press.

In an article that appeared in the Los Angeles *Examiner*, Burbank is quoted as calling the experts at the Bureau of Plant Industry in Washington D. C. a batch of "low-browed, narrow-gauged and pin-headed employees, who have to keep shouting to hold their places. . ." His insults then become more direct:

> . . . a certain David Griffiths, after visiting my grounds on several occasions, awoke at last with a shock and took occasion to publish a bulletin on the 'spineless prickly-pear'; it's whole end and aim and too-evident purpose being only to deride and belittle the long and very expensive experiments which have been made here before he or the department had awakened from its drowsy indifference to the great value of this long-neglected gift of nature, which now promises to be of as great or even greater value to the human race than the discovery of steam."

Whew! What a public tirade. (Actually, Burbank had done a reciprocal visit to Dr. Griffiths's large cactus plantation as well.) A rather tongue-in-cheek comeback from the Agricultural Department appeared in the Chico, California, *Chico Record*, under the banner headline, "*WHY BURBANK HAS BECOME PEEVISH ABOUT GOVERNMENT'S CACTUS WORK.*" Quoting a news dispatch from Washington DC, the article reads in part:

> Burbank, huh! If you claimed to be the inventor of the only spineless cactus known to man, and were selling cuts of it all over the country at from $2 to $5 a cut, and

someone wrote a pamphlet declaring that there is no
such thing as a spineless cactus at all, wouldn't it make
you mad? That's what's the matter with Burbank.

If you were selling the cuts and the pamphlets said that
. . . the cactus that has outgrown most of its spines is an
ancient plant that grows all the way from Malta to
Mexico and is unpatentable, it would make you still
madder, wouldn't it? Well, that's some more of what's
the matter with Burbank.

With these words, the Bureau of Plant Industry dismissed
Burbank's charges, noting that their free distribution program of
nearly spineless cacti "places them in the hands of people willing to
make the most of them for themselves and the productiveness of the
nation, regardless of the private business of Mr. Burbank."

As a parting shot, they also add that "as a matter of fact, the
largest growers of cactus for fodder prefer certain varieties of the
spiny cactus. . ." To Burbank, this must have been a bit like waving
a red flag under a bull's nose.

THE SPINELESS SPECULATORS

Burbank's temper would not let him back down and so the
controversy over spineless cactus continued to heat up. There is also
an old saying that there is no such thing as "bad" publicity - just
"publicity" - and Burbank was receiving plenty of that.

This debate also attracted a host of spineless cactus promoters,
many who had get-rich-quick schemes of their own. "In 1912, for
example, a former cattle ranch in the San Joaquin Valley was divided
into 20-acre lots and renamed Oro Loma, the Spineless Cactus Land,"
says Jane Smith.

The developers advertised that buyers could turn virgin
desert into profitable farms by planting spineless cactus,
whose paddles would be provided with every purchase.
If the buyer didn't initiate cactus cultivation right away,
the sellers would still allow them to get into the market
on the ground floor by providing, for the paltry

102

additional price of $125, a quarter-acre plot that was fenced and planted with 100 cactus plants of several varieties. For some time, similar schemes had filled mailboxes and crowded the advertising pages of newspapers and popular magazines.

Here's how one eyewitness of the day summed it all up:

> The fakers now stepped in and tried to induce nice old ladies of both sexes to embark in the business of raising Burbank spineless cactus. As a result there sprang up acres and acres of this hybrid Opuntia all over the south land.

> Even now one may ride about Los Angeles and see abandoned acreage given over about twenty years ago to raising spineless cactus. Of course the tenderfeet were successful in raising the crop, but of what good was it after they had raised it? The promoters had painted vivid pictures of untold wealth to be derived from selling spineless cactus in bales by the ton to feed to cattle in lieu of hay. The suckers didn't stop to investigate. They never even so much as offered a slab to a cow.

Burbank appears to have openly encouraged this "cactus" speculation. It was certainly good for his own sales. In his last pamphlet just before The Luther Burbank Company was formed, he predicted that a grower's plantings of his spineless cactus, even on marginal land, should yield a "crop worth nearly or quite [close to] $400.00 per acre on the third and every succeeding year." ($400 in those days was equivalent to more than $10,500 today.) Little wonder why people clamored to buy Burbank's spineless cactus and start a cactus farm of their own.

Even back in his home garden, Burbank put on a continuing public show. "He took pleasure in rubbing a cactus slab against his cheek to show how harmless it was," Peter Dreyer observes.

> But visitors were so frequent that he could hardly cut a fresh slab for every demonstration, and [so] the same piece was used again and again, till it was polished smooth by repeated rubbings. The more observant

103

among his visitors sometimes noticed that there were numerous thorns on other parts of the same plant.

(He was prepared to suffer for his cactus project and remarked that he had been pricked so many times in the hands and face handling the slabs, that sometimes he had to shave the spicules off with a razor or rub them down with sandpaper, so that as what was left of them worked into the skin, they would not cause more than a minor irritation.) These ploys should have fooled only the ignorant and the unwary, but the journalists who took up the spineless cactus story so enthusiastically seem to have had no trouble accepting Burbank's presentation at face value.

AMERICA OPENS ITS ARMS TO THE WONDER CACTUS

Members of the 62nd US Congress also took Burbank's word at face value, and in 1912, Congressman Everis Hayes, who had witnessed the spineless cactus show at Santa Rosa, introduced a most remarkable bill before the House of Representatives. If passed, it would allow Luther Burbank to select up to 12 sections totaling some 7,680 acres (3,108 ha) of uncultivated and unproductive semi-arid public lands located in California, New Mexico, Arizona, and Nevada to demonstrate whether or not his spineless cacti "can be so grown as to be of great commercial importance to those regions which Mr. Burbank claims."

Although there were some flowery speeches praising Burbank's "great work" delivered to the members of the House, very little debate actually occurred. The bill passed easily and was soon ratified by the Senate. Obviously, Congress was enthralled by "this gentle man who has done so much for human kind."

Burbank now had his big chance to show the world what his cactus could really do. But one of the conditions on acquiring the deed to all this real estate was that it had to be planted with "at least 100,000 growing plants of spineless cacti of a character suitable for animal food upon said lands or some part thereof for the period of

104

two years." Upon approval by the Secretary of the Interior, he would then be allowed to purchase the property for as little as $1.25 per acre.

His attorney, Fredrick Wythe, in a letter to Congressman John E. Raker on behalf of Burbank, informed him that they had already reserved 150,000 slabs of spineless cactus for just this purpose and were making arrangements to spend about $10,000 on the experiment. "These slabs alone are worth between $10,000 and $20,000, being in excess of seven [train] carloads," he noted.

There was no hurry, though, Congress had given Burbank up to five years in which to scout out and choose the lands on which his great experiment would be fulfilled.

BURBANK GETS "CACTUSED"

Meanwhile, The Luther Burbank Company was beginning to implode. Although dividends as high as 12% had been paid to stockholders in 1914, business was definitely slowing down. The main problem was that neither Rollo Hough and W. Garner Smith had any previous experience in the seed and nursery business.

Although Smith made sales tours through the eastern and middle-western states, they were essentially relying on the overwhelming public enthusiasm for Burbank's products to carry them through. Spineless cactus, however, sold exceptionally well. . . perhaps too well.

It was company policy that all orders were to be filled regardless of whether or not they had the proper stock on hand. As backorders piled up, workers soon resorted to deception. When they didn't have enough spineless cactus to fill their orders, they brought in ordinary spiny prickly-pear, removed the prickles with wire brushes and sandpaper, and shipped them out to their unsuspecting customers.

Of course, this outrageous fraud was revealed as soon as the plants began to grow. Ultimately, The Luther Burbank Company collapsed into bankruptcy in early 1916, less than four years after it had been created.

Although he had little to do with the company's sales policies, Burbank bore the blame for this scandal because his name was on the product. (I'm sure that his health suffered greatly as a result of all of this turmoil, but he doggedly continued to work day after day with his beloved plants.)

Ten years after the collapse of The Luther Burbank Company, on the evening of March 24th, 1926, Burbank suffered a heart attack. After a week had passed, when he seemed to be recovering, he suddenly began to suffer nonstop spasmodic hiccoughs.

Peter Dreyer recounts that "During the week that followed, he rallied again, but the medical reports indicated 'an exhausted nervous system' . . . The slow decline continued. Burbank was worn out, unable to eat, wracked by ceaseless hiccoughing. By Saturday, April 10th, he had fallen into a coma. He died without waking at 13 minutes after midnight that Sunday morning."

Looking back, Burbank was apparently never able to completely validate his great spineless cactus experiments on those lands that Congress had so generously offered him.

There exist relatively few documents pertaining to the project, but a letter dated November 17th, 1922 from Mr. E. Lyders, with whom Burbank had granted complete power of attorney over the project, reported that he "had traveled extensively over Arizona looking for locations for the grant of twelve sections and have several in view which I may select shortly." (Apparently, Congress had given Burbank a time-extension on the land grant.)

Lyders had previously made a selection of some 80 acres located 15 miles (24 km) north of Wickenburg, Arizona, simply because it was located near an already existing grove of spineless cacti. "The cuttings of which I have purchased," he explained, "And will commence the planting about the first of February."

After each selection had been duly planted with spineless cactus and title to the land secured, Burbank's attorney was then authorized to sell the "improved" property to anyone who wished to purchase it. But, once again, things didn't go according to plan. At that time, Arizona was suffering from a financial depression caused by a sharp drop in the price of two of its primary commodities: cotton and copper.

"Under these circumstances," Lyders wrote in summary, "It is difficult to find anyone who desires to acquire more land, but I hope to have the whole grant located before the spring and will be able to pay you some money as the locations are made though I will have to use some of the first payments to defray the expenses of locating the land and planting the cacti."

I have no information that indicates whether or not Burbank ever received payment for any of Lyders's efforts. The whole thing may have ended as just another failed business deal. Adding this to the collapse of The Luther Burbank Company and all the other controversies - especially those surrounding the spineless prickly-pear - appears to have been just too much for the gentle "plant wizard."

THE LEGACY OF RUTLAND'S SANTA ROSA ORCHARD"

Half a world away in Australia, John Rutland was still tending his fruit orchard and stands of spineless cactus. Late in 1912 - nearly four years after Burbank's original cactus and fruit tree shipment had arrived in the country - a reporter from *The Sydney Morning Herald* came to visit Rutland on his property.

"From the very modest start of five 'leaves' there are now growing about a million, which cover an area of about five acres," he wrote. "He (Rutland), however, is not yet ready to make public, nor discuss, his object in propagating these cacti here."

Yet Rutland was happy to show the man around his farm. Describing one of Rutland's animal-feed experiments with spineless cactus, the reporter recounts:

> . . . he had fed 14 pigs on second-quality "leaves" for five to seven months this year, and the swine are doing very well on them. The pigs were given as much water

107

as they required, but during the periods stated they had been given nothing else but the cactus . . . The quantity which had been fed to the pigs when they had been kept on the cactus exclusively was eight pounds (3.6 kg) a day.

The newspaper man eventually went home impressed by all that he had seen. Rutland's parting comment to him was his prediction that, "The curse of the land they reckon is going to be the salvation of the country." Unfortunately, what actually occurred was very opposite of this vision.

In April 1915, the *Melbourne Leader* reported that botanical experts attached to the various State departments were viewing "the Burbank [cactus] creation with suspicious eyes." They contended that there was danger that the spineless cactus would revert back to a spiny type. Subsequently, they rather easily convinced the Federal government to entirely prohibit its importation.

The big problem with this "rear guard" action, however, was that there already were a great number of Burbank's cactus and similar plants growing around the country. But to Rutland in particular, it was a big disappointment, for he had been hoping for widespread acceptance of the spineless cactus.

In the wake of this import prohibition, the editors of the *Leader* sent their agricultural specialist out to see Rutland. After his visit he reported that:

> In spite of an unprecedented drought, the spineless cacti were flourishing . . . The spineless cactus has now been in continuous growth at Mr. Rutland's farm for eight years. During the whole of that time it has remained entirely free of spines. There has been no reversion to an older and less desirable type. In every respect the plant has redeemed that which was promised of it. It has proved to be prolific, hardy, and a producer of a large quantity of stock fodder.

He also notes, although the cacti had not been watered, that "Mr. Rutland estimates that their yield of edible matter is at the rate of 100 tons to the acre." In conclusion, he says:

Eight year's experience of the spineless cactus on this Kiewa farm justifies the optimistic statements made by Mr. J. H. McColl six years ago. It certainly promises to be an exceedingly valuable addition to the fodders of Australia, and the fact that it will thrive here in arid and adverse conditions should make it the more acceptable to our stockmen.

Exactly what happened to Rutland's spineless cactus efforts will probably never be known. On his farm, Rutland was able to keep his Burbank varieties true to their original form by using their pads (cladodes) as propagules.

In this way, every plant was a clone, genetically identical to its parent. But this could change when spineless cacti - the Burbank varieties and others - were shipped about the country for growing by individual farmers and graziers. Rutland may have had the "rights" to the Burbank cacti, but once they were sold he couldn't control what happened to them.

Eventually, most likely through neglect, some of these plants were allowed to flower and set fruit. Their sweet seed-laden fruits were then eaten by crows and other birds. Unharmed by their passage through the birds' digestive systems, the cactus seeds were scattered far and wide via their droppings.

Some of the seeds sprouted and grew. Most resembled their parents, but because they had come from hybrid stock, a few of these seedlings displayed something alarming: numerous large spines and needle-like glochids. The old fear of reversion had come true.

Burbank seldom recorded the parentage of his cactus crosses; he was much more interested in results. Some of his productions were the result of five or six parents. Likewise, many of the "fake Burbank" and other spineless cacti that were being sold around Australia during this time had similarly obscure pedigrees. A few were even derived from the wheel cactus (*Opuntia robusta*), which is still considered a serious pest in some parts of Australia. Most, however, were just varietal forms of our long-cultivated old friend from Mexico, the Indian fig (*Opuntia ficus-indica*).

When these spiny "pears" began to persist and then later turn into pests, one particularly widespread spiny variety soon became known as the "Mexican pear." Australian botanists, in a reflection of the ongoing confusion in cactus nomenclature and systematics, promptly named it *Opuntia megacantha*, the large-spined prickly-pear. (Although *Opuntia megacantha* is now considered to be a synonym for *Opuntia ficus-indica*, this variety still exhibits its big spines.)

As you will see in the next chapter, it really didn't matter what names these cacti were given. Australia's diverse mix of prickly-pears (and several other types of invasive cacti) usually meant only one thing to the landholder on whose property they grew: a life of difficult and oppressive labor spent trying to get rid of them.

Chapter 5: Coping With the Green Invasion

The Government told the farmer
There was no time to spare.
If he wanted to keep his home,
He had to beat the prickly-pear.
They slashed it, burnt it, and
Laboriously grubbed the ground,
But the pear quickly came back
After each and every round.

"Weeds are penalties of civilization, " wrote Joseph Maiden in 1895 as he watched prickly-pear begin its takeover of huge sections of eastern Australia. "Weeds march over the country like a victorious army. They have their outposts at which they rest, get a firm hold, and then proceed to further attacks on hitherto unconquered country."

Succulents - like prickly-pears and other cacti - generally have a long lag phase before becoming invasive. In South Africa, it took close to 150 years for the spiny variety of Indian fig (*Opuntia ficus-indica*) to even become recognized as a problem plant.

Likewise in Australia, prickly-pear was not generally regarded as a pest for more than 80 years after its first introduction. Then, in the year 1870, it suddenly began to spread rapidly from New South Wales northward into Queensland. It had reached "critical mass."

"People were staggered by the rate the pear swept every-thing before it," wrote a reporter for the *Australasian Post*. "It was as if an irreversible ocean was moving over the land and nobody knew what to do." On open ground, the pear often averaged 10 feet in height (3 m), but in scrub country it could be 20 feet high (6 m) or more.

In many places it grew up to the road in a dense wall, making it very difficult for wagons and other vehicles to pass when they met on these narrow lanes. (An irate shouting match as to who would have to back up to a slightly wider portion of road often ensued.)

All across southern Queensland, huge tracts of good farmland soon became so thick with prickly-pear that one witness despondently wrote, ". . . it does not seem possible that it will ever be trodden by man again."

FIRST LEGAL REMEDIES

When, in 1882, a member of the Queensland parliament voiced alarm at the rate of prickly-pear's spread, fellow politicians scornfully laughed at him. Many of them still held the old belief that prickly-pear was worth tolerating simply because it was a valuable fodder for cattle during periods of drought. (During that same year, however, prickly-pear was legally declared to be a nuisance by over 22 local government jurisdictions.)

Still, it would take another four years of intense persuasion before the nation's first legislative attempt, aimed at specifically controlling prickly-pear, was passed by the New South Wales colonial government.

Known as the "Prickly Pear Destruction Act of 1886," this measure unfortunately had many serious flaws which set the stage to virtually guarantee a long, difficult struggle for the humble "man on the land." More than ten years later, Queensland passed the "Lands Act of 1897" which contained similar criteria as a condition of land tenure.

The main problem with these laws was that they obligated the landowner or tenant to clear their property of prickly-pear

112

themselves, under threat of a large fine. (This was later increased to the penalty of forfeiture for properties leased from the government.) The government, at least at first, offered no assistance other than by dictating exactly how the pear was to be destroyed.

Regulation #4 of the Prickly Pear Destruction Act of 1886, for example, states that the prickly-pear:

> ... may be stacked in large heaps, not to exceed 24 feet (7.3 m) in width, built so that all portions of the plant bearing fruit are turned inwards and covered, to prevent birds or animals from obtaining access to and disseminating the seed. . . Heaps or stacks may remain on the ground and be added to from time to time as the work of clearing progresses, until the land is cleared of prickly-pear, after which they shall be burned.

There were additional rules that made clearing the pear even more onerous. For instance, two of these stacks of cut prickly-pear could not be built within 300 feet (100 m) of each other on any land belonging to the same owner or occupier without special permission from the government minister.

If permission were denied, as it often was, it was an even tougher prospect for the landholder. (We're talking about the hand-clearing of a very heavy and spiny plant. Densely infested lands often grew more than 800 tons of the prickly stuff on every acre.)

Furthermore, if any piece of prickly-pear appearing on the top or sides of a stack were judged by authorities to be bearing fruit, the "owner or occupier shall be deemed guilty of a breach of the Act." This was a particularly tough rule, for as we have seen, these plants can reproduce under some of the harshest conditions imaginable.

In the long run, these regulations and even the laws themselves proved to be useless in curbing the prickly-pear invasion. The average farmer simply could not keep up with the spread of this plant over his property. Also, there was no provision for dealing with prickly-pear on abandoned or otherwise unoccupied land.

Road easements, riverbeds, Crown Land reserves, and open grazing country all became safe havens for the proliferating cactus.

113

From these refuges, the pear could spread back as seed onto the occupied properties, oftentimes even as they were being cleared.

A retired farmer from Queensland's hard-hit Chinchilla district bitterly voiced his disappointment on this matter in his memoirs: "By backbreaking and heartbreaking manual labor the pear was stacked on wood and burned, and when one had got a few acres cleared, he looked back to see a regrowth of hairy seedlings was following along."

Even after special clauses in the regulations empowered local authorities to deal with prickly-pear on the roads and public reserves under their control, little clearing was actually done. These jurisdictions simply could not afford the cost of labor in their under-developed, often heavily infested territories.

In his annual report for 1886, the land commissioner for the Warwick district of Queensland, Mr. A. McDowell, wrote: "This very question of the increase of prickly-pear is one of great and growing importance and of tremendous magnitude - the expense of eradicating it or [even] keeping it within bounds will be enormous."

ANOTHER LEGAL BLUNDER

By 1900, during the period when the various Australian colonies were confederating to form a new national identity (the Commonwealth of Australia), prickly-pear had already infested nearly ten million acres (4 million hectares) of arable land.

Joseph Maiden, the outspoken botanist for New South Wales, called the spread of this cactus "a vegetable smallpox," adding that he refused to believe that the legislators had done all they could to stem this terrible pest.

He was right. A year later the Queensland state government passed the "Prickly Pear Selection Act." Designed to encourage destruction of pear on heavily infested land, this act allowed for a ten-year-long lease that supposedly provided the tenant enough time to clear the pest from selected properties up to 2,866 acres in

114

size. After this period - if the land was found to be free of prickly-pear - the tenant would be granted deed to the property.

Unfortunately, the act was a complete failure. In total, only ten people committed themselves to the program. Obviously, few people would willingly sign up for a future that guaranteed nothing but a decade of extremely difficult labor.

A REWARD FOR A CURE

It was becoming more evident every day that colossal sums of money would be needed to wipe out this pest by any known conventional means. In 1901, the government of Queensland offered a reward of £5,000 "for the discovery of an effective method of destroying prickly-pear." (This was the equivalent of around US $600,000 today.)

The reward was not to be paid until the applicant had destroyed all of the pear in a preselected test area and had shown that the method was cost-effective. Furthermore, the pear was not considered to have been destroyed if it showed "any signs of vitality within three months of operation."

Free railway passes were issued to inventors and their equipment, so they could personally demonstrate the value of their methods to the government officials.

Applications soon came pouring in, but most of them did not seem very promising. So in 1907, the government doubled the prize to £10,000. The announcement of this huge prize in several major newspapers, such as *The Sydney Morning Herald* and *The New York Times*, soon riveted the attention of inventors from all over the world.

All told, between 600 and 700 schemes to destroy prickly-pear were lodged, but again, not one them was deemed economical when put to practical test. Entries included traction engines, machines with a million mirrors, electrocution devices, steam boilers, knives attached to an electric car, and flame-throwers.

Typical of many of the applications received, here's a published comment on a suggestion tendered by a farmer/inventor for an "oven" mounted on a wagon that would singe and bake the prickly-pear when drawn over it:

> The idea of the inventor is to develop in the interior of the oven a 'high-heat' and then to have the apparatus driven by two horses over the prickly-pear area . . . The inventor has sent a fairly lengthy description of his proposed invention, but he has omitted to state several particulars. For instance, how does he intend the heat of the furnace to *descend* instead of ascend, as it has a habitual way of doing? Nor, how does he propose to prevent the horses having their tails singed? It would be interesting, also, to know on what part of the roasting vehicle the driver would sit. . .

In another hopeful attempt, a party of scientists from Germany directed mustard gas onto the pear. (This is the same stuff that would be used so devastatingly against Allied Troops ten years later during World War I.) After "gassing" the neighbors' cattle and several men who were employed on the project, the Germans went home disappointed.

So finally, after witnessing a long succession of failed demonstrations, the government quietly withdrew its reward offer in 1909.

THE PLAGUE APPARENT

Throughout this period, the pear continued to expand its domination over the landscape, causing ever-increasing anxiety. Occasionally, however, there were incidents that allowed this cactus some respite from the "hate" that was slowly growing in the general population. During the great drought of 1902, for example, the pulped succulent pads of prickly-pear were fed to livestock in a desperate attempt to keep the beasts alive until the rains returned.

The tactic worked, saving tens of thousands of animals that otherwise would have most certainly perished. But it was later

116

realized that the practice actually accelerated the spread of the cactus, because landholders who originally had none of the stuff on their own properties carted it in to feed their cattle.

Meanwhile, out in the grassy wilds of Queensland's Darling Downs region, something new was developing. Two different species of prickly-pear had apparently hybridized and the resulting cross - with its hybrid vigor - was beginning to spread. "It only needed the right trigger," John Eggleston, historian for the Jondaryan Woolshed (located in the heart of the Downs) told me. "The floods that followed the drought were that trigger. The plants were dispersed all along the watercourses by the flood waters, setting the scene for an explosion of this hybrid prickly-pear that left landholders dumbfounded." (See Plate 8)

Nearly every cattle and sheep station or rural community had its own story about the advance of the pear. Hector Munro describes what he saw after returning to Boondooma Station in Queensland after an absence of eight years:

> Up to about 1880 . . . the spread of the pear was very slow. We knew of a few clumps on different parts of the run . . . I returned to Boondooma in 1888. General war had been declared against the pear, burying or burning being the methods of destroying it. Men were constantly engaged clearing it. All station hands were instructed to make note of any plants and on the first spare day to go out and stack dry wood on and around the plant, so that the first bush fire would burn it out. These bush fires kept the pear in check for years, but now we have no fires. . .

On Billa Billa Station, located north of Goondiwindi (also in Queensland), stockman and writer John Nicholes describes what happened in the late 1880s, just after the station owner's new home and outbuildings had been built:

> The owner and his wife went for a trip to southern California. They returned with many kinds of ornamental cacti for their rock-garden, among which was a plant called prickly-pear, otherwise known as Opuntia.

117

The plants in the rock-garden were a huge success, especially the prickly-pear, which grew at an alarming speed. As new leaves formed, old ones fell off and took root, no matter where they fell. It was not long before the place had a hedge of prickly-pear. It came out in flower and was very beautiful. Visitors came to see it and took plants away for their own gardens.

Soon there was little but prickly-pear in the Billa Billa garden, and the more it was cut, the faster it grew, until it had covered the outbuildings and the homestead. Every piece that fell took root and sent out leaves, to fall and grow again, until the whole property was an impenetrable wilderness. It was left to the pear.

The toughness of these soft-looking, succulent plants, was often deceiving. Mr. William Coates, who spent most of his life farming in the Chinchilla region, clearly remembered his long-running battle with the pear:

> It looked so easy to chop; the only drawback seemed to be those formidable big thorns. But though we . . . chopped and grubbed and chopped and grubbed, it fought back with those accursed prickles. The big ones, like pins, were bad enough, but those little fellows - about 1/5 of an inch long (5 mm) - in their myriads came virtually flying through the air at us.

> What a wonderful plant was that prickly-pear! We grubbed it out and every leaf took root as it lay on the ground. We stacked it up on wood and it thrived in the air. Every small part of it was obstinate. A leaf broke off and it took root. A leaf got broken up into a dozen small pieces and every one rooted. The green flower buds got knocked off and they rooted where they fell. The hateful yellow flower fell and it, too, took root. Then we had the green fruit. Something knocked it off and it grew. The fruit became ripe and the myriad of seeds in it grew. The crows and emus ate the fruit and the pear passed through them, but every seed grew. Came good season, came dry season, but still the cursed pest kept on.

In New South Wales, the actual rate of prickly-pear's spread across one primary location was officially measured. An area called the Mungle Scrub, located on the Moree Plains in the north-central part of the state, was surveyed in 1908 and thought to contain about 42,000 acres of prickly-pear.

Two years later, a new survey traverse revealed that the pear had advanced about a half a mile in a solid mass on a frontage of about four miles. "That is to say, in two years in that one spot," *The Sydney Mail* declared, "a piece of land four miles long by one-half a mile in breadth had been lost."

MORE INEFFECTIVE LEGISLATION

Every few years, the prickly-pear affected states - particularly Queensland - came up with more ill-conceived legislation in an attempt to stop the pear. In 1906, the "Closer Settlement Act" was created to allow people to farm smaller, more manageable-sized properties that averaged about 640 acres, all of which was required to be fenced in.

Lands covered with prickly-pear were later marked out as "Prickly-pear Selections" and offered for occupation through special leases in the hope that the new tenants would clear the land of the dreaded pear. They rarely were able to accomplish that goal.

"There were additional weaknesses in the legislative approach adopted by state governments," says Donald Freeman, associate professor of geography at York University, Ontario, Canada. "Concessions and compensations for prickly-pear clearance were never sufficiently attractive to induce whole-hearted cooperation by tenants on leasehold lands. Subsidies to help landholders clear the prickly-pear were virtually nonexistent."

Even if the landholder did successfully clear his property of pear, he was often penalized by having his rents or land-taxes raised due to a perceived increase in the value of the land.

In that same year, the government of South Africa (which

was experiencing a prickly-pear problem of it own) also decided to require compulsory cactus eradication by landholders, but with one notable difference. Landholders were to be provided with state aid issued on a graduated scale according to the severity of the infestation. Once an area was "clean," however, it would be the owner's responsibility to keep it so. This strategy seemed to work much better, at least in the beginning. But as the territory occupied by prickly-pear increased, so did its rate of spread.

In 1911, the New South Wales government commissioned an official map of the state's prickly-pear affected areas. The map showed that over 2.5 million acres of land were being impacted. Eleven years later, a new map indicated that the prickly-pear region had more than doubled in size.

During that time, Queensland's prickly-pear zone had grown to be nearly five times as large. Kathleen Johnston, writing for the *Toowoomba Chronicle*, described this vast prickly-pear region as a "dreary land of ghost farms, lumpy-jawed cattle, death and desolation."

Despite the landholders' best efforts, the line of invasion was only temporarily checked. As settlers gave up hope and abandoned their holdings, the pear quickly overran nearly every spot of ground that had been previously cleared. Soon, even the settlers who had elected to stay and continue the fight were completely surrounded by pear. Clearly, eliminating this pest by coercing people equipped with just hand-tools was just not going to work.

The inadequacy of these government policies to effectively deal with this agricultural crisis was becoming more obvious every day, and it began to create a great deal of political turmoil. "With scores of farms and grazing properties being abandoned every week," says Donald Freeman, "a rising crescendo of accusations that the governments were not doing enough, mingled with plaintive appeals for help for farmers losing the battle against prickly-pear."

The new attitude towards these government programs is echoed in a letter from a Mr. D. Groeneweg to the editor of the *Maryborough Chronicle*:

> The love of Government for the 'man on the land' - called by many 'the foundation of our community'- is and always was <u>nil</u> . . . For example, in September 1910, I left my piece of ground at Gayndah after nine years of trouble and slavery. At that same time on the same Woodmiller Road were living six other families - sober, hardworking people. Today, nobody is living on that road. Hundreds of acres of clean and cultivated land have gone to waste as a result of prickly-pear, droughts, and lack of help from the Government.

It's been estimated that from the years 1910 to 1930, some 40 to 50% of the settlers in central and southern Queensland were driven off their land by the rapid advance of prickly-pear and poor government management.

In reading the handwritten minutes made during an emergency council meeting in the town of Miles, I learned that nearly 80% of that area's residents had already been "cactused out." The assembly had been called to decide whether or not what was left of that community should continue on as an "incorporated identity."

Commenting on the continuing abandonment of homesteads, *The Sydney Morning Herald* asked:

> Can it be conceived that there should be in Queensland a good homestead standing on and surrounded by fertile soil, the roof of the house to be seen in the distance, but no man able to approach it? Impossible, most people would say. But we have it on good authority that it is only too true. A barrier of prickly-pear shuts it in, so dense that nothing can force a way through it but the rabbits, for which it proves a safe breeding ground. It could be cleared, of course, but the cost of clearing is greater than the value of the land and who will undertake it on those terms?

LOOKING FOR COUNTRY

In March 1923, the *Brisbane Courier* published a detailed account of a Queensland farmer's impressions of his travels through prickly-pear country. Having heard that the soils of the Dawson Valley were extremely fertile, he had gone there in the hope of securing some first-class land for growing cotton on.

"I got as far as Juandah, which is the terminus of the railway from Miles," he recounted. "Looking around Juandah and seeing practically nothing but prickly-pear, I decided to head for Taroom. I was told that I could not possible get off the road, as I only had to keep between the pear and that there were only two bunches, each 42 miles (68 km) long on each side of the road."

> After traveling about 16 miles (26 km) I reached the old Rochedale cattle station, which has been abandoned for years, the pear having taken possession of everything. A few miles further on I came across a clearing in the pear with a house and yards on it. This place is called "Linger and Die," and is used as a halfway accommodation house between Juandah and Taroom.
>
> Taroom is a town with a population of about 200 and is surrounded with prickly-pear. Sooner or later the residents will have to cut their way out. . . I was now 40 miles (64 km) from the railway, so thought it would be wise to try to secure suitable land within ten miles (16 km) of Taroom. Although I went about ten miles in many different directions, I did not get out of the prickly-pear. My regret is that I had to return without procuring any country on which to grow cotton.

DEATH ADDERS

Prickly-pear did prove to be a great breeding ground for rabbits. It also provided ideal habitat for many other small mammals and birds. . . and their predators, including various kinds of snakes. Most notorious of those snakes was the common death adder (*Acanthophis antarcticus*). Imagine a short, fat, extremely poisonous

122

banded snake, from one to three feet long (0.3 to 0.9 m), having a large triangular head, long fangs, vertical pupils, and possibly the fastest strike of any reptile in the world.

When hungry, death adders do not actively hunt their prey but rather lie in ambush. Masters at camouflage, they bury themselves in whatever substrate is handy - leaves, sand, or dirt - leaving only their head and tail exposed. There they wait, often for many days at a time.

The tip of its tail is a different color from the rest of the body, and when wriggled, uncannily resembles a small worm or grub. When an unsuspecting bird or small mammal comes over to investigate - "wham!" - it gets bit. (This snake can go from strike position, to injecting its prey with deadly venom, and back to strike position again in less than 0.15 of a second.) It then waits for the victim to die before eating it.

Returning from work one day in the Billa Billa scrub, writer John Nicholes saw a death adder under a bush with the tail feathers of a dove protruding from its mouth. "I had been told that in this state they could be picked up with safety, as they could not disgorge a half-swallowed meal. I have always been a doubting Thomas, so I tried poking him with a stick first, and out came the dove like a champagne cork!"

As the pear increased its spread exponentially, so did the numbers of death adders. Fortunately, they were rarely as aggressive as their reputation made them out to be. "I worked in the belah and brigalow scrubs of northern New South Wales and southern Queensland when the prickly-pear was there," recalls Nicholes. "During that time I saw perhaps thirty death adders and nearly all of them were within inches of my hand or foot. The camouflage of the adder is so effective that it is next to impossible to see it, except by remote chance."

Occasionally one of these snakes did bite someone, and the person often died as a result. "One fellow about twelve miles (19 km) from here got bit and he had to chop his thumb off to save his life," remembers retired farmer Walter C. Schroder. "He nearly bled to death and was in the hospital for a long time before he recovered. But what else could you do?"

Children on their way to school often carried strong sticks against the many snakes they were likely to encounter. Others, anticipating that they might be confronted by snakes barring their path on the narrow tracks winding through the prickly-pear, would leave sticks at frequent intervals so that there would always be a weapon handy.

In the southern Queensland town of Tara, death adders became so plentiful that the owner of the local pub and hotel was forced to keep a half-dozen lanterns out on the verandah. At night, as soon as a guest arrived by either car or horse-drawn sulky, he would call out to "wait!" until someone brought out a lantern, so they could safely pick their way through the snakes that were lounging in the parking area.

"Throughout this region, no one would dream of walking out at night without a hurricane lantern, for fear of treading on one of these reptiles," wrote a local historian. In the village of Polardo, it was said that the railway men were most reluctant to leave their trains when stopped at the station, for fear of treading on a death adder.

Later, after the cactoblastis moth had done its job of clearing away the pear, the death adders began to vanish.

"I think the cactoblastis was responsible indirectly for the disappearance of the adder from these parts," Nicholes wrote. "When the pear died, it left behind a mass of highly combustible material, sometimes feet deep over the whole area of these vast scrublands. Bush fires sprung up all over the place and it was not long before the scrubs were just a memory. The birds that frequented this type of country disappeared, taking away the adder's main source of food." With this, death adders virtually vanished from the scene.

AN EXPLORER IN THE PRICKLY SEA

War correspondent, photographer, polar explorer, naturalist, geographer, climatologist, and aviator: the life of Sir Hubert Wilkins reads like some kind of romantic adventure novel.

Born in South Australia in 1888, young Wilkins grew up on a farm and spent considerable time in the nearby bush. He also studied electrical and mechanical engineering, and at seventeen, became interested in motion picture cameras. After touring Europe and America as a reporter and photographer, he took up flying and was one of first men to take photographs from an airplane.

Best known for his bold innovativeness, Wilkins began his Arctic career in 1913 when he was invited to join the three-year-long Canadian Arctic Expedition. He later became the first man to fly across the Arctic (also the first to walk back from a downed plane in the Arctic), the first to fly over the Antarctic (luckily, he didn't crash during this endeavor), and the first man to attempt to take a submarine under the polar ice.

After returning to the warmth of Australia, Wilkins led his own expedition into the relatively unexplored wilds of that country's tropical far north in 1923, collecting specimens for the British Museum and living, for a while, with the aborigines.

"At the time, much of the area in inland Queensland where we first penetrated in automobiles was covered with a kind of cactus that grew so thick that it was impossible for a man to pass through it. This barrier of cactus is unbelievable until it has been seen," he wrote. (See Plate 6)

In a biography compiled by the equally well-known reporter and journalist, Lowell Thomas, Wilkins vividly describes some of his experiences with the "pear":

> In full daylight, it was here and there possible to find one's way through the cactus on foot along narrow paths that had been broken by the wild cattle roaming the area. But once headed on a path, even the cattle found it impossible to turn around and many times we

were confronted with these untamed creatures and had to lie down with our faces buried in our arms until the cattle lost their fear and finally rushed past us.

Wilkins's team was traveling by automobile and most of the avenues that led through this prickly-pear wilderness had to be created as they went along. "We carried sharp machetes strapped to our belts, but since the cactus grew to a height of 30 feet (9 m), and their thorny leaf points spread outward from the stem close to the ground, it was almost impossible to clear a way in daylight, and absolutely impossible, even with headlights, to chop one's way through at night," Wilkins recalled.

He did not mention how many flat tires - caused by needle-sharp cactus thorns - that his team had been obliged to repair. Perhaps he felt that it was best to forget that part of the adventure.

Wilkins later returned to polar exploration. Ironically, his most famous expedition was a failed attempt to sail under the arctic ice to the North Pole in a decommissioned navy submarine that he renamed the *Nautilus.* Wilkins eventually did make the trip, however.

In November 1958, after he unexpectedly died in his hotel room in Framingham, Massachusetts, the U.S. Navy decided to honor this intrepid polar (and prickly-pear) explorer by transporting his remains under the ice to the North Pole in the nuclear submarine *USS Skate.* Here in this vast desolation, in the teeth-chattering temperature of minus 26° F. (-32° C) with a wind speed exceeding 30 knots, his ashes were scattered in a solemn, but necessarily brief, ceremony.

LIFE IN THE TALL CACTUS

Prickly-pear thrived in the Warra-Chinchilla region of Queensland so extremely well that it was soon considered one of the worst areas of infestation. The whole province was covered in a dense mass ten feet high (3 meters) and more in places. It was so thick that stock and people got lost in it for days at a time.

126

For example, there is the story of a woman - Mrs. Edmunds - and her three children who came out to visit her parents at Boonarga. They had traveled by train and the engineer obligingly stopped close to her parents' property to set the little party down. They quickly headed off across the paddock for the house. "As they followed the path, Mrs. Edmonds father's bull came bellowing and tossing his head and she scurried off the track into the pear," recalls Vera Genge, a lifelong resident of the area.

> In a short time they were hopelessly lost, the pear towering over Mrs. Edmond's head. They wandered about in that dreadful wilderness, so thirsty that the six-year-old's tongue was swelling. All were crying from the painful thorns. At last they stumbled onto the railway line and Mrs. Edmonds took the two-year-old's red dress and waived it at a passing train. It didn't stop, but the guard did report the sighting and a man eventually came looking for them. All their clothing had to be burnt. They were stiff with thorns.

In another way-back section of Queensland, a narrow lane hemmed in by dense pear along both sides eventually led to a small schoolhouse. After a day's incessant rain, the track had closed up due to the rapid growth of the prickly-pear.

"Neither teacher nor scholars could get home from the school until some of the settlers came with brush-hooks to cut the pear and liberate them from their prison," a local newspaper reported.

There were so many incidents like these that, over time, the prickly-pear began to develop a kind of "mystique" about it. One popular saying was that "it could grow anywhere, even on a barbed-wire fence." Another was "it was so thick that a dog could run across the tops of the pear." What it did to the dog's paws, we can only guess.

A few of the stories do seem a bit fanciful. Take this one for example: "A true story!" the headline in the newspaper known as *The Gundagai Independent*, assured its readers. "Last week when Jeff Dodd returned from a picnic up north, he found the point of a pear in his leg. He got it out and threw the point on the ground. Four days later a prickly-pear plant was found growing where the piece of pear from Jeff's leg had been thrown." (This seems a bit fast, even for a rapid-growing plant like prickly-pear!)

Indeed, some stories were unbelievably tall, a sure sign of the very real concern that generated them. In a letter (signed "Pincushion") sent to the editor of *The Western Champion*, the writer claims to have come to a place "where a house should be, but saw only mounds of pear."

> Yet, by the meerest chance a movement was noticed. Closer investigation revealed a man high up, with a heavy waddy (wooden club), trying to keep a small space clear and such an alarming battle was in progress. I hailed him and learned that he had retired to bed early, but during the night the prickly-pear had grown up around his house, seemingly fastening him in. There he stood, a shipwrecked mariner surrounded without any means of escape. I threw him all the biscuits I had and hurried for help. Fortunately for him, a flying machine (airplane) was passing and the pilot threw him a rope and rescued him. [Otherwise] his bones would most assuredly have been bleached on this pinnacle of horror . . .

The readers of Pincushion's letter must have had a quiet chuckle, as they knew only too well the harsh reality of the "Green Hell," as it was often called.

By that time, hundreds of farmers had already been driven off their properties when the pear encroached to the very doors of their homes. Eventually, those deserted houses were smothered and crushed beneath the ever-advancing cactus.

Arthur Graham tells another story (true this time) that brings this point to the point. Please keep in mind that this incident took place in the early 1900s, in an age of extreme modesty, and in a very conservative farming community. The occasion must have been the talk of the town and the butt of many off-color jokes for at least a month:

My father and I were going to town in the sulky (horse buggy). In those days the road was only a track in and out of the pear. We had just come around a corner and there in full view were two brothers (our neighbors), one of whom had his bare behind well exposed, with his brother shaving pear prickles off his backside with a pocket knife! This debacle had happened because the two men were taking cattle to town, having sold them to the local butcher.

One of the beasts broke away from the mob and dashed into the pear. One of the brothers set off to block the animal. The horse hit the beast, the beast rolled, and horse and rider rolled over the top of it with the rider landing in a big patch of pear. If you have never had pear prickles in you, you may never know the agony of it. Hence the other brother trying to relieve his brother's anguish before mounting their horses to get the cattle into town.

Many settlers took up land that was covered with both scrubby brush and prickly-pear. To cut the scrub on their land they had to wade through the pear, which sometimes towered over their heads. They took time off only to remove the largest pear thorns. The bunches of smaller prickles were left to fester out.

"I know this," old Herbert Heilig wrote decades later, "because as a bush worker in the prickly-pear country of those days, I had first-hand experience. Willingly or otherwise, I endured more than my share of prickles as well as the still more irritating prickly-pear thorns."

"This plant created so much misery, there is no way to ever measure it," Thomas Foster, who also grew up in pear country, told me. "As the prickly-pear spread, there was less and less pasture available to feed livestock. So we fed them prickly-pear. It involved cutting the pear, pitching it into a dray (heavy wagon) and bringing it home. Then with Mum turning the forge, Dad would hold the pear over the fire with a pitchfork to burn off the prickles before feeding it to the milking cows and other livestock."

Having very little grass to feed their stock, especially during droughts, the people at Jondaryan Station eventually resorted to using old sailing ship's water tanks to prepare prickly-pear for their mob of hungry cattle.

Nearly a dozen of these huge cast-iron tanks salvaged from derelict vessels were purchased and laboriously hauled inland from the coast. Once at the station, they were set up so that a wood-fire could be built underneath them and then they were filled with water and fresh-cut prickly-pear. Boiling softened the prickles so that the cattle could safely eat it.

Most often, however, the prickly-pear wasn't cut and prepared beforehand; the cattle were just turned out into the thickets to survive as best they could. Many of them didn't. By contrast, when the station was first settled back in 1842, the rich pasture of native grasses grew up to 12 feet (3.6 m) high.

"They had to learn to eat it," retired farmer Clarence Kerr of Chinchilla, Queensland, told me. "After about three or four days we'd have to go out and pull the pear prickles out of their tongues. We would put them in the "crush cage" to immobilize them and then reach in there with our fingers and pull them out real easy. They were deadly things. If you didn't do it, the prickles would kill them. The beast would die."

In prickly-pear country one could often see cattle with swollen tongues hanging out of their mouths and bloated carcasses lining the roadways.

But not all of the stock seemed to suffer from eating prickly-pear. Very fat, aged, wild cattle were frequently found in the pear scrubs. Such cattle did not have to travel out of the pear forests to find water to drink either, because the high liquid content of the cactus sustained them.

Often several generations of these "scrub" cattle would occupy a particular pear thicket. With a lot of luck (and pluck), some of these wily beasts could occasionally be rounded up by men on horseback and sold at auction.

Surprisingly, because of the animal's exclusive diet of prickly-pear, the meat had a very mild flavor and was exquisitely tender. Because of this, it commanded a premium price in the larger cities and was always in great demand. However, most of the time the stock couldn't be mustered in spite of all efforts, including the use of thick leather coats to protect men and horses from the thorns.

"Of the great number of ways suggested for utilizing the pear, the only one which has proved satisfactory is that of feeding to stock," wrote W. B. Alexander in an early agricultural bulletin published by Australia's Institute of Science and Industry. He quickly added, however, "If all the cattle in Australia were fed entirely on prickly-pear, it is doubtful whether they would be able to keep pace with its annual increase alone."

To eradicate the pest, people needed to look to other methods. In fact, it was the cattle which were most responsible for the great spread of the pear during this time. Cattle were often moved from paddocks that had prickly-pear growing on them to "clean" paddocks that contained no pear. But as the animals were moved around, their droppings contained scores of prickly-pear seeds. Surrounded by rich manure, those seeds soon sprouted and flourished.

Chapter 6: A Country at War With the Pear

They dug it out, burned it up,
And sprayed deadly poison by the ton.
But many a man walked off his land saying,
"This is a battle that can't be won."

Poorly equipped for an all-out conflict, the invasion was initially met with an assortment of knives, hoes, spades, plows, poisons, and a hodgepodge of improvised mechanical devices. Unfortunately, none of these weapons had much effect on slowing the spread of prickly-pear on a national basis, yet down on the local level, it often seemed that the cactus really could be beaten into submission.

On fairly level land with good soil, for instance, crushing the massive thickets of pear with a "roller" could frequently be quite effective. A large, very heavy eucalyptus log, fixed at a slight angle to chains, was dragged across the cactus growth by a bullock team of as many as twenty animals. Attached in such a way that the log worked to one side of the beasts, the roller did not really roll, but passed over the pear with a sliding motion in an attempt to bruise and crush the cactus as much as possible.

It was said that one crushing could kill up to 60% of the pear. This was usually followed by two more crushings to finish off the rest of the mess. Sometimes the "rolled" pear was then plowed into the ground. But the farmer had to act fast. Plowing the crushed and broken pear underground only stimulated the plant's ability to propagate vegetatively and those broken-up pieces readily produced new roots and shoots. It was a constant struggle to keep the ground clear long enough to grow even a single crop on it. Sometimes the land had to be plowed three times in the year before being sown.

Of course, there were some temporary successes. According to one newspaper account, a farmer near Pallamallawa (for correct pronunciation, try saying "Pallamallawa" with your mouth full of crackers) in northwestern New South Wales, had cleared over 700 acres in this way and then quickly planted the land in wheat. At the time of the report, he was hoping to harvest some 6,000 to 7,000 bags of wheat, which he reckoned would more than cover his cost of clearing the land in just that one growing season.

However, the rolling method did not work well where the ground was rough and uneven. In these places, the pear was hacked out root and branch, care being taken to remove every particle of the plant. These were stacked on straddles built of timber and then the whole pile was burned.

Across a vast landscape monopolized by prickly-pear, there were many places where this pest had been driven back to the limits of the farmer's boundary fence - the result of years of unremitting toil. However, the pear would not stay confined and soon continued its inexorable advance. "It was like a very slow tsunami," Gary Ryan, a retired member of the former New South Wales Prickly Pear Destruction Board, once told me. And it was almost as unstoppable.

CHINESE WORK-GANGS

As the prickly-pear consolidated its dominance over the land, extra labor was often imported into some of the hardest-hit regions in a desperate attempt to win back lost ground. In the early days, British laborers were used. But as one contractor disclosed in his testimony to a commission of inquiry, he had "found British labor

very unsatisfactory and had consequently employed Chinese."
Using the highly-skilled Asian labor, he had already successfully
cleared between 25,000 to 30,000 acres of land, at a cost that averaged
only half the amount of his old system.

The Chinese who came to Australia in the late 1800s and
early 1900s, like numerous other people from around the world,
were often following the lure of the young nation's rich gold fields.
When the mines began to play out, many of these Chinese took
employment as house servants, cooks, and gardeners. They would
work for lower wages than the other locals, and they were much
maligned as a consequence.

Some of them settled along rivers and established market
gardens, which often became the only source of fresh produce in
many country towns. Others managed work-gangs of fellow Chinese,
who would go out onto the properties, make a camp, and then cut,
stack, and burn prickly-pear for days on end. (See Plate 7)

"It was hard, horrible work," Rita Gall of the Mungindi district
in northern New South Wales recalled. Continuing, she added:

> They once had one such camp at Dandaraga Station. It
> consisted of fifteen men. The contractor was the well-
> known George Gett, whose headquarters were at the
> Gardens in the town of Mungindi. He was very fair and
> considerate to his workers of whom he had a great many
> many, good, honest, and friendly men. Their camp was
> always clean and tidy and their meals were good with
> lots of imported luxuries, such as ginger, dried fruits,
> and spices . . . I always think the Chinese in those days
> contributed so much to outback Australia. I feel sad that
> their work had so little reward.

There were quite a few Chinese work-gangs scattered throughout the prickly-pear districts of New South Wales and Queensland.
Some of these groups consisted of large teams of 30 to 40 or more
men, who, for a reasonable wage, would labor like slaves to clear
away the pear in remote locations for weeks or even months at a
stretch.

135

During the first decade of the 20th century, a private proposal to import into Australia some 2,000 <u>indentured</u> Chinese workers annually from mainland China was repeatedly submitted to the Queensland government. Each worker could only stay for a maximum period of five years, then would have to return to China. Yet the proposition failed to clearly state whether or not these people would even be paid for their long toil.

"My reason for suggesting Chinese is that they do not seem to mind working amongst the prickly-pear, whilst I most undoubtedly consider and further unhesitantly say that the clearing of prickly-pear land is the cruelest work that white men were ever asked to do and I do not blame them for shunning such work whenever they can, no matter how good the wages are," the author of the proposal wrote. Fortunately, the governors of Queensland had the good sense to ignore this bid for slave labor.

RESEARCH STATION AT DALUCCA

The first positive step in Australia's official campaign to control prickly-pear was taken in May of 1911, when Queensland's government created the Queensland Board of Advice on Prickly Pear Destruction. The "Board of Advice," as it came to be known, was chaired by Professor Bertram Steele of the University of Queensland in Brisbane. After nearly a year of studying the problem, Steele and his fellow board members made two important decisions.

In 1912, they formed the Queensland Prickly-Pear Traveling Commission and sent its two principal members on a year-and-a-half-long, round-the-world trip to study prickly-pear (and prickly-pear's biological enemies) in every country where it occurred.

However, the hard-won advice that the "Traveling Commission" brought home with them would not reverberate in this war against the prickly-pear pest until more than a decade later. (A more detailed look at the Traveling Commission can be found in the following chapter.)

In that same year, the Board of Advice (with help from the Department of Lands), set aside 645 acres (261 hectares) of otherwise useless, prickly-pear choked land, located a mile (1.6 km) northwest of the village of Dalucca in south-central Queensland. It was to be an experimental field station in a newly-launched scientific search for the best ways to eradicate the pear. Dr. Jean White, a thirty-five-year-old botanist from Melbourne, was appointed to be officer-in-charge of carrying out these investigations.

Born in 1877, Jean White was the seventh of eight children born to Victorian astronomer Edward White. In 1909, she became the second woman ever to earn a Doctor of Science degree from the botany department at the University of Melbourne for her work on the enzymes and latent life of seeds.

Wearing a broad-brimmed sun hat, she arrived alone at the Dalucca field station to discover that "with the exception of the clearing of a cart track and the pegging out of the sites for three railway tents in part of the reserved area, no steps had been taken towards the construction of the Experimental Station."

It took nearly a month before she got the tents erected, one of which was to serve as her temporary laboratory. A month later, Dr. White hired a foreman and three laborers to work as her staff. She immediately put them to work clearing away prickly-pear to make a space for her permanent laboratory buildings. By mid-November of that year, the buildings were finished, complete with a tidy fenced-in yard.

Now, Dr. White could get to work on the real problem at hand. Earlier, a wish-list detailing the scope of her investigations had been handed to her from the Board of Advice. It included documenting the growth habits of the various prickly-pear species from seeds and cuttings, investigating the influence on seed germination after ingestion by animals (principally cattle and birds), natural factors influencing growth such as injurious insects and diseases, the nature and exact mode of action of various poisons, mechanical devices for destroying prickly-pear, and finally, exploring ways to beneficially utilize the cactus.

This was a very tall order to expect from someone who had no staff with any scientific training and was still sleeping in a tent. So, by the time her second annual report (for the work period from July 1, 1913 to June 30, 1914) was duly sent back to the Board of Advice, she had sensibly narrowed her research down to just two channels of investigation: "The observation of the effects of various chemical substances applied to the pear plants by various methods" and "the acclimatization and propagation of the wild cochineal insects forwarded to Queensland from Ceylon (now Sri Lanka) and South Africa by the Prickly-Pear Traveling Commission."

Yes, once again the cultivation of cochineal was being attempted in Australia. This time, however, it was not for the rich red dye these insects produced but for their damaging effects on their host plants, the prickly-pear. And this time the insects did not prematurely die out.

COCHINEAL ONCE AGAIN

In northern Queensland, a treelike kind of prickly-pear (*Opuntia monacantha*) grew in huge thickets throughout the Charters Towers region. (If you recall, *monacantha* is the same species of cactus that is thought to have originally been brought to Australia by Captain Arthur Phillip in 1788.)

Having observed that the cochineal which had been sent to her seemed to do very well on this type of cactus, Dr. White decided to conduct an experiment with them near the town of Charters Towers, at a locality known as Sandy Creek. A house-like frame covered with "breathable" fabric (burlap) was constructed over a clump of *monocantha* and a few pads infected with white, fluffy, cochineal insects were then attached to the plants.

"The experiment looked so futile that it was really taken as a joke, but as time went by the small, fluffy snow-white balls increased at a miraculous rate," a reporter from the *Charters Towers Northern Miner* wrote some fifteen months later. "Still, the area of pear was so vast that even with the enormous multiplicity of the cochineal insects, the task set them was considered too Herculean. However, they stuck to their work and today the huge clump is just a mass of tumble-down fiber with no vestige of life."

Encouraged by these results, the insect culture was then transferred to a bank of the same prickly-pear growing along the creek. "The open air treatment evidently agrees with the cochineal," the news article continues. "For they have attacked this pear so thoroughly that everywhere can be seen signs of its inevitable destruction. Every clump of pear has busy insects on it, and on a couple of acres the pear is already fading out."

Indeed, within a few years this particular variety of prickly-pear was brought under such complete control throughout the entire district that it was no longer considered to be a nuisance. While press reports intimated that the nation's pear problem would soon be relegated to the dark corners of history thanks to this bug, this was in fact not to be.

Some species of cochineal insect are very specific on which sort of prickly-pear they can live. When these particular insects were placed on the much more widespread "common pest-pears," (*Opuntia stricta* and the so-called *Opuntia inermis*) they literally starved.

Although there was some lingering hope that the insects would in time become acclimatized to feed on these other varieties, ultimately they could only be induced to live on the *monocantha* prickly-pear.

Still, this was the first time in Australian history that a biological agent had successfully been used to control a pernicious weed. This experiment would eventually pave the way to winning the Great Cactus War.

SEARCHING FOR THE PERFECT POISON

Meanwhile, back at Dalucca Experimental Station, Dr. Jean White was busy working on the primary task in her assignment portfolio. Throughout Australia, plant poisons had been used for many years to clear and maintain lands free from unwanted tree and shrub growth.

As early as 1898, the general-use poison known as "Scrub Exterminator," a mixture of arsenic and caustic soda, was being advocated in the *Queensland Agricultural Journal* for destroying prickly-pear. One of the first compounds developed specifically for getting rid of pear is said to have been developed by Mr. J. C. Brunnich, a chemist with the Department of Agriculture and Stock. This, too, was based on a mixture of arsenic and caustic soda, but with the addition of common salt. Although it worked reasonably well, the poison was so expensive that removing the pear often cost more than the value of the land.

In 1903, the "*Journal*" also reported that the Reverend Maitland Wood had "invented a pill and a kind of gun for introducing the pill into the plant, which completely dies out by this treatment." The article advised it readers, however, that "it has not been tried, we believe, on a large scale."

Over in South Africa, where an ongoing battle with intro-duced prickly-pear was also taking place, another injectable chemical preparation was patented a few years later. For some reason, this is the first and last we hear of either of these inventions. Perhaps their manufacture was just too expensive for use over broad areas.

At the Dalucca field station, a complex series of experiments on the effects of plant poisons were carried out by Dr. White and her staff. An enormous number of substances thought to be poisonous were tried, either in the form of sprays, injectables, or as gaseous vapors. By the end of 1913, more than 1,500 experimental plots had already been marked out. (In order to separate and allow access to each individual numbered plot, a series of parallel pathways had been cut through the pear.) In total, more than 10,000 experiments were eventually concluded there.

Many of the chemicals were discarded as being either too expensive or too hazardous. "It was found that in some cases the poison traveled inside the pear at the rate of three inches (7.5 cm) per minute, but this was most dangerous," one newspaper reported. "Dr. White's assistant unfortunately touched a spot of liquid with the end of one of his fingers. The burning pain was so intense that the finger had to be taken off at the first joint to save further consequences."

There were other problems, too. Dr. White was often criticized by visitors to her field station for the practice of "cleaning" up the experimental plots prior to treatment. They maintained that the poisoning should be only done under the natural conditions of growth for the pear. But in order to track the precise effect a particular substance had on the cactus, all of the undergrowth and any seedlings, fallen segments and fruit must first be removed. This left the plot clear of everything except the individual plants to be tested.

This was done because the first effect of most poisons was to cause the shedding of the affected segments and fruits, Dr. White would explain to her critics, and that she needed to keep track of just how many of these fallen pieces retained sufficient vitality to sprout and form new plants.

After Australia entered into World War I in 1914, a large part of the nation's resources were diverted to the war effort. As a consequence, many of the chemicals that Dr. White needed for her experiments became scarce and difficult to procure. And as the war dragged on, this scarcity became even more pronounced.

However, in spite of being partially crippled by lack of materials, the field station's research effort limped on, month after month, as best it could. But Dr. Jean White's future was about to radically change. A few months before the war broke out, a young American chemist named Oliver Cromwell Roberts had arrived with his family in the little village of Dalucca to set up a research operation of his own.

EXPERIMENTAL GAS TRIALS

Roberts had read of the widespread devastation that prickly-pear was causing in Australia and became convinced that he could provide a chemical remedy to the problem (and get rich at the same time). Initially rejecting the spray-method of poisoning the plants as too labor-intensive, he moved from San Francisco to Queensland to begin investigating the use of poisonous gases.

His preliminary experiments were made at Deagon, some 11 miles (18 km) north of Brisbane. The initial apparatus he used was crude - just a boiler that created toxic fumes - yet it was enough to encourage him to proceed on a larger scale.

After having depleted his own savings on this project, Roberts soon obtained substantial financial backing from a company located in Melbourne. This helped him create a company named "Cactus Estates Limited," with himself nominated as the company's managing director.

Moving to Dalucca, he reserved part of the top story of the Dalucca Hotel as a suite for his wife and children and quickly set up a laboratory located near the railway line.

After having first secured an initial 50 acres, then over 200 acres of pear-covered land located close to the government experiment station, Roberts eventually received a lease from the Queensland government for ten blocks of land consisting of 10,000 acres each. All of this property was badly infested with pear, but if Roberts could somehow clear away the cactus through his experiments - and keep it clear for just two years - he would be awarded title to the entire holding. As a show of good faith on the part of the government, Roberts was even provided free carriage of his chemicals via the railroad.

Forty men were employed to cut miles of access roads

through the pear and scrub. Roberts's plan was to release clouds of deadly arsenic trichloride gas ($AsCl_3$) from boilers mounted on horse-drawn wagons that were driven along these tracks. (See Plate 10) The chemicals were placed in the boiler together with salt and the resulting vapor escaped out into the surrounding air. Being heavier than air, the fog soon settled on the pear, causing many of the aboveground portions to die. In spite of being extremely hazardous to the operator, nearly every day for weeks on end - unless there was a stiff breeze or if it was raining - Roberts's poison engines pumped large volumes of this mist out over the pear.

For a time, this technique really did appear to be working. "Though the machine is very crude, the results are marvelous," the *Maryborough Chronicle* reported on October 6th, 1913. "But Mr. Robert's gain, even if it makes him a millionaire, will be very small compared with what the state gains."

Mr. Arthur Temple Clerk, a prickly-pear activist who tirelessly campaigned for the eradication of the pear, had recently visited Roberts and was subsequently interviewed for the *Daily Mail*.

"He has just returned from Dalucca, where the gas process has been used by Mr. Roberts," the reporter wrote. "He spent many days closely examining the pear and wandering the large area which had been treated. He was more positive than ever that his gas formula was none other than absolutely fatal to the whole of the pear."

So it seemed at the time. However, the tenacity of the prickly-pear had again been underestimated and its vigorous regrowth from underground rootstocks the following spring clearly indicated that the answer had not yet been found. Cactus Estates Limited went into liquidation two years later and Oliver Cromwell Roberts moved to Brisbane, where he continued his investigations on how to beat the pear with chemicals.

But before his experiments with arsenious chlorine gas were concluded at Dalucca, a serious relationship between Dr. Jean White and Cliff Haney, a member of Roberts's staff, had evolved. They were married in February of 1915. (In her last two reports to the Board of

Advice, she would use her new name, Dr. Jean White-Haney.)

Dr. White-Haney's preliminary investigations had indicated that a specific compound of arsenic (arsenic pentoxide) appeared to be the most effective chemical to poison prickly-pear. The trouble was that the chemical was only obtainable in extremely limited quantities (what with the war on) and for a long time, her conclusions could not be backed up by sufficient scientific evidence.

Now that she was linked to O. C. Roberts's enterprise through her marriage to Cliff Haney, she somehow procured, "nearly a ton of the crude specific for the purpose of further experimental research and since then no time has been lost in repeating my experiments on a larger scale." (Very likely, the same Melbourne-based company that had been providing Roberts with operating funds and large amounts of arsenic compounds for his own field-trials had also supplied Dr. White-Haney for her experiments.)

After thoroughly testing arsenic pentoxide in a variety of ways, such as dusting the plants with the powdered chemical, mixing it with water and spraying it in on, or injecting it as a liquid directly into the plant, Dr. White-Haney could finally say that "as a result, I am now glad to be in a position to state without hesitation that I am confident of having demonstrated the most generally effective pear-killing specific which has ever been tried."

With research funds drying up because of the ongoing war and the added responsibility of becoming a new mother due to the birth of a baby boy into the White-Haney family, the Board of Advice decided to close the research station at the end of June 1916. Although Dr. White-Haney had discovered that arsenic pentoxide was superior to other chemicals in destroying the pear, it was also very expensive.

In her final report, she cautioned that the only real solution lay in discovering "some parasitic insects or organism capable of bringing about the destruction of the different species of prickly-pear as completely as the *Coccus indicus* has done for the *monocantha* species in north Queensland." (This cochineal is now known as *Dactylopius ceylonicus*.)

144

"The need for further investigations is imperative on account of the rapidity with which the pest is spreading," she warned. Continuing, she added:

> Millions of acres of good land are rendered useless in Queensland . . . large tracts of land in New South Wales are monopolized by the pest, and the danger in that state is a grave one. In parts of Victoria, notably about Melton, South Brighton, and Essendon, a species of pear is quickly gaining a hold. The Director of Agriculture in South Australia informs me that he does not [thus far] consider the pear a pest in that state, though two species are prevalent there. The acting director of agriculture of Tasmania states that the pear has not escaped from cultivation there, yet. I have also been unofficially informed that a species of pear has run wild on Thursday Island. Whether regarded as a pest or not, in certain states it can only be considered as a dangerous plant which needs stamping out completely in the shortest time possible.

O. C. Roberts shared Dr. White-Haney's sentiments in many ways. He was also worried about the exponential spreading of the pear, but he felt that the best way to fight it was with chemicals. At the time when his own experimental headquarters had closed, Roberts held two patents for pear-destroying machines. These he had tested and modified during his trials at Dalucca. Although he had strongly advocated the use of arsenious chloride gas all the while he was there, he later went on to develop a commercial poison based on arsenic pentoxide, almost exactly as Dr. Jean White-Haney had recommended.

ROBERTS'S IMPROVED PEAR POISON

Eliminating prickly-pear by gassing it proved to be a hit-or-miss technique. This was primarily because of uneven distribution of the poison by fickle breezes. Also, a sudden change in wind direction could envelope the poison-machine's operator in a cloud of toxic gas, thereby threatening his own health. Eventually, these and numerous other shortcomings convinced Roberts that this system was just not going to be commercially viable.

For all of his intense effort, Roberts still had not completely removed the pear from even one of his 10,000 acre leasehold blocks near Dulacca. If only he could develop a relatively inexpensive chemical treatment that would actually clear the land economically, the entire state then could move ahead into a prosperous future.

Abandoning the gas idea, Roberts now threw himself into the task of perfecting a new prickly-pear poison. As Dr. White-Haney had discovered earlier, arsenic pentoxide really did appear to be the most effective compound. So Roberts followed her counsel and while the violence of World War I was drawing to a close, he developed and patented what he came to believe was the very best formulation for destroying prickly-pear.

It was a liquid mixture that contained 80% sulfuric acid and 20% arsenic pentoxide. In test after test, it did indeed prove superior to any other chemical known at the time. The treatment, he explained, worked in a twofold manner: the acid eroded the prickly-pear's tough cuticle, which then allowed entry of the arsenic compound into the plant, thus killing it completely.

Just a few years later, the newly-financed and reorganized "O. C. Roberts Company" built a factory in Wallangarra, Queensland, which immediately began producing this poison by the ton. (The governor of Queensland had even performed the opening ceremony.)

The arsenic portion of Roberts's poison formula, which originally had to be imported from Japan, was soon locally available from a mining complex on the Mole River. As demand for arsenic and arsenic pentoxide increased, another arsenic mine opened at Jibbinbar near the town of Stanthorpe in southern Queensland.

Although the new poison was very effective, it also could be dangerous to those who used it. A few drops of the mixture would eat a hole into leather and it utterly destroyed any clothing it came into contact with. Not only would it create a rash on the skin,

146

repeated exposures would sometimes cause one's fingernails to fall off. Yet with reasonable care, Roberts advised, the poison could be handled safely. Initially skeptical, state governments began testing and retesting the new poison on various patches of prickly-pear.

Directed by the New South Wales Department of Lands, one series of field trials concluded that "although the poison was severe on the skin . . . the effect was immediately nullified by immediate application of water . . ." W. J. Roper, the person in charge of these particular experiments, reported that the men employed in applying the spray appeared to be in excellent health and showed no ill effects from the use of this compound. But what it did to the prickly-pear was another matter.

"One is at once struck with the apparent destruction wrought by this poison," he wrote in his final report. "Within about an hour of being sprayed, the pear begins to show black spots where the drops have lodged. In a day, the joints show black and the plant quickly falls . . . Where the pear has been sprayed or infected for a month or more, it is dead and rotting."

While these results were certainly very encouraging, the bottom-line was still the actual cost of this poison to the settler. Roberts knew very well that if the expense of clearing the pear were going to be more than the value of the property - which was often worth less than $50 US an acre in today's terms - very few people would even try his product. (And because the pear would always find ways of returning, this was actually an ongoing expense.)

This problem was finally resolved when he cut a deal with the government, which announced that it would subsidize the cost of supplying his poison to the landholders. Not only would the government bear the balance of the cost of the poison, it offered free carriage by rail for delivery of the stuff to the nearest railway station. In bulk form, the poison was to be supplied in 100 pound (45 kg) drums. Eventually, the poison was available in a range of smaller container sizes, from diminutive earthenware jars to 10 and 20 pound tins (4.5 to 9 kg).

147

Roberts now appeared to be on the road to riches. His new poison worked well and enormous quantities of it were being manufactured and sold. Even before the official opening of his factory in Wallangarra, he had already marketed the stuff to over 1,350 users who had cleared "no less than 234,000 acres" of pear-covered land.

Two years later, the O. C. Roberts Company had a contract to supply 1,100 tons of this chemical at £34/8s a ton (totaling more than $2.5 million US). Roberts's poison business was booming. The *Brisbane Courier* discretely reported in its financial section that the company's net profit in just that one year was almost a million dollars.

There were various estimates on just how much of Roberts's poison it would take to destroy a given amount of prickly-pear. When used as a surface spray, one ton of the poison was said to be able to kill about 4,500 tons of pear.

This was the equivalent to about five and a half acres of land covered in dense pear. Yet when injected directly into the cactus, this same ton of poison could clear as many as 25 acres (about four times as much cactus) having the same density of growth. The problem with both methods, however, was getting access into those impenetrable spiny thickets to even poison anything. But on old, tough plants or where the pear grew in scattered clumps, the poison worked wonders.

After several design changes, the handheld atomizer used to apply Roberts's poison as a surface spray was finally perfected. It contained a five-liter tank (approximately 5 quarts) slung under the arm that was pressurized by a hand pump. A metal wand that distributed the misting spray was controlled by a spring-loaded thumb-trigger. All the operator had to do was walk around and squirt it on the pear in one-second-long doses.

"A light spraying of the leaves only is necessary, as the circulation carries the poison to the bulb," *The Sydney Morning Herald* advised its readers in an article on how to kill prickly-pear with Roberts's poison. "The pear should not be slashed or broken as this destroys the circulation. The slashing of access lanes should [also] be carefully avoided and is a waste of time. In very dense pear the accessible part will fall quickly after spraying and permit access."

For use as an injectable poison, farmers began carrying Roberts's arsenic mixture around in wide-mouth pickle jars suspended with a piece of twisted wire. One pound of this toxin was sufficient to destroy 10 tons of pear or about 500 two-year-old plants. The poison was applied by dipping a sharpened flat steel file into the solution and then jabbing several "leaves" of the pear. That was it; the poison did the rest.

Eventually, safer and more efficient commercial pear-stabbing devices that acted like giant hypodermic syringes began to supersede this primitive technique. But to many small farmers, these were luxury items that cost more than the income from the sale of one of their prize bacon pigs. They stuck grimly to the old file method until the government began subsidizing the purchase of both the new pear-stabbers and the atomizers. (See Plate 13)

Along the way, there were constant challenges to Roberts's little poison monopoly. First on the list was the state government itself. It was paying Roberts nearly four and a half times the subsidy rate for his patented liquid poison and it wanted to find a (legal) way around the deal.

The solution lay in the Jibbinbar mine, which was state-owned and operated. From there, hundreds of tons of elemental arsenic were converted into powdered arsenic pentoxide and sold directly to the landholders at a very cheap rate. Once on the farm, the poison was then mixed with water and applied to the pear.

"The price the farmer has to pay is all out of proportion to the value he receives. The advantage of a concentrated poison in powdered form is in mixing, cost of transit by rail, cost of packing, and moreover it is less dangerous," the Minister for Mines announced in defense of this move. From then on, in a kind of "right pocket, left pocket" shuffle, the Department of Lands paid the Mines Department the so-called difference in market price. In reality, the money never left the government's coffers.

After witnessing the national merchandising success of Roberts's pear poison, numerous other entrepreneurs (and charlatans) tried their hand at developing a "better pear poison." They were marketed under names like "Perfection Pear Poison," "Dr. Botteral's Prickly Pear Gas," and "King's Pearicide."

One of these, which for a brief time attracted considerable attention in the press, was called "Save Our Soil Prickly Pear Poison," (or "S. O. S." for short). It appeared to work well, and the company's test plots indicated that this special chemical mixture would completely kill the pear within six weeks.

One demonstration of the effectiveness of "S. O. S." was even attended by Walter Wearne, a leading member of the New South Wales state parliament. "The butts, crowns, and roots of the plants were dug up and thoroughly dissected and the consensus of opinion was that not one vestige of pear remained alive," reported the *Brisbane Courier*. "The singular features of 'S. O. S.' are that it is non-corrosive and can be delivered in ordinary petrol or kerosene tins," the news-article crowed. "It is non-injurious to clothing or boots and can be sold to the man on the land at half the price charged for any other specific which is effective on pear."

But all of this news turned out to be just clever "smoke and mirrors" publicity. A year later, the manufacturer of "S. O. S." was being sued by a Dr. Ernest Deck in order to recover damages from the company's misrepresentations of the effectiveness of the poison. In the lawsuit, Dr. Deck claimed that these untruths induced him to purchase shares in the company, which later had become worthless.

Also, during a revisit of the same test plot where a demonstration of the poison's effect had been shown to him, he found that the prickly-pear was still growing. Unsurprisingly, not much concerning "Save Our Soil Prickly Pear Poison" was seen or heard again.

ARSENIC ON THE LAND

Records indicate that during the twenty-year period between 1912 and 1932, more than 3,300 tons of arsenic pentoxide powder and Roberts's Improved Pear Poison were subsidized and shipped free by rail to landholders in Queensland. Huge amounts were also sent to New South Wales.

Some local districts received as much as 12 tons of these materials in a single consignment. Even after the prickly-pear invasion had been beaten back by the introduction of *Cactoblastis*, pockets of resistant growth were sprayed with poison to bring them under control. In fact, arsenic-based herbicides were still being widely used for general weed control right up until the early 1960s.

What effect did this widespread dousing of arsenic for more than 45 years have on Australia's rural landscape? Apparently, the jury is still out on this question. Perhaps because it is such a potentially controversial topic, my queries directed to two of Australia's leading experts on environmental toxins went unanswered. However, I have come across numerous reports of groundwater being contaminated, cattle dying, and workers suffering from long-term symptoms of arsenic poisoning.

Arsenic (*As*) is the 20th most abundant element on earth and occurs widely distributed in the earth's crust. The greatest commercial use of arsenic is as an ingredient in wood preservatives, termiticides (for killing termites), leather-tanning solutions, some explosives, and in the manufacture of glass and electronic semi-conductors. Although many naturally occurring arsenic-based compounds can be found, there are two basic forms of the material: organic and inorganic.

Small amounts of organic arsenic are present in all living organisms, mostly from dietary uptake. You may be surprised to learn that measurable amounts of arsenic occur naturally in many of our foods, including cereals, vegetables, and especially seafood. (Average concentrations in fish and shellfish are often greater than

151

five ppm [parts per million] and can exceed 30 ppm.) However, within three days after consumption, most of this "background" arsenic is eliminated from your body.

Inorganic arsenic is essentially found in soil and rock but it can leach into groundwater. The natural sink of this "arsenic in solution" is in the sediments, usually within a wetland system, where it forms insoluble complexes with iron precipitates and organic matter that become permanently trapped.

Arsenic and its many compounds are also transformed by microorganisms. One case study of a wetland's ability to clean arsenic from contaminated seepage coming from a gold mine waste dump located in Australia's Northern Territory showed more than a thousand-fold decrease in this substance when measured at the points where the water entered the wetland and where it exited, due to the work of the microorganisms.

When ingested or absorbed through the skin into an animal's body, arsenic is transported into most of the organs by binding to the so-called "globin" portion of hemoglobin in blood cells. Acute arsenic toxicity in mammals can interrupt ATP synthesis in cells and act as a capillary poison, causing circulatory failure. Symptoms of acute arsenic poisoning include abdominal pain, vomiting, diarrhea, limb incoordination, and hypothermia.

On the other hand, long-term exposure to arsenic in doses just slightly higher than what an animal's system can eliminate will eventually lead to chronic accumulative poisoning. This appears to be what happened to many of the people who used arsenic pentoxide to clear their land of prickly-pear. In a poignant letter, Queenslander Thomas Foster told me of his own family's heartbreak associated with the prickly-pear eradication:

> My grandfather, Harry Foster, developed arsenic
> poisoning from handling drums of arsenic, [that] were
> delivered by rail. Often the drums were leaking and
> my grandfather would carry them on his shoulder. As
> a result Grandfather was constantly exposed to the
> arsenic as it soaked into his body. He was very ill for a

long time and almost died before he recovered. My grandmother nursed him at home. She used to massage milk and other additives into his shoulders.

It wasn't just people who developed chronic arsenic toxicity. Writer Eric Rolls describes the results of attempts to clear pear by spraying it from horseback:

> The horse's legs were bound to protect them from the spines and a pressure tank fitted with a hand-pump, nozzle and hose was strapped to the saddle. The mixture destroyed what pear it could be sprayed on. It also destroyed the men's clothing, their boots, their saddles, and eventually their horses, who lost their hair and developed sores that would not heal.

"How dangerous this practice was, with misting poison drifting over the workers and their horses," Thomas Foster's letter concluded. "They would be saturated with arsenic and their wives would also be contaminated with arsenic when washing their clothes."

"There was a terrible lot of danger with it, because if you sprayed it on yourself it would eat your clothes away. And the mist would get into your eyes," Clarence Kerr, a retired farmer from Queensland's Chinchilla district told me during an interview. "It was the worst bloody stuff that you ever had anything to do with." Many years after he had stopped using the arsenic sprays, poor old Clarence went blind.

Because arsenic is so toxic, many of the farmers who used it began expressing concern about what it might do to their crops or stock. To allay their fears, a bulletin published in 1919 by the Institute of Science and Industry attempted to address this issue. Referring to some of the experiments undertaken at Dulacca, the publication assured the reader that:

> Crops of wheat and lucerne (alfalfa) raised on plots on which pear had been poisoned with arsenic, then burnt and dug in, did better than crops raised on land from which the pear had been removed without poisoning.

Analyses of the plants grown on land where the pear had been poisoned showed that no appreciable quantities of arsenic had been absorbed by them, so that it is fairly certain that the arsenic does no harm to subsequent crops and that the burnt poisoned pear when dug in is distinctly beneficial.

Another publication stated that landholders often "allow stock to graze in the paddocks that are being poisoned and have no losses. The poisons are applied so sparingly that it would be difficult for stock to eat enough pear to be poisoned." Because of these kinds of statements, it became generally assumed that cattle could safely eat prickly-pear in a wilted state just three days after it was poisoned.

But some plants can apparently concentrate arsenic within their tissues. After one of my "prickly-pear talks" in the town of Chinchilla, Queensland, a farmer told me how he had lost cattle that had fed on couch-grass growing in an area containing arsenic residue. During my own visit to Dulacca, another farmer showed me the spot where he had recently lost dozens of calves due to residual arsenic poisoning.

Clearly, long-term impacts to the soil have resulted from the widespread spraying of arsenic compounds around the region. Summing all this up in his memoirs of the prickly-pear days, South Queenslander Bill Varidel simply wrote, "I think it did more harm to the men than the pear."

So, how safe is Australia's water supply today? According to the National Water Quality Management Strategy, raw sources of potential drinking water typically contain concentrations of arsenic ranging from <0.001 mg/L to 0.03 mg/L.

Because the national guidelines state that concentrations of arsenic in public water systems should not exceed 0.01 mg/L, it is easily reduced using an efficient coagulation process with equipment that is certified to perform to 0.01 mg/L or less. Actually, you might receive a larger dose of arsenic when you eat that tempting extra shrimp sizzling on your backyard barbecue.

THE PRICKLY-PEAR SELECTIONS

Throughout the regions dominated by prickly-pear, state governments attempted to make settlement of the land more attractive. This was especially true in Queensland, where there was already a strong push towards what was known as "closer settlement." From the 1860s onwards, a considerable number of schemes aimed at breaking up the large land estates were being devised.

Promoted as "building blocks for a stronger nation" which would make the land more productive and profitable, settlers were to be provided with properties "large enough to make a living, yet small enough to promote a sense of community." Also, some of the closer settlement acts passed by parliament in the 1900s were specifically aimed at diversifying land production from merely grazing beef-cattle to producing wheat, cotton, sugar, fruit, dairy products, and market garden vegetables.

The Prickly Pear Selections Act (1901), for example, was one of the first of a long series of schemes to offer prickly-pear infested land to would-be settlers essentially rent-free. (Known as peppercorn leases, the government charged "the rate of one peppercorn per year, if demanded.")

There were also various incentive bonuses for clearing a portion of the land each year. However, before they could occupy it, anyone who had selected a particular block of land (which became known as a "selection") was required pay a substantial fee for having it properly surveyed.

Subdividing these huge blocks of prickly-pear-infested land was an extremely difficult task. The dense growth created a formidable barrier through which the surveyor had to clear his boundary lines. Working through the 1920s, surveyor John Meek recalled that "the pear itself had nasty spines and if you were scratched by these, your skin could become infected. We disliked working in dense pear country. It was impossible to walk through, so we had to hack out a path, not difficult with such a soft plant, but very time consuming."

A few of the more innovative surveyors had special leather suits made for them. But because these garments could be god-awfully uncomfortable even during a normal day - let alone a hot one - most of the surveyors just put up with the annoying prickles.

The end of World War I created another problem for Australia. What to do with the thousands of unemployed returned soldiers? During the war, there had been a severe drought that promoted a huge surge in prickly-pear growth. "Many families walked off their properties, leaving them to the invading menace," wrote Val Tongs in the *Australasian Post*. "Even large pastoral holdings became a deserted wilderness of spikes."

Because the sea of prickly-pear had spread over such huge areas of new land while they were overseas, many of these young men could not even locate the homesteads where they had grown up. Those who did find their old homes, often discovered that living there was all too difficult and soon walked away, abandoning their farms once again to the "menace."

With the nation's cities, towns, and villages filling up with idle men hoping to find something to do to make a living, the government began offering land, in blocks ranging from 640 to about 900 acres (259 to 364 hectares), nearly free to almost anyone who would work it. But the men who took up these "soldier settlements," as they came to be called, often had grown up in cities and literally had no experience whatsoever at farming.

When they realized that they had been beaten by the pear, many soldier settlers ended their farming careers by forfeiting the land. Others survived for a while by finding work clearing pear on large estates in return for wages. And because the only time they had for fighting their own pear was during Saturday and Sunday, they often could not meet the improvement conditions stated in their leases and ultimately ended up forfeiting as well.

ZIFF WEARNE'S WILD TRAIN RIDE

"They spend hours leaning over fences, looking at the pear and hating it. They hold single hates. They hold community hates. The pear is impervious to both," the *Sydney Sun* declared in June of 1924. "It is at their paddock fence one day and the next morning in their backyard. It spreads so rapidly. The trouble with some people is that they spend so much time hating the pear that they forget to harness up the bullock team and roll it."

Unfortunately, this was a common attitude of many of the people who lived in Australia's largest cities during the reign of the pear. They were aware that prickly-pear was a widespread problem out in the countryside, yet to them it was an issue that could be easily cured with the right combination of willpower and "elbow-grease."

Echoing this attitude, it was perhaps the primary reason why Parliament had failed to effectively respond to this issue for so long. Very few of the lawmakers had even seen the prickly-pear invasion full-on and close-up.

Walter "Ziff" Wearne was the Minister for Lands and a leading member of the New South Wales State Parliament at the time that *Sydney Sun* article appeared. He also knew what prickly-pear was really like; although born in Sydney, he had grown up in Bingara, in the very heart of some of the state's worst pear country.

To gain support for his proposal for a bill that might lead to the eventual control of prickly-pear, Wearne invited his fellow-members of parliament to accompany him on a tour of the state's prickly-pear lands. They were mostly city-dwellers who knew next to nothing about the problems connected with prickly-pear.

Expecting to lead a party of only a dozen people on a regularly-scheduled train, Wearne was pleasantly surprised when nearly 30 of his fellow parliamentarians expressed their keen desire to go and see. To cater to such a large group, though, Wearne found it necessary to charter a special train. This immediately got the attention of the press, which severely criticized the trip as a "public excess." (See Plate 12)

157

"As each member was paying his own way," Mr. Wearne hastened to assure the reporters, "the trip would not cost the government anything." One newspaper scathingly replied in an editorial, "It would be rude to dispute the declaration of a Minister, but we would like to bet a new hat that their contributions fall far short of the cost of the trip . . . Even now, when the advance of these pests on uninfected land could be stopped by a man with a hoe, nothing is done, except organizing picnics of blasé politicians."

Wearne and his colleagues completed their 1,100 mile (1,770 km) journey in just four days, but those days were crammed with a firsthand look at just how serious the pear situation really was. During their initial briefing, the parliamentary group was informed that some seven and a half million acres of land in New South Wales had already been overrun, and the "horror" was advancing across the state at a rate of over a half million acres per year. But this hardly prepared them for the reality of the situation.

After transferring to a fleet of a dozen cars, the party got their first real sight of the prickly-pear plague at Pallamallawa, where it was "seen in absolute control of thousands of acres." Near a place called Myall Creek, the whole retinue of automobiles was brought to a sudden standstill by a barricade someone had made by stacking cut prickly-pear across the road. "When the members jumped out to see the obstacle," *The Sydney Morning Herald* reported, "They were amused to read the words scribbled on a note, 'Good morning gentlemen, we are here to greet you'."

In one district, the only space clear of pear was a 15-foot-wide (4.5 m) swath used by road traffic. In total, the group traveled nearly 200 miles (320 km) by car over the next two days and were completely impressed by the fact that the battle currently being waged against prickly-pear was a losing one.

Indeed, all the members of Wearne's tour group were unanimous regarding the need for government action. Known as the "Prickly-pear Act, 1924," Wearne's bill easily passed through parliament when it was introduced. It may have been a step in the right direction but, unfortunately, it still obligated the landholder to bear the cost of dealing with the pear.

There were some significant changes, however. Owners of large areas of land heavily infested with pear had been previously expected to clear the entire property within a given time. As that task was utterly impossible, the pest was essentially allowed to continue spreading. Under this new bill, the rate of clearing was much more relaxed, and now the landholder was only compelled to keep clear land that had already been cleared.

Whatever its shortcomings were, this bill did help pave the way for the creation of the New South Wales Prickly Pear Destruction Commission later that year. Beginning its operations in 1925, for more than 60 years its employees actively provided useful information, poison, equipment, physical labor, and insects in helping to control prickly-pear infestations, right up until it was disbanded at the end of 1987.

THE DREADED PRICKLY-PEAR LAND RANGERS

In the neighboring state to the north, a similar body called the Queensland Prickly Pear Land Commission (the PPLC) also got its official start in 1924. However, unlike the New South Wales commission, this organization was given broad judicial and administrative powers to deal with the pear problem.

With a guaranteed annual budget that started at £100,000 (around $6.5 million US today), the commission's three principal officers received ten-year long appointments with annual salaries ranging from £800 to £900. ($49,000 to $55,000 US) per year. Their authority extended to all pear-infested areas in the state. Eventually, the PPLC would be administering a territory almost the size of Italy.

Initially, they began to purchase the most effective prickly-pear poisons, including Roberts's improved pear poison, and distribute them to landholders often at cost price. (In one form or another, most of that poison came from the state's own arsenic mine.)

159

In Queensland's worst-affected districts, local governments were offered a subsidy of £2 for every £1 that they spent on prickly-pear removal.

But the PPLC still held to the widespread yet mistaken belief that landholders, both private owners and those with long-term government lease agreements, were still responsible for clearing the pear from their properties. This proved to be a gross underestimation of the problem. Where the pear growth was dense, determined farmers could clear 10, 20, 100, occasionally even 1,000 acres or more, but the land would remain clear only for a short time unless that effort was being constantly enforced.

The Prickly Pear Land Commission became that "enforcer." Functioning as an independent body, responsible only to Parliament, the commission's "Prickly Pear Court" could regulate the rights of Crown tenants (people who rent public lands), fix their rent rates, determine the annual land-clearing requirements, open pear-infested land for settlement - and most importantly for people living within their jurisdiction - evict landholders who were unable to comply with their strict pear-clearing conditions. This often meant confiscation of whatever other improvements, such as dwellings, roads, outbuildings, fences and corrals, that the former tenants were forced to leave behind.

The PLLC's tough approach was moderated somewhat when it eventually agreed to review many of the leases in their jurisdiction and to offer inducements for continued occupancy by lowering rents or extending the lease itself. This was a slow, laborious process. For many years, about every two weeks, the latest lease adjustments were announced in the regional newspapers. Here's a typical one that appeared in the June 25th, 1926 edition of the *Brisbane Telegraph*:

> The Prickly Pear Land Commission yesterday issued a
> further batch of decisions in cases in which the lessees
> have sought relief under 'The Prickly-pear Land Acts,
> 1923 to 1926.' The schedule comprises a total of 177
> cases . . . situated in the Gayndah, Roma, Rockhampton
> and Dalby districts.

160

Two weeks later, the crowded prickly-pear court had processed another 172 cases "situated chiefly in the Rockhampton and Roma land agent's districts." And so it went, until more than 10,000 lease-holders had sought relief.

To enforce their decisions, the PPLC maintained a detachment of some 80 or more prickly-pear land rangers, whose job was to regularly inspect properties for compliance with conditions set forth in the landholders' leases. "If the pear wasn't kept in check, you were reported to the 'Higher Powers,' who promptly told you what to do about its destruction," wrote Kathleen Johnston in the *Toowoomba Chronicle* some years later. "If you didn't comply - or were unable - you either got your walking orders or walked off without waiting for them."

Figures compiled from land rangers' annual reports indicate that, on average across the state, only 63% of lease holders were able to comply with their clearing conditions. The other 37% often got into serious trouble. Even owners of private properties were not exempt. Although they could rarely be physically evicted, they could receive hefty fines for not clearing enough pear.

Having reverted back to the Crown, the confiscated properties were not cleared of the offending prickly-pear in order to make the land ready for the next settler. "Instead," continues Johnston, "It was leased out at a cheap rate to any enterprising person who cared to take it up for fattening bullocks, but who were not obliged to do anything whatsoever in the pursuance of pear extermination." When they were finished running cattle on it, the land was simply left to the invading cactus.

"Some of the land rangers were quite officious and harassed the farmers for not doing enough to clear more areas," wrote Clarence Ulm in his letter to me. "They became despised by the farmers, when they had enough to contend with as it was." Another retired farmer told me that he wouldn't have been surprised at all if one day he'd heard that his own district's prickly-pear ranger had been found under a bush with his throat cut. "Actually, I'm kind of surprised that he wasn't," he added.

In his letter to the editor of the *Maryborough Chronicle*, Mr. D. Groeneweg comments on the vicious cycle that most settlers faced:

> The average man who takes up land - prickly-pear land in particular - is poor or next door to it. He starts to clear a piece of land . . . and [then] a dry spell sets in. Result: No crop and that man has to look for a job from shire or town council or neighbor. After some months, the man finds his clean lands again infested with pear and has again to start clearing. The inspector comes and does his duty and complains that the necessary amount of land is not cleared.

Fighting the pear was often a full-time job that left little time or opportunity to make a reasonable living from farming. One settler who took up a prickly-pear selection near Chinchilla, wrote in his diary that he felt that he and his family "were trapped on the property - deliberately by the government, as it should have known. The conditions imposed were worse than slavery and impossible to be accomplished. Conditions imposed meant 20,000 tons of prickly-pear per annum to clear and keep clean."

Assuming an average growth of 400 tons of prickly-pear per acre, that meant he had to clear nearly an acre of land every week, and then keep it free of return growth. An onerous task like this certainly wouldn't leave a person much spare time to earn even a basic living.

Proud of their vigorous policies, however, within just a few years of its inception the PPLC began to publish announcements that the continued spread of prickly-pear had been definitely been arrested. Citing the effective use of poison over the region, their figures indicated that "nearly one million moderately-sized pear plants are now being destroyed daily." Unfortunately, their success had been grossly overestimated; in reality, the pear invasion was still continuing its implacable expansion.

1. Title page from Thiery de Menonville's 1799 book on how to raise cochineal.

2. Early view of prickly-pear in Australia. Painting is titled "Double Bay, Port Jackson, 1852." (Courtesy National Library of Australia)

3. William Bell Carlyle's 1823 "Satur House," near Scone, New South Wales. This is where the prickly-pear plague is thought to have gotten its true start.

4. Granny Sutton, who as a young woman, tended her employer's prickly-pear plants with loving care. (Photo from a 1899 newspaper obituary, clipping source unknown.)

5. Dense forest of velvety prickly-pear located near Gogango, Queensland. Commonwealth Prickly Pear Board photo by H.W. Mobsby, circa 1928.

6. Driving in the Gogango Range in Central Queensland, through a forest of velvety prickly-pear (*Opuntia tomentosa*). Some plants are over 20 feet high (6.5 meters). [*The Queenslander*, February 19, 1921, photo by Vernon White.]

7. Prickly-pear neatly stacked by Chinese workers for eventual burning.
(Photo courtesy the Coward family)

8. Rescuing sheep from a flooded and prickly-pear choked river.
("Wongalee Station") Photo courtesy the Coward family.

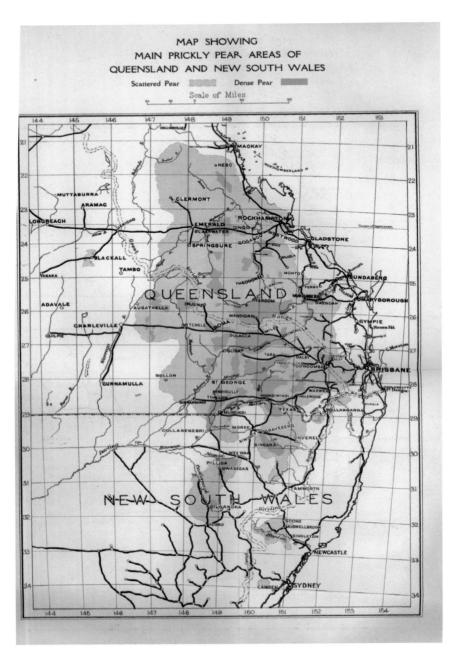

9. A late 1930s era Commonwealth Prickly Pear Board map of the worst prickly-pear affected areas in New South Wales and Queensland. In reality, the cactus had already spread far beyond the range of this map, but it was not yet considered to be a serious economic problem in those regions.

10. Arsenic gas generator. Location is unknown, but is most likely part of O. C. Roberts' pear-poison research that was conducted near Dalucca, Queensland, in mid-1914. (Photo courtesy National Library of Australia)

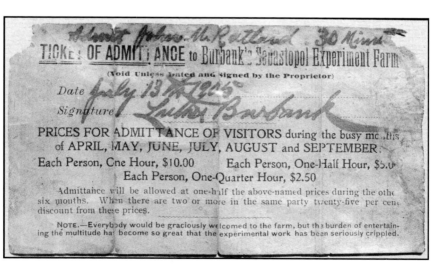

TICKET OF ADMITTANCE to Burbank's Sevastopol Experiment Farm

(Void Unless Dated and Signed by the Proprietor)

Date July 13 1905

Signature Luther Burbank

PRICES FOR ADMITTANCE OF VISITORS during the busy months of APRIL, MAY, JUNE, JULY, AUGUST and SEPTEMBER:

Each Person, One Hour, $10.00   Each Person, One-Half Hour, $5.0

Each Person, One-Quarter Hour, $2.50

Admittance will be allowed at one-half the above-named prices during the other six months. When there are two or more in the same party twenty-five per cent discount from these prices.

NOTE.—Everybody would be graciously welcomed to the farm, but the burden of entertaining the multitude has become so great that the experimental work has been seriously crippled.

11. Photo of the original "Ticket of Admission" that allowed Australian John Rutland to speak to Luther Burbank in person. (Courtesy of Luther Burbank Home and Gardens, Santa Rosa, California)

12. A cartoon lampooning Ziff Wearne's train trip to show members of Parliament what the prickly-pear plague was like. (*Daily Guardian*, June 6, 1923)

13. An arsenic pentoxide-filled "pear stabber" in use. After stabbing the prickly-pear, a trigger (covered by the man's right hand) delivered a measured dose of the poison into the plant. Bingara, New South Wales, June 7, 1924. (CPPB archive collection)

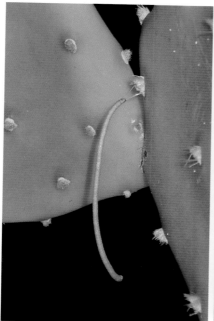

14. Cactoblastis eggstick attached to a prickly-pear plant (*Opuntia stricta*).

15. Alan Dodd, the man most credited for winning Australia's war on cactus.

16. The boldly-colored caterpillar of *Cactoblastis cactorum*.

Collecting the eggs from the cages at Chinchilla, Q. October 1929.

17. Daily collection of Cactoblastis eggsticks at the Commonwealth Prickly Pear Board's field-station in Chinchilla, Queensland. (Photo: CPPB archives.)

18. One day's harvest of approximately five million Cactoblastis eggs at the Chinchilla, Queensland, field-station. (Photo: CPPB archives.)

19. A consignment of Cactoblastis eggs being trucked to the railway for dispatch to landholders. Chinchilla field-station, Oct. 1929. (Photo: CPPB archives.)

20. Digital reconstruction of faded newspaper cartoon depicting Cactoblastis caterpillars coming to work on the "pear." (CPPB archives.)

21. Dense pear in a brigalow scrub country research plot near Chinchilla, Queensland, before Cactoblastis was introduced. October 1926. (CPPB archives)

22. Same area in October 1929 after Cactoblastis was introduced. Note almost complete destruction of the prickly-pear. (CPPB archives.)

23. A memorial to a moth: Cactoblastis Hall at Boonarga, Queensland

24. Cactoblastis poster, USDA. (Courtesy of Joel Floyd)

25. Boxes of artificially reared Cactoblastis moth caterpillars grow in an incubator room in a biosecure facility located in Gainesville, Florida, USA.

26. Wearing a "space suit" to provide protection against inhaling airborne moth wing-scales, a lab worker sexes cactus moths that have been chilled into a torpor.

27. USDA workers destroying Cactoblastis-infested prickly-pear with special propane-fired torches in southern Louisiana.

28. At risk of extinction by Cactoblastis, the unique semaphore cactus exists only in a few isolated locations in the Florida Keys.

29. Members of a USDA/ARS research team check for the presence of Cactoblastis moths in an Argentinean prickly-pear orchard.

30. A vision of things to come? Part of a stubborn infestation of snake cactus (*Cylindropuntia spinosior*) in north-central Queensland, Australia.

A BOUNTY ON BIRDS

One of the Prickly Pear Land Commission's most ill-conceived and controversial decisions was to place a price on the head of several bird species that were accused of aiding the spread of prickly-pear. This included the flightless emu (Australia's national bird), the crow, and the pied currawong (locally known as the "scrub magpie"). Disregarding the expert advice of naturalists, the PPLC insisted "that the emu and crow were amongst the chief agencies by which pear seed is spread."

To justify their action, they listed six reasons why the birds should be eliminated. "Each of these birds is a voracious eater of pear fruit," the Commission wrote in its second annual report. "The pear seed when passed uninjured through the digestive tract of these birds germinates much more rapidly than the seed of ripe pear fruit merely fallen to the ground. Each of these birds has a wide feeding range. [For example] . . . marked crows have been known to travel a distance of 40 miles (64 km)."

At the top of the PPLC's list of reasons, however, was the statement that "the vast majority of landholders desired the destruction of these birds, which were present in the pear belt in large numbers." (Actually, I think that most of these landholders simply saw this as a practical opportunity for an additional source of income from their embattled properties.)

The bounty was rather generous. With various local government offices acting as honorary receivers of the dead birds' heads and their eggs, a farmer could earn £0/2s/6d (about $8.00 US today) for every emu that he killed and £0/1s (about $3.00 US) for every emu egg collected. (An emu nest might contain up to 20 eggs or more.) A dead crow could earn him the equivalent of around $2.00 US.

Beginning on February 1st, 1926, the PPLC's bounty scheme ran for a period of nearly two years. During this time, more than 226,000 birds and some 109,345 emu eggs were turned in for the reward. To fuel this wholesale destruction of native bird life, the PLLC paid out a total of £12,982/12s/6d (nearly $800,000 US today).

"I wish to enter a most emphatic protest over the destruction of this noble bird," wrote H. Greensill about the emu in the *Brisbane Courier*. "The reason put forward for its destruction is that it spreads prickly-pear. Well, I admit that the emu does eat the pear fruit, but I affirm that not one bunch of pear in a thousand is grown by this means . . . Balance the enormous amount of good done by these birds in the destruction of grasshoppers and other insect pests and it will far outweigh the damage done."

The wisdom of the PPLC's bird-killing program began to be openly questioned in a heated debate that frequently spilled over into the press. In an article entitled "Birds and Prickly-pear" which appeared in the regional publication, *Pastoral Review*, author Neil McGilp argued strongly for the birds' destruction, stating that "it is hardly possible to estimate the loss to our country caused by the prickly-pear and if it is proved, as I'm afraid it is, that the Emu, the Crow, and the Scrub Magpie are agents for spreading the pest-pear, they must go."

Just below this article, however, appears a telling note from the editor of the *Pastoral Review*. He asks, "Anyway, what sense is there in destroying Emus when cattle, which certainly spread pear, are running in the same country? It behooves bird-lovers, and indeed all good Australians, to see that these remarkable birds are not unduly victimized." Fortunately, the "bird-lovers" finally prevailed and in due course the bounty was discontinued.

The PPLC "ruled" over its prickly-pear provinces for just eight years before it was merged into ineffectiveness within the Land Administration Board in 1932. Their coercive approach to land tenure had failed, essentially because there had been little or no provision for keeping prickly-pear from spreading onto unoccupied lands. From these refuges, the pear could easily re-colonize any nearby property that had been previously cleared.

Even so, the Queensland Prickly Pear Land Commission did survive long enough as a functioning organization to be able to take part in some of the greatest biological experiments in human history. The unexpected success of one of those experiments was, in truth, the primary reason why the "Commission" eventually went out of business.

Chapter 7: The Search For a Biological "Cure"

So, naturalists observe, a flea
Has smaller fleas that on him prey;
And these have smaller still to bite 'em,
And so proceed ad infinitum.

From "On Poetry: a Rhapsody" by Jonathan Swift, 1733

The first person in Australia to advocate the use of insects to control prickly-pear was English naturalist Henry Tryon, who in 1880 - after having abandoned his medical studies - decided to immigrate to Queensland. In his new country, Tryon quickly established a name for himself in the Brisbane scientific community. Just three years after arriving, he became the founding secretary of the Royal Society of Queensland.

Tall and of medium build, he was frequently irascible and over-critical in both personal and public relationships. In meetings of scientific organizations, he was said to be "the terror of inexperienced or ill-prepared speakers." Not surprisingly, these behaviors often led to intense personal conflict.

However, Tryon was also a precise, intelligent, meticulous scientist, who used Carl Linnaeus, rather than Charles Darwin, as his role model. Because his favorite area of research was in plant pests, he was eventually appointed to act as the government's entomologist in 1894 and in 1896, he became the state's plant pathologist. Tryon held this post until his retirement at age seventy-three.

It was well-known among his scientific colleagues, that Tryon believed most botanical pests could be controlled by the use of insect herbivores. As early as 1899, he began making repeated suggestions to use this tactic against the advancing prickly-pear.

So it probably came as no surprise to him when, thirteen years later, "the Queensland government finally saw the light and set up the 'Prickly-Pear Traveling Commission' to find an insect enemy of the pear." Henry Tryon would be part of that investigation.

The so-called "Traveling Commission" consisted of just three men. Dr. Thomas Harvey Johnston, from the biology department of the University of Queensland, was the commission's designated chairman. Affectionately known as "T. H. J.," Johnston was a gentle, clear-thinking man with a slow, quiet sense of humor, who eventually published nearly 300 scientific papers about Australian parasites.

He was the perfect counterpart to help keep Henry Tryon's mercurial irritability within reasonable bounds. The third member of the commission was Mr. C. W. Holland, who acted as secretary yet apparently did not accompany the other two men on their year-and-a-half-long overseas quest.

After first visiting some of the worst locations in Queensland's pear-infested country, the "prickly-pair" (as Johnston and Tryon were christened by the press) headed for Sydney's Botanic Gardens. Here they sought the advice of Joseph Maiden, the government botanist for New South Wales and director of the gardens. Maiden, you might recall, had been actively studying prickly-pear cacti for many years.

During their tour of the botanic gardens, Maiden showed the commissioners his impressive collection of spineless cactus, which also included at least two Luther Burbank varieties. Yet even as he propounded on their possible use as a source of fodder for graziers in the parched western lands of the state, Maiden cautioned his guests that many of his spineless forms would develop a heavy armament of prickles under the dry climatic conditions that existed out there.

Two days later, the "Commission" left Sydney by steamship bound for Java, via Singapore, on the first leg of its far-ranging assignment to investigate prickly-pear cacti and its enemies wherever they occurred. It was a journey that would also include visits to Ceylon (Sri Lanka), Malaysia, India, South Africa, the Canary Islands, Spain, the Mediterranean Littoral, Egypt, Syria, the USA, the West Indies, and South America.

From Sri Lanka, the investigators forwarded several packages containing two varieties of wild cochineal that they had discovered, along with their host plants, back to the Board of Advice in Brisbane. Accompanied by detailed notes for their propagation, it was one of these species that made Dr. Jean White-Haney's experiments in destroying the tree pear *Opuntia monacantha* in northern Queensland so successful.

By the time Johnston and Tryon reached India, they had decided to split up and work separately, ostensibly "in order to cover the field more expeditiously." One of them worked in the northern part of that country while the other confined his efforts to its southern states. This strategy probably saved their working relationship. (Incidentally, during his journey from Calcutta to Delhi by rail, one of the men actually saw the Great Hedge, then commonly referred to as the "salt-wall," that had been planted to prevent the smuggling of salt.)

Meeting up at the port of departure, the "Commission" then toured South Africa and the Canary Islands on their way to the Mediterranean's coastal region. As they left Spain, they split up once more: One would go to Sicily and Italy, while the other traveled through Morocco, Tunisia, Algeria, Malta, Egypt, and Syria. Some months later, they met again in England.

Johnston and Tryon arrived together in New York City on October 10th, 1913, where they immediately arranged a meeting with Nathaniel Britton, the director of that city's botanic gardens. (Dr. Britton, in collaboration with Joseph Rose of the Carnegie Institute, was a leader in the study of cacti.)

At the time of his visit, Mr. Tryon was described as being "apparently about 60 years of age, with a closely-clipped grey beard, and quite markedly hard-of-hearing." Perhaps it was this hearing problem that made him so cranky.

From New York, the Commission traveled to Washington D. C., where they met with David Griffiths and his colleagues, and then moved on to slowly explore Texas, New Mexico, Arizona, and California. While in California, they visited Luther Burbank at his nursery in Santa Rosa. Although they had dearly wanted to inspect the prickly-pear regions of Mexico, a civil war raging in that country prevented them from visiting any more than just a few cities located near the northern border. By then the team had already discovered over a dozen cactus-eating insect species that they felt deserved further study.

After returning to Washington D. C. to conduct more interviews, Johnston and Tryon then turned south for Key West, Florida. There they split up again. One of them, they decided, would explore the Caribbean islands of Jamaica, Trinidad, the Lesser Antilles, Puerto Rico, Haiti, and the Virgin Islands, while the other would travel through South America.

Although the official report of the Prickly-Pear Traveling Commission is written anonymously and does not specifically name who went to South America, in all probability it was Henry Tryon. Back in 1911, Tryon had informed the Board of Inquiry about two deadly enemies of prickly-pear - a fungus and a caterpillar - found in Argentina that he had learned of through correspondence. (I'm sure that he would have wanted to see them for himself.)

THE FIRST ATTEMPT FOR CACTOBLASTIS

Aided by Dr. C. Spegazzini, a well-known Argentine botanist whom Tryon had met while he was making inquiries about prickly-pear back in Italy, Tryon eventually managed to collect "a considerable number of more or less fully-grown caterpillars and a supply of one of its food plants" from the Buenos Aires Botanical Gardens located at La Plata. These were the cactus-boring larvae of a small moth,

170

known at the time as *Zophodia cactorum.* (This species would later be renamed *Cactoblastis cactorum.*)

On the journey back to Australia, Johnston and Tryon were delayed for two weeks in Hawaii while they waited for a ship to arrive from San Francisco. During their voyage and subsequent wait, many of their caterpillars pupated and, after about three weeks in the cocoon, had emerged as adult moths.

A few of the moths laid eggs, and it was from these eggs that a small colony of new caterpillars was started. This little nucleus ended in failure, however, when all of the insects eventually died in Brisbane after several months of intense care. Johnston would later quip, "It is very possible that we loved them to death."

"This apparently is the outcome of certain of its habits being unknown and accordingly not taken into consideration," the Traveling Commission wrote in its final report published on November 25th, 1914. When introduced to the common pest-pear, the caterpillars seemed to eat it with relish.

Yet they constantly emerged from the interior of the stem-joints, and "wandered around spinning a little silk as if to pupate." However, they did not pupate. Tryon later came to believe that the insects were actually attempting to hibernate, but Brisbane's weather at the time was just too warm.

Although this first attempt at introducing *Cactoblastis* into Australia was unsuccessful, the Prickly-Pear Traveling Commission had discovered the extremely important fact that these caterpillars would actively feed on the common pest-pear.

Be that as it may, when Australia entered World War I nearly four months earlier, the nation's priorities had been suddenly altered. In the pressing tumult of the war, the Traveling Commission's findings were tabled and largely forgotten. Seven long years would pass before another attempt at bringing *Cactoblastis* into Australia would occur.

In 1922, Thomas Harvey Johnston was appointed professor at the University of Adelaide, South Australia, where he became a world authority on flatworms. Later, he would be invited by Sir Douglas Mawson to serve as chief zoologist on the joint British, Australian, and New Zealand Antarctic Research Expedition of 1929.

Instead of immediately moving to South Australia, however, Johnston chose to remain in Queensland until early 1923 so he could provide direction to a new government-funded program that would ultimately see the success of his cranky traveling companion's seemingly radical notion of controlling a pest by directing its own natural enemies against it.

THE NOTION OF BIOLOGICAL CONTROL

Henry Tyron's idea of "biocontrol" actually had been around for more than 1,500 years. As early as 300 AD, for instance, citrus weaver ants (*Oecophylla smaragdina*) were being employed in China to regulate pest-insects in orange groves. These communal insects are still used today in Thailand and Vietnam.

In southern California, another orange-grove problem created by a cottony-cushion scale insect (*Icerya purchasi*) was brought under control in the 1880s by the introduction of a ladybird beetle (*Rodolia cardinalis*) from Australia. In 1902, a mix of herbivorous insects were used to control lantana, a serious weed that had established itself in the Hawaiian Islands.

The first intentional use of an insect to control prickly-pear over a large region occurred in southern India in 1863, when Henry Tryon was just seven years old. (Perhaps he had heard about it.) Following the abandonment of India's cochineal industry, one species of prickly-pear (the tree-pear *Opuntia monocantha*) became rampantly invasive. Just six years after the wild cochineal insect (*Dactylopius ceylonicus*) was introduced to this cactus, huge territories that were formerly impenetrable because of thick growths of prickly-pear were again fit for cultivation.

Commenting on this radical change to India's landscape, Joseph Maiden wrote, "Its destruction made such a difference to the

172

face of the country that writers promptly noticed and recorded what was happening . . . *Opuntia monocantha*, thanks to the cochineal insect, which is still with us, is now a comparatively scarce plant." A couple of years later, the same experiment was successfully repeated in Sri Lanka.

But in 1903, a similar attempt to establish this insect in Australia had failed. Ten years later, the first shipment of cochineal sent to Australia from Sri Lanka by Johnston and Tryon's Traveling Commission also perished. However, enough insects from their second backup consignment survived just long enough to be successfully bred and released into northern Queensland by Dr. Jean White-Haney's team.

Unfortunately, the significance of this cochineal's striking success in eradicating the *monocantha* pear in Australia was eclipsed by the "Great War," and a long delay in the search for additional prickly-pear biocontrols followed.

"A NATIONAL PROBLEM"

Shortly after the end of World War I, Australia began to take stock of itself as a nation. Because so many young sons had been killed, almost every family had been affected by the fighting. War memorials were being erected in nearly every community.

Resolutely turning its face towards the future, the nation was shocked when it learned just how much land had been lost to the invading prickly-pear and of the plight of former soldiers who were attempting to return to their rural homes. Some accounts estimated that the "green menace" had conquered an additional five million acres during the four years and three months when the country's attention had been diverted overseas by the war.

Following much public discussion that even involved Australia's prime minister, it became generally acknowledged that the prickly-pear scourge was "not a shire council matter only, nor a state matter only, but a national matter to be treated in a national way." In response to this consensus, during the final month of 1919 an accord between state and federal governments was reached that allowed for the creation of a new organization whose sole purpose was to investigate the use of biological control agents against prickly-pear.

The Commonwealth Prickly Pear Board (CPPB) was formed as a result of this agreement. Comprised of representatives from state and federal agencies, the CPPB held its first meeting in April 1920.

Half of the Board's initial funding of £8,000 per annum (around $430,000 US) would be paid by the federal government, while the state governments of Queensland and New South Wales each would contribute one-quarter of the total funds. This yearly amount would be raised to £12,000 in 1926 and to £18,000 in 1928. When the Board's efforts were terminated in late 1939, the total cost of its prickly-pear biocontrol research and implementation program would exceed £168,600 or about US $11.5 million.

An ever-popular choice, Professor T. Harvey Johnston was promptly appointed to the position of "Scientific Controller" of the Board's activities. (He would remain in that role until he was forced to resign in early 1923 because of conflicts of duty concerning his appointment as professor at the University of Adelaide.)

The broad outline of the Board's charter was to search in both North and South America for any insect that attacked prickly-pear, then to study the life-histories and habits of those insects. After selecting species of potential value and determining their food preferences, the insects were to be subjected to starvation trials on plants of economic importance, such as lettuce, cotton, tomatoes, grapes, and oranges. If they passed those tests by starving to death, the species could then be sent to Australia for retesting, acclimatization, and possible mass distribution into the field. There was also to be a survey of bacterial and fungal plant diseases.

A SECOND ATTEMPT FOR CACTOBLASTIS

Within a very short time, the Commonwealth Prickly Pear Board had two people actively searching for prickly-pear-eating insects in South America. Professor Johnston, himself, had left Australia in August in order to meet up with Mr. W. B. Alexander, a British biologist from Western Australia who was canceling his return visit to England in order to join the CPPB. Johnston was very keen to pick up where he and Henry Tryon had left off before the war.

Essentially that meant just one thing: Collect some more of those *Zophodia* (*Cactoblastis*) caterpillars, and this time get a successful breeding colony established back in Australia. Johnston had been very impressed by Tryon's "damage report" of what these caterpillars could do to the native prickly-pear in Argentina.

Both Johnston and Alexander arrived in Buenos Aires, Argentina, on December 6th, 1920. Wasting no time, just two days later they were at work in the botanical gardens at La Plata, where Henry Tryon had collected his insects before the Great War. Carefully examining prickly-pear plants for evidence of damage by these caterpillars, they found what they thought were indications of previous activity, yet were unable to locate any of the larvae.

Stymied, Johnston and Alexander went to see the British Consulate and through its assistance managed to get an interview with Argentina's Minister of Agriculture. Unfortunately, apart from providing an expansive welcome to his country, he was not much help. A visit to the Agricultural Museum the next day again turned up no special information about cactus insects or diseases.

Eventually, however, their daily meetings with various Argentine departmental heads began to pay off. The chief of Agricultural Protection (Defensa Argricola) promised to assign one of his men, entomologist E. E. Blanchard, to assist with Johnston and Alexander's research and to act as interpreter.

A visit with Henry Tryon's old friend, Dr. Spegazzini in

La Plata, ended with another trip to the botanic gardens. This time, the two men learned that the damaged cactus they had seen earlier had not been caused by caterpillars at all, but rather by a fungus called *Sclerotinia*.

"But certainly, Señors, the moths and their caterpillars would appear within a few months," the trio were assured. Satisfied that he was leaving his caterpillar quest in Alexander's capable hands, a few days later Johnston boarded a ship for passage to England and his eventual return to his duties in Australia.

Born in 1885, Wilfred Backhouse Alexander was a serious-minded man who had been introduced to natural history by his two uncles when he was a boy. His two main interests, it was said, were "birds and bugs." Soon after receiving a Master of Arts degree in 1911 from King's College, Cambridge, England, he took up a position with the Western Australian Museum in Perth.

Recently invited to work with the Commonwealth Prickly Pear Board, it was Professor Johnston who had requested that Alexander join him in South America for his first assignment with the organization. (Later, Alexander would direct the CPPB's research effort for several years before permanently leaving Australia in 1926 to complete the work on his book, *Birds of the Ocean*, the world's first ornithological field guide, which was published in New York. Apparently, his long days aboard slow-moving steamships had not been spent in idleness.)

Keen to explore new territory, Alexander did not wait for the caterpillars he was seeking to reappear in La Plata's botanical gardens. Two days after Christmas, following more than a week spent in various consultations about where they should go, Alexander and Blanchard headed south by train for the coastal city of Bahia Blanca. Arriving at 9:30 a.m., by that afternoon the two men were tramping around in the nearby hills, busily examining cacti for insects. Their efforts did not yield anything of particular interest.

So began a pattern that was to continue week after week: Travel to a region, check into a comfortable hotel, then go out and explore the district looking for cactus insects, and from time to time, return to Buenos Aires for expert advice in identifying specimens that they had collected and to visit La Plata in hopes that the caterpillars had reappeared.

One day, while examining several boxes of old records from the Commonwealth Prickly Pear Board, I came across Alexander's red-leather-bound, handwritten notebook that recorded his daily efforts during those five months he spent in Argentina. Here's a selection from a typical page:

> *Carmen de Pategones* (Argentina)
> Dec. 30, 1920 - The *Opuntia* was very severely damaged, apparently by a fungus whose effect appears to be identical with that of *Sclerotinia* as seen at La Plata. . . In many cases whole clumps of the *Opuntia* had been killed as effectively as if sprayed by arsenic, only the dead white epidermis of the joints being left with the remains of the fiber inside . . . A *Coccus* [cochineal insect], giving a red stain when injured, was also present in small quantities on the *Opuntia*, but did not seem to be doing any damage.
>
> Numerous specimens of a *Coreid* bug, in all stages from small larvae to adults, were also found on the *Opuntia*, but not on the adjacent bushes. No damage attributable to them could be observed. (Specimens labeled "C.P. 30/12/20 Opuntia joint") . . . The day was cool, and rain was falling most of the time, and in consequence various insects were found sheltering on the plants, including numerous specimens of a *Bombid* bee (bumble-bee) in the flowers, a syrphid fly, [and] a small beetle. . . Some flowers were found full of red ants which were cutting up and carrying away the petals.
>
> Dec. 31 - I was not feeling well and remained at home. In the afternoon Blanchard walked out onto the hills to the east of town. He found most of the same species of cacti as we saw yesterday. Much damage due to fungi was seen again, and the *Coccus* was again found on the *Opuntia*.

As they traveled together, Alexander and Blanchard collected many cactus-eating insects, including various flies, boring moths, beetles, weevils, scale-insects, and of course, wild cochineal. But finding the *Zophodia* caterpillars continued to be problematic. Then, on February 9th, 1921, near the small town of Andalgala, in the north-western province of Catamarca, they discovered them. Alexander's diary records their find:

> There were about seven of these larvae in each of the plants. In one they had only excavated a comparatively small tunnel near the base and their pale yellow excreta had been discharged on the surface. In the other, they had almost destroyed the interior of the plant and their excreta filled nearly half the interior of the plant, which was dying. These larvae ranged from about 1 to 2 inches long (2.5 to 5 cm) and are deep red in color with a black transverse stripe on each segment.

The team continued to explore and collect cactus-eating insects for another month. During this time they encountered the caterpillar twice again. On April 15th, Alexander sent a triumphant telegram message to Professor Johnston that read in part: "Have collected 300 *Zophodia* (Cactoblastis) larvae. Shall I bring these to Australia during the winter? Steamer sails Cape of Good Hope in a few weeks." (Remember that the seasons in the southern hemisphere are reversed from those in the northern hemisphere.)

After having received no answer for more than a week, Alexander then sent another message informing Johnston that the "Steamer sails for the Cape 3rd May. No other for two or three months. Will sail if I do not hear to the contrary."

As Alexander waited in Buenos Aires for a reply, some of his caterpillars were being looked after by friends in a nearby research facility. Although there had been a number of losses, most of the larvae still seemed to be doing okay.

Being at loose ends, Alexander decided to do one more field trip before leaving the country, then suddenly changed his mind and canceled his train ticket to Tucuman so that he could examine his berth when the steamer arrived.

Good thing that he did, because his bed on that ship was just a couch with no room. After speaking to the captain and the purser, it was agreed that he could keep his containers of insects in the small hospital located aft, which also contained two bunks. "I suggested I should occupy one of these so to be with my things," Alexander later smilingly wrote.

With still several days to spare, Alexander resumed his trip to Tucuman, arriving there on April 27th. The next morning, he walked out to the Agricultural Research Station to inquire about a batch of caterpillars that he had left in that facility's care at the beginning of April. They hadn't done very well. In one box, only four or five larvae remained alive from the hundred or so that had been placed in it just three weeks previous. Not a very good beginning for their long overseas journey to Australia.

Undaunted, Alexander arrived by train back in Buenos Aires on May 1st, to find himself in the midst of a general labor strike. He quickly discovered that there were no vehicles available to transport his luggage and insect cage filled with prickly-pear over to the ship. "However, I induced a porter to help me carry the heavy cage to the dock, and, after considerable difficulty in locating the boat, got it on board the *Kanagawa Maru* about 10:00 p.m.."

Less than twenty-four hours before the ship's scheduled departure, a cable finally arrived from Brisbane. It tersely read: "Referring to your telegram 25th, provided you satisfied exploration work completed, bring all material, otherwise remain. Telegraph reply."

"It seemed too late to cancel the arrangements that I have made," Alexander wrote in his diary. "So I propose to reply: 'Satisfied it is no use exploring during the winter. Bringing material.'"

On the day of departure, Blanchard dutifully brought Alexander a batch of *Zophodia* eggs that they had collected earlier, "which had darkened in color as if about to hatch." In the late afternoon, after getting the remainder of his luggage aboard and saying his "good-byes," W. B. Alexander stood at the rail and watched the city of Buenos Aries recede into the distance as the steamer slipped

179

away. The seas were smooth and his precious caterpillars were on their way to Australia.

Each morning as the ship followed its route, Alexander meticulously inspected his insect charges, noting any changes in their condition. They arrived in Rio de Janeiro on the 8th of May and tied up to the wharf, where they were unfortunately delayed for nearly two weeks. Constantly worried about the condition of his caterpillars, Alexander wrote in his diary:

> *Rio de Janiero*
> May 8, 1920 - The hot sun on the hospital seems to cause the larvae to emerge from their food plant and crawl about the cage. In the middle of the day about 20 were visible. Nearly all of the eggs have now hatched and the young larvae penetrated the [cactus] joint.
>
> May 9 - One larvae outside the cage this morning. I think someone must have reached in through the porthole and opened the top door of the cage as both the boys with access to the room deny having touched it. At least six of the larvae have died since yesterday from no obvious cause. . .
>
> May 10 - No more larvae seem to have died in the cage, only two were visible and I hope the remainder are feeding again. Most of the young larvae have reentered the joint and are feeding near the top of it, much fresh excreta having been discharged from a new, rather large, hole there.

All of this concern might seem a bit excessive to a casual observer, but Alexander was very much aware that thousands of people and hundreds of communities, indeed the future of a large part of rural Australia might depend on the success of his mission.

On May 14th, Alexander reported that "All the larvae are now feeding in two fresh joints. I removed the first joint which had been completely destroyed." The next day he noted that the larvae were continuing to feed well and, being a very wet day, he had put the cactus plants out in the rain to water them. Overall, the trip seems to have been going fairly well by the time he arrived in Capetown,

South Africa, on the 3rd of June.

Immediately after the ship was tied to the dock in Capetown, the government's inspector of plants came on board to offer Alexander any possible assistance. "With his help," Alexander noted in his diary, "I conveyed the specimens to one of the stores on the wharf where he has an office, the key of which was left with the storekeeper so that I could gain access to it at any time." Here he waited for nearly two more weeks for the next ship bound for Western Australia.

His daily checks on the caterpillars indicated that they still appeared to be doing well, although some periodic housekeeping of replacing partially eaten and rotting prickly-pear joints was necessary from time to time. Most of the remainder of Alexander's time in Capetown was spent comparing notes with some of the officers and entomologists who were involved in prosecuting South Africa's own war on prickly-pear. He would gain a lot of useful information from those meetings.

On the afternoon of June 16th, after having again installed his collection of insects in the ship's hospital, Alexander sailed out of Capetown's harbor on the *S. S. Carina* and immediately encountered a strong sea that caused the ship to roll violently. The following morning, Alexander reported that "in spite of the rolling during the night, everything seemed all-right this morning and the wind now being behind us, we are rolling less." His daily checks on the caterpillars also seemed to suggest that they were also doing well.

Imagine Alexander's shock, when during a routine inspection on the morning of June 19th, he discovered that a tragic accident had taken place among his diminutive charges:

> The larvae in the jar were still crawling about on the joints this morning. I made a small hole in the side of the [prickly-pear] joint and in a short while they were all congregated about it beginning to feed. I thought therefore that probably the larvae in the cardboard box also required food and decided to replace them with a fresh joint. On opening the box I found them all apparently dead and the cause was at once apparent. I had taken the

box out of the suitcase in which a box of naphthalene [the toxic ingredient of moth balls] had come open, and though I think that none had ever been in the cardboard box . . . enough vapor was present to give a distinct odor of the substance and to kill the caterpillars.

"Some of them exhibited slight signs of movement when placed in the fresh air in the sun, so possibly a few will revive," he noted after moving the caterpillars to a fresh cardboard box fitted with a cloth cover.

Two days later he was greatly relieved that "the revivified larvae have begun to feed and some of them now look none the worse." But the chemical fumes must have weakened the insects, because at the following morning's inspection Alexander discovered that nearly 30 were dead and he had to throw them away.

Yet by the end of the month, Alexander was again feeling more hopeful. He noted, "Most of the healthy larvae have now disappeared into the joint . . . I fear that the naphthalene has been fatal to about 50, whilst rather more than that have recovered."

The ship carrying Alexander and his ailing prickly-pear insects arrived in Fremantle, Western Australia, on the 6th of July. Immediately after clearing Customs, his collection was driven by car to the museum in Perth for temporary housing. For the next week or so, Alexander divided his time between making sure that his insects were kept fed and the packing of all his belongings for the move to his new home in Brisbane.

Leaving Perth by train on the evening of the 19th, Alexander arrived in Melbourne two days later, where he transferred onto a waiting express train to Sydney. From there, he proceeded north to Queensland. Having been briefed in advance by government officials on the importance of Alexander's mission, the railway authorities did everything they could to expedite his overland journey.

On the 25th of July, almost three months after leaving Buenos Aires, he finally arrived in Brisbane. Professor Johnston was on hand to meet him in the central train station and together they conveyed the case of precious insects to his laboratory at the university.

The caterpillars did not do well in their new home. Even though Alexander needed to find new lodgings for himself and unpack his belongings, he checked on the caterpillars as often as he could. His journal records what he saw:

> Aug. 2, 1921 - Five larvae were walking about in the jar, apparently having emerged from the smaller [prickly-pear] joint. I pierced a hole in a new joint and placed them upon it and they immediately entered it and commenced to feed. I opened up the [old] joint but found no more larvae, so that the 15 that entered on June 19th have somehow been reduced to five. No signs of dead ones appeared.

> Aug. 3 - Six larvae emerged from the larger joint during the day. When placed in proximity to the hole into which the five went yesterday, they immediately entered.

> Aug. 11 - Four dead and shriveled larvae were on the soil in the bottom of the jar this morning, another was still alive but much shrunk and obviously dying. It died later. Two others were crawling about the surface of the joint, one of which was clearly in an unhealthy condition. This latter and the dead ones were handed to Prof. Johnston for examination as to the causes of death.

> Aug. 15 - Another dead larvae was on the soil in the bottom of the jar this morning and was handed to Prof. Johnston. Only four larvae now remain alive. . .

> Aug. 26 - The joint is badly attacked with the bacterial rot which is so prevalent in the laboratory. On opening it I found the whole internal contents more or less liquid and the bodies of two drowned caterpillars. Doubtless the other two have been overwhelmed.

Below this final entry Alexander dejectedly scribbled, "The attempt to introduce *Zophodia* (Cactoblastis) to Australia has thus <u>failed</u> once more!"

THE WORK OF THE BOARD

Discovering an effective enemy of prickly-pear was the

183

Commonwealth Prickly Pear Board's top priority and it wasn't long before it dispatched another entomology team back to America. In the United States, near Uvalde, Texas, they set up a field station to serve as a convenient overseas base and began a systematic hunt for cactus-eating insects.

Because two previous attempts at establishing *Cactoblastis* in Australia had already failed, this species was deemed to be too delicate to warrant further consideration for the time being. Accordingly, the Board instructed its field personnel to concentrate their efforts in the prickly-pear regions of the USA and Mexico (now that the civil war had been resolved).

During the nearly 18-year-long course of these investigations, between 150 and 160 different kinds of cactus-eating insects were eventually found. Of these, at least 50 turned out to be new to science. About a third of these species appeared to cause enough damage to prickly-pear to justify an attempt at establishing them in Australia.

Consequently, over a period of several years, large numbers of selected insects were sent overseas. Eventually, more than a half-million individual insects would be dispatched from the Uvalde railway station in special containers known as "Wardian cases." Waiting for the next westbound train to arrive, carts filled with these insect cages became a familiar sight on the station's loading dock.

The Wardian case was a modification of a shipping container originally used by people who collected exotic plants for botanic gardens. Measuring around 40 inches long, 18 inches wide, and 24 inches high (100 cm x 45 cm x 60 cm), it had a handle fitted at each end for easy lifting and carrying. Its peaked roof prevented it from being placed wrong-side-up by those who handled them *en route* and its fine wire screen windows provided ventilation, while at the same time preventing the escape of any insects. After a bit of trial and error, this unit soon became the standard container for sending any cactus-feeding insect on an overseas trek.

"For the long journey from America to Australia, the bottom is first filled with sterile sphagnum moss, a material that absorbs water like a sponge and retains it for a long period," Alexander explained in a newsletter. "In this moss, freshly cut pear is planted securely and wedged in to prevent movement - which might crush the insects. The pear soon sends out roots into the moist sphagnum and help to keep it from shaking. The insects are then introduced and the top firmly screwed down."

During the years that the USA field-station was in operation, hundreds of Wardian cases were shipped by train from Uvalde to San Francisco. From there, most of the insect cages were sent to Sydney via the *S. S. Sonoma*, of the Oceanic Steamship Company of San Francisco, whose owner generously provided transportation (and return of the empty cases) free of charge.

Upon arrival in Sydney, the insect cages were immediately placed on a northbound train, to be transferred onto a Queensland train at Wallangarra (because of differently gauged rails) and delivered to CPPB personnel in Brisbane. On average, the trip took approximately six weeks from the time insects were put into their cages in America.

Still, shipping insects overseas presented many unforeseen problems. In addition to time delays that might cause the insects to perish because they had run out of food, there was the danger of too cold temperatures, or of drowning after being left out in the rain, or simply being cooked to death if the cages were exposed to the hot sun too long. Even so, most of the time the insects arrived in fairly good condition. Success was much more likely if the insects reached Australia in the late spring or early summer.

During its second official meeting, the Board had chosen the abandoned explosives reserve at Sherwood (a suburb of Brisbane) for the site of its new headquarters, laboratory, and quarantine and breeding station. Throughout the construction period, any insects that happened to arrive from America were temporarily housed nearby at Queensland University, "which granted, gratis, two whole rooms and part of a third."

185

By January 1922, the laboratory and breeding facilities were ready for operation. Here, all newly arrived insects would be held in quarantine until it was certain that they could be bred and that their natural parasites had been eliminated.

Over the next two years, field-stations equipped with hundreds of cages for the mass rearing and release of cactus-eating insects were set up in the very heart of prickly-pear country. Locally called "bug farms," each of these stations added substantially to the local economy by providing employment for a carpenter or two and dozens of general laborers.

There was one at Westwood in central Queensland, another at Biniguy in New South Wales, and still another at Chinchilla, 200 miles (320 km) west of Brisbane, in southern Queensland. (After a while, for various reasons, the Westwood station was later moved a few miles down the road to Gogango and the Biniguy center was transferred to Gravesend in the same district.)

After the success of *Cactoblastis* became apparent, a fourth field-station was built in southwest Queensland at Goondiwindi. In April 1930, a final station was opened at Scone, not far from the very place where the prickly-pear plague had begun nearly a century before.

With its main laboratory, insectaries, quarantine facilities, and field-stations poised for action, all the Board had to do now was to find a very destructive cactus-feeding insect, breed it up into its millions, release it on the prickly-pear, and watch it annihilate the "green menace."

This, of course, would prove to be no easy task. Of the 50 or so insect species that had been sent over from America, only about 12 were deemed worthy enough to be introduced into the "field of battle." Even so, acclimatization was an ongoing problem and most of these insects did not establish populations in the wild for any significant length of time.

There were several very important exceptions, however. So, with the knowledge gained firsthand from these ongoing experiments, the Board began to stake its greatest hopes on just two species of insects and a minute red spider mite. Indeed, in just a few years the combined effect of these three herbivores would decidedly slow the spread of the pear and in some districts, actually bring it under complete control.

As the work with insects progressed, it was the field-stations that brought the research to the people. But convincing the public was an uphill battle. Curious visitors openly scoffed at the efforts to raise "tiny bugs that were supposed to clear away a wilderness of pear." Referring to the Biniguy field-station, the *Sydney Sun* wrote:

> At the laboratory there is a little staff who are referred to by the young ladies of the district as 'cranks.' Having been born amongst the pear and had prickles in their ankles before they were three years old, they naturally know more about it than simple scientists. That is the feeling locally. It is the fashion to laugh at the laboratory scheme, so they laugh heartily at the little *Chelinidae vittigera* and *Chelinidae tabulata* - two bugs which are held in such high esteem by Mr. Alexander, the federal prickly-pear expert.

Chelinidea tabulata, a sap-sucking bug from Texas, was one of the first insects to be introduced into Australia's prickly-pear country. Usually colored brownish-yellow with yellow legs, the adult measures around half-an-inch long and about half as wide (13 mm x 6.5 mm). They puncture the cuticle of the pear with their long proboscis, and in sufficient numbers can kill the plant by literally sucking it dry.

Often destroying the fruit before the seeds could mature, they would contribute greatly in slowing the spread of the pear. Although it seemed to prefer the pest-pear (*Opuntia stricta*), this insect also fed freely on most of the other kinds of cactus that had become naturalized in Australia.

Chelinidea was very easy to establish. Cage-rearing at the field-stations was soon halted when the insects began appearing in huge numbers on their own throughout many of the prickly-pear districts. Near the town of Palardo, for instance, these bugs had increased to many millions spreading over thousands of acres after just 100 of them had been liberated less than five years earlier.

From 1927 to 1929, the Queensland Prickly Pear Land Commission (PPLC) hand-collected some twelve and a half million adult *Chelinidea* bugs from early release sites and redistributed them in some of their worst prickly-pear choked areas. Prickly-pear authorities in New South Wales did likewise. The Commonwealth Prickly Pear Board also made repeated attempts to establish another species of *Chelinidea* (*Chelinidea vittigera*) without much success.

Another group of insects that showed great promise, at least at first, were the cactus-boring caterpillars of certain moths in the *Melitara* and *Olycella* genera. These relatives of *Cactoblastis* were given considerable attention and hundreds of thousands of them were released. Although they initially bred well in captivity and reportedly did a lot of damage to the pear, their numbers gradually decreased with each succeeding generation. After numerous imports of these insects from Texas eventually failed, the work with them was reluctantly abandoned.

The prickly-pear spider mite (*Tetranychus opuntiae*) was accidentally introduced in 1922, when it arrived unnoticed in a consignment of insects from Texas. Being no larger than the head of a pin, it was first observed in the rearing cages at Chinchilla station, where it soon escaped and established a breeding colony amongst the stands of prickly-pear surrounding the facility.

After a short time it also appeared in New South Wales and was soon found to have spread widely at many points throughout the pear district. "The ravages of the red spiders among the pear are becoming more and more pronounced daily," reported the *Brisbane Courier*. "The spider attacks the pear in the vicinity of the spines and eats its way into the stem, thus causing the leaves (pads) to drop and rot." Plants damaged by this mite form distinctive "corky" scars.

By and large, the little spider mite only augmented the much more extensive damage created by yet another cochineal import, misidentified at the time as *Dactylopius tomentosus* and now known as *Dactylopius opuntiae*. One of the most successful introductions of a cactus-eating insect ever, it was first carried out by a private individual and not by a body of government researchers.

ARTHUR TEMPLE CLERK

Mr. Arthur Temple Clerk was so consumed on finding a way to beat the prickly-pear plague that it bordered on fanaticism. He had spent two weeks closely examining Oliver C. Robert's arsenious gas operations in Dulacca. Most notoriously, he was also that controversial author of the proposal for importing indentured Chinese workers to clear pear.

In 1913, he had self-published a 40-page booklet titled "The Prickly Pear Problem," in which he outlined the extent of the growing cactus "menace" and his suggestion to import Chinese labor to combat it. Also in that year, he compiled a comprehensive book of photographs depicting the various kinds of prickly-pear which occurred within the state. A copy of that book was carried by the Traveling Commission to show people in other countries what the situation was like in Australia.

"I landed here in 1875 and went to north Queensland, where I was engaged in sugar-growing in Ingham. My partner, Mr. W. B. Ingham, after whom the town was named, was murdered and eaten by blacks," he recalled during an interview shortly before his own death. "I was asked by the late Mr. J. T. Bell to join the [Queensland] Lands Department and concentrate on the prickly-pear problem, which I did. I remained in the Department for 16 years, when I had to retire on account of a complete breakdown of my health." (One history-researcher maintains that Clerk was actually forced out of government because of his obsession with prickly-pear and that he was still advocating for indentured workers as late as 1923.)

Apparently, Mr. Clerk first worked for the "Department" as a land ranger and then later became a lands inspector. During this time he had ample opportunity to witness the effects the prickly-pear plague had on the local people.

189

As far back as 1907, Clerk had also been in correspondence with David Griffiths of the United States Department of Agriculture in Chico, California. To learn if the American scientist could identify them, he shipped Griffiths some live samples of Queensland's worst prickly-pear varieties. Those samples were duly planted at Griffiths's research-station and for nine long years Mr. Clerk heard no more about them. Then he received a letter informing him that a wild cochineal insect had attacked one of those pear plants.

Eventually, Griffiths dispatched a number of the cochineal infested prickly-pear pads back to Mr. Clerk, but the first consignment was a failure. (Sound familiar?) Finally, one pad with attached insects reached Sydney safely through the post. With assistance from his friends in the agricultural department, the package was quickly passed through customs and personally handed over to Clerk. Half of this material was given to Professor Harvey Johnston, who was still in charge of the government prickly-pear investigations. That sample was sent to the laboratory at Sherwood. Mr. Clerk kept the other half and went home to breed them.

Clerk had a serious health problem. Faced with approaching blindness, he soon decided it was time to distribute the cochineal, which he now referred to as the "Chico," the name of the town from where they had been sent. He took some to Nebo Tableland in northern Queensland and released some others at Westwood in the central part of the state. He also placed a few individual insects on the separate properties of Mr. B. H. Corser and Mr. Norman Culliford.

Besides receiving a total of 20 adult cochineal insects, Culliford was also given special permission to sell their offspring, if he wished. The proceeds of any sales, however, were to go for the education of Culliford's children, Wallace and Jean, whom Clerk had known since they were babies.

"I may never see the result. I do not know whether they are going to be a success or failure, but they are here and they must take their chance, live or die," Clerk reportedly said as he handed over the cactus pads carrying his precious charges. "At any rate, I am pleased and gratified to think that those whom I have been so anxious to help, have now a relief in sight from the depredations of the prickly-pear."

In a 1923 newspaper interview, Mr. Culliford was quoted as saying, "Those 20 cochineal insects have in the last two years increased to many billions. I have already infected 700 acres of prickly-pear on my land . . . and I have also sold many thousands of insects to various people who were anxious to destroy pear on their land."

Continuing to suffer from failing eyesight, Mr. Clerk paid Culliford a final visit a year later. The Prickly Pear Land Commission was also eager to learn the results of his experiments, and gifted Clerk with a first-class train ticket for his trip. While he was there, Clerk soon learned that Culliford's cochineal business was booming. In fact, more than 15 local governments throughout the region had recently ordered cochineal-infested prickly-pear pads from him for the purpose of establishing their own cochineal nurseries.

Close to the nearby community of Palardo, two young men from Brisbane - who also foresaw a business opportunity of their own - took up a prickly-pear lease of 40,000 acres on a 50-year tenure. They purchased £5 (about $315 US) worth of cochineal from Mr. Culliford and distributed them about the property. The insects increased so rapidly that, within a year, they had infested 500 acres of pear. The men were confidently predicting that the insects would go on to infest another 3,000 or 4,000 acres within the next 12 months. Eventually the entire property would be cleared, they declared, without any of the backbreaking labor usually required to clean up just one acre of land.

In a statement published by the *Brisbane Courier,* Culliford said that he could supply over 200,000 kerosene tins of infested cactus pads at any time without perceptibly reducing the rate of destruction of pear on his own land. (In those days, kerosene for lighting, cooking, and tractor fuel was sold in large square cans that held about four gallons (18 liters). When empty, the useful tins were often recycled a half dozen times or more.)

"Mr. Culliford expects in a few years to see his holding entirely free from the pest," the newspaper article continued. "He has photographs showing the pear so high as to obscure fences and gate posts, but these spots today are open and clean."

For a short while, Culliford continued his brisk cochineal business. Some of his transactions were said to earn him as much as £1 ($63 US) per infested segment. But his sales opportunities soon ended when the cochineal spread far beyond his property's boundary line onto other lands.

Not only did Arthur Temple Clerk go totally blind before he died, but he did not see that his "Chico" cochineal was, indeed, causing widespread damage to the pear. Although Clerk's introduction of cochineal into Australia - which did not go through "proper testing or proper channels" - was strongly criticized by most government prickly-pear workers, he was much admired by the folks who were helped by his Chico cochineal. The people of Dulacca showed their appreciation by naming two of the town's thoroughfares in his honor: Temple and Clerk streets.

This same insect would later be supplied to other landholders by government agents. In its typically high-handed management approach, the Queensland Prickly Pear Land Commission (PPLC) at first denied its tenants the right to claim the use of cochineal in the performance of their pear-clearing duties. Later, they reversed this edict and made it compulsory for all landholders to infect their property with the insects.

"In the event the lessee or occupant fails to infect the pear within the time and in the manner specified in the notice served upon him, the Commission may perform the work and recover the cost thereof," the new regulation threatened.

To their credit, however, the Prickly Pear Land Commission distributed thousands of cases of cochineal-infected prickly-pear along the frontage of hundreds of miles of pear-choked public roads. On some of these lanes, there were long stretches where vehicles did not even have enough room to pass each other.

192

Two of Clerk's original liberation sites were kept under close observation by several members of the Commonwealth Prickly Pear Board's staff. "At Dulacca, Mr. Clerk infected a dense patch [of prickly pear] growing in a clump of brigalow (a type of shrubby tree), and two years later all the pear had become thickly covered with cochineal, though it was still practically impenetrable," they reported. A year later, "a good many of the large plants had collapsed and many joints had been killed. The clump was now traversed by cattle tracks and the cochineal has spread widely over the plants in the paddock."

At the Westwood site, Clerk's Chico cochineal also became widespread yet it did not seem to create nearly as much destruction in this region. Even so, the CPPB was forced to admit that "the [Chico] cochineal in these instances undoubtedly held the plants in check and any joints that fell off onto the ground or seedlings that sprang up in their vicinity were quickly destroyed ."

In the meantime, the Board had successfully imported two other strains of this wild cochineal species (*Dactylopius opuntiae*) from America. They were nicknamed the "Texas," and the "Arizona." It was soon discovered that the three breeds of cochineal reacted very differently to the various types of prickly-pear.

Clerk's Chico was very destructive to the common pest-pear (a variety of *Opuntia stricta* that scientists at the time called *Opuntia inermis*) yet did much less damage to the spinier varieties. The Texas strain, on the other hand, proved especially destructive to the spiny form of pear but had little affect on anything else. In the long run, the Arizona insect was not very effective at all.

What these insects would or would not do in different localities soon became common "table-talk" in most rural communities. The time it took for cochineal to affect the cactus varied greatly. It might take only a few months or sometimes up to several years before they even started to reduce the pear.

Insect numbers were usually at their lowest in the month of October, the peak growing-season for prickly-pear. Yet under ideal conditions of constant dry weather and warm temperatures hovering around 86° F (30° C), the cochineal colonies could double their population every five days.

Predations by indigenous ladybird beetles (*Cryptolaemus montrouzieri*) and attacks by ants took their toll and occasionally retarded a colony's spread. But a sudden heavy rain or hailstorm could be utterly devastating, wiping out most of a locality's cochineal stock within an hour.

For nearly six years weather conditions overall seemed generally favorable for Australia's cochineal program and a great deal of progress was made against the pear. Then in late 1927, six long months of heavy rain began to fall. By June of 1928, most cochineal colonies throughout the region had been destroyed. Yet, there were a few survivors that struggled on and when conditions eventually improved, their numbers began to increase again. Twelve months later, the insects had almost completely recovered from this setback and were again rapidly spreading through the dense stands of prickly-pear.

Eventually, the Commonwealth Prickly Pear Board (without ever giving him direct credit) would admit that Arthur Temple Clerk's cochineal had brought nearly half of the nation's prickly-pear scourge to its knees. Australians were finally beginning to realize that stopping the rampant spread of the great green "octopus" was now possible through the actions of a couple of "lowly little bugs and a tiny mite." The *coup de grâce* would soon be delivered by another small insect named *Cactoblastis*.

Chapter 8: Cactoblastis

Eventually, scientists in the Argentine found a moth
Whose bright-colored larvae ate the pear with glee.
Within the span of just a few short years,
It rendered the infected land nearly cactus-free.

"The road was being shelled behind us and just as we reached Bellevarde, 'Fritz' (the Germans) dropped a number of coal boxes (heavy artillery) perilously close, shooting earth and shrapnel all over the dugout," wrote stretcher-bearer Alan Parkhurst Dodd in his World War I diary.

"Next moment my ears were ringing, my head singing, and for a minute I lay blinded and half suffocated with smoke. Then I heard a shout, 'For God's sake, come and get us out!' The shell had caught the edge of the dugout, smashing it in and burying us under sandbags and earth. Luckily, most of it burst outwards. The patient we had just laid beside us was killed. In the other dugout, three of our bearers were wounded, one mortally."

Conscientiously refusing to bear arms, Alan had volunteered nearly two years earlier to become an orderly in the medical corps of the FirstAustralian Imperial Force. Although he survived the conflict, this sensitive young man witnessed a great deal of death and destruction.

How could this obscure participant in the "great war to end all wars" even dream that within seven years he would become "Officer in Charge" in prosecuting yet another war, this time against a silent but unyielding invader called "prickly-pear"?

195

The third son of Frederick Parkhurst Dodd, Alan was born in Brisbane in January, 1896. Frederick, a keen self-taught naturalist, was attempting to make a name and a living for himself by capturing and rearing rare Australian butterflies and moths for sale to wealthy European collectors.

As his business and fame increased, he soon was able to quit his job as a bank teller and move his growing family north to Townsville so that he could be closer to the insects of the tropics. In consequence, all of his children, including Alan, grew up in a family environment where natural history and rare insects were subjects of everyday conversation. These early years were to have a huge impact on them, especially young Alan.

One day in 1903, when Alan was only seven, cyclone "Leonta" destroyed their house. He later wrote of the experience:

> About 1 PM a terrific gust tore the ceiling and roof off in one piece . . . shortly after, while we were making our escape . . . another gust lifted the house off its low blocks and slammed it against the kitchen . . . the lattice door flung shut and knocked [Mother] back inside and unconscious for a while. With Father out in the street, we were picked up by each succeeding gust, carried along as through space, then dropped flat. Shelter was found . . . behind a low earth bank where after a while we were joined by . . . my mother, streaked with blood from numerous deep cuts. We terrified youngsters . . . hid our faces in Mother's lap.

Forced to move, the family traveled further north into the heart of tropical Queensland to settle in the small town of Kuranda. Surrounded by lush plant-growth and rich biodiversity, this proved to be the perfect place for a budding naturalist to grow up.

At first, Alan attended school in Kuranda's little one-room schoolhouse, then later spent two years at the Townsville Grammar School. "This was a meager education by modern standards," says Geoff Monteith in *The Butterfly Man of Kuranda*. "But entomologically he had come through the 'school of life' with the family at Kuranda and when he left school he was precocious and confident."

196

In 1912, when he was just 16 years old, Alan Dodd was offered the job of assistant entomologist with the state's Bureau of Sugar Experiment Stations. There, under the tutelage of a brilliant but erratic American entomologist named Alexandre Girault, young Dodd was inspired to study a group of minute parasitic wasps of the family Scelionidae. (Many years later, Girault's eccentricities would eventually morph into complete madness and his final days were spent in an asylum for the insane.)

At the "Sugar Bureau," Alan soon began publishing lengthy papers that described new species of these nearly microscopic-sized insects. "His output was phenomenal considering his age and limited training," Monteith declares.

"At 17, Alan published four papers totaling 78 pages and at 18, he published eight papers totaling 140 pages. His work was soon independent of Girault and is still regarded to be of high standard." Alan also did some significant work on the beetles that attack sugar cane while he was there. In 1915, he was elected Fellow of the Royal Society of South Australia.

At the close of World War I, transportation for homebound Australian soldiers was practically nonexistent. Many of them were forced to wait nearly a year before passage could be arranged from war-torn Europe. To prevent boredom among the idle troops - and to help them reenter civilian life - many were posted to training positions in an effort to improve their former occupations.

"If they had been dairy farmers, we will send them to Denmark to learn the latest trends in dairying, or if they were mechanics before the war, we will arrange for them to learn the latest techniques in their field," declared General John Monash, then Commander-in-Chief of Australia's armed forces in Europe.

For Alan Dodd, this became an exciting opportunity to spend three whole months studying butterflies, moths, and other insects at the famous British Museum in London before he, too, was shipped out and eventually discharged from military service back in Brisbane.

197

Alan returned to his research position at the Sugar Bureau soon after arriving home from England. Although he still had no formal education beyond primary school, in 1921 Alan applied for a job with the Commonwealth Prickly Pear Board.

In response, the scientific controller of the organization, Professor T. Harvey Johnston, offered Dodd a position as an entomological assistant. When Alan complained that the starting salary was too low, Johnston increased his offer, explaining to the other members of the Board that Dodd was a "highly desirable man with wide experience in insect work."

Young Dodd was soon busily engrossed in his duties at Sherwood Laboratory. Later, he would be stationed for a short while at the Biniguy field station near Moree, New South Wales, just before becoming the "acting" officer-in-charge of the Westwood field station. Progressing rapidly up the organizational ladder, Dodd soon rose to the position of "Assistant Entomologist" and was placed in charge of the Chinchilla field station.

Barely eight months later, in April 1924, he was sent to Uvalde, Texas - now at the rank of "Senior Entomologist" - to become officer-in-charge of the North America field station. "With his family background, particularly in the rearing of insects," Jeoff Monteith maintains. "Alan Dodd was the perfect choice to tackle the task of finding an insect to control the pear." (See Plate 15)

THE THIRD TRY WAS THE CHARM

Tall and lanky, with a determined purposeful stride, Alan Dodd arrived in Uvalde, Texas, in mid-June of 1924. Here, this serious-looking 28-year-old would spend the next four months reorganizing his "Australian bug-station," as the locals called it.

New insect cages had to be built, the small staff needed to be briefed, the food-preference experimental garden enlarged, and numerous field-trips to search for cactus-eating insects organized. But the daily toil often had a lighter side, as evidenced in the steady stream of letters Alan sent back to his family in Australia.

In one letter dated "Thursday Evening, August 22nd, 1924," addressed to his sister Katie, he recalls his meeting with an iconic species of Texan wildlife:

> T'other morning when out collecting cactus weevils shortly after daybreak, a queer little armadillo came fossicking round. He couldn't have seen me, so I stood stock-still and watched the quaint little chap in his coat of armor. So close he came that I touched him with my foot, when he bounded in the air, turned somersault, and bolted. Chee, he was a scared animal!

In another letter sent to his mother, we get an inkling of Alan's dry humor when he was presented with a guest ticket to a local play in nearby Brownsville, Texas:

> T'was quite a good performance too. I enjoyed it. Now for a joke. As I did not know anyone in the audience, the gentleman next to me had been instructed to introduce himself. He inquired how long I had been in America and learning that it was less than a month, asked if I had not been here before. 'But,' he said, 'You speak very good English.' Then after a pause, 'You must have studied English thoroughly.' I thought the Barbers (Alan's hosts) would go into hysterics when I told them. T'was humorous, wasn't it?

With the Uvalde field-station in satisfactory order, Alan Dodd soon received further instructions from the Commonwealth Prickly Pear Board to head for New York City to catch a steamer bound for Argentina. The "Board" and W. B. Alexander, who was now scientific controller for the organization, had decided that it was time to make another attempt at importing *Cactoblastis* into Australia.

In a letter dashed off to his mother just before he departed, Alan complains, "Then I'm to return to North America for the summer. So, Mum, 'twill be another twelve months before I sail for home. You bet I'm disappointed but it can't be helped. I can't afford to throw away the present salary I'm getting . . . I expect I'll be in South America for about three months, for I'll have to be back in Texas before the end of March."

Immediately after arriving in Buenos Aires in late November of 1924, Dodd went to work by performing a quick trip to Mendoza to visit a site where Alexander had collected *Cactoblastis* during his own attempt to bring them to Australia more than three years earlier. Unfortunately, this time the insects were not located.

Also, the Argentine government once again assigned Mr. E. E. Blanchard to act as official guide and interpreter for the Australian prickly-pear investigation. (Originally from the USA, Blanchard would eventually become a distinguished figure among Argentinean entomologists during his long scientific career that spanned more than 50 years.)

In a letter to his sister Bess, Alan offhandedly mentions that Blanchard, "is a nice chap and we got along famously." Later, he tells her that "Blanchard is a wonderful pianist, a regular genius. 'Tis a treat to hear him play. One evening at Mendoza he was in his best playing mood. Classic after classic, without any [sheet] music, among them such difficult things as Chopin . . . And yet he makes no attempt to make money from his talent." Impressed by each other's abilities, the two men soon became good friends.

After returning from Mendoza, the pair of insect hunters then proceeded to Uruguay for a month. Near the end of January 1925, at Concordia, Entre Rios, Argentina, opposite the Uruguayan town of Salto, they found *Cactoblastis* larvae infesting the local prickly-pear and collected some of them.

After successfully transporting the fully-grown caterpillars back to Buenos Aires, the men erected several breeding cages on the grounds of Blanchard's home in the riverside suburb of San Isidro and quickly installed the insects. Then they made a second trip to Mendoza.

By now, it was becoming apparent that there were actually more than one species of *Cactoblastis* in this world. Although Dodd was certain that the material he had collected at Concordia was indeed *Cactoblastis cactorum*, he was just as equally certain that the

Cactoblastis insects that Alexander had collected earlier in Mendoza had not been of the same species. Although the two varieties are very similar in appearance, Dodd was able to note some subtle differences.

In all of his reports and correspondence that followed his South American trip, Dodd refers to the Mendoza variety as *Cactoblastis bucyrus*. Specimens of this variety were also brought back to Buenos Aires with him and installed in some of the insect breeding cages located at Blanchard's home. (Today, five species of *Cactoblastis* have been described, including one known as *Cactoblastis doddi*, which was named after Alan Dodd. At least two of these other species were eventually imported into Australia, but neither of them proved to as be effective at controlling prickly-pear as *Cactoblastis cactorum*.)

From February 20 to March 10, Dodd was kept fully occupied with breeding his *Cactoblastis* and preparing them for shipment to Australia. In a worried letter to his father, he explained that the larvae he had collected at Concordia had provided him with over 500 cocoons yet he was in a quandary as to what generation he was dealing with. In their native habitat, *Cactoblastis* can produce three, possibly four, generations per year. "It seems to me that February is too early for the last generation to emerge; there should be time for another generation before winter. And if the insects are not of the over-wintering generation, the shipment will probably prove a failure."

In late February, some 450 adult moths emerged from his 500 *Cactoblastis* cocoons. After mating, they duly laid their eggs for the next generation and soon died. Sensing that this might be his best opportunity, Dodd quickly packed six Wardian cases full of prickly-pear cactus and then affixed approximately 3,000 of these moths' eggs on the pads. "There is a boat leaving here somewhere between March 10-15, via Rio de Janeiro to Capetown, thence tran-shipment to Australia," he hastily wrote to his father.

201

After getting his cactus-filled Wardian cases transported to downtown Buenos Aires, Dodd settled in to wait for the steamer's arrival. "The weather is beautiful. Have been in town all week. Have to hang around until I get off the shipment of insects early next week. I hate loafing about with little to do. Also, I'm not fond of sitting by myself meal after meal. Solitary eating doesn't agree with a noisy person like myself," he grumbled in another letter.

At last, on March 10th, 1925, Alan Dodd was able to ship his cases of prickly-pear and *Cactoblastis cactorum* eggs. Placed in a sheltered spot on the vessel's deck, the consignment traveled unaccompanied, with no one to present oversee their welfare. The eggs soon hatched and the resulting larvae began to eat the prickly-pear that filled the Wardian cases.

Just four days after he had shipped his history-changing cargo of *Cactoblastis*, Alan dashed a letter off to his sister, Bess, telling her that he had suddenly changed his travel plans. He was now endeavoring to return to his US field station in Uvalde, Texas, as soon as possible. "Had a busy two days, running around this city fixing up tickets, passports, etc. Now most everything is done. Have sent off my trunk, been out to say 'goodbye' to the Blanchards. Leave in the morning for Chile to catch the steamer from Valparaiso on Wednesday, thence up the west coast, through Panama, change steamers and direct to New Orleans. Should be in Uvalde on April 7th or 8th."

In a letter to his father written after his return to Uvalde, Dodd seem positively buoyant. "Well, I think I shall be back in Australia before the end of the year, according to the last letter from Alexander," he enthused.

> I've got a busy season ahead of me . . . In March the Board again expressed its approval of the manner that I am carrying out the duties entrusted to me. And they have accepted my plan for the season's work, which includes the purchase of two motorcars. Yes, we're going going to be busy right enough, and I've got to accomplish results . . . which reminds me that the new

Melitara (moth) from New Mexico has been named *Melitara doddalis*. Hope to send lots of insects to Australia this year.

Meanwhile, his consignment of *Cactoblastis* was still on its plodding way to Australia.

"On arrival at Capetown, officers of the South African Department of Agriculture examined the cases and reported that the material was in excellent condition," Dodd wrote later. "Before reconsigning the shipment, they removed a few colonies of the larvae to maintain a small reserve in the event of the main supply suffering misadventure during the remainder of the voyage."

The remaining lot of approximately 2,750 *Cactoblastis* larvae arrived at Sherwood Laboratory in "splendid condition" in May of 1925, after having traveled over 14,000 miles "without scientific supervision" during its ten-week-long journey.

The larvae, which by now were nearly half-grown, were quickly removed from their travel cases and placed in quarantine cages furnished with a fresh supply of local pest-pear. Historically, this would be the only consignment of *Cactoblastis cactorum* to be successfully imported into Australia.

The caterpillars were reared to maturity in the quarantine insectary and host-tested by John Mann, who, in Alan Dodd's absence, had become acting-officer-in-charge of the laboratory. Mr. Mann was, indeed, the right man for the job and so became the first person to successfully breed *Cactoblastis* in Australia.

"I'd been breeding insects since I was fifteen, so there weren't really many difficulties with *Cactoblastis*, although we were working under very Spartan conditions," he told a magazine reporter more than 50 years later. "All we had was an old wooden building with wooden floors, lino (linoleum), and one antique telephone. I had to run an electric light cable from the main house down to the quarantine cages. I then put whatever number of electric light bulbs inside the insect cages that I estimated would give the warmth that they required

203

to breed. As long as I kept them properly warm, they bred quite easily."

The first generation of caterpillars gave a return of 1,137 cocoons, from which 1,070 moths emerged. Of this group of adult moths, some 527 were female, and after a short time, they had laid more than 100,000 eggs. The second generation of moths yielded a staggering two and a half million eggs.

Soon, surplus *Cactoblastis* eggs were being sent to field stations located in both Queensland and New South Wales. Then in March of 1926, almost one year to the day when Alan Dodd had placed his six insect cases aboard a steamer in Buenos Aires, the first wild release of more than two million *Cactoblastis* eggs was made at 19 trial sites in Queensland and New South Wales.

"The introduction of *Cactoblastis cactorum* changed the whole outlook regarding prickly-pear control," Dodd commented later. "Had that one shipment given poor results, one can but wonder to what extent the success of the biological campaign would have been prejudiced or at least delayed."

WHAT'S UP WITH JOHN MANN?

Just before he was due to return to Australia, Alan Dodd received a cable informing him that Alexander had just resigned. "Don't know what has happened and I'd dearly like to know," he said in a note to his mother. "Well, I must rest my mind in patience for the next few weeks. Weather hot and dry. Very hot today." Of course, Dodd would eventually learn that Alexander had left for America to publish his groundbreaking field-guide to seabirds.

With several of the Commonwealth Prickly Pear Board's top spots suddenly vacant and with Dodd still overseas, a scramble for better job positions began within the organization. L. F. Hitchcock became acting officer-in-charge of all the investigations, replacing the outgoing Alexander. Mr. A. R. Taylor was placed in charge of the Chinchilla field station, and Ronald Mundell took charge of the

Gogango field station. Meanwhile, John Mann did everything he could to bolster his position as acting officer-in-charge of Brisbane's Sherwood Laboratory.

News of the shuffle slowly trickled into the Uvalde, Texas, field station. "Yes, I heard that Veitch has been appointed to succeed Tryon. I suppose Edmund Jarvis thought he would get the job, but he should be satisfied with what he has. I knew that Burns had resigned . . . don't think Alexander has a very high opinion of Burns," Dodd confided in a letter to his father.

In late 1925, soon after he had arrived back in Australia, the Commonwealth Prickly Pear Board offered the hardworking Dodd their top job: "Officer-in-charge of Investigations." He would hold this position until the Board was disbanded in November of 1939. (In the same month of 1939, the Queensland Department of Lands was reorganized to include a section designed to further the science of biological control. Dodd was given the job as that unit's director, where he continued on for another 22 years until his retirement.)

Meanwhile, John Mann was knocked back to his old position of senior assistant at the Sherwood Laboratory, after being the acting officer-in-charge of that research facility for almost a year. This action was probably at Dodd's request. (From talking with people who knew these two men, it became obvious to me that they held a great dislike for each other.) Although Mann did not resign when he was forced to resume his former job, he appears to have nursed a smoldering hatred for Alan Dodd for the remainder of his life.

Even so, just four years later in 1929, he again became the officer-in-charge of Sherwood Laboratory. But Mann's exalted tenure in this position lasted for less than a year before he was abruptly transferred out west to the Chinchilla field station with the upgraded title of "Research Entomologist." This transfer was apparently a deliberate attempt by Alan Dodd to keep Mann "out of sight and out of his hair."

John Spencer Mann was born in Queensland in 1904. His father died just one month after the child was born. As a young boy,

John took solace in collecting all manner of insects. While he was teenager, he moved to Sydney to finance his external university studies by catching and breeding butterflies for an amateur collector named Dr. Waterhouse. Eventually, it was Dr. Waterhouse who recommended him for his first job with the Commonwealth Prickly Pear Board.

After returning to Brisbane in 1923, this 19-year-old young man accepted a position as laboratory assistant at the Biniguy field station. A year and a half later, Mann was promoted to the rank of senior assistant and transferred to the Sherwood Laboratory in Brisbane. With the course of his career apparently set, John never did go back and finalize his degree. (After the CPPB was disbanded, Mann also began working for the Biological Section of the Queensland Lands Department and was rehired at the position of "Entomologist.")

Mann had a "portly figure, was a dapper dresser, and usually wore a bow-tie and a neat little mustache." He was also described by his colleagues as being "rather pompous and full of airs." In contrast, the "workaholic" Alan Dodd wore plain clothes and simply had no time for "such nonsense from a junior."

Alan Dodd and John Mann were both self-taught entomologists; that much they certainly had in common. But the schism between them ran much deeper. Dodd had long accepted Darwin's classic theory of biological evolution in both his working and personal life.

Mann, on the other hand, remained a staunch Christian creationist, who rejected evolutionary theory because it was based on "99% imagination and 1% fossils . . . So I maintained that as a Christian, I would believe in the Bible until somebody could come up with any definite proof that men had evolved from animals," he once told an interviewer.

When the Commonwealth Prickly Pear Board was disbanded in 1939, the king of England awarded Alan Dodd one of that nation's highest metals. For his outstanding role in rescuing so much of rural Australia from the cactus menace, Dodd received an M. B. E. (Member of the Order of the British Empire). Except for one or two obscure published reports, however, there was little mention of John Mann's part in the campaign.

Just before Dodd retired from active civil service in early 1962, Queen Elizabeth awarded him an even higher honor in the form of an O. B. E. (Officer of the Order of the British Empire). At this slight, John Mann could barely contain his outrage; he would spend the rest of his working career - indeed the rest of his life - seeking and garnering recognition for his work.

After Dodd's retirement as head of the Biological Section of the Department of Lands, John Mann received an appointment to replace him in that coveted position. For nearly nine years, Mann basked in the "director's limelight." Finally, upon his own retirement in 1970, Mann was awarded an M. B. E..

During his farewell dinner, after almost a decade of being in charge of Ph.D. scientists doing research on insects and biological control, the fact was announced that Mann did not even have a basic university degree. At that, one professor is said to have leaned over to him and kindly whispered, "Well, it never showed."

Thirteen years after his retirement, John Mann was awarded an honorary doctorate from the University of Queensland. (The smug look of satisfied revenge was the first thing that I noticed when I saw a newspaper photo of him taken during the award ceremony.) From that moment on, he insisted on being addressed as "Dr. John Mann." Alan Dodd, on the other hand, had simply placed his honors and royal metals in a drawer and rarely looked at or ever mentioned them again.

There were other problems at the laboratory and research stations, some of which became chronic irritations. For example, Dodd had a love for cats. "There were all these bloody cats around the place," retired entomologist Graham Donnelly confided to me. "They were strays that Dodd would befriend and feed. But Taylor, who managed the Chinchilla research station, hated cats. Apparently, he would stick cyanide in their food and poison them."

207

Tall and rangy in physique, Dodd's face usually wore such an expression of utter seriousness that some people often mistook it for anger or sulleness. He rarely laughed outright in public, but at home he often entertained and was the life of the party. "He smiled a lot when his family and friends were around," his niece, Janice Perry, told me. "His eyes fairly twinkled."

Although Dodd had a tremendous knowledge of insects, his management approach at work left a lot to be desired. He was totally committed to the job at hand and he could be very difficult and autocratic, especially with people with degrees. "He had a lot of young scientists come to work for him, but the fact that they had a university degree didn't automatically impress him," Robert Baldwin, a great nephew, told me. "Just because you had a degree didn't make you a good scientist."

"I think in terms of his work life, it was probably fair to describe Alan as single-minded," Baldwin continued. "After all, I doubt anyone could have achieved what he did without a significant degree of determination, persistence, concentration, attention to detail, and strong focus. Certainly in his later years, he retained a very sharp mind and definite, rigid, views on how things should be done . . . My memories are of a man who was a real gentleman and a bachelor who was very much set in his ways."

THE BIG "PUSH" BEGINS

It was against this background of tensions and divided loyalties that the labor-intensive work of mass-breeding and distributing *Cactoblastis* into Australia's prickly-pear-dominated landscape began in earnest. Demonstrating a food preference for just prickly-pear, the caterpillars had already passed routine starvation tests on commercially useful plants with flying colors . . . by literally starving to death.

Cactoblastis caterpillars are colored bright orange or reddish-orange, with black spots that are often fused into rings. (See Plate 16)

They live in colonies that tunnel freely through the prickly-pear plant, one segment at a time, and can cause rapid decay within the affected parts. The adult caterpillars often spin their white cocoons in or under the litter of dead and drying prickly-pear pads that usually accumulates beneath affected plants.

In due time, small, rather plain-looking, brownish-grey moths emerge from the cocoons. They have no functional mouth parts, so cannot feed. In the few days before they, too, starve to death, the moths' primary task is to mate and lay eggs to begin the next generation.

The eggs are laid in curious chains, known as "eggsticks." (See Plate 14) Although a female moth is capable of laying from 100 to 300 eggs, most eggsticks contain an average of between 40 to 75 eggs. When viewed with a microscope, these flexible and rather durable eggsticks appear to be made up of stacks of tiny coins glued together, one on top of the other. Each little "coin" is an individual egg.

In Australia, there are normally two generations of *Cactoblastis* annually: a long-lived over-wintering generation and a shorter-lived summer one. A particularly good year, however, may see three generations.

For the mass breeding of these moths, the CPPB's normal insect enclosures quickly proved unsuitable. A special *Cactoblastis* breeding cage soon evolved and at the peak of the nation's rearing program some 2,500 of them were in use. At the same time, dozens of large open-air galvanized-metal sheds, each measuring 100 feet by 30 feet, (30.4 m x 9.1 m) were constructed at the field stations to protect the cages' occupants from the worst effects of the sun and weather. (See Plate 17)

The breeding cages consisted of a simple wooden framework covered with fine-mesh wire screening, with a removable top, but no bottom. A large wooden "platform-tray" fitted with legs was covered several inches deep with soil or sand, on which a prickly-pear plant was placed. As a protection from ants, each leg of the tray was placed in a water-filled tin. Then the open-bottomed breeding cage was dovetailed over the cactus sitting on the tray. These cages came in several sizes, the most common one measured six feet long by three feet wide and two feet high (183 cm x 91.4 cm x 61 cm), although many smaller ones were also used.

When the female moths in the breeding cages began to lay their eggs, the eggsticks were collected on a daily basis. (See Plate 18) With an incubation period between three to five weeks long, there was usually ample time to permit the eggs to be transported from the *Cactoblastis* breeding facilities out to the most remote prickly-pear infestation before they hatched. (See Plate 19)

"In the last six months, some two and a quarter million of these insects have been liberated in various parts of Queensland and New South Wales," the *Brisbane Courier* reported on September 28th, 1926. "Mr. Dodd emphasized that the liberations of these insects are purely experimental; to show how they act on different pear in different localities."

On December 22nd, 1926, the *Daily Mail* reported that all of the nearly 100 thickets of prickly-pear in the Leslie District where *Cactoblastis* had been released just a month earlier were now showing signs of decay. "A recent visit to the locality showed that the caterpillars' operations on the pear were well up to expectations."

On August 1st, 1927, the *Daily Mail* further reported that a year and a half earlier, "twenty thousand eggs were liberated on Mrs. Donnelly's property (near Emerald, Queensland), and a good hatch resulted . . . [They] are now spreading at a great rate, having already covered an area of three miles (4.8 km) in radius and in some places are found as far as five miles (6.4 km) away."

Australia's prime minister, Mr. S. M. Bruce, who exhibited a considerable interest in these ongoing experiments, soon paid the unflappable Mrs. Donnelly and her *Cactoblastis* a visit, which, "in conjunction with the cochineal insect, had completely exterminated some large clumps of prickly-pear." (See Plate 20)

By the first quarter of 1927, more than nine million *Cactoblastis* eggs had been distributed in selected places throughout the prickly-pear region. Within two years of these releases, the increase in *Cactoblastis* numbers at these sites had become so great that cage-rearing at the field stations was no longer required. It appeared that *Cactoblastis* was becoming firmly established in Australia and that their eggs could now be collected in bulk in the wild.

"As evidence of the enormous increase of *C. cactorum*, mention can be made of the fact that at Emerald, Queensland . . . 22,000,000 eggs were gathered . . . by five men in one week," Alan Dodd wrote. At this point, the CPPB also discontinued much of its egg distribution effort and turned the bulk of that task over to the various state agencies.

However, the CPPB's research stations continued to provide most of the eggs. Although the moths were no longer reared in captivity, hundreds of thousands of their cocoons were being collected in the field to be put in cages, where the emerging moths would soon lay their eggs. The eggs were then conveniently gathered and put in boxes for mass distribution.

"A gang of about 50 men has commenced collecting *Cactoblastis* cocoons at the prickly-pear nursery near Emerald," the Brisbane *Telegraph* reported in January of 1929. "Last year a similar number of men were employed for about three months collecting cocoons."

In another locality, where 100,000 eggs had been liberated in February, 1926, over 300 million eggs were collected four years later. One man was said to have harvested nearly four million eggs, or about 60,000 eggsticks, in just eight hours.

"To give some idea of the scope of the operations," Alan Dodd remarked. "In one month alone, one field station housed 6,500,000 cocoons and secured 81,500,000 eggs, of which number over 4,000,000 eggs were laid in one night."

HOME GROWN ENTREPRENEURS

By 1929, the CPPB's workforce had expanded to well over 200 people. A boon to the local economy, nearly 70 of them were employed in just the small community of Gogango. Across the state,

211

a fleet of seven trucks and over 100 men delivered packages of *Cactoblastis* eggs.

The cost of distributing eggs raised at the research stations was calculated to be £15 for every million eggs. (About $910 US in today's terms.) However, collecting them in the field reduced that cost to only £5 for every million eggs. After learning of this fact, many local men and schoolboys sensed an opportunity to earn some extra cash and began collecting *Cactoblastis* eggs and cocoons in their spare time.

Soon the *Cactoblastis* business was booming. Workers from the town of Chinchilla, for instance, were paid 15s/6d per day (about $47 US) to collect eggs and cocoons in kerosene tins. "Even the kids were hired, and if they could get a matchbox full of eggs, they were paid ten shillings," retired farmer Clarence Kerr told me. Those were very good wages in the days when the national economy was sinking into the Great Depression.

"A few people conducted the business on more extended lines," Alan Dodd recalls in his 1940 book, *The Biological Campaign Against Prickly-pear*. "They purchased the eggs in small lots from local collectors and hawked the bulk-supplies by motorcar for selling in districts where the insect was not yet present in quantity."

At the edge of one small town, two enterprising boys set up an office in a dilapidated hut. On the door they had inscribed, "*Cactus Blastus Agints*." In order to pursue their little venture, I imagine they had missed more than one day of spelling and grammar at school.

"As soon as evidence of the insect's destructive powers became apparent," Dodd continues, "Landholders were eager to see the same results reproduced on their [own] properties." For the next two or three years, as word spread across the prickly-pear dominated countryside, the trafficking of *Cactoblastis* eggs was a profitable enterprise.

GETTING TO CRITICAL MASS

In the early days of *Cactoblastis* distribution, the eggsticks were simply attached to small squares of gummed paper about the size of a postage stamp which were pinned directly to the prickly-pear plants. But there were two serious flaws to this method. Firstly, the eggs remained exposed to the weather and to predation by ants or other insects. Frequently, when nearing the hatching point, the eggs would simply die in the direct heat of the summer sun.

The second problem revealed itself more slowly. Although most landholders realized the value of liberating *Cactoblastis* eggs in a timely manner on their prickly-pear-choked properties, it often seemed too much trouble to paste each little eggstick to a small piece of paper and then fasten them, one by one, onto the plants. "Hence, millions of purchased eggs were wasted by being broadcast amongst the prickly-pear," Dodd dryly observed.

Later on, a much higher rate of hatching success was achieved by enclosing the eggsticks in small water-resistant waxed-paper tubes, about the size of a cigarette. These paper "quills" were then pinned directly onto the pear plant, where the little caterpillars exited through a small hole after they had hatched.

At the field research stations, rows of men sat for hours each day at long tables busily rolling *Cactoblastis* eggsticks into waxed-paper quills. When finished, the quills were placed in boxes which held around 100,000 eggs each.

Each box was marked with a "use by" date and included pins and a printed instruction sheet to help guide the landholder in the correct method of liberation. All that was necessary to receive one of these boxes, free-of-charge, was to fill in an application form, obtainable from the district land office or the local prickly-pear ranger. If the application were approved, a supply of eggs would soon be posted to you.

When they released their own package of *Cactoblastis* eggs, "Dad and Mum made sure that it was a family outing," Eric Geldard of Miles, Queensland, told me. "We went around poking them onto all these leaves, then had a cup of tea and some bickies (biscuits), and that was it."

But sometimes the egg deliveries got delayed in the mail. Grace Lithgow remembers when her grandfather had ordered his box of *Cactoblastis*. "Grandfather lived on a remote property and the mailman used to come out only once a fortnight (every two weeks). The eggs had arrived at the post office on the wrong weekend, so they sat in the post office for a full week."

The eggs had hatched during this period and by the time the mailman arrived late in the afternoon on the appointed day, the tiny caterpillars had dispersed all through the inside of his mailbag in their desperate search for something to eat. "And so the bag was emptied onto a tarp spread out over the table. They were inside the letters and inside the papers that were all rolled up . . . they were inside everything."

"The men went to bed, with their horses out in the yard, while the women sat up all night and gently placed these little caterpillars into small paper cylinders that they had fashioned. They also took two [cloth] suger-sacks and sewed them into shoulder bags . . . and that's where the caterpillars in their paper vials went."

Around two-thirty in the morning, the women woke the men up. Sleepily, they trooped out into the darkness and distributed the caterpillars across the property. "They pushed the little paper vials onto a cactus spine to make a hole in it and then pushed it onto another spine to keep it there," Grace explained. "They wanted the little caterpillars to get into the pear before the birds woke up."

"Our farm at Brigalow was one of the first to be allotted a batch of the larvae and in a short space of time the results were amazing," Clarence Ulm informed me in a letter. "As the *Cactoblastis* multiplied, large areas were soon covered with heaps of rotting pear. The farmers were simply overjoyed. In the space of a few years the countryside was transformed." (See Plates 21 and 22)

214

THE GREAT COLLAPSE

With the research stations now coordinated with gangs of men collecting cocoons and eggs from the field, it did not take long for *Cactoblastis* liberations to "saturate" the worst regions of prickly-pear infestation. By 1930 it was estimated that a total of more than three billion eggs had been released. The results were nothing short of stupendous. In some precincts, in the span of just four months, the areas of destroyed prickly-pear had increased more than tenfold.

It has been estimated that it takes about two thousand *Cactoblastis* larvae to destroy a medium-sized prickly-pear plant and around 25 million of them to clear a single hectare of growth (2.47 acres). By the end of June of 1930, nearly half a million acres (200,000 hectares) of pear had been totally destroyed.

While most farmers and landholders greeted the arrival of *Cactoblastis* as their savior, others protested the wholesale destruction of the pear. "What folly is here! We had a fodder plant of the utmost value that did not require to be planted or cultivated, that was always on hand in unlimited quantities, free from insect foes and disease, an absolute guarantee against losses in the droughts, and an abundant feed to keep up the flow of milk and general condition of animals whenever grass gets dry," a full page article in the *Brisbane Telegraph* complained. "Instead of recognizing these marvelous qualities, possessed by no other plant, we try to get rid of it when we ought to use what little brains we have and utilize it. . ."

Traditional mindsets are often hard to change, as witnessed in the following incident: "Reports indicate that the 'official mind' is liable to be even a greater menace than the pear," the *Rockhampton Bulletin* disclosed after certain regulations of the Queensland State Lands Act were enforced to the letter-of-the-law. During a prosecution hearing for failing to destroy prickly-pear on their land, the landholders testified that 90% of the pear on their property was infected with *Cactoblastis* and that nearly all the cactus was dying.

"Yet the [land] holding was recommended for forfeiture," the

Bulletin continued. "To avoid coming under the ban of official wrath, other landholders are now poisoning their pear together with millions of the insects that are being fostered by the federal government to destroy the pear." This regulatory conflict was soon corrected, however, and *Cactoblastis* again continued its march across the prickly-pear dominated landscape almost unimpeded.

Despite *Cactoblastis* having been imported into Australia supposedly free of its natural predators and diseases, the moth soon encountered some formidable native enemies in its new home. "Several species of birds tear open the pear segments in which larvae are feeding and eat whole colonies, others scratch around among debris and find cocoons," reported John Mann. "Mice frequently make holes in the cocoons and eat the pupae. Ants and cockroaches occasionally destroy the eggs."

In another report, this one written by Alan Dodd, bacterial and fungal diseases also caused considerable losses, especially among the densest *Cactoblastis* populations. Moreover, two of the 20 species of internal parasites found to infect the moth's pupal stage caused mortality rates of up to twenty-two percent. In addition to these biological hazards, wildfires (especially the widespread bush fires of 1928) also created considerable havoc amongst the caterpillars. Sustained by this specie's amazing powers of reproduction, however, these setbacks were simply overwhelmed by sheer numbers.

By mid-1932, huge areas of prickly-pear throughout Queensland and northern New South Wales were being reduced to decaying pulp. "The rapidity of the onslaught was astonishing," Dodd wrote. "Mile after mile of dense growth collapsed under the concentrated attack of phenomenal numbers of the larvae." It was said that you could stand in a patch of prickly-pear and hear them eating.

Although the *Cactoblastis* caterpillars caused a lot of damage to the pear, it was actually a secondary infection comprised of a mixture of bacteria and fungi that usually caused the cactus to collapse. The disease organisms are transported on the skin of the larvae and their net effect is to create liquid putrefaction inside the affected

216

prickly-pear pads. No longer able to bear its own weight, an infected plant will suddenly fall to the ground in a slimy, decaying heap.

As millions of acres of prickly-pear lay rotting, a strong odor began drifting across the landscape. Likening it to the stench of dead cattle, one retired farmer told me that "you could drive for days in any direction and never get away from that smell." The aroma persisted for weeks and even months as the pear decayed into the ground. Its rankness was often so strong that it caused people to want to leave the region. Certainly, those who were subjected to this fragrance never forgot the experience.

"The collapse of the prickly-pear menace was so fast and so dramatic that at first the people on the land couldn't believe that it was finally beaten," historian John Eggleston told me. "Eventually, the rotting pear turned into dry brown heaps that covered the ground in dense masses. In many places, tremendous fires broke out and raged across the countryside, leaving the land covered with a dense layer of ash. Following the rains, almost miraculously, the grasses and herbage returned again." Land that had been useless for decades was now cleared and planted with grain and other crops.

Fertilized by the rotting pear, these supercharged soils were soon yielding bumper harvests. "The soil was so rich that for 40 years we did not have to use any fertilizer on our farm at Warra in Queensland, " Walter Schroder told me. The Warra district formerly had been one of the worst of the prickly-pear areas.

In another district of the same region, Eric Geldard's property had originally been leased to his father as a prickly-pear selection, with the standard condition that they had to keep it clear of pear. Like so many families, they simply couldn't do this on their own, and eventually half of their 1,280 acres was forfeited back to the Crown. But when Eric's father learned of the increasing success of *Cactoblastis*, he applied for the return of his forfeited 680 acres. Not only did he get that block back, he also acquired another piece of land next door.

After the Geldards had introduced *Cactoblastis* onto their

property, the pear began to collapse and disappear, almost like magic. "While digging post-holes for a new fence," Eric recalled, "my brother Burt told me that he never once stood on the earth; he was standing on rotting pear the whole time. That's how thick it was!"

Alan Dodd summed up the vast scene of devastated prickly-pear with a description of his own experiences along Queenland's Moonie River:

> In August 1930, for 150 miles (241 km) along the river, [the] prickly-pear was in its full vigor, its continuity almost unbroken by clearings; the road which followed the stream being a mere lane walled in by the pest . . . Exactly two years later, in August 1932, when I traveled the same road, the transformation was extraordinary. Ninety percent of the pear had collapsed. For mile after mile one saw nothing but masses of rotting pulp.

"Country that was absolutely impassable for many years can now be traversed on foot with ease," one newspaper boasted. An extract from a report of the prickly-pear warden for the Goondiwindi land district reads, "The twelve months under review has made a wonderful difference in the pear country in this district, due largely to the splendid work done by the Cactoblastis . . . and now land which twelve months ago was covered with green pear is free from pear."

The warden for the Charters Towers district also happily reported that, "generally the conditions are satisfactory and the pear is not making any headway. The Ranger always carries his [arsenic] stabber and treats any odd plants that come under his notice." While over in the Ingham district, the warden there disclosed that, "no further occurrence of pear along the coast has been reported. The Ranger has made numerous inquiries and always keeps a lookout when on patrol work, but no pear has been found."

Arthur Hurse of Chinchilla remembers that when he was a boy, the stands of prickly-pear had been reduced "to an eerie forest of skeletons, white and frail, and ready to disintegrate at a touch." Tempted to fill his pockets with the brittle stems, Arthur still vividly

218

recalls suffering the consequences as the sharp spines penetrated his tender skin.

After having made a tour of southern Queensland and northern New South Wales, the Commonwealth Prickly Pear Board became so impressed by the progress of prickly-pear destruction that they issued a statement declaring it was "inevitable that the *Cactoblastis* insect will achieve complete victory over the pest."

So confident of their program's eventual success, the Board even produced a 16-minute-long black and white "talkie" motion picture, *The Conquest of Prickly Pear*, which was released for viewing in movie theaters all across Australia and throughout the English-speaking world. Its star was an animated "Willie Cactoblastis, hero of the greatest plant invasion of all time." The governor of Queensland was among those who witnessed its first screening and was reported to have been "visibly impressed."

Meanwhile in North America, the *San Francisco Examiner* devoted more than half a page on Australia's success story with *Cactoblastis*. "A tiny caterpillar is doing a big job that men armed with chemicals and machines failed to do. And when the soldiers in the insect army have won the war, they will conveniently eliminate themselves, having no enemy to devour," predicted the reporter.

"They will have the consolation of the Glutton, who said that not even Heaven could take away from him the memory of the dinners that he had eaten; they have some gorgeous eating before them before the time comes to starve," the *Sydney Sun* quickly rejoined.

REGROWTH

In 1933, seven years after the initial trial liberations had been made, the last big area of primary prickly-pear in Queensland finally succumbed to *Cactoblastis*. The caterpillars had finally exhausted their food supply and now they were starving to death in enormous numbers, decimating their population. But as the public would soon learn, however, the Great Cactus War was far from over.

In desperation, some of the famished larvae attacked nearby fields of green tomatoes and watermelons. Invariably, this strange diet killed them before they could do more than negligible damage. Yet farmers were clearly getting worried and scientists from the Commonwealth Prickly Pear Board were asked to investigate these incidents.

During one well-publicized case, the CPPB found that the *Cactoblastis* larvae had originally been liberated in a stand of dense pear that lined both sides of a creek. Just upland from the prickly-pear was the cultivated land of a Mr. M'Meiken, who was growing tomatoes on it at the time. After the pear had been completely eradicated, the starving caterpillars then spread out in a desperate search for more food. The researchers determined that they had "attempted to feed on the green tomatoes, but had not touched the ripe fruit or injured the plants in any way."

In the meantime, prickly-pear's strong recuperative powers were becoming more evident every day as new infestations began to appear from sprouting seeds and underground stems. "The regrowth grew extremely rapidly," Alan Dodd observed. "A field of apparently dead pear at the end of the winter might be covered with green pear 12 to 18 inches high (30 to 46 cm) by the end of summer and three feet high (1 m) a year later."

Very quickly, the prickly-pear began reclaiming much of its old territory and soon appeared to be as formidable as the original infestation. This was a real worry to country folks and scientists alike.

Initially, the reduced *Cactoblastis* population was far too small to have any noticeable effect on the surging regrowth of prickly-pear. Comments predicting the failure of the biological control campaign began trickling into the press. But the new prickly-pear was a very succulent type of growth, which did not seem to possess the insect-resistant qualities of the original plant. "And it proved most palatable to *Cactoblastis*, which was able to increase at a faster rate than in the original infestation," Dodd notes. "By 1934, it was obvious that the insect had regained ascendancy."

"One of the strongest characteristics of this insect is its ability to increase from very small to very large numbers in the course of a generation or two, when food and climate requirements are favorable," Dodd explains.

The most widespread areas of regrowth were brought under control by the end of 1934 and there have been no large-scale recurrences ever since. "Regrowth has appeared in many places and has remained for a few years in certain areas, but since 1933 its incidence has not given rise to apprehension."

Seven years later, during a meeting of the Historical Society of Queensland, Alan Dodd formally announced that the war against prickly-pear was over. Although it had taken more than five decades to actually achieve this victory, for the past several years it had become readily apparent to most people that prickly-pear was no longer a threat to the rural landscape.

With success now assured, the Commonwealth Prickly Pear Board had been disbanded and various state agencies appointed to complete the "mop-up." Prickly-pear's economic importance was reduced to not much more than that of an ordinary weed.

"Queensland has been freed, to all practical purposes, from this great plant octopus," Dodd informed his rapt audience. Declaring that it was no exaggeration that over 95% of the former pest had already been eradicated, he assured them that "all that remains in most districts are scattered, often very widely scattered plants. Over many extensive belts of what was impenetrable prickly-pear, there is no trace of the plant's survival." *Cactoblastis* had done its job well.

LIFE AFTER VICTORY

"Little remains to remind one of the grey-green dragon which once drew millions of acres into its greedy maw," the *Toowoomba Chronicle* announced. Around the world the success of the biological campaign against prickly-pear was proclaimed in newspapers and discussed in scientific journals. For Australia, the new science of

221

biocontrol had finally been proven and its poster boy was *Cactoblastis*.

In the words of Queensland's minister for lands at the time, "It is astonishing to realize the great transformation that has taken place over the vast area that was then regarded by many as irretrievably lost to prickly-pear . . . It is doubtful if the historical records of any country could reveal a biological experiment that could approach the magnitude of this one."

"The miracle wrought by *Cactoblastis*, after decades of failed government measures, astounded even the scientists who introduced it," says Professor Donald Freeman, adding that "The governments of Queensland and New South Wales were not bashful about taking credit for the spectacular success of their program . . ."

Certainly, no one anticipated the remarkable success of *Cactoblastis*. "Had *Cactoblastis* not come into the picture, the earlier insects would have justified the biological experiment, for they were already beginning to exercise a definite measure of control in reducing the density of impenetrable areas, in killing seedlings and individual older plants, and in destroying immature fruit," Dodd told his many listeners. But the *Cactoblastis* moth had performed "even better than good."

"A wave of the scientist's wand has rung down the curtain on a scene of hopelessness and desolation and raised it on a new scene full of promise and prosperity," *Walkabout Magazine* extolled. Suddenly, millions of acres of arable land had become available for cultivation.

The state governments made the reclaimed land available in two classes. Blocks ranging from 640 to 5,000 acres were offered for farming and dairying, while larger areas up to 25,000 acres were granted for raising beef cattle or sheep.

A constant stream of settlers soon began arriving to take up these newly available lands. For surveyor John Meek, like many in his profession who had previously struggled through vast wildernesses of prickly-pear, a new era of steady (and easier) work came available as vast tracts of land that had only recently been

222

infested with cactus were divided up into smaller blocks for "selection."

Competition for these selections was often fierce. "Four prickly-pear selections which were opened for selection under perpetual lease tenure at the Chinchilla Court House again attracted applicants from all over the state," the *Chinchilla News and Murilla Advertiser* reported. "So great was the number (490 primary and 829 secondary applications), that the Prickly Pear Warden had to postpone the ballot." The waiting crowd was so large that it spilled out into the street.

Winning a selection was often very much like winning the lottery. On another day at the same Chinchilla Court House, nine blocks of land went up for selection. For these, there were nearly 500 applicants. One block alone received 183 applications. "And the lucky drawer for that block was Eric Brown," the local newspaper reported. Now with over a thousand acres of rich farmland on which to live and work, Mr. Brown's life had suddenly made a turn for the better.

In less than five years, many of the towns and villages in former prickly-pear country had doubled in size. Agricultural production also increased exponentially. "For example, at Chinchilla in 1926 - the year that *Cactoblastis* was first released - a small factory produced 400,000 pounds of butter," Dodd writes. "In 1939, a modern factory produced 3,100,000 pounds of butter. This sevenfold increase can be attributed solely to the disappearance of prickly-pear."

Nearly all the lands in both Queensland and New South Wales, where for so many years prickly-pear had reigned supreme, were brought back into production.

"The unwanted trees have been killed over millions of acres, many hundreds of water catchment excavations have been formed, thousands of miles of new fencing have been erected," Dodd continues. "Homes of new settlers, wool sheds, dairy sheds, barns, etc., have appeared everywhere." This vast region had now become some of Australia's richest and most productive farmland.

MEMORIALS TO A MOTH

In March 1938, a drawing of a single-story wooden building set on low blocks appeared in the syndicated *"Ripley's Believe It or Not"* section of newspapers all over the world. "Erected in honor of an insect!" its caption read.

The small farming community of Boonarga, Queensland, had been nearly smothered out of existence when prickly-pear dominated the landscape. As the town "got back on its feet" after *Cactoblastis* had destroyed the pest, people wanted to do something that would permanently memorialize their "savior."

Now prosperous, the little town was growing and needed a community hall for meetings and social events. Land for the proposed hall was donated by Mrs. Fahey, a resident of Boonarga.

A local farmer, Stewart Oliver, is credited with promoting the notion of dedicating the hall to the *Cactoblastis* moth. The idea quickly won over the district's grateful residents and funds were raised through bake-sales, community dances, and pledges from several prominent citizens.

They employed a carpenter who, with help from volunteers, spent two years building the structure. It was officially opened on February 21st, 1936, with a grand reception replete with long-winded speeches, followed by a festive dance. (See Plate 23)

"They built a bloody hall to commemorate the cactus being gone!" writer and author Craig Walton told me during a lunchtime meeting in downtown Brisbane. "That's not something a community does if they're not tearfully celebrating. Sixty, seventy, eighty years ago and more. . . it's almost out of living memory, but it's still very much in the cultural memory out there."

Over the years, the hall has been used for numerous official meetings, weddings, birthdays, and community dances. Esmé Davis, who grew up near Boonarga, happily remembers going to some of those dances when she was a young girl: "There . . . that's where you met your boyfriends and girlfriends. We had a dance every second

224

Saturday and Mum and Dad and all the kids went. Everyone went," she told me. "Everybody got to know other people . . . not sitting in front of the computer like today. The dance bands were all local people."

"We danced the "dipsy-dos," the barn dance, the waltz, the Canadian three-step, and the Canberra two-step," Esmé continued. "I had a crush on a boy who was a good dancer, but I was somewhat younger than him, only about 11 or 12, but I would make it my business to have a dance in the 'progressive' waltz. When the music stopped, you changed partners."

"That's when you got to dance with <u>that</u> boy?" I asked.

"That's when we'd dance with all the teen-aged boys that we had a crush on," she smilingly averred before resuming. "In between dances, the younger kids would be all over the dance-floor, slipping and sliding. A lot of the oldies who couldn't dance just came and sat for the social interaction."

"We always had supper at about 11:00 o'clock at night with homemade cakes, sandwiches, and a cup of tea. Some of the men sat outside on stumps - or whatever they could find - around the fire that we used for boiling water and smoked, drank a bit of rum, and told lies. . . I suppose."

Since those early days, the hall has been extended by one-third and the dance floor replaced. Otherwise, it remains fairly unchanged. The building is now listed on Queensland's historical register.

Another local resident, R. D. Dyke, eulogized the hall in a poem. The final part of it goes like this:

Two hundred miles from Brisbane, along the Western Line,
Where the land was infested in the days of auld lang syne,
At a little railway siding where farmers take their cream,
There's an edifice that stands as a token of esteem.

In memory of the Cactoblastis which achieved so much,
And the residents with a grateful and reminiscent touch,
Have named it with an aptitude which is approved by all,
The Boonarga Cactoblastis Memorial Hall.

Now at the dance popular which every week they hold,

Whilst younger folk are dancing, the older ones, I'm told,
Will often get together, and as the dance band plays,
They talk of when the pear was thick, back in the olden days.

There have been at least three other memorials created to honor Australia's smallest hero. In 1965, the people of Dalby, Queensland, erected a large cairn to record their "indebtedness and gratitude" to the little moth. In 1985, sculptor Rhyl Hinwood's bronze statue of a prickly-pear bush being attacked by *Cactoblastis* was formally presented to the Miles Historical Society. And near Chinchilla, a commemorative wall with informative plaques was erected near the site of the old "bug farm," one of the Commonwealth Prickly Pear Board's former field stations.

DYNAMIC BALANCE

Actually, *Cactoblastis* never did get rid of the prickly-pear. It simply vastly reduced its quantity on the landscape. (One study estimated that the weight of the destroyed prickly-pear was over one and a half billion tons, which is equal to more than 32,300 *Titanics*.) In any case, it's suicide for an animal to eat all of its food supply.

Today, *Cactoblastis* and prickly-pear (*Opuntia stricta*) are still present in scattered populations on unused ground all across the enormous region of Australia that was formerly dominated by the cactus. By and large, a kind of balance has been achieved in the relationship between this insect and its food plant. *Cactoblastis* typically maintains a low population level and its damage is seldom noticed.

In years when favorable environmental conditions encourages the prickly-pear to spread, the cactus moth "comes out of hiding," and reduces the growth back to its former lower levels. Despite occasional regional outbreaks, this system of dynamic balance seems to work so well that there is no longer any official monitoring of the weed by state authorities. "The farmers are not complaining about prickly-pear," I was told by a New South Wales agriculture representative. "So why should we?"

"There is a constant bout between the climate, the micro-climate, the cactus, and *Cactoblastis*," weed biocontrol specialist Dr. Rachel McFadyen explained to me. "For example, in the 1960s people said it was not working because it was a very dry time. And again, in the 80s, people said that it's not working. Always it was the same story, it's either a very dry year or a very cold one. Once you get warmer weather, or wetter weather, suddenly it works. Certainly, my view is that it's working no better and no worse than it ever did."

There are places where *Cactoblastis* has had little effect on the prickly-pear. For example, it is not able to control the cactus in cooler regions, such as the New England highlands of New South Wales, where the moth cannot complete at least two generations a year. (In some of these areas cochineal has proven to be an effective alternative, however.) The same is true for regions where it is hot most of the time, when the prickly-pear segments often become dehydrated.

Alan Dodd recognized at least three varieties of insect-resistant prickly-pear that seemed to contain abnormally high levels of mucilage and starch. One form that *Cactoblastis* found nearly impenetrable, which he dubbed "vigorous resistant pear," has much thicker stems than normal. Another one, commonly known as "bull pear," also has thick segments and sports prolific sterile fruits.

A third mucilaginous form of less vigorous growth, known as "yellow pear," is a product of the nitrogen-poor soils of the open basaltic plateaus of New South Wales, particularly in the Hunter River Valley and the Bingara-Inverall country to the north. Usually stunted and rather sickly looking, when the young *Cactoblastis* larvae bore into its yellowish-colored pads they are quickly drowned by a flood of excreted mucilage. Plants of this sort that have been artificially fertilized, however, soon regain a normal appearance and *Cactoblastis* usually has no problem invading it.

"The solution to the problem was secured by killing the standing timber which absorbed the available nitrogen in the soil," reported Dodd. "The application of this practice has resulted in a

227

very marked reduction in the acreage under yellow pear" (and a significant decrease in tree cover).

Although new hormone-type weed killers, such as 2,4-D and 2,4,5-T, became widely available after the end of World War II, they have proved to be very expensive in the long run - both environmentally and price-wise. On some holdings, the cost of spraying these chemicals to control Cactoblastis-resistant prickly-pear exceeded the full value of the property. For a long time, the New South Wales Prickly Pear Destruction Commission shared the cost of spraying with the landholders. But since the "Commission" was decommissioned in 1987, the responsibility for prickly-pear control has now mostly reverted back to the occupants of those properties.

With no one monitoring the continuing effectiveness of *Cactoblastis*, we have little idea of how the relationship between this remarkable insect and its food plant is evolving.

"In most instances, it has reached an equilibrium situation," offers entomologist Graham Donnelly. "Prickly-pear fluctuates up and down, population-wise, and so does *Cactoblastis*. It is sort of a density-dependent situation." And changes to that equilibrium will eventually occur in this delicate relationship. Whatever they may be, it is very likely that prickly-pear and many of its cactus relatives will be present in Australia for a very long time to come.

Chapter 9: The Good Bug Goes Bad

Cactoblastis cleared the pear,
Saving many an outback farm.
Surely sharing this grub with others
Would certainly do no harm.
They sent the moth to Africa, Pakistan, Hawaii,
Even tiny Nevis, where it jumped the queue
And began eating <u>native</u> cactus in the USA;
Who knows how much damage it will do?

Let's fast-forward exactly 90 years from that day in 1925 when Alan Dodd sent his historic shipment of *Cactoblastis* to Australia. As the camera zooms in, I am standing in the middle of a large cultivated prickly-pear plantation in an agricultural district called "El Virqui." It is located some 30 miles (48 kilometers), as the crow flies, northeast of the city of Catamarca in northern Argentina.

The biting midges and flies are particularly bothersome today, and I have foolishly worn only a short-sleeved shirt, shorts, and sandals for protection. By dinnertime tonight my fingers, lips, and eyelids will be swollen and misshapen from the toxic effects of my insect antagonists. At the moment, however, I am staring intently at one of these cactuses towering above me, nearly as big as a tree.

There are four of us here, busily locating and counting the little eggsticks that *Cactoblastis* moths have attached to the prickly-pear plants. My hosts on this adventure are Drs. Jim Carpenter and Stephen Hight of the United States Department of Agriculture's ARS (Agricultural Research Service).

They have been studying methods of controlling *Cactoblastis* for nearly a decade. Normally based in the southeastern United States, Carpenter and Hight have come here, along with a new ARS colleague, George Fox, to collect data from an ongoing experiment and to look for an insect enemy of *Cactoblastis*. Most particularly, the one they especially want to collect is a minute parasitic wasp only a few millimeters long, named *Apanteles*. It can kill *Cactoblastis* caterpillars.

But wait a minute. . . . Why would they want something that would kill *Cactoblastis*, the poster boy of the science of biological control?

By halting the relentless spread of prickly-pear cactus across the landscape, *Cactoblastis* had literally become the savior of a large portion of rural Australia. Did something in the prickly-pear biological control program go wrong? To some people, the short answer is a definitive "yes."

But to learn about the events that led to that conclusion, we'll need to backtrack for a new examination of the Commonwealth Prickly Pear Board and Sherwood Laboratory's surviving records from the 1930s, 40s, and 50s.

We will also look at later information published outside of Australia by researchers around the globe to bring us up-to-date, and the reason for our little group's presence in this Argentinean prickly-pear plantation, counting little *Cactoblastis* moth eggsticks.

THE CACTOBLASTIS "INTERNATIONAL TRAVEL CLUB"

News of Australia's great success at controlling its crippling prickly-pear plague during the Great Cactus War spread fast. As early as 1928, when victory actually seemed attainable, the Commonwealth Prickly Pear Board (CPPB) began to be besieged for information from other countries where prickly-pear had also become a weedy pest. When it finally became clear that *Cactoblastis* had indeed turned the tide on the advancing pear menace, Australian scientists were ready and willing to share their "wonder grub" with the world - and requests came pouring in.

India was one of the first countries to get in line. "Inquiries show that details of the method of pear eradication being practiced in Queensland have been sought from [such] places as India, Ceylon (Sri Lanka), and parts of Canada and America, as well as from South Africa," reported Brisbane's *Daily Mail* on May 20th, 1929.

Two months later, the *Brisbane Courier* noted that the "Indian Government is considering a proposal by the Bombay Government to import the insect, *Cactoblastis cactorum*, from Australia for the destruction of prickly-pear."

Following the abandonment of India's failed cochineal industry in the early 1800s, at least two species of prickly-pear (*Opuntia dillenii* and *Opuntia elatior*) had become widespread pests that extensively damaged crops and forests, particularly in the southern part of the country.

"Official" records from the CPPB are scanty as to how the Board actually responded to the request from India. Yet it is very likely that the CPPB also included some *Cactoblastis* eggsticks along with the destructive cochineal, *Dactylopius opuntiae*, which <u>was</u> recorded as being "dispatched to India."

"As a result of this effort," wrote Alan Dodd in *The Biological Campaign Against Prickly-pear* in 1940, "Marked destruction of these two prickly-pears has taken place in Ceylon (where the insects were also sent) and in many districts in India." (Today, *Cactoblastis* is apparently absent in both of these countries.)

Suddenly, the race to acquire *Cactoblastis* was on. South Africa was next on the list. In 1927 and again in 1932, the South African government sent one of their best entomologists, Dr. F. W. Pettey, to Australia to study the CPPB's prickly-pear control work firsthand.

"He returned to South Africa taking with him 12,000 eggs of *Cactoblastis* the first time and 112,600 eggs the second time," wrote John Mann. The first batch of eggs actually ended up being destroyed due to an acrimonious "diversity of opinion" among farmers as to what its effects would be if the cactus moth were to become established in that country.

On the second go-around, Dr. Pettey had either gained a consensus or, more likely, his government employers simply overruled any opposition, and *Cactoblastis* was again brought to South Africa.

The initial target for *Cactoblastis* was our old friend, the Indian fig (*Opuntia ficus-indica*), which by then had become so widespread that it occupied more than 2.2 million acres (900,000 ha) in Cape Province alone. The opposition for eradication came from the thousands of farmers who grew this useful treelike cactus on small plantations or utilized wild-growing plants for food and stock fodder.

In spite of the objections from farmers, the South African government forged ahead with an intense *Cactoblastis* rearing program, releasing some 580 million eggsticks between 1933 and 1941. The results, however, were clearly not up to expectations. The host plants in South Africa were larger, woodier, and tougher than those in Australia, and *Cactoblastis* could do little more than exert a retarding effect on the spread of the cactus by reducing its fruiting ability.

Cactoblastis also encountered an unexpected predator in South Africa. Troops of free-ranging baboons, which normally feed on prickly-pear fruits in the summer, soon discovered that the moth's little caterpillar was a very tasty morsel. "[Baboons] now throng the infected areas, breaking open the leaves (pads) and eating the grubs," a syndicated column reported in newspapers around the globe. "As the baboons have also developed the habit of killing lambs, thus doing more damage than jackals, the farmers are organizing to exterminate them."

Eventually, the ever-practical South African farmers learned to control *Cactoblastis* invasions in their cultivated stands of Indian fig prickly-pear simply by physically inspecting the plants and removing the conspicuous eggsticks which had been deposited during the moth's two egg-laying seasons (February-March and in September-October).

In South Africa, *Cactoblastis* was also used with some success to control another old acquaintance, the "pest pear" (*Opuntia stricta*), which had invaded some of that country's more remote regions, such as Kruger National Park. However, similar attempts to establish *Cactoblastis* as a way of controlling prickly-pear in Kenya, Israel, and Pakistan ultimately ended in failure.

Also in 1932, in the South Pacific island nation of New Caledonia, the CPPB supplied the Noumea Chamber of Commerce with 10,000 *Cactoblastis* eggs. A year later, they received a further 25,000 eggs.

One early progress report (originally written in French) indicated that in "Noumea there are three generations annually [of *Cactoblastis*], as compared with the normal two" and that within "a year after its introduction, in the third generation, *C. cactorum* has become well established in one locality. At other points, establishment does not appear to have been so successful and a further attempt will have to be made." Eventually, after several repeated trials, *Cactoblastis* became so well founded across the island that prickly-pear was brought under complete control.

The Indian Ocean island nation of Mauritius received its *Cactoblastis* directly from South Africa's breeding stations in 1950, and then in 1950 or 1951, the Hawaiian Islands (which had not yet been granted statehood) received a gift of over 190,000 *Cactoblastis* eggs from Australia. (Apparently, these were hand-delivered by Alan Dodd, himself.)

Hawaii has had a long history with prickly-pear. Locally known as "panini" (supposedly meaning "fence wall"), the cactus was most likely brought to the islands sometime before 1809 by Don Francisco Paul de Marin, a resident of O'ahu who introduced fruit trees and many other cultivated plants to the Hawaiian Islands.

Originally intended to serve as living fences and cattle fodder, by 1910 several thousand acres of the Indian fig prickly-pear (*Opuntia ficus-indica*) were being grown in Hawaii. True to form, the cactus eventually escaped cultivation and became naturalized on five of the main islands. There are also two other species of introduced cactus present in the Hawaiian Islands: one is a prickly-pear (*Opuntia cordobensis*) and the other a spineless variety of cochineal cactus (*Nopalea cochenillifera*).

On the big island of Hawaii, the Indian fig spread at an alarming rate, covering the lowlands almost solidly in many areas. It also spread into the better pastures of the upper elevations. Maui and at least one of its neighboring islands also became nearly over-run with prickly-pear.

By 1930, the cactus was being openly called a "menace" by some of the ranchers, particularly W. W. Carter, the former manager of the huge Parker Ranch on the island of Hawaii. Hearing of Australia's great success in tackling its own prickly-pear problem, Carter turned to the local government to start a similar program. The scientists at Australia's CPPB could not be more accommodating.

However, many of the ranchers on smaller properties opposed the introduction of cactus-eating insects. They firmly believed that the cactus could be very useful as fodder during times of drought, so why eliminate it? It took years of vociferous debate to eventually over-come this bit of opposition.

In due time, by using a combination of cochineal insects and *Cactoblastis* moths, Hawaii's prickly-pear control program was finally launched. Within five years, the campaign was declared a success, with "substantial to complete control" of the pest cactus being reported in many localities.

By 1965, for instance, the 66,000 acre (26,700 hectare) cactus infestation on the Parker Ranch had been reduced to just 7,600 acres (3,075 hectares). In some regions on the island of Hawaii, such as from Kawaihae to the lower limit of Waimea, the invading prickly-pear had been simply eliminated.

To most biological-control practitioners working during this period, these developments were welcome news for their fledgling science. They were truly "on a roll" with the cactus-moth. So when a request for *Cactoblastis* to control native prickly-pear that had become superabundant due to overgrazing by goats was received from the Caribbean island of Nevis, no "red-flag" questions were even considered.

TO NEVIS WITH LOVE

Nevis is a roughly cone-shaped island, approximately seven miles (11.5 km) in diameter, that is capped by a potentially active volcano - known as Nevis Peak - which soars to 3,232 feet (985 meters) in height. The island is located in the Caribbean Sea due north of Venezuela and composes one of the arc of islands that form the Leeward Islands chain of the West Indies.

During the 17th and 18th centuries, much of Nevis's lowlands were deforested to clear the way for sugar plantations. Sugarcane fields once stretched from the coast up to the mid-slopes of Nevis Peak, where it became too steep to farm.

For nearly 300 years, intense cultivation by the sugar industry and later the cotton industry, greatly changed the island's ecosystems. Extreme land erosion had swept much of the topsoil away. What little pasture that remained was often heavily overgrazed.

A complex of native cacti, dominated by a prickly-pear known as the "Spanish lady cactus" (*Opuntia triacantha*), had found these barren lands perfect for colonization and were forming increasingly dense thickets that often excluded all other plants.

In late 1956, *Cactoblastis* was sent by British entomologists from South Africa to a rearing station located on the northern South American island of Trinidad. After six months of captive breeding, the first of several shipments was released on Nevis in 1957.

The overall effect soon became dramatically apparent. In short, *Cactoblastis* "gave very effective control of the indigenous cacti." The impact was so significant that one researcher noted that it "was difficult to find clumps more than one foot in height. . ."

Following the great success of Nevis's cactus-control program, in 1960 infested cactus pads containing *Cactoblastis* were sent from there to the surrounding islands of Montserrat and Antigua, where again it was apparently very effective. Ten years later, Grand Cayman Island also received a shipment of *Cactoblastis* from Nevis. A shipment was also made to Saint Helena Island in the South Atlantic Ocean in 1971, and two years later, the cactus moth was sent from Saint Helena to neighboring Ascension Island.

The first inkling that something might be going wrong and out-of-control with these very successful biocontrol projects occurred in 1963 when *Cactoblastis* was reported in the US Virgin Islands and in Puerto Rico: places where the cactus moth had not been officially sent.

Then a year later, it was found on Saint Kitts, a close island neighbor of Nevis. From these locations, the moth apparently "island hopped," with no known human assistance, to many other islands in the Caribbean basin, including the Bahamas, Hispaniola, the Dominican Republic, and Cuba, where it began attacking and destroying native *Opuntia* species.

In Cuba, one of its native prickly-pear species (*Opuntia stricta* variety *dillenii*) had become a serious weedy pest by the early 1970s. But concerned about what was happening on other Caribbean islands, the Cubans wisely decided not to import *Cactoblastis*.

Unfortunately, their decision made little difference; *Cactoblastis* made its own way onto the island. The first instance of the cactus moth being reported in Cuba was in 1974, when it was anecdotally disclosed that the moth had attacked some *dillenii* prickly-pear and was said to have given "good control of the infestations." (This state-ment begs the question as to whether or not it had been intentionally brought to the island.)

Two more unverifiable reports of *Cactoblastis* in Cuba surfaced: first in 1980 and again in 1988. Then in mid-December of 1992, Cuban botanist Alberto Areces collected *Cactoblastis* from a small colony of a rare cactus species, *Opuntia dilloni*, near Bibijagua Beach on Isla de la Juventud, off the southwestern coast of Cuba. This time, the find was officially verified. (Within a few days of Areces's discovery, all of the plants in that patch of *Opuntia* were

236

dead and their pads shriveled up.)

Over on the southeast end of the island, the cactus moth quickly became superabundant in the Guantanamo region, where it decimated thick stands of the weedy *dillenii* prickly-pear which had invaded some 76,600 acres (31,000 hectares) of overgrazed pasture-land.

Back in the autumn of 1961 - after the failed CIA sponsored "Bay of Pigs Invasion" - Fidel Castro had ordered his troops to plant an eight-mile-long (13 kilometer) barrier of prickly-pear cactus along the northeastern section of the fence surrounding the US Naval Base at Guantanamo Bay. This was done in an attempt to stop Cuban citizens from escaping and taking refuge on American-held ground.

The big cactus patch became widely known in the press as the "Cactus Curtain," an allusion to Europe's "Iron Curtain" and the "Bamboo Curtain" of East Asia. Apparently, *Cactoblastis* has also decimated whatever had remained of this famous cactus patch at Guantanamo Bay.

COMING TO THE UNITED STATES OF AMERICA

It is important to remember that *Cactoblastis* was originally restricted to a relatively small region in South America: portions of Argentina, Uruguay, and Paraguay. Although suitable prickly-pear host species were abundant in neighboring Chile, the high Andean mountain chain apparently prevented the cactus moth from extending its range to the west.

The primary reason that this particular cactus moth was so devastatingly effective, both in Australia and in the Caribbean basin, was that the cactus species in those places had never before been exposed to its predations. Most of the cacti simply had not evolved adequate defenses against the ravages of *Cactoblastis* caterpillars. At least not for the short term. . . as we shall see later.

In Texas, many ranchers still feel that they have a serious problem with prickly-pear invading their own, often overgrazed, range lands. Overgrazing by livestock often creates perfect conditions for rapid prickly-pear colonization.

Following Australia's success with *Cactoblastis*, the United States Department of Agriculture (USDA) was repeatedly petitioned by various stockmen and farmers to import the "cactus moth." The idea was formally considered in the 1960s but still no releases were made. This was primarily because of serious concern for the security of Mexico's commercial cactus industry and for the possible deleterious effect the moth could have on indigenous wildlife. (In their native ranges, some prickly-pear species function as "keystone species" - those species that create habitat or provide food for a large number of other plant and animal forms. If a "keystone species" is eliminated, then all in the ecosystem are threatened.)

The cactus destroyer arrived in the USA anyway. Although some confusion exists on this point, apparently the first authenticated record of *Cactoblastis* in the States was a single female adult moth collected in Florida by lepidopterist Terhune (Terry) Dickle, on Bahia Honda Key in October of 1989. A few months later, the moth was also found on Little Pine Key. Since those first two detections, *Cactoblastis* has continued to spread widely.

Fearing that a devastating *Cactoblastis* plague was about to descend on the native prickly-pear populations of the southern United States, which could threaten the ecology of the region concerned, entomologists from the USDA and various state agencies and universities soon mobilized. Initial assessments for potential damage ranged from moderate to complete annihilation of some of the native prickly-pear species.

One early report suggested that the moth was dispersing into new territory in the Southern United States at the alarming rate of nearly 160 miles (257 kilometers) per year. Later studies brought that prediction down to a more conservative pace of somewhere between 24 to 45 miles (38.6 to 72 kilometers) per annum.

In comparison, during a two and a half year recording period in Australia, *Cactoblastis*'s average annual rate of spread in dense prickly-pear was only about 10 to 15 miles (16 to 24 kilometers). In

South Africa, the unaided dispersal rate of the cactus moth over a similar duration of time was even slower, just 1.8 to 3.7 miles (3 to 6 kilometers). (Note that cactus-moth dispersals were actively encouraged in both of these two countries.)

But what exactly was happening in America, and would the researchers have adequate time to address the invasion? During 1991 and 1992, in response to the various dispersal predictions for *Cactoblastis*, inspectors from the Florida Division of Plant Industry (and other "bug" people) conducted extensive on-the-ground surveys all across Florida. They were able to document what they had been suspecting: the cactus moth was already present throughout the Florida Keys and the southern half of the state. So much for the slower dispersal rate.

The surveyors also found that all six species of the state's native prickly-pear were being attacked by *Cactoblastis*. At least two species, *Opuntis stricta* (this is the same one known as the "pest pear" in Australia) and *Opuntia humifusa*, were being literally "hammered out of existence." Because of their poor defenses to resist the cactus moth's invasion, these two cacti were rapidly disappearing from their native habitats.

Almost 90 species of prickly-pear cacti are found in the United States and Mexico. Nearly all of these species could be severely impacted, if *Cactoblastis* found its way to them. Some researchers worried that the potential for profound changes to the country's desert ecosystems was enormous and unpredictable.

Between the years 2000 and 2003, official concern over the spread of *Cactoblastis* jumped up another notch. The "front edge" of dispersing moths was found to have moved more than 290 miles (466 kilometers) during that time, indicating that the moth's dispersal rate had accelerated. If the spread continued at this speed, the cactus moth could be waltzing into the dense prickly-pear country of Texas within four or five years. This would probably make some Texas ranchers very happy. They would love to get rid of that pesky cactus that was overtaking their grazing land!

239

Against the backdrop of official environmental concern, interest for the possibility of using *Cactoblastis* to control unwanted prickly-pear on private lands continued to crop up again and again. In 2002, a delegation of Texas ranchers approached a Hawaii Department of Agriculture entomologist to inquire about the likelihood of obtaining the cactus moth from him. Even a Texas-based agricultural scientist, who apparently sympathized with the ranchers, began making inquiries about the possibilities of moving the cactus moth from Florida to Texas. To date, none of those people appear to have been successful in obtaining *Cactoblastis* as a "take-home" for installation in their own back paddock.

However, based on the genetic analyses of a number of *Cactoblastis* populations, it appears that this moth had already been introduced into the United States at least two or three times, perhaps more. Whether this movement was by human agency, or not, is unknown. The adult moths could have easily flown over from Cuba (carried on a storm front) or they might have simply been brought over in commercial shipments of cacti that were infected with them.

The USDA/APHIS Plant Protection and Quarantine inspection station in Miami, Florida, reported that during the 13-year period from 1981 through 1993, *Cactoblastis cactorum* was intercepted in 17 shipments of *Opuntia* cacti nursery-stock coming from the Dominican Republic and Haiti. (There is an extensive horticultural trade between Caribbean suppliers and US buyers.) Since only about 2% of each consignment is ever examined by inspectors, the invading moth larvae could have easily escaped detection in many of those shipments.

In June, 2000, a consignment of cactus plants at a Wal-Mart store located near Pensacola, Florida, was found to be infected with *Cactoblastis*. The store's location was some 125 miles (200 kilometers) west of the current leading edge of the cactus moth's expanding range. Also in that year, baggage containing *Cactoblastis* infested plants was intercepted at the Dallas International Airport in Texas.

240

In spite of these successful interdictions, the moth continued its unrelenting spread. By 2009, *Cactoblastis* had already chewed its way through Florida and up the eastern seaboard to mid-South Carolina. It had also eaten a path along the Gulf Coast through Alabama, Mississippi, and part of Louisiana. In the moth's wake was left a great deal of dead and rotting prickly-pear.

One of those prickly-pears may very well be the most endangered native plant species in America. Already rare before *Cactoblastis* arrived, at one point the world's entire known population of semaphore cactus (*Opuntia corallicola*, also known as *Consolea corallicola*) was reduced to just 12 mature individuals located on one small island in the Florida Keys. The "arms" of this treelike plant are reminiscent of a railway semaphore signal. (See Plate 28)

Fortunately, new plants can be easily propagated from cuttings or fallen pads in a nursery facility and an outplanting program that has attempted to reestablish them in habitats similar to their original is showing some success. In the meantime, an additional small natural population of semaphore cactus has been discovered on another one of the lesser Florida Keys. Even so, the semaphore cactus is still considered to be critically endangered and facing possible extinction.

"SIT, NOW STAY!" - A BIOCONTROL APPROACH

When I first met Jim Carpenter and Stephen Hight, they were driving out to a test plot of prickly-pear to see if their sticky-traps had caught any male *Cactoblastis* moths. They were in the process of testing a synthesized pheromone of the female cactus moth. Any males caught in the traps could be evidence that they had gotten the chemical formula just right.

Banners of scent waft away from the moth when she releases a special compound. Embedded in those banners are chemical messengers (pheromones) that tell their male recipients to "come hither." It is a very powerful perfume, even when spread into the air in ratios of parts per trillion. Perhaps it could be used lure the male moths to their doom? "Only trial and error will let us know," Carpenter assures me, "and that takes time."

At the moment, however, time seems in short supply. Carpenter and Hight are quick yet thorough in their assessment of the nearly one acre pheromone test site and are soon ready to move on. But luckily for me, they are willing to pause their quick pace to amicably answer some of my questions about the nature of their work.

Even as we speak, another one of Carpenter and Hight's cactoblastis control projects is already in full swing. This is their SIT (sterile insect technique) program. The goal of this policy is to make the advancing front of the *Cactoblastis* invasion "stay" where it is rather than continuing to expand out-of-control.

Hundreds of thousands of adult *Cactoblastis* moths are raised in captivity and then sterilized by subjecting them to a pulse of intense radiation. The moths are then chilled to slow down their metabolism and movement, dusted with fluorescent dye, and shipped out in this refrigerated condition to the release sites, where they are warmed up and soon fly away.

Since *Cactoblastis* moths must mate within a day or two after emergence from the cocoon, the big hope is that there will be many more matings with a partner who is sterile than with those that are fertile. In this species, the female won't lay her eggs if they are infertile.

So, continuing to raise and sterilize cactus moths and filling the air with them at the right time and place, should see the *Cactoblastis* population decline, if not actually plummet. This technique of using sterile insects to interrupt the reproductive cycle has worked well in controlling other nuisance species, such as the codling moth and certain parasitic cattle flies. At the moment, it also appears to be effective with *Cactoblastis*.

In 2009, the *Cactoblastis* moth made a move that was symbolically, if not historically important to American cactus-moth researchers. It had flown across the Mississippi River and seemed poised to invade the nation's western states. Colonies of the cactus-eaters were already being discovered in southern Louisiana.

A detection network consisting of some 76 sentinel sites was set up across the country and was being monitored regularly in order to provide early warning should the vanguard of the cactus moth's invasion arrive at one of its locations. Carpenter and Hight's SIT program also uses this network to help determine where the next releases of sterile cactus moths should take place.

The most critical element of the SIT program - actually breeding and raising the *Cactoblastis* moths - is accomplished at a climate-controlled mass-rearing facility, operated by Florida's Department of Primary Industry in Gainesville. "Right now we can raise about 50,000 cactus moths a week," administrator George Schneider says while showing me the high-tech rearing process from egg to adult. (See Plates 25 and 26)

Instead of cactus pads, the caterpillars are fed on blocks of artificial food made from beans - a sort of tofu - that have been covered with beeswax to mimic the cactus plant's cuticle. It's a good imitation, too. The larvae enter the "tofu" chambers and eat out their interiors just as if they were real prickly-pear plants. As soon as the adult moths emerge from their cocoons, they are readied for shipment out to the "Western Front."

In the field, the battle to hold the *Cactoblastis* line in Louisiana was being directed by Joe Bravada, officer in charge of the USDA Plant Protection and Quarantine center in New Orleans. (See Plate 24) *Cactoblastis* is not his primary duty, as his agency must also monitor and document the huge shipments of export grain moving through the port. But stopping *Cactoblastis* is important to Bravada and his crew.

I joined up with them one morning in September 2011 as they headed out by motorboat into the bayous of Madison Bay for their biweekly patrol. Later that afternoon, I watched as thousands of sterile moths woke from their cold torpor and flew into nearby cactus patches at the various release sites.

243

Along the route, we periodically stopped to check pheromone-baited monitoring traps for the presence of "wild" *Cactoblastis* moths. At one site, using propane-fired weed burners that roared like jet engines, Bravada's crew scorched a *Cactoblastis* infected patch of prickly-pear to the ground. Most likely, the cactus would eventually recover by sending new growth up from the roots, hopefully *after* the cactus moths have long gone. (See Plate 27)

At this time, the USDA's effort appears to have halted *Cactoblastis*'s westward advance. But since prickly-pear cactus is not an important agricultural crop in the USA, annual funding for this program has become yet another victim of ongoing federal budget cuts. The *Cactoblastis* regional management program has subsequently been canceled.

Our neighbors to the South in Mexico are clearly worried about this. Prickly-pear (called *nopal* in Spanish) is a major agricultural crop here, as well as a national icon that is even featured on the country's flag. Currently, as many as 210,000 farmers tend over 204,000 acres devoted to raising *nopalitos* (edible cactus pads that taste a bit like green beans) and *tunas* (the sweet pear-shaped cactus fruits). Nearly 1.25 million tons of these products are consumed in Mexico each year. The national average consumption of cactus fruit alone is more than 8 pounds (3.7 kg) per person annually.

According to the most recent estimates that I have received from representatives of the Mexican government and online news sources, their commercial *nopal* harvest is estimated to average about 800,000 tons annually. Mexico's cactus industry is now worth more than US $175 million annually and growing. In addition, the export volume of their cactus commodities has also increased rapidly and now exceeds US $80 million in value every year.

Mexico's concern about *Cactoblastis* invading its *nopal* farms is so great that in a curious reversal of foreign aid policy, the Mexican government had been providing the USDA's cactus moth program with $5 million pesos (about $275,000.00 US) in matching funds. But with the termination of the USDA's *Cactoblastis* abatement program, the Mexican funding has also been withdrawn.

Cactoblastis has already made its way into Mexico twice. Back in 2005-2006, for instance, it was discovered on two islands near Cancun. By aggressively removing infected plants and "flooding" the islands with sterile insects, a joint USA/Mexico response team was able to eradicate it completely. However, the next time the cactus moth shows up in Mexico, it is likely that there may not be sufficient funds or expertise available to tackle an infestation with such thorough determination.

So, what about finding a self-sustaining biological solution to the problem? Why not enlist the aid of the insect enemies of *Cactoblastis*? Something like that tiny wasp, *Apanteles*, which parasitizes the cactus moth? To answer these and several other urgent questions, Carpenter and Hight traveled back to *Cactoblastis*'s homeland in Argentina.

THE ARGENTINEAN CONNECTION

In addition to the SIT program, for the last few years Carpenter and Hight have also been working to perfect other methods that might disrupt *Cactoblastis* matings. This is not their first trip to Argentina. They have been here several times before.

One of their ideas for an effective disruption technique uses pheromone-soaked yellow-colored wire-like plastic tags to flood the cactus plantations with enough scent to disorientate the male moths so that they will be unable to find a female to mate with.

The perfect place to test this idea is in the cultivated prickly-pear plantations in regions where the cactus moth naturally occurs. If damage to the cactus plants by *Cactoblastis* can be reduced or even stopped, the technique might also work in the *nopal* plantations of Mexico or even on wild prickly-pear in the United States. This new approach is rather expensive, however, and involves a lot a time and labor. Yet, it's certainly worth a try.

"It took two days of hard work to hand-place over 18,000 pheromone dispensers on just that one big plantation near Santiago de Estero," Hight tells me. Most of Carpenter and Hight's joint research effort is focused on two large *ficus-indica* plantations and half a dozen smaller cactus orchards. "While we're here in Argentina, we will be constantly traveling back and forth between these mating disruption sites."

As we drive along some very bumpy roads on our way to the next prickly-pear plantation, Dr. Jim Carpenter, who grew up in Alabama, talks with facile eloquence about the ongoing work with *Cactoblastis*. His words are punctuated with the "twang" of his southern accent.

Following his first four years of college, Jim had taken a laboratory technician's job with the USDA's Agriculture Research Service (ARS) in Tifton, Georgia. After about a year there, he found the work so fascinating that he took a leave of absence without pay and went back to school to complete his Masters Degree. When he returned to work at the lab, he was soon promoted to the position of research entomologist and later completed a work/study program to earn his Ph.D.

Dr. Stephen Hight is also an ARS research entomologist, but is stationed in Tallahassee, Florida. With his long flowing beard and broad-brimmed hat, he looks a lot like Gandalf, the fictional wizard in J. R. R. Tolkien's *The Lord of the Rings*. His scientific interest centers around the biological control of weeds.

To learn more about this work and to take my mind off the uncomfortable jolting of the vehicle that we are riding in, I begin a debate by reciting some of the most spectacular failures of the science of "biological control" with him. Stuff like the sugar industry's introduction of South American cane toads into Australia and Asian mongooses in Hawaii, both of which failed to do their predicted jobs and have since become serious pests in their own right. Stephen is unabashed and responds good-naturedly by making a case in favor of his science.

As usual, Stephen is at the wheel of our borrowed Peugeot "Boxer" van. He likes to do the driving and talks over his shoulder to me, while waving a hand now and then to illustrate a point. He is a fast yet safe driver, slowing down when approaching curves and for the occasional horse-cart plodding along. In most of Argentina, the rules of the road seem to dictate that the faster vehicles get the "right-of-way." On the highways, we pass slow-moving heavily loaded trucks as if they are tortoises.

Much like Carpenter, Stephen Hight also found work with the ARS fascinating. After growing up, receiving a basic education, and getting married in southeast Kansas, Hight then moved to North Carolina to get a degree in botany and soon began working for the USDA.

"I did a Masters project on honeybees and started working with a woman who did pollination work," Hight tells me. "The ARS has a really big research facility, so I was put with her and she was also doing biocontrol of weeds. When she left during a crisis, they gave me the responsibility and I liked it; the guy that I worked for was really encouraging. I worked there for 12 years before he finally convinced me to go back [to school] for a Ph.D. The people in biocontrol research are great! They're exceptional. Even though this *Cactoblastis* work is insect control, I still think of myself as a 'biological control of weeds' person."

"How did you two get together and begin collaborating?" I ask both of them.

"The way we got started . . . was that the Cactus and Succulent Society of America became really concerned about *Cactoblastis* and their president had called the USDA's Animal and Plant Health Inspection Service (APHIS) to voice their concern," Carpenter explains. "To follow up on the whole issue, APHIS organized a meeting . . . brought in people from all over, including South Africa and Mexico, just to explore how big the problem was . . . and things like 'What do we know?' and 'What did we need to know?'"

"Around that particular time," Carpenter continues, "Three

247

of us - Ken and Stephanie Bloem and myself - initiated the first research. Then Stephen joined us, and not too long after that, the Bloems moved on to other things. Stephen had a lot of enthusiasm for the work, so we continued our collaboration."

"I wanted to be involved as a proponent of biocontrol of weeds," Stephen Hight tells me almost defensively. "This is not 'biocontrol gone bad' as some people are starting to publish . . . *Cactoblastis* is simply a pest that was put into the Caribbean and got here on its own volition, either by a hurricane. . . or through the nursery trade, most likely. It's similar to how so many other pests get here."

"So I was interested in the insect from the angle of [acting as] a 'protector' of the good work of the biocontrol of weeds," Hight continues. "And, as it has turned out - for most of my career in Tallahassee - *Cactoblastis* has been the main thing that I've worked on. . . it's just gotten bigger and bigger."

After arriving at the next cactus plantation, we go into a huddle before beginning work. "We're measuring the efficacy of mating disruption in two ways," Carpenter tells me. "One way is: 'Does it reduce the number of males that go into a trap?' Loaded with an artificial pheromone, the trap essentially represents a female that is sitting and calling."

"So that's one method we use to see whether or not mating disruption works," Carpenter continues. "But we're also looking at whether or not there's a reduction in the number of eggsticks the female lays. We know that the female isn't going to lay any eggs if she hasn't mated."

At this, our little group spreads out to locate the first number-marked *ficus-indica* prickly-pear plant that they are monitoring. (See Plate 29) No eggsticks are found on Plant #1. We move on to Plant #2. Stephen finds two eggsticks; Carpenter locates one. The eggsticks are plucked from the plant and placed in plastic cups and we move on to plants "Three," "Four," and "Five."

"A total of three eggsticks on four plants. Number Five is zero," Hight announces. We move on to Plant #6, then #7, and soon begin searching for plant number eight located somewhere within the dense grove.

At cactus plant #9, George Fox finds the first eggstick. "One!" Carpenter: "Two!" After a pause "Three!" "It's so hard to find them," Hight observes. "It's pretty amazing. They can be right in front of your face and don't see it until someone else comes up and points it out to you." "Five!" "Six!" "Seven!"

"Place your bets, place your bets." I joke. "Seven on Nine, Seven on Nine."

"I think there's another one in there," George declares.

"You feel it?" asks Hight.

"Yes!" George affirms.

"Every gambler says that," I mockingly rebuke.

"There it is!" Hight announces. "Eight!" Smiling, I wear a false "shameface."

In all, we found over 100 eggsticks that day.

A TRIP TO FUEDEI

The first time I visited FuEDEI, I had traveled there by rail from Buenos Aries shortly after my arrival in Argentina in March of 2015. I was waiting for word from Jim Carpenter and Stephen Hight, who were out in the field somewhere in the northern part of the country. I had some time on my hands before I joined up with them and had been assured that my little sojourn would be a worthwhile diversion.

The 45-minute train ride itself was highly entertaining. A magician put on a show in the alcove near the door. Hawkers patrolled up and down the aisles, talking loudly and placing packages of wrapped candy or plastic combs on people's laps or the empty seats beside them. I quickly learned, however, that if I dared to open one of these little parcels, that was the signal that I had just purchased it.

249

Then when someone called out in English, "Watch your bags!,"
I quickly turned to stare down a man who had been hovering over
mine. With a gratuitous smile, he backed away and soon left the
carriage. I leaned my elbow on my day pack and camera bag for the
rest of the trip.

At my designated station-stop in the suburb of Hurlingham,
I was met by a handsome young woman riding a bicycle with her
toddler in the child-seat behind her. Her name was Laura Varone. She
is part of the staff at the Fundación Para el Estudio de Especies
Invasivas (Foundation for the Study of Invasive Species) or "FuEDEI"
for short.

We talked as we slowly walked, both the bike and the toddler,
back to the laboratory. Laura's young son, however, still wanted to
ride on the bicycle and was vociferously reluctant to stroll.

"Our lab used to be called the "South American Biological
Control Laboratory," Varone informed me over the squalling. "Back
then, it was actually part of the USDA." This research station was
established in 1962, originally to study the natural enemies of aquatic
weeds. Later it began to focus on pest insects. The USDA-ARS has
also founded several other overseas biological control laboratories.

Actually, the very first one was started in 1919 just outside
of Paris, France. Currently, it maintains facilities in Beijing (China),
Montpellier (France), and Queensland (Australia). Varone has been
working at the Argentinean laboratory for more than 14 years.

"Our funding used to come through the American embassy
at Buenos Aries," Varone explained. "We exported insects to control
pests that were a problem in the USA . . . after we had done all the
research. But at one point we started having regulatory problems
with the Argentinean government, and they stopped giving us export
permits for insects. So, they obliged us to reorganize as a private
foundation. We still do the same research, and we still get funds
from ARS, but now it comes directly to our lab. We don't receive any
funding from our own government."

After passing through a security gate located on a quiet side street, we enter a group of low white buildings with metal bars placed across the windows. Inside, I am introduced to Dr. Guillermo Logarzo, who was a student when he started working here over 20 years ago. He motions for us to sit down and we immediately begin discussing all things *Cactoblastis*.

"I conducted *Cactoblastis* life-table studies on *ficus-indica* here, and I compared them with life-tables made in South Africa," Logarzo tells me at one point in the conversation. "The main difference in mortality is in ant attacks. The ants in South Africa kill 70% of the larvae. Here in Argentina, only five-percent."

A life table study provides a snapshot of the age-specific mortality rates for any given population. Also known as a "mortality table," it is often used to estimate the probability that a person of your age will die before his or her next birthday. Insurance companies rely heavily on these tables to set their premiums. Perhaps this difference in ant-caused mortality was the primary reason why it took *Cactoblastis* so long to get established in South Africa?

THAT LITTLE WASP!

A week later, in the middle of a grove of tree-sized *ficus-indica* prickly-pear plants located somewhere near Santiago del Estero, the four of us - Jim Carpenter, Stephen Hight, George Fox, and myself - are clustered around and staring at a cactus pad that has recently become infested with *Cactoblastis*.

By working as a cooperative team, the small newly-hatched caterpillars have managed to chew through the plant's tough cuticle, and now the group of larvae is occupying a small hollowed-out chamber located just beneath the skin's surface.

Frisking around near the caterpillars' little shelter-cave is a minute dark-colored female wasp, called *Apanteles opuntiarum*. Just recently described by scientists, this tiny insect measures only around one eighth of an inch in length (3-3.5 mm). As she moves over the surface of the prickly-pear pad, she rapidly taps the cuticle with both of her antennae in her search for suitable caterpillar hosts into which she will deposit her eggs.

Collectively, we hold our breath when she suddenly inserts her elongated ovipositor through the cuticle "window" located above the caterpillars' chamber. One caterpillar comes to the entrance hole and sticks its head out momentarily. The wasp is there in an instant, but the caterpillar has already withdrawn inside. Again the ovipositor is jabbed through the plant's cuticle and quickly withdrawn.

The caterpillar that came out to have a look will now probably be doomed when the eggs that have just been injected into its body by the wasp begin to hatch. As they grow, the wasp's larvae will slowly eat the caterpillar's viscera until it succumbs.

For a minute or two, no one speaks as we watch the drama unfolding on this little stage. Another female *Apanteles* soon arrives, and conflict flares when the two wasps eventually meet. Finally, the wasp interloper flies away, presumably to find her own batch of just-hatched *Cactoblastis* caterpillars.

We continue to stare at the spot until Carpenter suddenly announces, "I've got to get some photos!" Then the spell is broken, and we all begin speaking at once.

"When she does that little injection, it's very quick. . . Brrrrt! . . . like a machine-gun," George says.

"Yes, like a machine-gun," Hight agrees.

"How many eggs does she put into each caterpillar?" I ask.

Carpenter, focusing his camera on an *Apanteles* wasp that is still exploring the prickly-pear pad, answers with a tentative, "I'm willing to say 10 to 25."

"We've counted over 50, but our average is closer to the 20 mark," George amends.

Dr. George Fox has suddenly become much more animated than usual. This little species of wasp is what he has traveled so far to see in the wild. And at last, here it is.

"*Apanteles* is our best candidate to date for possible biological control of *Cactoblastis*," Carpenter tells me.

Back in the USA, Dr. Fox has been tackling the job of raising these parasitoid insects in quarantined captivity. Under artificial conditions in his laboratory, he has been able to successfully breed many generations of these tiny wasps. But for some unknown reason, each successive generation contains increasing numbers of males, until finally they are all male and the colony dies out.

Dr. Fox will be taking his field observations and some of these "wild" wasps back with him to start a new and, hopefully, successful breeding colony. He will also try to determine what other insects, if any, these little wasps parasitize. It might take months or even a couple of years of exposing them to perhaps hundreds of other species before he can be certain that *Cactoblastis* is truly this wasp's only host.

If *Apanteles* were released into a new environment and was not truly host-specific, then it could attack other species of insects that are part of the established biological community. This, in turn, could lead to unpredicted and potentially serious ecological changes in the region.

During the next few days, we eventually manage to fill several small plastic containers with bits of cactus covered in dead *Cactoblastis* caterpillars. Surrounding each caterpillar's corpse are one to two dozen *Apanteles* pupae. We also had collected several hundred *Cactoblastis* eggsticks and, for good measure, a few prickly-pear pads with the living caterpillars inside them. Alan Dodd might have been proud of us. But now it was time to go.

The return trip to FuEDEI was a two-day-long blur of fast driving, whizzing landscapes, and not-so-fast food. But lovely Laura Varone was there to greet us when we drove up to the gate in the van, which Carpenter and Hight were returning. It had been borrowed from here more than a month earlier.

A Christmas-like excitement permeated the air as boxes of specimens were unloaded and carried into the lab for examination. Other staff members dropped what they were doing and came to see what we had brought in.

Someone boiled water for a pot of yerba maté, the strong Argentinean tea, and a wooden mug fitted with a curved silver straw was soon topped up and passed around from person to person. It was the first time I'd ever drunk yerba maté and true to its reputation, it was potent. In my memory, most of that afternoon also seems to be a warm yet fuzzy blur.

At one point, however, I vividly recall Laura Varone exclaiming as she peered into one of the plastic *Apanteles* specimen boxes, "Ah, there they are. It looks like. . . it looks like. . . Oh!. . . (pause) They're flies!"

"What!!" We all cry in unison.

"Those are flies!" Varone insists.

"Flies?" asks Hight, incredulously.

"What do the *Apanteles* look like?" Carpenter demands light-heartedly.

Varone (laughing): "Like a wasp!"

"Are you sure? Aren't there wasps in there? I thought for sure. . .," mumbles Hight.

"George said there were wasps in there . . . I didn't even look at them," replies Carpenter.

"It's George's fault?" Hight asks.

"I never looked at them!" Carpenter answers in mock defense.

Hight: "Right!" (more laughter) "Some kind of fruit fly?"

"Yeah, they do look like some of these are fruit flies," George answers.

Carpenter: "Open it up and let's get the real thing about it. We wondered why they came out of the pupae stage so quickly."

"Yeah. . . they are all flies, I'm sorry," Varone apologizes.

Hight: "No. . . Thank you!" (more laughter).

Luckily, the very next specimen box brought out for examination contained plenty of *Apanteles*. So in the end, it appears that Dr. George Fox did not have to go home empty-handed.

Two days later, as my own return airline flight climbed away

254

from Buenos Aires and leveled out high over the sprawling Argentinean Pampas, it seemed I could still taste the yerba maté tea and hear the echo of scientific mirth during that afternoon at FuEDEI.

****

Several months before my trip to Argentina, I had received an e-mail from Jim Carpenter briefing me on the results of their previous year's mating-disruption trials.

"Our program has evolved from a 'stop-the-spread and/or eradication program' to the development of sustainable management options that minimize the long-term impacts of the moth on native desert ecosystems and commercial cactus production areas in the USA and Mexico," he wrote. "In El Virque, we saw a significant reduction in eggstick production - from control to treated areas - by over 90%. In Porton Blanco, male capture was significantly reduced by more than 90% and eggstick production was reduced by more than 99%." Put in simple terms, fewer eggsticks means that fewer *Cactoblastis* moths will bother your cactus plantations.

This may prove to be a premature judgment, yet to me it appears very likely that Carpenter and Hight's continuing Argentinean experiments will eventually result in a biological control success story of one sort or another, even if there is no eventual funding available to implement it on a wider scale. Perhaps our little wasp, *Apanteles*, will tip the scales in its favor as an effective agent of biological control.

In practice, biological control takes advantage of a target organism's weaknesses. Very seldom, however, will a control agent completely eradicate the target organism. *Apanteles* has not wiped out *Cactoblastis* in its native habitat.

In part, this is because the two species have co-evolved together and *Cactoblastis* has developed defense mechanisms that allow it to maintain a more or less stable population. *Apanteles*, too, has its own diseases and enemies that keep its population under control. Under these constraints, *Apanteles* is also evolving new behaviors and mechanisms for its own continued survival.

If released into a new locality without its normal load of parasites, pathogens, and predators, it is quite possible that this parasitic wasp could breed up into huge numbers that greatly exceed those in its home range and bring about a significant reduction in the USA *Cactoblastis* population. That is, if *Apanteles* does not move on to alternative host species. Then we may be in even greater ecological trouble.

THE BIOLOGICAL CONTROL DEBATE

Although biological control has long been touted as an environmentally friendly alternative to chemical pesticides, the practice carries some inherently serious risks. Despite a 1987 National Academy of Sciences report that strongly argued that biological control should become the primary method for pest control in the USA, many conservationists are clearly worried that a few of these non-indigenous pest-control species might disrupt sensitive ecosystems or cause the extinction of some native species.

"Biological control practitioners have rebutted these warnings, arguing that they rest on unproven cases and hyperbole; that biological control need not be risky, and that current procedures minimize the already low likelihood of unforeseen disasters," wrote Daniel Simberloff and Peter Stiling in an article published in the journal, *Biological Conservation*. In fact, "many workers in the field see themselves as conservationists," the authors added.

Biological control agents are usually self-sustaining once they have been introduced into the environment of the target pest. Unlike pesticides, they normally do not need to be continually reapplied, and there is no toxic residue that can affect other non-target plants and animals. In many cases, little or nothing more needs to be done.

After release, these biological control agents can spread on their own to penetrate locations, such as creek beds, cliff faces, and rocky bush lands, that are normally inaccessible to most other forms of pest control. Ideally, ongoing costs will become minimal or non-existent after such a control program is fully operational.

So what kinds of unforeseen problems can the introduction of a biological control agent create? I've already mentioned the releasing of the cane toad into Australia in 1939 and the Asian mongoose into Hawaii in 1883. Those two exotic animals continue to be problem pests to be sure, but are there any more recent issues that have resulted from biological control efforts?

Actually, there are several interesting cases that quickly come to mind. Biological control of one species can sometimes have subtle, yet far-reaching effects on other so-called "innocent" species that share the same general environment. Consider the introduction of the *Myxoma* virus to control rabbits in Great Britain. The virus reduced rabbit numbers, all right, but it also led to the extinction of England's large blue butterfly, *Phengaris arion*.

It appears that the butterfly's predatory caterpillar needed to feed and develop in the underground nest of a certain species of ant, *Myrmica sabuleti*. These ants do not colonize overgrown areas and are only found in flower-strewn grassy meadows and other open habitats.

But in the wake of changing land-use patterns that has seen reduced grazing by livestock, browsing by rabbits had become the primary means by which these open places were maintained. When the rabbit populations were reduced by the introduced pathogen, plant regrowth surged, open land disappeared, ant numbers declined, the caterpillars could not complete their development, and so the butterfly vanished. (Fortunately, this butterfly species is also found in continental Europe and has since been successfully reintroduced to a dozen or so sites located in southwestern England.)

In a less dramatic example, a European weevil (*Rhinocyllus conicus*) introduced into North America by Canadian authorities in 1968 for control of musk thistle and other non-native thistles is now damaging native thistle populations located as far away as Nebraska and California. The scientists responsible for this bio-control effort justified the weevil's release on the basis that several tests indicated that it had a strong preference for non-native thistles.

Even though the researchers knew very well that the weevil could also complete its life cycle on native thistles, they successfully argued that the insect would have no significant impact on the native plants because of this tested preference for non-natives. Time and experience have since proven them wrong. This is a good example of why biological control practitioners must adhere to the highest standards of evidence, not faith, before releasing a novel organism into the environment.

To combat a wide variety of insect pests, over 1,000 species of biological control agents have already been introduced into new environments worldwide. Also, during the past 100 years or so, more than 350 kinds of living organisms have been released in a bid to control some 135 weed species. These last efforts are said to have resulted in the successful control of around 40 species of those weeds, and another 40 species have been reduced to some degree.

These numbers might sound impressive against the backdrop of a few failures. . . "But it is often difficult to explain the success or failure of a biological control agent, and even more hazardous to attempt to predict them beforehand," warns Australian weed bio-control specialist, Dr. Rachel McFadyen. (Given its history with the prickly-pear crisis, it is interesting that Australia is the first nation in the world to legislate specific laws aimed at regulating biological control.)

Another potential problem with biological control agents is the simple fact that they are living organisms. . . which means that they, themselves, are still evolving and increasing their resilience. Some of them, like the Australian gall wasp (*Trichilogaster acaciaelongifoliae*) have recently expanded their range of host species. Other biological control agents have increased their tolerance for chemical pesticides in their environment.

Also, a pathogen like a virus or a fungus can change its

virulence quite suddenly, and with dramatic effect. The Japanese fungus *Entomophaga maimaiga*, for example, was originally introduced into Massachusetts in 1910 to control gypsy moths. It was not seen again until 1989, when it reappeared in a much more aggressive form that caused a massive die-off in gypsy moth populations all across the northeastern United States. To most people concerned with gypsy moth control, this was seen as a good change. Yet it could have played out otherwise, especially if this pathogen had jumped to a different host while it appeared to be absent.

Although most biological control programs have actually been relatively problem-free, there is a lot of room for error - and evolutionary change - when dealing with living organisms. Even "simple" life forms, when looked at closely, are not that simple. Advances in technique, however, such as undertaking pre-release studies in the country of origin, improving non-target testing, long-term post-release monitoring, and the use of modern genetical analysis to determine genetic variability in introduced populations can greatly help in a biological control program's success rate.

In their native environments, plants and their various parasites co-evolve, so that a kind of balance between the "eater" and "eatee" is struck and both are able to survive in sufficient numbers to sustain the species involved. As with the prickly-pear of Australia, plants without their burden of parasites often become "weeds" when they are introduced to new areas because there are less factors to limit their growth and reproduction. In this way, they frequently have a competitive advantage over other plant species in their environment.

Once established, some of these new arrivals can become agricultural weeds that compete with farm crops for water, nutrients, and light. Or, they may invade native vegetation and become environmental weeds that alter the composition of the original ecosystem. From the moment they "set foot" on a landscape, introduced plants and all other exotic life-forms become part of the dynamics of that region's ecology and evolution. In fact, very few places exist on our planet's surface that have not been modified by this process.

EVOLUTION FAVORS "RESISTANCE"

Although they are composed of mostly water (around 90%) which is stored primarily in their succulent pads, prickly-pear cacti are actually very durable plants. Their ability to survive drought, flood, wildfires, poison, being chopped into hundreds of pieces, and most herbivores, is legendary. They can regenerate from decapitated rootstocks, a fallen fruit or flower, a single pad that touches the ground, or even a small portion of that pad.

Their seeds can wait for decades for the right conditions before they germinate. In fact, there is even evidence that some of their seeds are programmed for delayed germination. Although most sprout as soon as environmental conditions are favorable, some seeds (perhaps even from the same parent plant) seem to be equipped with delayed "timers" and will wait - good conditions or not - for two, three, four, 10, 20. . . possibly 60 to 100 or more years before sprouting. As a group, prickly-pears seem to have all their reproductive bases covered.

Let's reconsider the state of Australia's prickly-pear population for a moment. *Cactoblastis* was purposely bred and released in plague proportions in an intense government-sponsored campaign in the late 1920s and early 1930s, yet it did not eliminate the pear. The moth controlled the rampant growth of the cactus, to be sure. But it did not completely remove prickly-pear from the landscape. It's still out there and relatively easy to see, yet in most parts of the country it is no longer considered to be a serious pest.

Moreover, a study conducted in 2007 by ARS researchers Robert Pemberton and Hong Liu on the tiny Caribbean island of Nevis (whose native prickly-pears were thought to be seriously at-risk at being decimated by *Cactoblastis*) revealed that the moth has not eradicated any of the island's cactus species at all.

260

These native cacti not only had survived more than 50 years of predation by *Cactoblastis*, in some locations they actually seemed to be thriving. "Our analysis of this historical biological control," the authors of the survey wrote in summary, "Suggests that the potential impact of *Cactoblastis cactorum* on native North American and Mexican *Opuntia* (prickly-pears) will be significant and variable, but not necessarily catastrophic."

For some regions of the southern USA that had been hard-hit by the *Cactoblastis* invasion, this last comment is now proving to be an understatement. During my most recent visit to several "post-Cactoblastis" zones in southern Mississippi and northwestern Florida, I found that the dead and dying adult prickly-pear cacti had been replaced by a myriad of healthy little cactus seedlings. In some locations, they almost seemed to be everywhere. Many were scattered throughout the tall grass or hidden under bushes and low trees. This regeneration of cactus was very impressive, and I have little doubt that some of these plants will survive long enough that they, too, will be able to reproduce themselves.

These examples of prickly-pear's continued survival in spite of *Cactoblastis* serve to remind me of one of evolution's most persistent conundrums: You have to continually "out-evolve" your enemy, or both of you might perish.

Chapter 10: The Song of the Prickly-pear

In some parts of the world I am known
As a noxious and pernicious weed,
But in other countries I am the friend
To turn to in times of great need.
I must protect my lovely blossoms and sweet fruit
That so many creatures cherish.
Without my armament of spines and prickles,
I most certainly could perish.

"The problem with prickly-pear is that it is such a bloody useful weed," an Australian agriculturist once told me over the telephone. "For instance, it can be used as fodder for stock, food for people, and medicine. . . the list is growing all the time. Since it seems to be here to stay, we really need to find a way of making it economically valuable."

When I heard this, I instinctively felt that this enlightened opinion was quite true, yet I also knew that it was not one which is shared by most of his colleagues around the country. A weed is simply something to be gotten rid of, or at least brought under control.

Even so, in the outback homes throughout the vast territory of prickly-pear besieged Australia during the early 20th century, many practical uses were found for this cactus. Its sticky juice, when added to whitewash paint, prevented flaking and peeling. Soap and glue were also made from the juice extracted from the pads.

Some varieties of pear produced spikes that became useful

263

substitutes for the old-time steel gramophone needle, producing a pleasing mellow tone when properly fitted. The dark red juice from overripe fruit was often used as ink for writing letters and for producing a heady home brew sometimes known as "Drover's Ruin."

"Did you eat the pear fruit?" I once asked Clarence Kerr, a retired farmer who grew up in the heart of prickly-pear country. "Oh yes! We ate prickly-pear jam and jelly. Every woman in the country made the stuff. . . and it was pretty good, too," Clarence responded enthusiastically. "Prickly-pear jam was part of our land rights."

The basic recipe that most folks used for making prickly-pear jelly in Clarence's neighborhood went something like this:

Ingredients: 4 dozen prickly-pear fruits.
Juice of 3 lemons.
3/4 cup sugar for each cup of prickly-pear juice.

Directions: Rub the fruit with a coarse canvas cloth to remove the prickles. Cut each pear into 2 to 3 pieces and place into a large kettle. Cover with water and boil for 1 hour. Strain well. Measure the resulting juice and add 3/4 cup of sugar for each cup of juice. Return to stove and boil until a cooled tablespoonful of juice will jell. Add lemon juice and boil for an extra 3 minutes while stirring. Bottle and seal. Burn the cloth that was used to rub off the prickles.

I've tried this recipe and it works. The resulting "jam" was a beautiful deep red and quite tasty. (However, I didn't strain the cooked fruit well enough to be able to call the mixture "jelly.")

****

Part of the bush-lore that was passed down in this region dictated that if you became lost in the "pear" wilderness, prickly-pear fruits would sustain you until you made your way out to civilization. During one well-publicized incident, this notion was put to the test. In late February of 1940, a Swedish watchmaker named Max Fries, disappeared into the bush for more than two weeks.

When finally located by a search party at Pinedale Station near Chinchilla, Queensland, he "had subsisted for 16 days on prickly-pear fruit [which] he had eaten both boiled and raw . . . In view of the privations that he had suffered, Fries was in good physical condition," a local newspaper reported.

POWER ALCOHOL

In 1856, a commercial distillery that produced ethanol as a potable spirit from prickly-pear fruit was established in Sicily. Average output of alcohol from the distillation process was said to range from 6 to 8 1/2 quarts (6 to 8 liters) for every kilogram (2.2 pounds) of fruit.

Unhappily for the island's many ardent consumers of this product, the local government's imposition of a very heavy excise tax crippled the enterprise, and it soon failed. Another early attempt at commercially manufacturing alcohol from prickly-pear - this time in Granada, Spain - met a similar taxed-to-death fate.

But the very idea for using prickly-pear for creating alcohol was eagerly noted by Australians T. H. Johnston and Henry Tryon when Sicily and Spain were visited during their worldwide fact-finding mission for the Queensland-sponsored "Prickly-Pear Traveling Commission."

Unfortunately for Johnston and Tryon, when their final report was published in November of 1914, the advent of World War I had diverted the government's attention away from the country's prickly-pear problem, and so their recommendations fell on deaf ears.

Five years after the end of the war, the idea for manufacturing alcohol from prickly-pear gained traction again. . . this time in South Africa. As reported in the Australian press, the South Africa Department of Commerce "has found that an excellent substitute for oil fuel can be made from prickly-pear juice mixed with other chemicals. It can be retailed for half the price of petrol (gasoline) and has an average of 22 1/2 miles per gallon (9.5 kms per liter) in a six-cylinder car. It starts easily in cold weather. Its manufacture is being kept a closely guarded secret."

265

The old method of producing commercial alcohol for fuel - a practice used in Sweden on a large scale at the time - had involved grinding up sawdust, wood shavings, and waste lumber into a pulp consisting of cellulose and water.

The cellulose is chemically changed to dextrose, which is then fermented into alcohol. But this new alcohol manufacturing method, discovered by a German chemist, consisted of a novel type of ferment that allowed the cellulose pulp to change directly into alcohol without any intermediate process. It was faster and required less energy in the production process. The news sparked a frenzy of motor spirit or "power alcohol" investigations across Australia.

"This is the psychological moment to start the production of motor alcohol in Australia, and in our prickly-pear jungles we have raw material resources almost as valuable as oil beds," the *World's News* reported in March 1924. "The demand for the product is absolutely assured. It is increasing every day and the world's supply of motor fuel is visibly shrinking."

Frank Cotton, a staunch advocate for power alcohol, enthusiastically wrote in his letter to the *Sydney Telegraph*, "Curiously enough, an analysis of the pear plant shows that, roughly speaking, it is composed of 20% cellulose matter and 80% water. This cellulose in the pear plant is in far better natural condition for pulp-producing purposes than the wood-waste which is used in Europe. On a very conservative estimate, an acre of average prickly-pear would produce 1,000 gallons (4,550 liters) of power alcohol."

By early 1926, power alcohol was starting to be manufactured on a small scale, mostly for practical demonstrations to politicians and the public. But the promise of 1,000 gallons (Imperial) of power alcohol per acre of prickly-pear proved to be wildly inaccurate. Only about 10 or 11 gallons of alcohol (45 to 50 liters) could be derived from an entire ton of pear, which meant that the productively of a typical acre of prickly-pear could be expected to be only about 110 gallons (500 liters), far less than previously estimated.

Even so, prickly-pear alcohol was still lauded as the power-source for Australia's motor vehicle future. Senator H. S. Foll, after witnessing a demonstration of an alcohol-powered car in Melbourne, stated that "in view of the price of petrol . . . and the increasing number of motor vehicles, it was urgent and imperative that every possible avenue whereby power-alcohol might be produced should be thoroughly investigated."

The idea of manufacturing unlimited amounts of power alcohol from prickly-pear to fuel Australia's increasing vehicle traffic came to a fever-pitch in April 1926, when a proposal of a reward of £5,000 (about US $307,000 today) to "the individual who first produces 100 gallons (450 liters) of power alcohol from prickly-pear on an economically sound and commercial basis," was announced in the *Brisbane Telegraph.*

Curiously, this generous offer to effectively "put up or shut up" proved to be the death knell for the whole power alcohol movement in Australia. It appears that no one was able to manufacture prickly-pear alcohol on anything even approaching a profitable basis. Eventually the whole idea of powering the nation's automobiles with cheap fuel derived from this weedy cactus quietly faded out of public concern.

"The South African venture offers little or no solution to Australia," one critic wrote. "The alcohol is apparently got from the fruit, which is hand-picked by native labor. There are hundreds of thousands of acres in Australia that men could not get into to pick the fruit [even if they wanted to]."

A WORTHY FRUIT FOR SO MANY SOULS

In Chapter 9, I mentioned that prickly-pear fruits and "leaves" (pads) were important food items in the culture and commerce of Mexico. Farmers in that country have been cultivating various types of these edible cacti, particularly the Indian fig (*Opuntia ficus-indica*), for thousands of years.

They typically appear in such dishes as *"huevos con nopales"* (eggs with cactus leaves) and *"carne con nopales"* (meat with cactus leaves). Several other Central and South American countries also include prickly-pears in their traditional cuisine.

"In Mexico, the *nopal,* or prickly-pear, is a key feature of our landscape, our diet and even our beliefs," wrote Alberto Ruy Sánchez Lacy in his essay about special plants in Mexican culture. "It is harvested, used for many purposes, and admired. It is a symbol and has even been considered a deity. It is an everyday thing, but it is naturally included among the unique manifestations which make up our country's culture."

When Hernan Cortés and his fellow conquistadors arrived in Central America in 1519 to destroy the Aztec Empire two years later for the "glory of Spain," they found the humble peasants' pear-shaped *nopal* fruits very much to their liking. But if you eat enough of these delicious "Indian figs," it can turn your urine a bright red color. This can be a big surprise if you are not expecting it.

At first, this aroused great fear among the conquering Spanish. Gonzalo Ferdandez de Oviedo, an administrator during the early days of occupation, graphically recalled that when his own urine turned blood-red after eating some Indian figs, he was quite stunned and petrified. He became convinced that he had either caught some unheard-of disease or that all the veins in his body had burst and the blood was flowing into his bladder.

But after this urine-coloring effect proved itself to be completely harmless, serving large quantities of prickly-pear fruits to newcomers from the homeland soon became a favorite prank for many of the more established residents of "New Spain."

Today, prickly-pears are grown for their fruits in over 30 countries. The Indian fig (*Opuntia ficus-indica*), one of a half-dozen or so long-domesticated prickly-pear species, is the most widespread and economically important of these cactus crops.

Besides Mexico, the primary centers for commercial cultivation are in Spain, Italy, Sicily, Brazil, Argentina, Bolivia,

Chile, Algeria, South Africa, and the United States, particularly in California. However, no country's production rivals that of Mexico. Mexican farmers are said to produce nearly a half-million tons of cactus fruits annually.

Cactus fruits, called *tunas* in Mexico, do not have the large spines like those sometimes found on the rest of the plant, but they often have tiny hair-like glochids that can be very irritating to the mouth and throat if they are not removed before the fruit is eaten.

One technique that some harvesters use to accomplish this is to spread the fruit on sandy soil and then vigorously sweep them back and forth with a handful of leafy branches. Another common method of removing the little spicules is to place a quantity of the fruit into a bucket and "twirl" them with a powerful jet of water coming from a garden hose fitted with a nozzle. Many others prefer to peel them before eating or simply slice them open and spoon out the often brightly-colored "meat."

Most of the commercially-produced *tunas* that I encounter in supermarket produce departments have already had their glochids mechanically removed before they were shipped to the store.

For the millions of people in Mexico and Central America for whom prickly-pear fruits are an important item in their diet, botanist Lyman Benson noted in his book, *The Cacti of the United States and Canada*, that:

> The tunas are considered a blessing, especially to the poor, who are dependent on them not only during the season when they are fresh and among the few foods available, but also later when the preserves (dried fruit) are a staple food. Individuals are reported to eat as many as 100 fresh fruits during a day. However, the flesh, like that of a watermelon, contains a large percentage of water along with the sugar and other nutritive materials. The numerous relatively large seeds are eaten with the flesh, and they seem not to be injurious.

To prepare cactus fruits for drying, the outermost layer of the epidermis must first be removed so that the fruit's moisture can

269

evaporate. Léon Giguet describes this process in his 1928 French classic, *Les cactacées utiles du Mexique*. The following is an English translation:

> This rather delicate operation, which consists of peeling the fruit with a knife in a single swift movement, is carried out very rapidly given the dexterity of those who are accustomed to performing it. Once their protective cover has been removed, the fruits are exposed to direct sunlight on racks made of bamboo or other long bush branches tied together with leather strips or pita thread. Desiccation takes about 15 days; one knows the procedure is complete when the fruit has exuded a thin ashy coating of sugary, mucilaginous matter. These dried tunas are then packed in woven baskets or small wooden boxes, where they can be kept as long as other dried fruits, such as figs, raisins, peaches and guavas.

Most cactus fruits around the world are eaten fresh, however. In 1884, British author Lewis Castle noted that in England "they are esteemed by some persons, but they are more usually employed as a curiosity in dishes of dessert . . . in recent years they have been so abundant that they occasionally appear in the street stalls and barrows (two-wheeled handcarts) in London at the popular price of two for a penny." Unfortunately, most Anglos today are completely ignorant about the value of prickly-pears and their tasty fruits.

In his essay, "In Praise of the Humble Excellence of Tunas," Mexico City writer, Eugenio del Hoyo, extolls the virtues of eating prickly-pear fruits. "Tunas can be eaten at any time of day, though there are certain preferred moments, like tea in England," he observes. "At home they are eaten at midmorning. . . However, great tuna banquets with appetizers and desserts are usually held at sundown, while comfortably seated at one of the large traditional stands, carefully choosing the fruit and heeding the order in which the different varieties must be eaten."

A chemical analysis of tunas from a very delectable Chilean prickly-pear cultivar that was being test-grown in the United States revealed that its fruits had a pH of 5.8 (acidic) and contained 12% sugar

(0.2% sucrose, 7.0% glucose, 4.8% fructose). Furthermore, a taste panel comprised of 10 people gave these particular fruits an average flavor rating of 7.6 on a scale of zero to nine.

The total caloric value of most prickly-pear tunas is on par with other fruits, such as pears, apricots, and oranges. So is their vitamin C content. However, they also contain enriched levels of certain mineral micro-nutrients such as calcium, phosphorus, magnesium, and selenium. Especially selenium.

Selenium is an essential micro-nutrient for all animals, including humans. The importance of selenium to human health cannot be overstated and is currently of global concern because many inhabitants of Europe, Australia, New Zealand, India, Bangladesh, and China receive insufficient amounts of selenium in their daily diet. This is largely due to inadequate concentrations of selenium in the soils and crops grown in those regions. In total, nearly 15% of the world's population now exhibits symptoms of selenium deficiency, leading to weakened immune systems, heart disease, and hypothyroidism.

Prickly-pear fruit has long been considered to be an excellent source of mineral nutrition and it also exhibits chemotherapeutic qualities that have been shown to boost human immune responses, help treat gastritis, arteriosclerosis, diabetes, prostate enlargement, and apparently even helps prevent several different types of cancer.

One experimental variety of spineless prickly-pear (*USDA No. 248*) appears to be exceptionally salt-soil tolerant. It also can accumulate higher than normal levels of selenium in a biologically available form, which may make this plant extremely valuable as a selenium-fortified source of food in the near future.

Recent investigations have indicated that the seeds contained in prickly-pear fruit are rich in iron, phosphorus and zinc, and that they also contain an edible oil that can be extracted, possibly on a commercial basis. Chemical analysis has shown that prickly-pear seed oil contains high levels of polyunsaturated fatty acids, similar to that of sunflower and grapeseed oil.

271

The discovery of this oil is not new. As early as 1914, chemists in Queensland, Australia, were examining prickly-pear seeds (which comprise from six to eleven percent of the fruit) for useful attributes. Samples of seed from various locales were found to contain as much as eight percent oil. However, because of the "low percentage [of oil] present, the seed can have no commercial value," the report flatly stated in its summary.

Nonetheless, someday an entrepreneur will seize the opportunity and begin extracting a healthful gourmet cooking oil from the tons of "wasted" seeds, like those currently left over from making prickly-pear fruit puree for the restaurant industry. Perhaps they have already begun.

COOKING UP CACTUS "LEAVES"

It is the very young prickly-pear pads (botanically known as cladodes) that are usually chosen for culinary purposes. In Mexico the pads are called *nopalitos* (literally "little nopals"), but in the United States and several other English-speaking countries, they are most often known as "cactus leaves" in the marketplace and kitchen. Outside of Mexico and Central America, you can often find fresh cactus leaves for sale in local supermarkets, or if you have prickly-pear growing wild nearby, you can harvest some yourself.

All common prickly-pear species are edible, but they are not always palatable because some of them have an extra heavy armament of thorns and prickles. Choose a variety that is more or less spineless, such as the Indian fig (*Opuntia ficus-indica*), the pest pear (*Opuntia stricta*), or the wheel cactus (*Opuntia robusta*).

Bringing along an experienced person or an illustrated field-guide to cacti with you could be very helpful, but not really necessary. I've eaten more than a dozen species of prickly-pear and most of them were quite good. A few were downright excellent. I simply avoid the nasty-looking heavily armored varieties.

Usually it's the smaller pads that grow high on the mother

plant in the springtime that are the best for eating. This new growth is often easy to spot, as it appears softer and darker green than the older pads growing beneath them.

Although the young pads often seem to be thornless, be careful of the little clumps of miniature spines, called glochids, that are sprinkled over the pad's surface. These tiny spinules can be very irritating if they get under your skin. Those little bumps (called aerioles) that contain the glochids will have to be sliced off the pad during preparation back in the kitchen.

Now, if you haven't been intimidated into skipping the whole idea of harvesting *nopalitos* on your own, you are ready to go. That is, once you remember to bring a good pair of heavy gloves, a strong set of cooking tongs or a long-handled fork, and a sack or box to put your goodies in. A cardboard shoe box is my favorite container for this job. You might also want to bring along some tweezers for sticker removal, just in case.

The best time of day to harvest a young prickly-pear pad is after they have been exposed to at least a couple of hours of direct sunshine. Because of these plants' special metabolism (CAM), this is when they will taste the sweetest.

To harvest a *nopalito*, simply grab it firmly with your tongs (or stab it with your fork) and rock it back and forth until the pad breaks off at the joint with the older pad. (Some people prefer to use a knife and slice it off at the joint.) Then drop your prize into the box. When you feel that you've gotten enough for a meal or two, head back to the kitchen for final preparation.

There are several ways of clearing away those little clumps of glochids and the occasional larger spine. I simply hold the *nopalito* down on a cutting board and remove the raised bumps containing the spinules with a sharp knife, slicing just beneath the surface of the skin. With practice you should be able to prepare a prickly-pear pad for safe handling within two minutes or less. Before I finish, I always trim the outer edge of the pad to lessen the chance of encountering any "hidden" glochids.

273

Two other methods of preparing *nopalitos* for eating include scraping the prickles off with a knife while holding the pad under running water and singeing the prickles over an open flame. These methods may work for some people, but I prefer the slicing technique. Whether they were purchased in a produce market or wild harvested, your cactus leaves are now ready for use.

Especially tender *nopalitos* can be cut up into bite-sized pieces and added raw to salads, where they will add a kind of lemony-flavored zesty crunch. Most often, though, they are sliced into green bean-sized strips and added to cooked dishes of many sorts. When fried with eggs, for example (my personal favorite, known in Spanish as *huevos con nopalitos*), the cactus imparts a light, slightly tart flavor and a hard-to-describe crisp yet mucilaginous texture.

Many people love this okra-like texture, including me. (But if you overcook this cactus, it loses its crispness and becomes quite slimy.) You can also boil it and then drizzle melted butter over it, with salt and cracked pepper, or fry it with diced onions. In more complex dishes, such as cactus creole (see below), the mucilaginous liquid is usually absorbed in the cooking.

The inspiration for the cactus creole recipe that follows originally appeared in a 1984 issue of the *Mother Earth News*. My "improved" version is similar, but with a few important additions:

CACTUS CREOLE
Ingredients: 2 cups of diced cactus leaves.
1 pound (450 grams) of minced kangaroo (cooked), or
1 pound ground beef (cooked and then drained).
6 ounces (170 grams) of tomato paste.
1/2 cup coarsely chopped onion.
1 diced jalapeño pepper (medium hot).
6 ounces (170 grams) of fresh shrimp (shelled).
6 ounces (170 grams) fresh fish fillets (cut into bite-sized pieces).
1 cup of water.

Directions: Mix all the ingredients together in a pan and cook over medium heat for about 15 to 20 minutes. Stir often to keep bottom of pan from scorching. Serve hot over a bed of brown rice or noodles or in a folded tortilla. Easily serves two to three people. For larger parties, simply double the recipe.

****

In Mexico, where the consumption of cactus is so deeply embedded in the culture, over 600,000 tons of fresh *nopalitos* are harvested annually nationwide. Some modern cactus farms use intensive management techniques that involve close plantings in irrigated and fertilized beds that are often covered with plastic. Productivity on these farms can exceed 250 tons per hectare (2.47 acres) per year. (Customarily, the young cactus pads are harvested when they are between three and four weeks of age.)

On poorer, rocky soils, the older indigenous system based on heavy doses of cattle manure and continuous year-round pruning is normally used. This cultivation method can produce annual yields of up to 60 tons of fresh *nopalitos* per hectare (2.47 acres). On these dry and depleted soils, this is a productivity level that is simply impossible to obtain with any other crop.

Part of this harvest is traditionally pickled in a sweet-sour vinegar for local use. Commercially pickled *nopalitos* that have been processed in a brine solution are now commonly available in the Mexican foods section of many North American supermarkets.

Bottled prickly-pear juice mixed with other fruit juices, such as guava, has also become an expanding international industry and a great deal of this product is now being exported into the United States. Not long ago, I purchased a chilled bottle of this lovely cactus juice elixir in a convenience store in a small country village located out in the wilds of central Oregon.

THE MEDICINAL CACTUS

The first herbal medical book that included a description of medicinal uses for prickly-pear was produced in the "New World" in 1552. Known as the Badianus Manuscript (after the translator), it was

275

originally written in the Aztec language by a Native physician and translated by another Aztec into Latin. The Spanish were very much impressed by the medical lore of the Natives and this singular book had been created as a present for the viceroy of New Spain (later to become known as Mexico).

Eventually the book was sent to Spain, where it was housed in the royal library until the 17th century, when it somehow came into the possession of King Philip IV's pharmacist. Later, the book showed up Italy to become part of the Vatican's library. In 1939, William Gates "rediscovered" the book and translated it into English. Then in 1990 during a pastoral visit, Pope John Paul II formally returned the original volume to Mexico, 438 years after it had been created. An English language version of this book was published in the year 2000.

Although prickly-pear juice was mixed with other herbs to enhance its effect, what had most impressed the Aztec doctors was its ability, when used as an emollient (soothing topical ointment), to reduce swelling in an inflamed part of the body. The anointed member was then rubbed down with a mixture of honey and egg yolk as a follow-up.

The succulent prickly-pear may have been a complete novelty to many 16th century Europeans, but it soon found widespread practical use aboard sailing ships as a preventative from scurvy. Containing significant amounts of vitamin C, edible cactus pads would stay fresh even during extended voyages. It is very likely that this custom also greatly contributed to the Indian fig's (*Opuntia ficus-indica*) increased naturalized range throughout the arid and semi-arid parts of our planet.

Folk medicine using prickly-pear includes a wide range of applications. In India, for instance, the baked fruit is used in the treatment of whooping cough. The mashed pads are used as a poultice to relieve inflammation and to promote healing of guinea-worm abscesses, and heated joints are often applied to boils to accelerate suppuration (discharging of pus).

Around the world, prickly-pear is currently being used by traditional healers to treat over 100 different ailments, including asthma, skin burns, fatigue, corns, enlarged prostate, high blood pressure, chronic skin conditions, diabetes, urinary problems, diarrhea, dysentery, gastritis and other gastrointestinal disorders, nosebleed, obesity, snakebite, sore throat, inflammation of the eye, hangover symptoms, and liver damage following alcohol abuse. It's an impressive list, but is there any efficacy beyond the placebo effect in these practices?

Apparently, there is some value in using prickly-pear juice as a cure for hangover. A 2006 medical study found that the juice could "reverse gastric mucosal alterations during ethanol-induced chronic gastritis in rats." Perhaps, this stuff <u>can</u> actually relieve that painful "morning-after" gut-cramp that so many late-night partygoers experience, including me when I was a young man.

In alleviating the often accompanying "hangover headache," researchers in another study discovered that a flavonoid (quercetin 3-methyl ether), which is present in prickly-pear juice, appeared to be a potent neuroprotector.

So what about diabetes? The results of dozens of research studies seem to strongly suggest that there is merit in using prickly-pear to help control Type 2 diabetes. (In fact, a US Patent was issued as early as 1937 for the use of a boiled prickly-pear extract from *Opuntia phaecantha* to control diabetes.)

During a more recent investigation, a single meal of broiled pads of the prickly-pear species *Opuntia streptacantha* was found to decrease some people's blood-sugar levels by 17% to 46%. However, it is not yet known if daily consumption of these cactus pads will consistently reduce blood-sugar levels.

Another experimental study, this one using rats, has shown that supplementing the diet with cactus seed oil (25 mg/kg) can also decrease serum glucose concentrations. And in still another study, a group of rats with experimentally induced diabetes received both a prickly-pear extract and insulin supplements. Within two weeks, glucose levels in this group had declined to values found in a non-diabetic control group, while the two other experimental diabetic rat groups - one that only received insulin and the other which received only the prickly-pear extract - were still diseased with diabetes.

Experimental evidence also suggests that prickly-pear reduces cholesterol levels in human blood and can modify low density lipoprotein (LDL) composition. One such study, again with rats, found a decrease in plasma total cholesterol and LDL, with no effect on HDL cholesterol (the good cholesterol) concentrations.

In one small study of 29 human patients, prickly-pear significantly reduced cholesterol levels. During another study also involving human patients (this time they were suffering from extremely high cholesterol levels), significant improvement was observed after just four weeks of eating 250 grams-per-day (8.8 ounces) of the broiled edible prickly-pear pulp (*Opuntia robusta*) that was being added to their otherwise unchanged diet.

And for those few people whose blood cholesterol is actually too low, a daily dose of prickly-pear fruit pectin may prove effective in bringing it up to normal levels.

A lot of men develop prostate problems as they get older. Men with an enlarged prostate appear to have reduced bladder capacity and they feel the urgent need to urinate much more frequently. There is growing evidence that consuming dried prickly-pear flowers in powdered form can have a significant effect on reducing the uncomfortable symptoms created by an enlarged prostate. Just how the dried flower preparation works, though, is not yet known.

There have been numerous other scientific studies on the medical properties of prickly-pear. One of them found that *Opuntia streptacantha* contained an anti-viral agent that inhibits a number of DNA and RNA viruses such as the Herpes simplex virus Type 2, influenza, and HIV-1.

Other studies have demonstrated that prickly-pear fruit extract inhibits the proliferation of cervical, ovarian, and bladder cancer cells and suppresses tumor growth in mice. Wounds appear to heal more rapidly after extracts made from prickly-pear juice are applied to them. Many *Opuntia* species are diuretic or contain a complex polysaccharide that acts as an effective laxative. And at least five prickly-pear species have been found to contain psychoactive compounds, including trace amounts of mescaline.

As tantalizing as these findings may be, much more research needs be done before we can truly understand the broad-ranging medical potential of prickly-pears. In the meantime, there are thousands of traditional practitioners around the world who will continue to routinely cure their patients' illnesses with prickly-pear preparations and juices.

There have been several other intriguing developments concerning prickly-pear that have potential for far-reaching impacts on human health. Mosquito borne diseases, such as malaria, dengue, yellow fever, West Nile virus, Zika virus and Japanese encephalitis, cause a great deal of suffering and death worldwide.

In April of 1998, Dick Kunkle of Dallas, Texas, was granted a United States patent for a natural, nontoxic, environmentally-friendly, insect-repelling compound that was essentially an extract of prickly-pear juice mixed into a mineral oil base.

According to the patent's accompanying documents, the ideal formulation for repelling mosquitos with this mixture consists of 40% prickly-pear extract (by weight) combined with 45% mineral oil, with some emollients and coupling agents included to stabilize the product. An analysis of his cactus extract found that it contained a form of rodene, a natural insect repellent.

I recently tested a small bottle of a cactus-juice-based ointment labeled "Outdoor Skin Protectant Spray," that is now widely available in the United State and parts of Central America. To my surprise, it seemed to repel mosquitos and biting gnats quite well.

In another mosquito-related use for prickly-pear, people in

Algeria are said to soak chopped cactus pads in water and then pour the resulting liquid into pools containing mosquito larvae to kill them. The cactus juice is completely biodegradable and leaves no toxic residue behind.

Researchers from the University of South Florida in Tampa have learned that boiling slices of prickly-pear releases a thick mucilage that can act as a water purifier. When added to a container of dirty water containing sediment and bacteria, the mucilage combines with the contaminants and causes them to precipitate to the bottom.

It is reported that up to 98% of the bacteria can be removed from the water by this method. This water-purification technique might well find practical use in developing countries that do not provide clean drinking water outside of their larger towns and cities.

One groundbreaking study has even explored the usefulness of prickly-pear mucilage for removing arsenic in drinking water. High concentrations of arsenic in groundwater still threaten the health of millions of people worldwide. A series of laboratory experiments has demonstrated that prickly-pear mucilage will bond to arsenic in solution and transport it to the air and water interface. "This interaction can be optimized and harnessed for the removal of arsenic from drinking water," the researchers predicted in their summary.

PRICKLY-PEAR IN THE HANDS OF THE DESERT-MAKERS

No matter which side of the fence you might sit on concerning the ongoing and acrimonious debate about global climate change, if you look at the long-term history of our human species, it is clear that our collective activities have allowed us to excel at creating deserts.

Typically, we eliminate woodlands and forests either by wholesale cutting for timber and then not replanting them, or through land-clearing to create pasture and grain fields, or by the slow, inexorable cutting of trees for use as firewood. (It might surprise

280

you, but firewood for cooking and heating, particularly in Asia, Africa, and Central America, is one of the leading uses for wood in the world today.)

What happens next to those cleared lands is a far-reaching drama with many chapters and individual players. Overgrazing by livestock, long periods of drought, over-tilling, and salt intrusion are but a few of the numerous insults that can cause arable lands to lose its wildlife and vegetation, reach a "tipping point" and become deserts.

Desertification is considered one of the most important environmental issues in the world today. For instance, reports indicate that during the past 50 years, Africa has lost more than 250,000 square miles (650,000 square kilometers) of its productive agricultural land to desertification.

These events are also occurring in Australia, on the steep mountain slopes of Nepal, along the entire Peruvian shoreline, in Italy, Spain, and Turkey. All told, 168 countries are affected by this problem and that number will probably rise.

In China, the vast Gobi Desert is now considered to be the world's most rapidly expanding desert, with sand dunes swallowing more than 1,300 square miles of land (3,370 square kilometers) each year. Entire villages are being buried in the process, and this may be just a preview of things to come for the people of Beijing. Although the main body of the desert is still quite a distance away, there are already reports that huge sand dunes have formed less than 44 miles (70 kilometers) outside of that great city.

The development of sustainable agricultural systems and the cultivation of appropriate crops is critical for the successful future of nearly every populated arid and semi-arid region on our planet. Many of these areas will probably be threatened with desertification sometime soon, if they aren't already.

Because they are so extremely efficient at converting water into biomass, prickly-pear cacti (particularly *Opuntia ficus-indica* cultivars) are being increasingly recognized as ideal crops for these arid climates.

In many locations, top quality fruit can be harvested just four years after a cactus plantation is established. Full production of both fruits and edible pads normally occurs when the plants are around 12 years old and yields can often be held at this level for at least another 20 years.

In the Mediterranean region, people have been eating cactus fruits and pads for hundreds of years. Prickly-pear has become so much a part of their culture, that people there often believe that the cactus is native to their region.

In Sicily and North Africa, not only are cactus fruits of great importance, many farmers even make their fences with live cactus plants. For cultivating degraded and eroded land, prickly-pear cacti are the plants of choice in both in Mexico and northern Africa. For supporting arid-zone livestock development projects, large areas in Libya, Algeria, and Morocco have been planted with prickly-pear.

In Tunisia, the treelike Indian fig (*Opuntia ficus-indica*) is being used to retard wind erosion and to halt sand movement. On terraced slopes, the web-like root system of this cactus helps to stabilize the soil and impede water run-off during the occasional heavy rainfall event. (Land terraces here are easily damaged by water run-off.)

To accomplish this protection, two rows of prickly-pear are usually planted on the inner (or uphill) side of the terrace. Development of the prickly-pear's strong root-system is promoted by the water that often collects in the bottom of the terrace. Once it is established, the cactus will hold the soil in place, allowing for eventual restoration of the native plant cover.

In 1919, a report was published by the Australian Commonwealth government that described a practical method of using prickly-pear as a crop mulch in India. The technique involved digging a series of wide trenches, partly filling them with cutup prickly-pear, and then covering the trenches with up to two feet (60 cm) of soil. Any new growth that made its way above ground was reburied. After a few months the buried pear is converted into moist humus, which supercharges the soil with potash and mineral nutrients. Farmlands that received this therapy were said to produce much better crops than untreated areas.

This report was published at a time when much of eastern Australia's agricultural land seemed doomed. But there were a few people who took the hint and soon found great value in the prickly-pear that covered their property. Take the case of Mr. F. G. Couper of Westbrook, Queensland, who said in a newspaper interview:

> I do not now poison on land fit for cultivation, as the green pear plowed into the soil makes a splendid mulch and certainly helps with the crops, especially in these dry seasons. In 1922, I first tried cutting and plowing the pear under and got a heavy crop of corn and pumpkins.
>
> I have now managed to get a machine that will cut the densest pear level with the ground . . . I did the above work with a horse, but I am now using a tractor, finding it more suitable as the wheels help in crushing the pear. The cost of clearing pear by this method is just about the same as ordinary plowing.

Then there is the inspiring story of Phil Badier of Scone, New South Wales. (Scone is where Australia's great prickly-pear plague is thought to have begun.) Phil lived and worked on a 250 acre block of land that was practically a jungle of prickly-pear.

Deciding to see if he could utilize the pear in some practical way, Phil soon devised a portable machine that "minced up the pear and broke the brittle spines into dust." He soon found that he could harvest up to 200 tons of pear from an acre of land. The resulting mulch was fed to his dairy cattle and pigs. It was also used to fertilize his garden.

"When he settled down to this work, he was regarded as a hopeless crank by the neighboring settlers in the district, and 'Phil Badier's Prickly-pear Farm' was the theme of many jokes amongst local humorists," the newspaper, *The Australian Worker*, reported.

> He went steadily on with his work, quite unperturbed by either criticism or ridicule, and has won all along the line. He now has a good herd of dairy cattle, a pig farm,

an apiary, and a market garden, and turns out high-grade products for which there is a ready sale. He has converted a block of pear jungle literally into an area flowing with milk and honey, and made a comfortable income out of the business.

"Just before the breaking of the recent drought, he was not only keeping his own stock - and his bank account - in a prosperous condition by means of his pear-mincing machine, but he was also lending his neighbors a hand by supplying them with good succulent fodder at a very low cost," the article continues.

> Former scoffers were wending their way to Badier's Farm with motor lorries, carts, wagons, and drays for loads of minced pear for their starving stock. One and all were bemoaning the fact they had permitted the pear to be destroyed on their own holdings, under the mistaken idea that this valuable plant was a noxious pest.

> Today the position stands thus: During the past drought year (1935), millions of stock perished from hunger and thirst in New South Wales and Queensland in the very localities where hundreds of millions of tons of succulent fodder had been destroyed in accordance with the official advice given out by the Federal Bureau of Science and Industry. This is a stupendous fact, which surely demands thorough public investigation.

Prickly-pear cactus has been both praised and cursed in just about every location that it happens to grow: from Australia, Morocco and India, to its native lands in Texas, Mexico and Nevis. Many people see great value in these plants as a source of food, fodder, medicine and as a living tool for creating livestock fences or repairing degraded lands. Others just see a noxious weed with little or no potential. No matter which way you look at it, however, it is certain that this stubborn, spine-covered, fleshy plant with lovely flowers will be playing an important role in our species' future.

******

284

Epilogue

One morning in late March 2014, while sipping a cup of hot tea and watching a kookaburra feed its newly-fledged young near my riverside camp on the northern coast of New South Wales, I heard a news story over my transistor radio that completely transformed my mental day. Australia's parliament had just formally upgraded invasive cactuses to "weeds of national significance." Apparently, Australia's war on cactus was not yet over and had recently taken a new turn for the worse.

The problem was widespread, the narrator explained, and primarily affected the thinly-populated range lands across the wheat-belt and Goldfield regions of Western Australia, to the Flinders Ranges of South Australia, the Wimmera of Victoria State, and the lower Darling Basin and Lightning Ridge areas of New South Wales.

In certain localities in outback Queensland, impressively large stands of invasive hybrid cacti had created impenetrable spiny barriers that excluded all stock animals and were choking out much of the other plant life. As I absorbed this news, I quickly decided that this was something that I had to investigate and see for myself.

It wasn't long before I was speaking over the telephone with Mike Chuk, the former chairperson of the Australian Invasive Cacti Network, an organization that was created to help combat the cacti.

"The main problem species come from two different genera of *Opuntioid* cactus, and unfortunately *Cactoblastis* has little or no effect on any of them," he told me.

There are nearly two dozen species of *Opuntioid* cacti that are currently on that "Weeds of National Significance" list. These include several true prickly-pears (*Opuntia*); the most problematic of them being the Wheel cactus (*Opuntia robusta*), and the Tiger pear (*Opuntia aurantiaca*) which infests large areas in eastern Australia, including some 200,000 hectares (494,000 acres) in New South Wales.

Also on the list are eight species of *Cylindropuntia*. Commonly known as "chollas" in their native North American habitats, these cacti can be identified by their long cylindrical segmented stems (true prickly-pears [*Opuntia*] have flattened stems), an internal woody skeleton, and detachable papery sheaths that cover the spines. Two species of a similar-appearing genus, *Austrocylindropuntia*, also appear on that list. They can be recognized by their long non-segmented cylindrical branches and their unsheathed spines.

"Some of the worst *Cylindropuntia* invaders are the extremely spiny Hudson pear (*Cylindropuntia rosea*) which infests more than 60,000 hectares (148,000 acres) in the Lightning Ridge area of New South Wales, the hybrid Coral cactus (*Cylindropuntia fulgida* var *mammillata*), and the Snake cactus (*Cylindropuntia spinosior*), whose infestations in western Queensland are truly scary to behold," Mike Chuk informed me.

I told Mike that I really wanted to see some of that "scary stuff" and by the time our conversation ended, he had given me the contact details for a few of the people on whose properties the cactus had invaded. He also provided an introduction to the field managers of Desert Channels Queensland, a community-based natural resource management organization that does much of the cactus-control work in the region.

A survey of invasive cacti across Australia's rangelands by the Rangelands Natural Resource Management Alliance has indicated that the continued spread of these noxious plants can pose real challenges to primary production (cattle and sheep) in every mainland state. In several regions where there are already fairly large infestations, the cost of chemical control often exceeded the value of the land. (If this is beginning to sound reminiscent of when the "pear" dominated much of eastern Australia during the first decades of the 20th century, keep in mind that the area affected back then involved a immense region of over 60 million acres instead of a series of isolated colonies scattered across the continent. Even so, it appears that a new kind of cactus plague is now brewing in outback Australia.)

After a leisurely week of camping along our 2,400 kilometer long (1,440 miles) route from Sydney to Longreach, Queensland, my friend Jeff and I rolled into that bustling country town in Jeff's dust-covered four-wheel-drive rig.

We were both thirsty for something cold to drink and running very low on fuel. Since it was nearing late afternoon, we decided to check into the Desert Channels office first. Although it was almost closing time, we were introduced to several of the staff, including Peter Kleinsmith, who helpfully gave us directions to the first property that we wanted to inspect. (A few days later, Peter accompanied us into some of the areas where he had been doing weed-control spraying, so that we could witness firsthand the disappointing results of his ongoing chemical herbicide program aimed at controlling these invasive cacti.)

Our first stop the next morning was at Leander Station, where we met Peter Clark and his partner Liz. After a cup of tea and a quick chat, we were soon out in the midst of their personal plague of coral cactus (*Cylindropuntia fugida* var *mammillata*). This cactus is a cristated hybrid that rarely, if ever, flowers. It reproduces by fragmentation.

A cristated plant is a genetic monster that forms weird ribbon or crest-like formations when the cells of the plant's growing point begin to multiply erratically. Cristated plants are often highly valued by horticulturists (the cockscomb celosia is a popular example), and this coral cactus infestation most likely originated from someone's discarded potted plant. When encountered here in the wild, however, it's a nasty-looking plant that is well protected with spines.

"We've found quite a few dead lizards and lots of big moths - even birds - that were impaled on the spines," Liz comments as

I take close-up photographs of one particularly impressive plant.

"How large is your property and how much is infested with cactus?" I ask.

"There about 500 acres in this patch. . . but it's connected, going about four or five miles (6.6 to 8.3 km) down the river," Peter replies. "The property is 30,000 acres; a bit smaller than most of those in this area. At the moment we've only got about 1,000 sheep on here because of the bloody drought. We haven't had a decent rain since 18 months ago. If this continues, we'll completely destock in December."

"How long has your poison spray program been in effect?" Jeff asks.

"We started in 1990, and the bloody cactus is still here!" exclaims Peter. "At this point we're just trying to stop it from going any further. . . but it's gone mad. It's everywhere!"

Peter estimates that they have already spent over $500,000 (US $400,000) over the years trying to control this pest.

When I discussed our visit to Leander Station with Mike Chuk some weeks later, he told me that spraying the Cylindropuntias for weed control was particularly difficult because of their ability to shut off non-poisoned segments from poisoned ones, which meant that careful spraying is required. The cactus often spreads when live segments drop off larger established plants and take root. But the vast majority of propagules come from small juvenile plants, not from the older ones.

"Hence the rather unique situation where people go out spraying with their eyes focused on the larger plants - as one naturally would. But the smaller fist-sized cactus plant hides in the grass, has a dozen or more tiny segments the size of grapes, that when bumped by an animal literally explode across the landscape," Mike explained. "These can lay on the soil in a hot, dry environment for a long time before they take root and they go a red color that makes them look like pebbles."

"In places where we had removed the adult plants, the big

challenge was to go back, time after time, and painstakingly look for the little ones. If they are not removed, in a couple of good seasons the situation soon reverts back to the way it was. When you visit a paddock, you'll see dozens of big cacti, but it's the hundreds of little ones that you don't see that are the cancer."

During our next stop a day later, we met Ross McPherson at Bexley Station. Ross has been battling an infestation of snake cactus (*Cylindropuntia spinosior*) for more than a decade. Apparently, this cactus had been in the station-house rock garden when the previous owners "chucked it out and put it in the dump back in '82."

"We had it controlled pretty well up to about 1995 or '96. . . even brought some [cactus eating] bugs out. . . didn't do any good. Now it's spread over 10 or 12 acres, or more," McPherson tells us as we stand in awe while we gaze at the infestation from a small knoll. (See Plate 30) "The kangaroos get into it. . . sticks to their fur. You'll see little ones (cactus propagules) under the trees where the roos have been laying in the shade."

"This is one tough plant," McPherson continues. "I've got some hanging in the shed that's been there for seven or eight years and it hasn't grown much. . . but it hasn't died either."

Already, there are numerous other spotty infestations of *Cylindroputia* cactus growing around this region, and it is still spreading. This is ample evidence that Ross McPherson's, the Clark's, Desert Channels Queensland's, and local government's efforts at chemical herbicide control of this invasive cactus are failing.

"Oh, we're losing all-right! It's a full-time job and you've got to came back and do it all over within two years, no matter what," McPherson growled as we turned away to leave for a visit with yet another cactus "battler."

"The future of control of *Cylindroputia* cactus appears to be with biocontrol," Mike Chuk told me after our road trip was completed. In South Africa, where coral cactus has also become a problem, it has been very effectively controlled by using a strain (biotype) of the cochineal *Dactylopius tomentosus*. In Australia, three biotypes of this cochineal have been tested against several of the *Cylindropuntia* cacti species with promising results. At the time of this writing, however, their open release into wild Australia was still pending.

As the cacti colonies scattered across Australia's huge tracts of rangeland continue to hybridize and evolve over time, some of them will eventually become resistant to whatever insects that have been placed out there to control them. There is growing evidence that this is already happening.

As discussed earlier in Chapter 8, a number of "pest-pear" (*Opuntia stricta*) varieties are demonstrating resistance to predation by *Cactoblastis*. Tiger pear (*Opuntia aurantiaca*) or "jumping-jack" (so-called because of the way its segments break off and attach so readily to passing animals or car tires) was for a long time effectively controlled by two species of cactus moth (*Cactoblastis cactorum* and *Tucumania tapiacola*) and a species of cochineal from Argentina (*Dactylopius austrinus*). Today, some large colonies of this low-growing invasive cactus are spreading rapidly, seemingly unaffected by the continued presence of these three insect herbivores.

On 1,550 hectare (3,830 acres) Curtis Island, located along the central Queensland coast near the south end of the Great Barrier Reef, an infestation of pest-pear (*Opuntia stricta*) has become a reliable food-source for feral pigs. The pigs, in turn, are threatening nesting flatback sea turtles (*Natator depressus*) by eating their eggs. They are also a menace to a critically endangered bird species, the Capricorn yellow chat (*Epthianura crocea macgregori*).

The cactus, itself, also poses a danger to birds like the threatened beach stone-curlew (*Esacus magnirostris*). This species often nests where the vegetation meets the beach sand, and it is here where prickly-pear is most common on the island.

So far, insect biocontrol agents such as *Cactoblastis* or *Cochineal* have been completely ineffective in controlling prickly-pear on the island. The cactus here seems to have developed a much thicker cuticle than normal, perhaps to assist the plant in salt tolerance. This thicker skin appears to be impenetrable to many of the cactus-eating insects' larvae, leaving most them to starve to death as result.

Perhaps, in the fullness of time, a generation of insects will evolve that is able to penetrate this thick-skinned prickly-pear. Or perhaps not.

****

Jim Carpenter retired after more than 30 years of service to the United States Department of Agriculture. However, Stephen Hight is continuing his work with the cactus moth, *Cactoblastis*. A recently discovered trail-following pheromone is currently being investigated as a disrupter of newly hatched caterpillars following one another on the cactus pad.

"The young caterpillars need to work together to quickly chew a hole into the thick-skinned cactus pad and overcome defensive sticky plant fluids," Hight wrote in a letter to me. "On plants sprayed with a chemical that mimics the trail-following pheromone, caterpillars became disoriented, were unable to find one another, and perished before they could start feeding."

"In Argentina, Jim and I often felt that we were walking in the footsteps of Alan Dodd. From a hotel in Santiago del Estero where Dodd had stayed, to small towns that were mentioned in his letters, the spirit of Dodd was all around. It was to great delight that before we left the country, we toasted Alan Dodd's birthday in the large cactus plantation of El Virqui."

"How fitting that this book is entitled *The Great Cactus War*, because like any war, it is made up of battles: the battle to save the environment of Australia from invasive cacti, and our battle in the Americas to save the native cacti from an invasive cactus-eating moth," Dr. Hight concluded.

Who knows? If the current situation for invasive cacti in Australia gets completely out-of-hand and becomes a monumental problem resembling the great prickly-pear plague of the early 20th century, there might be a need to bring Jim Carpenter out of retirement and to truly apply Stephen Hight's skills as a "biological control of weeds person." Only time will tell and, as we are now all keenly aware, the "weed clock" is constantly ticking.

****

About the Author

A lifelong naturalist and conservation biologist, Terry is the author of the internationally acclaimed book *Bears of the World*, as well as *Kangaroos: The Marvelous Mob*, *The Last Thylacine* (his first work of fiction), *Natural Areas of the San Juan Islands*, *Wild Harvest: Wild Edible Plants of the Pacific Northwest*, and was photographer of *The Nature of Borneo*.

Terry's published work has received numerous awards, including the coveted Washington Governor's Writers Award, a Sigma Delta Chi award for "Excellence in Journalism," and first place in the World Photography Contest 1983. His articles and photographs have appeared in *Smithsonian*, *Natural History*, and in publications of the *National Geographic Society*.

When not traveling for research, he splits his time between Washington State's San Juan Islands and Port Stephens, New South Wales, Australia.

Notes

Chapter One: From Whence It Came... and the Secret of Grana

1 *One newspaper graphically described the plants*: Cactus Invasion.
2 *Joseph Maiden, one of Australia's leading*: Maiden, Preliminary.
2 *...civilizations of the original prickly-pear*: DeFelice, 873.
3 *Apparently, the Indian fig has been farmed for so long*: Griffith, Phylogeny, 1915.
3 *This seems to have led to the creation*: Anderson, Cactus, 51.
3 *"Like other ancient Mexicans"*: Greenfield, 40.
3 *Further south in Peru*: Donkin, 35; Sáenz-Hernándes, 222.
3 *...little doubt that Columbus and his crew*: Gibson, 532.
4 *Upon Columbus's return to Spain*: Hale, Edward, 58.
4 *...Columbus's entire original journal*: La Casas, 3-5.
5 *La Casas had access to Columbus's original*: Cabot, V.
5 *Because of prickly-pear's bizarre appearance*: Candolle, 275; Greenfield, 167.
5 *When the Moors were expelled*: Russell, 435.
5 *...first illustration and discussion of prickly-pear*: Oviedo y Valdés.
6 *Intrigued by this plant's most unusual form*: Gerarde, 1329-1330.
6 *...in 1735 that the Indian fig*: Miller, Vol. 2, Section "OP".
6 *...first established in botanical gardens*: Casas, 156.
6 *...royal botanical gardens in Poland*: Dubielecka, 7.
6 *Although cactus collecting*: Kunte, 7.
7 *...Sicily was particularly suitable*: Anderson, Cactus, 53.
7 *Yields up to twenty-two tons of fruit per hectare*: Maiden, Plan.
7 *In total, 20 species of prickly-pear have been naturalized*: Essi, 485-486
7 *After nearly 500 years of growing on rocky hillsides*: Anderson, Cactus, 67.
7 *An enduring botanical curiosity*: DeFelice, 872.
7 *Prickly-pear was first recorded in China in 1625*: Zehnyu, 210-211.
7 *...part of the landscape of the "Land of Israel"*: Nassar, 117.
8 *...they also built a number of forts*: Binggeli, 335-339.
8 *One indigenous group, the formerly nomadic Mahafale*: Kaufmann, 345.
9 *The French eventually annexed Madagascar*: Binggeli, 335-339.
9 *...prickly-pear became a focal point*: Kaufmann, 1-2.
9 *The issue came to a head in the early 1920s*: Binggeli, 335-339; Walters, 185.(One unusual effect of the cochineal introduction was that at certain times of the day the winged male cochineal insects would occur in huge swarms. One French lady was reported as saying that "swarming clouds cochineal would hit the car and windscreen and be crushed. The automobile seemed drenched in blood.")
9 *...original prickly-pear and two varieties*: Binggeli, 257-268, 335-339.
10 *Mature males and females look very different*: Alexander, Prickly Pear, 33.
10 *The eggs, laid beneath the female's body*: Mann, Cactus-feeding Insects, 143.
10 *Newly hatched male and female crawlers are*: Mann, Cactus-feeding Insects, 143-144.
11 *...along the arid coastal region of Peru*: Dutton, 9, 11. (Concerning the first human use of dye and the development of art: "The urge to create art is purely instinctive," insists my friend Beth Rahe Balas, who conducts art classes with very young children, "As soon as someone is able to make a mark, they will make a mark. I never have to encourage a child to make art.")
11 *Though all species of cochineal are known to yield*: Alexander, "Natural Enemies", 52.
12 *Although it resembled kermes*: Dutton, 18-19.
12 *...cochineal was carried by Aztec merchants*: Dutton, 11-12

12 ...*encountered Aztec artisans who used the red cochineal*: Dutton, 18.
12 *The Spanish called the dyestuff "grana cochinilla"*: Ibid.
12 ...*a 1438-39 accounting of King Henry VI's wardrobe*: Munro, medieval, 66.
13 ...*a successful Flemish master-mason*: Munro, luxury, 27, 75, 113; Munro, anti-red, 86.
13 ...*most expensive scarlet English woolen broadcloth*: Munro, rise, 51.
13 *Word of this new red dyestuff soon reached*: Donkin, 23, 37; Greenfield, 51-52.
13 ...*that "grana cochineal" was far superior*: Dutton, 20.
13 *After a long delayed entry* : Greenfield, 65-66.
13 ...*cochineal had become indispensable*: Greenfield, 77-78.
14 ...*soon found other uses for cochineal*: Greenfield, 81-84.
14 *Although most of the finished dyestuff*: Donkin, 13; Dutton 35.
14 ...*this disregard of edible crops*: Donkin, 29.
15 ...*"nopal" eventually became the general term*: Donkin 13-14, Dutton 132.
15 ...*insect colonies also had to be protected*: Donkin 13-14.
16...*stored in closed baskets under the roofs*: Donkin, 16-17; Dutton, 27.
16 ...*care was taken to harvest the cochineal*: Donkin, 16, Dutton 24.
16 ...*a great deal of variety in the quality*: Donkin, 17.
17 *Wild varieties of cochineal were also harvested*: Donkin, 14; Dutton, 24.
17 *The royal tribute system*: Donkin, 24; Dutton, 19, 36.
17 ...*eventually became focused on the Oaxaca Valley*: Dutton, 33-34.
17 *Once the cochineal was harvested*: Donkin, 18; Dutton, 36-37.
18 *The sheer amount of grana that was shipped*: Donkin, 29; Dutton, 21.
18 *Seville was a very busy port*: Donkin, 38, 51.
18 *Much of this middleman activity ended*: Greenfield, 108:
19 ...*often became the target of pirates*: Greenfield, 111-122.
20 ...*obscure the true nature and source*: Donkin, 44-45; Dutton, 40; Greenfield, 125-135.
20 ...*asked Antoni van Leeuwenhoek*: Donkin, 45; Greenfield, 146-147, 150.
21 *Another microscopist, Jan Swammerdam*: Greenfield, 148-149.
21 *Perhaps the earliest*: Donkin, 44.
21 ...*cochineal controversy droned on*: Donkin 44-45, Greenfield 158-163.
21 ...*the Spanish maintained a strict embargo*: Donkin, 3; Greenfield, 165-168.
22 ...*now knew that cochineal was an insect*: Alexander, Natural Enemies, 52.
22 ...*after America's declaration of independence*: Donkin, 46; Dutton, 42; Greenfield, 169.
22 ...*Nicolas Joseph Thiery de Menonville*: Greenfield, 169-171.
22 *After a sixty-six day voyage*: Greenfield, 172-173; Thiery, 753-754.
23 *It proved to be a rough voyage*: Thiery, 754-762.
23 *Impressed by Thiery de Menonville's botanical enthusiasm*: Thiery, 767-768.
23 ...*when he arrived in Mexico*: Greenfield, 174; Thiery, 773-774.
24 ...*found a plant that would make him locally famous*: Greenfield, 175; Thiery, 775.
24 ...*while visiting a merchant's home*: Thiery, 786-788.
25 ...*was not placed under house arrest*: Thiery, 789-791.
26...*one afternoon in the cabin of a shepard*: Thiery, 792-793.
26 ...*he took the time to observe*: Thiery, 795.
26 ...*after hiring horses and Indian guides*: Thiery, 811.
27 ...*in an attempt to purchase some cochineal*: Thiery, 826-827.
27 *Using a series of guides and hired horses*: Thiery, 837-838.
28 *The second incident took place at the Veracruz city gate*: Thiery, 848.
28 ...*both Thiery de Menonville's friends and enemies alike*: Greenfield, 179.
28 *The likely prospect of discovery*: Greenfield, 179-180; Thiery, 853-854.
29 *By the time Thiery de Menonville reached Saint-Dominque*: Thiery, 854-875.
30 *Colonial life and the troubles with breeding*: Greenfield, 181-182; Thiery, 875.
30 *Thiery de Menonville fell sick*: Greenfield 181-182.

30 ...*the wild cochineal persisted*: Donkin, 46; Johnston, Report, 129.
30 ...*Thiery de Menonville's notes on how to raise cochineal*: Greenfield, 183.

Chapter 2 : Royal Red In the Land Down Under

33 ...*the gout that had long*: Greenfield, 197; Lyte, 242, 244; Maiden, Sir Joseph, 221.
34 *Born in 1743 into a wealthy Lincolnshire*: Greenfield, 184; Hooker, xxiii; Lyte, 7-8.
34 *Two years earlier, at his own expense*: Fara, 78-79; *Sir Joseph Banks*, 66; Hooker, xxv.
35 ...*Banks returned to England*: Fara, 80; Greenfield, 184; Hooker, xxv-xxvi;
35 ...*becoming even more famous than Captain Cook*: Greenfield, 185.
35 ...*long audience with King George III*: Greenfield, 185; Maiden, Sir Joseph, 55.
35 ...*declined to join Cook on his second*: *Sir Joseph Banks*, 69-72; Smith, Life, 24.
35 ...*audience with King George III*: Greenfield, 185; Maiden, Sir Joseph, 55, Smith, Life, 21-22.
36 *In 1773, the king appointed him unofficial director*: Greenfield, 185.
36 *Banks's house truly was the "rendezvous*: Smith, Life, 90.
36 ...*introducing new and useful plants*: *Sir Joseph Banks*, 69, 88; Hooker, xxxiii.
37 ...*mastermind for the breadfruit scheme*: Smith, Life, 126, 129-130.
37 *To act as reservoirs for interesting tropical*: *Sir Joseph Banks*, 69,88; Hooker, xxxiii.
37 *During his life nearly 7,000 new plants*: Smith, Life, 96.
37 ...*contained a copy of Thiery*: Carter, 274; Greenfield, 188.
37 ...*England's dye works were using some 240,000 pounds*: Greenfield, 186.
38 ...*Banks received a letter from Madras*: Carter, 274; Greenfield, 186-187.
38 *Unfortunately for all concerned*: Greenfield, 187.
38 ...*posted a large reward*: Carter, 275; Greenfield, 189.
38 *India, it seemed to him*: Greenfield, 189.
38 *The East India Company then sent* : Alexander, Prickly Pear, 11-12; Greenfield, 189.
39 ...*been sent each year across the Atlantic*: White, 4-5.
39 ...*rising crime rate had left Britain's jails and prison hulks*: Lyte, 226.
39 *The severity of the English criminal law*: White, Part Two: 15, 21-22.
40 ...*eight years were to pass before* : Cameron, H.C., 180; Lyte, 228-229.
40 ... *no sooner did Captain Phillip*: Cameron, H.C., 180-181; Lyte, 230; White, 7.
41 *Joseph Banks and Arthur Phillip*: Carter, 234, 275; Lyte, 231-232; Mackaness, 28.
41 ...*in the port of Rio de Janeiro*: Carter, 232, 275; Maiden, Preliminary, 2; Phillip,
      Chap. IV; White, 37-38.
42 *Phillip's cabin was described as resembling a small greenhouse*: Carter, 232.
42 ...*visited aboard his vessel*: Alexander, Prickly Pear, 12; Johnston, Report, 127.
42 *On the 18th of January, 1788*: Marchant, Vol. 2; Smith, Life, 216-217; White, 7, 42-44.
43 *Occasionally teetering on the brink*: Lyte, 231.
43...*coax the precious cochineal-covered prickly-pear*: Carter, 275.
43 ...*long letters to Banks*: Carter, 233-234; Lee, 55-59; Lyte, 231-232; White, 19.
44...*permitted to leave Sydney late in 1792*: Lee, 55-59; White, 19.
44 ...*even sent him nursery stock*: Carter, 274-275; Greenfield, 189.
44 *Anderson took issue with Banks's secretiveness*: Carter, 276-277, Greenfield, 191.
44 ...*one of Banks's agents managed*: Carter, 275-276, 341; Greenfield 191-192.
45 *In 1795, as Smith was preparing*: Carter, 276.
45 ...*by the name of Captain Neilson*: Carter, 276; Greenfield, 192-193.
45 ...*placed them under Smith's care*: Carter, 276, Greenfield, 193-194.
45 ...*insects on some 600 potted*: Carter, 276.
46 ...*cochineal's breeding cycle only took*: Greenfield, 194.
46 ...*reluctant to grow cochineal*: Greenfield, 195-196.
46 ...*the East India Company shipped over 4,000 pounds*: Greenfield, 196.
48 ...*company directors finally accepted*: Ibid.

47 *But after his death in 1820*: Lyte, 244.
47 *...Mahatma Gandhi*: Andrews; Moxham, 181-182.
48 *...formed the "Inland Customs Department"*: Moxham, 70.
48 *It is not entirely known when the "Customs Hedge"*: Moxham, 97-98.
49 *...hedge would be from ten*: Johnston, Report, 27; Moxham, 7, 105.
49 *...contingent of around 12,000 men*: Moxham, 3, 113-114.
49 *...protest of the Salt Tax resulted*: Andrews.
49 *...impossible to say how many people were made ill:* Moxham, 134.
50 *...Mexican Revolution*: Donkin, 30, 35, 46-47, 50-51; Greenfield, 205-207; Prance, 377.
50 *...Dutch managed to smuggle dozens*: Greenfield, 210-214.
51 *The most spectacular cochineal transplant*: Castle, 78-79; Dodd, 15; Donkin, 30, 47, 52; Dutton, 42-43,47; Greenfield, 215-216; Russell, 435.
51 *In reaction to the glut of all this red*: Greenfield, 216-217, 219; Sáenz-Hernándes, 227-228.
51 *...noted German chemist*: Donkin, 6; Dutton, 37; Greenfield, 222-224, 228; Prance, 377.
52 *...industry collapsed*: "Cochineal is Near End", 6; Greenfield, 229-232, 241; Johnston, Report, 43-44.
52 *...cochineal is experiencing a comeback*: Greenfield, 243-244; Mulas.
52 *...world's leading producers of cochineal*: Bustamente, 21; Dutton, 48; Greenfield, 245-246; Portillo, 4; Sáenz-Hernándes, 228.
53 *...has been tentative speculation*: Alexander, Prickly Pear, 12.
53 *...plants growing in Sydney's Botanic Garden*: Australian Colonial Plants Search.
53 *A handbook on the culture of grapes*: Alexander, Prickly Pear, 12.
54 *...offered for sale in a Tasmanian nursery*: Bunce.
54 *...plants found on William Macarthur's*: Macarthur (1843), Macarthur (1850); Teale.
54 *...William was a surgeon in the British Navy*: Medical Pioneers Index; Carlyle (b); Carlyle (c), Colonial Secretary Index; Carlyle (d), jenwilletts.com; Carlyle (e), Australian National Library; Carlyle (g).
55 *For the prisoners, life aboard these transport ships*: Bateson, 41.
55 *Surgeons found employment in the convict service unattractive*: Bateson, 40-41.
55 *...instructions that amounted to a contract were issued:* Bateson, 47, 52-53.
56 *As a result of this intervention*: Bateson, 379.
56 *...land grant of 2,000 acres:* Medical Pioneers Index; Carlyle (d); jenwilletts.com; Carlyle (f); Hastings.
56 *...he was appointed county Magistrate*: New Commission of Peace; Carlyle (d); jenwilletts.com.
56 *...acquired a daughter*: Carlyle (e), Australian National Library; Carlyle (g); Sinclair, (March 6 & 12); ancestry.com.
56 *...arrived in Sydney in February of 1833*: Prince Regent; Sinclair, (March 6 and 12).
57 *During my research I found more than*: Alexander, Prickly Pear; Carlyle (e); Australian National Library; Carlyle (f); Hastings; Dodd, 19; Eggleston; Freeman; Graham, 21, Steele, Append. 3:37; Prickly Pear in New South Wales; Prickly Pear: Who Introduced It?; Walton, Reclaiming, 17-18.
57 *...on the coastal sailor Westmoreland*: Medical Pioneers Index.
58 *...keen on the subject of the growing of grapes*: Teale; Macarthur (1843); Macarthur (1850).
58 *...he too established a vineyard*: Medical Pioneers Index; Carlyle (f); Hastings.
58 *When Mary died near Scone in a house fire*: Granny Sutton (a); Granny Sutton (b).
58 *Unluckily for Queenslanders, Scone was*: Elverton; Sinclair (March 12).
59 *...came across a settlers' map*: Dixon.
59 *Dr. Carlyle passed away in 1844*: Medical Pioneers Index; Carlyle (b).
60 *...Queensland Agricultural Journal published*: Queensland Agricultural Journal, 135-136.
61 *Alan Dodd, a scientific researcher*: Dodd, 19.
61 *A plant or two of the pear will make its appearance*: Invasion of Australia, 8-9, 21.

Chapter 3 : What is Prickly-pear?

64 *Due to the spiny nature*: Bradley, 1, 9; Schuster, 158; Theodori, 1081, 1805.
64 *...the word "cactus" wasn't specifically assigned until*: Andersohn, 57; Linnaei, 466-470.
64 *...originates from the Greek*: DeFelice; Hecht, 14; Maund; Pizzetti.
64 *...great confusion over cactus classification*: Anderson, Cactus, 94; Andersohn, 57; Gibson; Griffith, Phylogeny; Kunte, 7; Rebman; Reynolds.
65 *...many cactus species have been renamed*: Andersohn, 60; Marshall, 62;
65 *Opuntias are believed have been named after*: Castle, 6, DeFelice; Gerarde, 1330.
65 *At last count*: Anderson, Cactus, 485; Griffith, Phylogeny; Pinkava; Reyes-Agüero; Wilson.
65 *...DNA profiling*: Graham, Cacti & Succulents, 14; Wallace, 11-12.
66 *...adapted to live*: Anderson, Cactus, 26-28, 30; Benson, 23; Graham, Cacti & Succulents, 7; Rebman, Opuntia; Socha; Top Ten; Wallace, 3; Walton, Reclaiming, 17.
66 *...crassulacean acid metabolism*: Anderson, Cactus, 37, Campbell, 223, 714; DeFelice; Nefzaoui, Forage, 200-201; Ocampo; Russell, 433; Socha; Top Ten.
67 *...unique to the cactus family*: Alexander, 6-7; Anderson, Cactus, 26-28; Andersohn, 233; Benson, 23; Flowering Plants; Charles, 120; Leese, 25; Rebman, Opuntia; Reyes-Agüero; Walton, Reclaiming, 17; Wilson.
67 *...adapted to many diverse habitats*: DeFelice; Dodd, Conquest; Domico, Native Cactus; Hosking; Majure; Rebman; Schuster, 174; Wilson.
68 *...almost no fossil record*: Becker; Brown; Caryophyllids; Chaney; Gorelick; Leese, 52.
69 *...small amount of physical evidence*: Anderson, Cactus, 37; Gorelick; Ocampo; Rebman; Uebergang.
69 *...rate of cactus DNA sequence changes*: Gorelick; Rebman.
69 *Most Opuntiod blossoms are*: Alexander, Prickly Pear, 7-8; Benson, 39, 43; Rebman; Reyes-Agüero; Wilson.
70 *...when prickly-pear stamens are touched*: Benson, 269; Maund; Reyes-Agüero; Wilson.
70 *...blossoms are self-fertile as well*: Rebman; Reyes-Agüero.
70 *...edible, plum-sized, pear-shaped fruits*: Alexander, Prickly Pear, 7-8; Australian Invasive Cactus Forum; Benson, 50; Rojas-Aréchiga; Reyes-Agüero; Wilson.
71 *...have been found in dead stumps*: Dodd, Biological Campaign, 23.
71 *...this "soil seed bank" can remain viable*: Reyes-Agüero; Rojas-Aréchiga; Ueckert.
71 *The oldest tree seed known*: Roach; Sallon; Shen-Miller; Yashina.
72 *...not all prickly-pear seeds will germinate at once*: Prickly Pear (d); Dodd, Biological Campaign, 144; Cunningham; Mandujano; Mann, Cacti, 21; Prickly Pear Pest, 9, 13; Rojas-Aréchiga; Ueckert.
73 *...information about seed longevity*: Cactus seeds are orthodox; Seed Longevity, 15, 24.
74 *...this process plays an important role*: Allendorf; Benson, 92; Rebman; Ueckert.
74 *One of the first to be noted was reported*: Alexander, Natural Enemies; Alexander, Variation, 9; Mann, Cacti, 16-17, 19, 21-22; Moree/Gwydir Examiner, Biniguy.
75 *...prickly-pear known as the wheel cactus*: Baker, Opuntia; McFadyen, Dodd.
77 *...people unwittingly brought dozens*: Green Octopus.
77 *Weeds are essentially a bi-product*: Weeds; Rolls; Green Octopus.
78 *...visiting the Japanese steamer*: Alastor.
78 *Less than 50 years after*: Dodd, 15; Frawley, Prickly Pear; Petherbridge; Rolls, 354-355.
78 *...prickly-pear's initial spread*: Delley; Dodd, Conquest; Emmerson, 145; Leese, 115; Mann, Cacti, 19, 23; Prickly Pear Menace (b).
78 *...Sydney Morning Herald published an interview*: Prickly Pear (a).
79 *...groups called "acclimatization societies*: Delley; Domico, Kangaroos; Rolls, 269, 354-355.
80 *...William Baynes*: Delley.
80 *...native to the south-eastern*: Alexander, Prickly Pear, 9-10; Alexander, Natural Enemies, 30-32; Benson, 499; Prance, 383; Mann, Cacti, 18, 22-23. (Australian botanist,

Ian Menkins, author of a paper titled "A Reassessment of the Type of Opuntia
Stricta, [accessed online in 2014 at http://opuntiads.com/zpdf/A_
Reassessment_of_the_Type_of_Opuntia_stricta.pdf] argues that the adoption
of *Opuntia stricta* as a species with no varieties has allowed ". . . all of the
previously indeterminate and confusing entities to be thrown into one
convenient pile. But it has done little to resolve the genetic diversity that many
botanists still puzzle over and find impossible to ignore.")
80 ...*also be found in Ecuador*: Global Invasive Species Database; Opuntia stricta; Prance, 383.
81 *The stems of this plant*: Benson, 497-501; Opuntia stricta; Mann, Cacti, 18; Prickly
Pear & Their Control.
81 ...*pest-pear's vast Australian territory*: Mann, Cacti, 19-21.
81 ...*one man's concerted effort to tame*: McColl; Australia's Opportunity.

Chapter 4 : Promises For a New World

84 ...*discovery of a natural genetic variant of potato*: Brown, 157; Harwood, 9-10; Howard,
Luther, 5; Janick, 154; Lazendorfer; Luther Burbank, Wikipedia; Luther Burbank,
Western Sonoma County Historical Society; Wickson, 20.
84 ...*when his father died*: Anderson, Vast Array, 161; Howard, Luther, 5; Luther Burbank,
Encyclopedia of World Biography; Luther Burbank, Western Sonoma County
Historical Society; Luther Burbank, Wikipedia; Smith, Luther.
84 ...*$150 for travel fare*: Harwood, 10; Howard, Luther, 5; Janick, 152; Luther Burbank,
Encyclopedia of World Biography; Luther Burbank, Western Sonoma County
Historical Society; Luther Burbank, Wikipedia; Smith, Luther.
84 ...*more than US $1.4 billion*: Brown, 157. (Ray Croc, of McDonald's restaurant fame,
who created what has often been called "the most delicious French fries in the
business," exclusively used Burbank potatoes in a special two-step frying
process.)
84 ...*managed to secure four acres in Santa Rosa*: Harwood, 14; Howard, Luther, 5;
Luther Burbank, Encyclopedia of World Biography; Luther Burbank, Western
Sonoma County Historical Society; Luther Burbank, Wikipedia; Smith, Luther;
Wickson, 9.
85 *He began with the ten Burbank potatoes*: Brown, 158; Wickson, 7.
85 ...*an order for 20,000*: Harwood, 14-15; Howard, Luther, 6; Janick, 154.
85 ...*creating new strains*: Harwood, 164; Howard, Luther, 8; Janick, 151; Luther Burbank,
Wikipedia; Preese, 201, 203; Smith, Luther.
86 ...*publishing a series of "announcements"*: Benson, 223; Janick, 154; Smith, Luther;
Wickson, 7.
86 ...*played the press like a violin*: Janick, 155.
86 *Burbank's approach to plant breeding*: Harwood 24-40, 169; Wickson 20, 22, 24-27, 36.
87 *Far too often the day with Mr. Burbank*: Harwood, 290.
87 *He had read Darwin's work*: Harwood, 18; Howard, Luther, 5; Smith, Luther.
87 *It was uncanny*: Harwood, 38-39.
87 *Burbank's sole object in making crosses*: Howard, Luther, 7.
87 ...*shorthand note-keeping system*: Harwood, 318-334; Howard, Luther, 8.
87 ...*grant from the Carnegie Institution*: Dreyer, 132; Harwood, 280-282, 362; Howard,
Luther, 132.
87 ...*Carnegie Institution hired a young biologist*: Dreyer, 132-133; Harwood, 285-287.
88 ...*friends with Thomas Edison and Henry Ford*: Janick, 156.
88 ...*people like Hugo de Vries*: Harwood, 363-364; Howard, Luther, 7; Smith, Luther.
88 ...*Academy of Sciences awarded Burbank*: Harwood, 360; Smith, Luther.
88 ...*Stanford University appointed him "Special Lecturer*: Janick, 155; Smith, Luther.

88 *Theodore Roosevelt is reported*: Dreyer, 193-194.
88 *In 1940, a US postage stamp*: Janick, 153.
88 *...nearly 800 letters a week*: Harwood, 297.
89 *...posted all of the gates*: Burbank, New Agricultural, 20-21; Harwood, 300.
89 *...required to purchase a "Ticket of Admittance"*: Harwood, 302.
89 *...bouts of nervous illness*: Dreyer, 117.
89 *...given a little potted cactus*: Harwood, 3-4; Wickson, 7.
89 *...collection of various kinds of prickly-pear*: Burbank, Luther Burbank's Spineless, 12; Dreyer 139-140, Smith, Luther.
90 *...Rose a giant cactus fully eight feet in height*: Harwood, 153-154.
90 *The fruit of these new cacti*: Harwood, 154-155.
91 *The leaves are to be fed to stock*: Burbank, Luther Burbank's Spineless, 7.
91 *The wild cactus is generally prepared*: Burbank, New Agricultural, 5-6; Burbank, Luther Burbank's Spineless, 7.
92 *Burbank then discloses that*: Burbank, Luther Burbank's Spineless, 7.
92 *Instead of selling to individuals*: Anderson, Vast Array, 162; Howard, Luther, 6-7; Smith, Luther.
92 *...Hybrid Lilies at an astounding $250,000*: Anderson, Vast Array, 161.
93 *...James McColl arrived back home*: McColl.
93 *...special commonwealth parliamentary report*: Ibid.
93 *Urging immediate government action*: Australia's Opportunity.
93 *...Rutland, a wealthy orchardist*: Howard, Luther, 6; Smith, Luther.
94 *...Rutland purchased a ticket of admission*: Original ticket held in Library of Burbank Home and Gardens, Santa Rosa, California.
94 *...the Australian orchardist came a-calling*: Gray, 26; LOC Box 32, Miscellany, 1894-1922 and undated, scrapbooks, Vol. 3. held in library at Burbank Home and Garden, Santa Rosa, California.
94 *Rutland's planting-stock order eventually grew*: Gray, 26-27; Dreyer, 132, 142.
94 *From the proceeds of this single sale*: Burbank, Luther Burbank: His Methods, 209-210; Dreyer, 142.
94 *...sent Burbank a farewell letter*: Letter dated Dec. 10, 1907, copies at Burbank Home and Gardens, Santa Rosa and in Manuscript Division, US Library of Congress.
95 *Searching through his home state of Victoria:* Gray, 27; New Fruit Trees, Western Mail.
95 *...task of selling his new cactus*: Burbank, New Agricultural, 15.
96 *...formed the Thornless Cactus Farming Company*: Dreyer, 168; Smith, Luther.
96 *...1,000 new plants each week*: Ibid.
97 *...The Luther Burbank Company, was formed*: Benson, 227; Dreyer, 191; Howard, Luther, 7; Smith, Luther.
97 *With his portrait forming part of a special seal*: Burbank, Luther Burbank's Spineless Cactus; Smith, Luther. [This portrait graced the front cover of the catalogue.]
98 *...less careful in his claims*: Anderson, Vast Array, 182; Dreyer 193.
98 *A letter sent to John Rutland*: Australia's Opportunity, 4.
99 *Responding to numerous inquiries*: Anderson, Vast Array, 183, 186; Dryer, 140, 142; Griffiths, Spineless, 3, 9-10; Smith, Luther.
99 *...state botanist Joseph Maiden declared*: Alexander, 19-20; Dryer, 140; Maiden, So-called, 52.
99 *...none of them is entirely spineless*: Benson, 229; Dreyer, 140, Griffths, Spineless, 10; Griffiths, Thornless, 17-18.
100 *...contribute to increase the spines*: Benson, 227-229, Griffiths, Spineless, 10-11.
100 *...in still another publication, Griffiths seems*: Benson, 229; Griffiths, Spineless, 3, 8-9.
101 *...Burbank is quoted as calling the experts at*: Benson, 230; Doubts Cast; Experts of U.S..
101 *Quoting a news dispatch from Washington*: Why Burbank Has Become.

102 ...*cattle ranch in the San Joaquin Valley was divided*: Smith, Luther.

103 ...*Here's how one eyewitness of the day*: Benson, 228-229.

103 ...*crop worth nearly*: Benson, 226; Burbank, Gold Metal Newest.

103 ...*rubbing a cactus slab against his cheek*: Dryer, 141-142.

104 ...*62nd US Congress also took Burbank's word at face value*: Dreyer, 193; Luther Burbank, Report # 821; Luther Burbank, Calendar #827, Public Laws, 507-508.

104 ...*but one of the conditions*: Public Laws, 507-508.

105 ...*in a letter to congressman John E. Raker*: Luther Burbank, Report #821, 7.

105 ...*was beginning to implode*: Dreyer 191, 193; Smith, Luther.

105 ...*brought in ordinary spiny prickly-pear*: Anderson, Vast Array, 186; Dreyer, 192; Smith, Luther.

106 ...*collapsed into bankruptcy in early 1916*: Dreyer, 201.

106 ...*Ten years after*: Dreyer, 214; Plant Wizard Dies.

106 *Looking back*: Lyders.

107 ...*reporter from the Sydney Morning Herald*: Thornless Cactus, Sydney Morning Herald, 4.

108 ...*various State departments were viewing*: DAIRY, Melbourne Leader.

109 ... *some of these plants were allowed to flower*: Benson, 227-228; Burbank, Luther Burbank: His Methods, 258, 260; Mulas. (It is interesting to note that Burbank admitted in his "methods series" that the return of spines was a constant problem with so-called spineless prickly-pears. He states, ". . . the spineless cactus does not breed true . . . there may be found among the seedlings of a spineless variety, plants that fairly bristle with spines, rivaling in this regard the best-protected of their wild ancestors." To those who claim that he did not understand genetic heredity, he goes on to say, ". . . it does not appear that the condition of spinyness acts as a simple Mendelian dominant. On the contrary, it appears that the hereditary conditions that govern the spiny condition in the cactus are very complex. The best interpretation would seem to be that there are multitudes of actors for spicules and spines, variously blended in the germ plasm of any given individual. The spiny condition, on the whole, tends to be dominate to the spineless condition. . .")

109 ... *were even derived from the wheel cactus*: Burbank, Luther Burbank's Spineless, 22; Howard, Luther, 45; Walters, 192.

Chapter 5 : Coping With the Green Invasion

111 *Weeds are penalties of civilization*: Maiden, Weeds, 152.

111 *In South Africa*: Walters, 17-18.

111 ...*in the year 1870*: High Hopes; Patterson; Prickly-pear Pest, 12; Samuel.

111 *People were staggered by the rate*: Cactus Invasion.

112 ... *it does not seem possible*: Centenary of Progress; Invasion of Australia, 8-9, 21; Parrington. (In the scrub districts, prickly-pear often grew up to the roads in an impenetrable solid wall. This made it very difficult for vehicles to pass, as there was usually not enough traffic to keep the way clear for more than one set of wheel tracks.)

112 *When, in 1882*: Freeman; Samuel; Walton, Reclaiming, 18. (Prickly-pear was increasingly being viewed as a serious pest. On May 3, 1881, tenders were requested for the clearing and destroying of about 200 acres of prickly-pear in the newspaper, *The Chronicle*, on behalf of James Davidson of Westbrook.)

112 ...*over 22 local government jurisdictions*: Dodd, 20; Freeman; Links With the Past..

112 ..."*Prickly Pear Destruction Act of 1886*": Freeman; Parliamentary Debates, 14; Maiden, Weeds, 152; Mann, Cacti, 4; Prickly-pear Pest, 12.

113 *Regulation #4*: Maiden, Preliminary, 1; Regulation of Prickly-pear Destruction Act of 1886.

302

113 ...*800 tons of the prickly stuff on every acre*: In Prickly Pear Land.
114 ...*By backbreaking and heartbreaking manual labor*: Coates.
114 *In his annual report for 1886*: Mann, Cacti, 4.
114 ...*a vegetable smallpox*: Prickly Pear, How It May Be Dealt With.
114 ...*"Prickly Pear Selection Act"*: Freeman; Land Acts 1897 & 1902.
115 ...*the act was a complete failure*: Freeman.
115 ...*offered a reward*: Australia's Victory; Links With the Past, 1; Mann, Cacti, 4;
    Prickly Pear Story; Reward, 258; Samuel.
115 ...*between 600 and 700 schemes*: Frawley, Prickly Pear, 323-338; Mann, Cacti, 4;
    Walton, Reclaiming, 19.
116 ...*an "oven" mounted on a wagon*: Singeing Move.
116 ...*a party of scientists from Germany*: Moss, 6.
116 ...*withdrew its reward offer in 1909*: Walton, 19.
116 *During the great drought of 1902*: Tongs.
117 ...*had apparently hybridized and the resulting cross*: Eggleston.
117 ...*after returning to Boondooma Station*: Munro, Pear Problem.
117 *On Billa Billa Station*: Nicholes, 112-115.
118 *Mr. William Coates, who spent most of his life farming*: Coates, Matthews, 183.
119 *An area called the Mungle Scrub*: Alexander, 14: Invasion of Australia.
119 *The 1906, the "Closer Settlement Act" was created*: Closer Settlement Act; Matthews.
119 ...*additional weaknesses in the legislative approach*: Freeman.
119 ...*the government of South Africa*: Compulsory Pear Destruction.
120 ...*map of the state's prickly-pear affected areas*: Prickly Pear: Control Methods, Bacteria.
120 *Kathleen Johnston*: Johnston, Day; Matthews, 207-210.
120 ...*farms and grazing properties being abandoned*: Freeman, Matthews, 180.
121 ...*a letter from a Mr. D. Groeneweg*: Groeneweg.
121 ...*the years 1910 to 1930, some 40 to 50%*: Dalucca; Fight; Parrington.
121 *Can it be conceived*: Items.
122 *Having heard that the soils of the Dawson Valley*: Taroom District.
122 ...*the common death adder*: Acanthophis; Cactus Invasion; Centenary, 20; Centenary
    of Progress, 23; Common Death Adder; M'Mahon; Nicholes, 131-132;
    Schroder; Those Pear Days; Walton, Reclaiming, 18. (In the vicinity of
    Brigalow, Queensland, a veteran herpetologist named Pambo Eades collected
    well over 100 death adders in just under three weeks during the heyday of the
    pear. These were used in a research effort to create an effective antivenom.
    Nowadays, death adders are seen around there only once or twice every couple
    of years. [Refer to *Toowoomba Chronicle*, Feb. 20, 1976])
125 ...*the life of Sir Hubert Wilkins*: Thomas, 158-159.
126 *Prickly-pear thrived in the Warra-Chinchilla region*: Centenary 1881-1981, 20.
127 ...*story of a woman - Mrs. Edmunds*: Genge, Lost, Matthews, 182.
127 ...*eventually led to a small schoolhouse*: Seagee.
127 *Last week when Jeff Dodd returned*: On The Land.
128 ...*where a house should be*: Pincushion.
128 *Arthur Graham tells another story*: Graham, Memories, 4.
129 ...*land that was covered with both*: Heilig.
129 *This plant created so much misery*: Foster, April 17.
130 ...*resorted to using old sailing ship's water tanks*: Eggleston.
130 *They had to learn to eat it*: Kerr.
130 ...*wild cattle were frequently found*: Eggleston; Pear Scrub Cattle.
131 ...*only one which has proved satisfactory*: Alexander, 5; Freeman; Walton, Reclaiming, 20.

Chapter 6 : A Country at War With the Pear

133 *Poorly equipped*: Mann, Cacti, 4.
133 *...crushing the massive thickets*: Alexander, 25; Brooks, Some Notes.
134 *...a farmer near Pallamallawa*: Fighting Prickly Pear in Northwestern NSW.
134 *It was like a very slow tsunami*: Ryan.
134 *But as one contractor disclosed*: Prickly pear: Cost of Elimination.
135 *...many of these Chinese took employment*: Frawley, Containing, 11; History of Mungindi, 257.
135 *It was hard, horrible work*: History of Mungindi, 257.
136 *...workers annually from mainland China*: Clerk, 38-39.
136 *My reason for suggesting Chinese*: Clerk, 39-40.
136 *...created the Queensland Board of Advice*: Matthews, 184; Walton, Reclaiming, 19.
136 *...Queensland Prickly-Pear Traveling Commission*: Matthews, 184.
137 *...be an experimental field station*: Mann, Cacti Naturalised, 5; Pear Pest: Dulacca Tests.
137 *Dr. Jean White*: Centenary of Progress: Dulacca, 26; Clifford, H. Trevor; Osmond;
      Walton, Reclaiming, 72.
137 *...with the exception of the clearing of a cart track*: White, Reports up to 30th June, 1913.
137 *It took nearly a month*: Ibid.
137 *A wish-list detailing the scope*: White-Haney.
138 *...narrowed her research down*: White, Report from 1 July, 1913 to 30 April, 1914.
138 *...conduct an experiment with them near the town*: Matthews, 190-191; Prickly Pear
      Pest: Eradication, Walton, Reclaiming, 71.
138 *...looked so futile that it was really taken as a joke*: Ibid.
139 *While press reports intimated*: Matthews, 190-191.
139 *...they literally starved*: Pear Pest: Dulacca Tests, Walton, Reclaiming, 71.
140 *...poison known as "Scrub Exterminator*: Qld Agricultural Journal 1898, 135.
140 *One of the first compounds developed specifically*: Matthews, 184.
140 *...the Reverend Maitland Wood*: Prickly-pear Country for Selection, 74.
140 *Over in South Africa*: Agricultural Journal of the Cape, 259.
140 *...more than 1,500 experimental plots had already*: Matthews, 187; Prickly Pear:
      Results of Experiments; Pear Pest: Dulacca Tests; White, Report from 1 July,
      1913 to 30 April, 1914.
140 *...a series of parallel pathways*: Matthews, 189; Prickly Pear: Results of Experiments.
141 *...10,000 experiments were eventually*: Walton, Reclaiming, 19.
141 *...poison traveled inside the pear at the rate*: Matthews, 187; Prickly Pear: Results of
      Experiments.
141 *Dr. White was often criticized by visitors*: White, Report from 1 July, 1913 to 30 April,1914.
141 *...in order to track the precise effect*: Ibid.
141 *...scarcity became even more pronounced*: Ibid.
141 *...Oliver Cromwell Roberts had arrived*: Prickly Pear: Destruction by Gas.
142 *Roberts had read of the widespread*: Matthews, 185.
142 *...preliminary experiments were made at Deagon*: Ibid.
142 *...obtained substantial financial backing*: Ibid.
142 *Moving to Dalacca*: Centenary of Progress, 25-26.
142 *After having first secured*: Centenary of Progress, 25-26; Dealing With Prickly Pear;
      Matthews, 185, 187; Prickly Pear Destruction; Prickly Pear: Queensland's
      Chief Enemy.
142 *Forty men were employed to cut miles*: Centenary of Progress, 25-26.
143 *The chemicals were placed in the boiler*: Alexander, 31; Matthews, 187; Prickly
      Pair Offensive; Prickly Pear: Results; Rolls, 355.
143 *Though the machine is very crude*: Matthews, 187; Prickly Pear: Results.
143 *Mr. Arthur Temple Clerk, a prickly-pear activist*: Matthews, 186; Prickly Pear Problem.
143 *...vigorous regrowth from underground rootstocks*: Centenary of Progress: Dulacca, 26;
      Prickly Pear Menace (b).

143 *Cactus Estates Limited went into liquidation*: Prickly Pear Menace (b).
143 *They were married in February 1915*: Clifford, Australian.
144 *...appeared to be the most effective chemical*: Alexander, 11; Mann, Cacti, 5; Matthews, 191; Walton, Reclaiming, 19; White-Haney.
144 *...she somehow procured, "nearly a ton"*: White-Haney.
144 *...Dr. White-Haney could finally say*: Ibid.
144 *...decided to close the research station*: Matthews, 191; Mayne, 57; Prickly Pear Eradication; Walton, Reclaiming, 71; White-Haney.
144 *She cautioned that the only real solution lay*: White-Haney.
145 *...held two patents for pear-destroying machines*: Matthews, 191.
146 *Abandoning the gas idea*: Matthews, 192; Pear Problem: Commission Busy; Walton, Reclaiming, 19.
146 *...built a factory in Wallangarra*: Battle With Pear; Centenary of Progress, 26; Matthews, 195; Prickly Pear Pest: Queensland.
146 *...had to be imported from Japan*: Cullen, 65.
146 *...another arsenic mine opened at Jibbinbar*: Pear Poison: State Arsenic Supplies; Prickly Pear Story.
147 *...one series of field trials concluded*: Matthews, 192; Prickly Pear: Good Eradication.
147 *...resolved when he cut a deal with the government*: Australia's Victory; Mann, Cacti, 12; Matthews, 183; O. C. Roberts; Prickly Pear Poison: Reduction; Pear Poison: Contract; Pear Problem: Commission Busy.
148 *...marketed the stuff to over 1,350 users*: Prickly Pear Pest: Queensland; Matthews, 195.
148 *...how much of Roberts's poison it would take to destroy*: Fighting the Prickly Pear; Information About Pear Poisons; QPPLC 2nd Annual Report.
148 *It contained a five-liter tank*: Tribute to a Grub.
148 *A light spraying of the leaves only is necessary*: Prickly Pear Destruction: Successful.
149 *...with a piece of twisted wire*: Information About Pear Poisons; Tribute to a Grub.
149 *The price the farmer has to pay*: Pear Destruction; Pear Poison: State.
150 *...tried their hand at developing*: Byrnestown; Laffey; Matthews, 197.
150 *...demonstration of the effectiveness of "S. O. S."*: Matthews, 197; S. O. S.: Prickly Pear Eradication: Closing; S. O. S.: Prickly Pear Poison; S. O. S.: War.
150 *...manufacturer of "S. O. S." was being sued*: Mr. Ley.
151 *...more than 3,300 tons of arsenic*: History of Mining; Parsons, 366; Pear Poison: St. George; QPPLC 2nd Annual Report; Raghu; Walton, Reclaiming, 19.
151 *...the 20th most abundant element on earth*: Arsenic; Arsenic in Drinking Water.
151 *...occur naturally in many of our foods*: Ibid. (Health food tablets and powders made from kelp have been found to contain up to 50 ppm arsenic.)
151 *Average concentrations in fish and shellfish*: Arsenic.
152 *...within three days after consumption*: Arsenic in Drinking Water.
152 *The natural sink of this "arsenic in solution"*: Noller, 132.
152 *...seepage coming from a gold mine waste dump*: Noller, 137-138.
152 *...arsenic is transported into most of the organs*: Noller, 134.
152 *...long-term exposure to arsenic*: Carn,17; Freeman, Walton, Reclaiming, 19.
152 *...Thomas Foster told me of his own*: Foster, Feb 14.
153 *...clear pear by spraying it from horseback*: Rolls, 355.
153 *And the mist would get into your eyes*: Kerr.
153 *...a bulletin published in 1919*: Alexander, 28.
154 *...graze in the paddocks that are being poisoned*: Information About Pear Poisons; Prickly Pear Pest: Official Poisoning Results.
154 *...Bill Varidel simply wrote*: Varidel, 6.
154 *...how safe is Australia's water supply*: Physical and Chemical, 400.
155 *...known as "closer settlement*: Australia Pacific; Frawley, Containing; Mayne.

155 *...schemes to offer prickly-pear infested land*: Prickly Pear Country.
155 *Known as peppercorn leases*: Kitson, 128; Lease of Prickly Pear Infested.
155 *...surveyor John Meek recalled*: Ibid.
156 *...had special leather suits made for them*: 1901 to 1920: Combating; Kitson,128.
156 *...thousands of unemployed returned soldiers*: Eggleston; Munro, Prickly Pear.
156 *...wrote Val Tongs*: Tongs.
156 *...abandoning their farms once again*: Eggleston; Prickly Pear: Queensland's Chief Enemy.
156 *...men who took up these "soldier settlements*: Munro, Prickly Pear.
156 *...only time they had for fighting their own pear*: On The Land: Pear Fighters.
157 *They spend hours leaning over fences*: In Prickly Pear Land.
157 *...although born in Sydney*: Clifford, Mary.
157 *...invited his fellow-members of parliament*: Dunnicliff; Prickly Pear Lands; Wearne, 72; With the Bug.
158 *...It would be rude to dispute the declaration of a Minister*: Notes of the Week.
158 *...land in New South Wales had already been overrun*: Australia's Cactus; Prickly Pear (b); Prickly Pear Menace (a); On The Land: Pear Fighters. (The Aug. 2, 1922 issue of *The New York Times* reported that the government of N.S.W. had drafted a bill which made it a penal offence to let prickly-pear grow on clean lands. Fortunately, that bill was not passed.)
158 *After transferring to a fleet of a dozen cars*: Dunnicliff; On The Land: Pear Fighters.
158 *...the members jumped out to see the obstacle*: Ibid.
158 *...only space clear of pear was a 15-foot-wide*: Ibid.
158 *...unanimous regarding the need for government action*: Prickly Pear: Board of Control.
158 *...Wearne's bill easily passed*: Prickly Pear: Board of Control. (This bill was passed as "The Prickly-pear Act, 1924.")
159 *...for more than 60 years*: Annual Report; Mann, Cacti, 12; Ryan; Tanner.
159 *...official start in 1924*: Dodd, 26; Mann, Cacti, 11-12; Matthews, 195; Pear Commission.
159 *...a territory almost the size of Italy*: QPPLC 5th Annual Report.
159 *...began to purchase*: Information about pear poisons; QPPLC 2nd Annual Report.
160 *...offered a subsidy of £2*: Pear Destruction: Vigorous Campaign.
160 *Functioning as an independent body*: Prickly Pear: The New Commission; Prickly Pear: Queensland's Curse.
160 *This often meant confiscation*: Clearing of Pear.
160 *...review many of the leases in their jurisdiction*: Held in Check; Science to Rescue.
160 *...the latest lease adjustments were announced*: Pear Lands: Reduction in Rents; Prickly Pear Land: Further Decisions; Prickly Pear: Rangers Appointed.
161 *If the pear wasn't kept in check*: Johnston, Day; Prickly Pear Rangers; Prickly QPPLC 2nd Annual Report. ("If a state government insisted on forfeiture of neglected lands, they were usually completely overrun by the prickly-pear in short order," says Donald Freeman. "Because no legislation obliged any government to clear them. Infested lands almost invariably failed to attract new tenants.")
161 *...compiled from land rangers' annual reports*: Prickly Pear Being Cleaned Up.
161 *...land rangers were quite officious*: Foster, personal correspondence, Feb. 14; Frawley, Containing; Ulm.
162 *...vicious cycle that most settlers faced*: Groeneweg.
162 *One settler who took up*: Seabrook. (This narrative, attributed to Thomas A. Cole II, was also seen in 2012 printed on an information sign located at the former site of the Commonwealth Prickly Pear Board's Chinchilla Field Station.)
162 *...began to publish announcements*: Fighting Prickly Pear; Prickly Pear Being Cleaned Up; Prickly Pear Menace Has Disappeared.
163 *...a price on the head of several bird species*: QPPLC 2nd Annual Report, 29.

306

163 *To justify their action*: Ibid
163 *The bounty was rather generous*: Ibid.
163 *...more than 226,000 birds*: Frawley, Prickly Pear Land; Parsons, 365; Prickly
    Pear Being Cleaned Up; QPPLC 3rd Annual Report; QPPLC 4th Annual
    Report, Walton, Reclaiming, 20.
164 *I wish to enter a most emphatic protest*: Greensil.
164 *...author Neil McGilp argued strongly*: McGilp.
164 *...appears a telling note from the editor*: Ibid.
164 *...eight years before it was merged*: Dodd, 26; Mann, Cacti, 12.
164 *...coercive approach to land tenure had failed*: Freeman.

Chapter 7 : Search For a Biological "Cure"

167 *The first person*: Conquering.
168 *As early as 1899*: Dodd, Biological, 8; Green octopus; Matthews, 180; Prickly Pear:
    Cost of Elimination; Walton, Reclaiming, 20.
168 *...Traveling Commission" consisted of*: Alexander, Prickly Pear, 15-16; Freeman;
    Green octopus; Guthrie; Howard, History; Logan; Mann, Cacti, 5; Professor;
    Sandars, Walton, Reclaiming, 21.
168 *...the "prickly-pair"*: Johnston, Report, pg. V; Logan; Sandars.
168 *...sought the advice of Joseph Maiden*: Frawley, Prickly Pear Land; Johnston, Report.,
    pg. VI., 1; Prickly Pear: Queensland Party. (Joseph Maiden's best known work
    today is his book, *The Useful Native Plants of Australia*.)
168 *...left Sydney by steamship*: Guthrie; Johnston Report., pgs. V-VI; Prickly Pear:
    Queensland Party.
169 *From Sri Lanka, the investigators forwarded*: Alexander, Natural, 56; Alexander,
    Prickly Pear, 33; Dodd, Biological, 27; Johnston, Report, 5, 7-8; Hosking, 434;
    Mann, Cacti, 80.
169 *...Johnston and Tryon reached India*: Johnston, Report, pg. V-VI, 8.
169 *...saw the Great Hedge*: Johnston, Report, 9.
169 *As they left Spain*: Johnston, Report, pg. VI.
169 *...a meeting with Nathaniel Britton*: Johnston, Report, 61.
169 *...Mr. Tryon was described as*: Howard, History.
170 *...met with David Griffiths*: Johnston, Report, 61.
170 *...visited Luther Burbank at his nursery*: Johnston, Report, 62.
170 *...a civil war raging in that country prevented*: Johnston, Report, pg. VII, 86.
170 *...turned south for Key West, Florida*: Johnston, Report, 62.
170 *...does not specifically name who went to South America*: Johnston, Report, 102.
170 *Aided by Dr. C. Spegazzini*: Cactus Invasion; Johnston, Report, 102, 105-106.
171 *...were delayed for two weeks in Hawaii*: Johnston, Report, 110.
171 *...all of the insects eventually died*: Dodd, Biological, 27; Johnston, Report, 106.
171 *This apparently is the outcome*: Johnston, Report, 106.
171 *...priorities had been suddenly altered*: Battle Against Pear; Conquering Prickly Pear;
    Freeman; Green octopus; Mann, 5, 53; Prickly Pear Story.
171 *...appointed professor at the University of Adelaide*: Prickly Pear: Control Methods,
    Bacteria; Sandars. (Dr. Johnston was quoted to have said on the day he left the
    CPPB, "I have no hesitation is stating that the indications for complete
    biological control of the prickly-pear pest are highly favorable. The laboratory
    results are very satisfactory and there is no reason to suppose that the
    organisms will be less deadly to the pear in the field than they are in the laboratory.")
172 *As early as 300 AD*: Ji Han; Pain; Walton, Reclaiming, 2.
172 *...a cottony-cushion scale insect*: Walton, Reclaiming, 2.

172 ...*used to control lantana*: Dodd, Biological, 30-31; Walton, Reclaiming, 3.

172 ...*use of an insect to control prickly-pear*: Holtcamp; Hosking, 433; Samuel.

172 ...*radical change to India's landscape*: Maiden, Prickly Pears, 864; Singh.

173 ...*was successfully repeated in Sri Lanka*: Singh. (At the present time, *Dactylopius ceylonicus* continues to control the *monocantha* prickly-pear in India and Sri Lanka.)

173 *But in 1903, a similar attempt*: Hosking, 433; Raghu; Walton, Reclaiming, 20.

173 ...*not a shire council matter*: Dodd, Biological, 27; Menance in the North; Prickly Pear: Control Methods; Prickly Pear Menace: Methods; Raghu; Walton, Reclaiming, 21.

174 ...*an accord between state and federal*: Dodd, Conquest; Fighting Prickly Pear: Pest Losing Ground; Prickly Pear Pest: Organising; Mann, Cacti, pg. V, 6-7; Walton, Reclaiming, 21.

174 *Half of the Board's initial funding*: Alexander, Natural, 13; Fighting Prickly Pear: Pest Losing Ground; Mann, Cacti, 6; Prickly Pear: Experimental; Prickly Pear Menace: Methods; Walton, Reclaiming, 21.

174 ...*Johnston was promptly appointed*: Alexander, Natural, 15-16; Fighting Prickly Pear: Pest Losing Ground; Howard, History.

174 ...*outline of the Board's charter was*: Dodd, Control; Hosking, 433; Mann, Cacti, 6.

175 ...*searching for prickly-pear-eating insects*: Alexander, Natural, 76; Mann, Cacti, 7.

175 ...*arrived in Buenos Aires, Argentina*: Alexander, Notes, 1.

175 ...*thought were indications of previous activity*: Ibid.

175 ...*interview with Argentina's Minister of Agriculture*: Ibid.

175 ...*entomologist E. E. Blanchard*: Ibid.

176 ...*by a fungus called Sclerotinia*: Ibid.

176 ...*later Johnston boarded a ship*: Alexander, Notes, 2.

176 ...*Alexander was a serious-minded man*: Alexander; Wilfred.

176 *Alexander would direct the CPPB's research*: Dodd, Biological, 28, 174.

176 ...*to complete the work on his book*: Alexander, Wilfred.

176 ...*for the coastal city of Bahia Blanca*: Alexander, Notes, 3.

117 ...*a selection from a typical page*: Alexander, Notes, 4

178 ...*near the small town of Andalgala*: Alexander, Notes, 23, 42, 45.

178 ...*Alexander sent a triumphant telegram*: Alexander, Notes, 50.

178 ...*so that he could examine his berth*: Alexander, Notes, 51-52.

179 ...*resumed his trip to Tucuman*: Alexander, Notes, 52-53.

179 ...*in the midst of a general labor strike*: Alexander, Notes, 55.

179 ...*a cable finally arrived from Brisbane*: Ibid.

179 *On the day of departure*: Ibid.

180 ...*arrived in Rio de Janeiro on the 8th of May*: Alexander, Natural Enemies, 24-25; Alexander, Notes, 56-60; Samuel.

181 *Immediately after the ship was tied to the dock*: Alexander, Notes, 62.

181 ...*strong sea that caused the ship to roll violently*: Alexander, Notes, 64.

181 *Imagine Alexander's shock*: Alexander, Notes, 65.

182 ...*arrived in Fremantle*: Alexander, Notes, 66.

182 *Having been briefed in advance*: Ibid.

183 *His journal records what he saw*: Alexander, Notes, 67 (Alexander didn't know it at the time, but the caterpillars that he had brought back with him were a new species of *Cactoblastis*. Although this species was established in Australia many years later, it never proved to be as successful or as destructive as *Cactoblastis cactorum*.)

184 *In the United States, near Uvalde, Texas*: Dodd, Conquest; Howard, History.

184 ...*between 150 and 160 different kinds*: Mann, Cactus-feeding.

184 ...*more than a half-million individual insects*: Mann, Cacti, 9.

184 *The Wardian case was a modification*: Alexander, Natural Enemies, 17-18; Mann, Cacti, 9.
185 *For the long journey from America to Australia*: Alexander, Natural Enemies, 17-18;
   Prickly Pears and Their Biological Control.
185 *...sent to Sydney via the S. S. Sonoma*: Alexander, Natural Enemies, 6; Mann, Cacti, 9.
185 *Success was much more likely if the insects*: Dodd, Biological, 73.
185 *...the Board chose the abandoned explosives reserve*: Alexander, Natural Enemies, 16;
   Dodd, Conquest; Donnelly; Fighting Prickly Pear: Pest; Walton, Reclaiming, 69.
186 *...field-stations equipped with hundreds of cages*: Alexander, Natural Enemies, 7-8,
   16; Dodd, Biological, 32-33; Dodd, Conquest; Mann, Cacti, 7-8; Prickly Pear
   Menace: Methods.
186 *There was one at Westwood*: Ibid.
186 *Of the 50 or so insect species that had*: Dodd, Biological, 3-4; Dodd, Conquest;
   Prickly Pear and Their Control; Prickly Pears and Their Biological Control.
187 *Curious visitors openly scoffed*: In Prickly Pear Land; Walton, Reclaiming, 73.
187 *...a sap-sucking bug from Texas*: Alexander, Natural Enemies, 50; Centenary of
   Progress, 27-28; Johnston, Report, 74; Prickly Pear, (c); Prickly Pear Menace:
   Factors in its Control; Prickly Pear Menace: Methods; Prickly Pears and Their
   Biological Control; Mann, Cacti, 69-71.
188 *...cactus-boring caterpillars of certain moths*: Alexander, Natural Enemies, 8; Army
   of Insects; Prickly Pear Menace: Factors in its Control; Mann, Cacti, 57-58.
188 *The prickly-pear spider mite*: Dodd, Conquest; Pear; Prickly Pear, (c); Prickly Pears
   and Their Biological Control.
189 *...was so consumed*: Clerk, Prickly Pear Problem; Donnelly; Johnston, Report, vii.
189 *...he recalled during an interview shortly before*: Frawley, Containing Queensland, 11.
190 *As far back as 1907*: Alexander, Natural Enemies, 56; Cochineal Insect; Fighting
   Pear: Cochineal at Work.
190 *...time to distribute the cochineal*: Centenary of Progress, 27; Clerk, Prickly Pear Problem;
   Cochineal Insect; Fighting Pear: Cochineal at Work; Insects and Prickly Pear;
   Fighting Prickly Pear: Pest Losing Ground; Mann, Cacti, 73.
190 *...Culliford was also given special permission*: Battle With Pear; Fighting Pear: Cochineal
   at Work; Cochineal Insect.
191 *...Mr. Culliford was quoted as saying*: Battle With Pear.
191 *...gifted Clerk with a first-class train ticket*: Cochineal Insect.
191 *...more than 15 local governments*: Cochineal Insect; Daclytopuis.
191 *...two young men from Brisbane*: Battle With Pear.
191 *...could supply over 200,000 kerosene tins*: Battle With Pear; Cochineal Insect.
192 *...was strongly criticized by most*: Pear Destruction: Value of Cochineal.
192 *The people of Dulacca showed their appreciation*: M'Mahon; Centenary of Progress, 27.
192 *Later, they reversed this edict*: Cochineal and Pear; Silent Workers.
192 *...distributed thousands of cases of cochineal-infected*: Campaign Against; Enemy of
   Prickly Pear; Is the Pear Doomed?; Pear Destruction: Value; Prickly Pear and
   Cochineal; Prickly Pear Battle; Prickly Pear: Cochineal Campaign; Prickly
   Pear Menace: Methods.
193 *...liberation sites were kept under close observation*: Alexander, Natural Enemies, 56.
193 *They were nicknamed the "Texas,"*: Alexander, Natural Enemies; In 10 to 15 Years;
   Mann, Cacti Naturalised, 74-75; Matthews, 197; Seagee.
193 *...insects would or would not do*: Alexander, Natural, 28; Fighting Prickly Pear: Pest
   Losing Ground; Is the Pear Doomed?; Mann, Cacti, 75-76; Pear Destroyers;
   Prickly Pear Insect; Prickly-pear Pest in New South Wales, 19; Silent Workers;
   QPPCL 2nd Annual Report.
194 *...six long months of heavy rain began to fall*: Alexander, Natural Enemies, 56;
   Fighting Pear: Parasites; Mann, Cacti, 76.

310

205 ...*he again became the officer-in-charge*: J. Mann Career Notes.
205 *John Spencer Mann was born*: John Mann Obituary.
206 ...*accepted a position as laboratory assistant*: John Mann Obituary.
206 ...*at the position of "Entomologist*: Dodd, Biological, 174-175; J. Mann Career Notes.
206 *Mann had a "portly figure*: Donnelly.
206 *But the schism between them*: Donnelly; Interview.
206 ...*rejected evolutionary theory*: Interview.
206 ...*the king of England awarded Alan Dodd*: McFadyen, Dodd; Man Who Helped.
207 ...*awarded him an even higher honor*: Ibid.
207 ...*John Mann received an appointment*: Donnelly; Little Brown Moth.
207 ...*Mann was awarded an M. B. E.*: Interview; John Mann Obituary.
207 ...*During his farewell dinner*: Interview.
207 *Thirteen years after his retirement*: John Mann Obituary.
207 ...*insisted on being addressed*: Mann, letter.
207 ...*Dodd had a love for cats*: Donnelly; Perry.
207 ...*such an expression of utter seriousness*: McFadyen, Dodd; Perry.
208 ...*management approach at work*: Baldwin, Robert; McFadyen, Dodd; McFadyen, audio.
208 *Cactoblastis caterpillars are colored*: Dodd, Conquest; Dodd, Report, 7.
209 *The eggs are laid in curious chains*: Dodd, Conquest; Freeman.
209 ...*breeding cage soon evolved*: Dodd, Biological, 33.
210 ...*the eggsticks were collected on a daily*: Freeman; Prickly Pears.
210 *In the last six months*: Destroyer; Dodd, Biological, 6, 111-112; Dodd, Conquest;
     Killing Pear; Pear Eradication, Valuable; Queensland Triumph.
210 *On December 22nd, 1926, the Daily Mail*: Enemy of Pear.
210 *On August 1st, 1927*: Poison Action.
210 *Australia's prime minister, Mr. S. M. Bruce*: Pear Destruction: Work of Cactoblastis.
210 ...*more than nine million*: Cactoblastis; Dodd, Biological, 113; Dodd, Conquest; Dodd,
     Progress; Mann, Cacti, 54-55; Pear Destruction: Work of Commission; Prickly
     Pear Menace: Methods; QPPLC 5th.
211 *To give some idea of the scope*: Dodd, Conquest; Prickly Pear Eradication; Prickly
     Pear Pest: Organising; Prickly Pears; Samuel.
211 ...*workforce had expanded to*: Raghu; Queensland Triumph;To Cost Less; Walton,
     Reclaiming, 25.
211 *The cost of distributing eggs raised*: Walton, Reclaiming, 25.
212 *Workers from the town of Chinchilla*: Chinchilla; Fuller; Walton, Reclaiming, 25.
212 *Even the kids were hired*: Kerr.
212 *A few people conducted the business*: Dodd, Biological, 116, Walton, Reclaiming, 25.
212 *On the door they had inscribed*: Ibid.
212 ...*attached to small squares*: Dodd, Biological, 111-112; Queensland Triumph, Rolls.
213 ...*often seemed too much trouble*: Dodd, Biological, 116.
213 ...*water-resistant waxed-paper tubes*: Queensland Triumph; To Cost Less; Walton,
     Reclaiming, 24-25.
213 *Each box was marked with*: Battle Against Pear; Dodd, Conquest; Mann, Cacti, 55;
     Prickly Pear Controlled.
213 *Dad and Mum made sure that*: Geldard.
213 ...*deliveries got delayed in the mail*: Lithgow.
214 *The men went to bed*: Ibid.
214 *Our farm at Brigalow was one of the first*: Ulm.
214 ...*more than three billion eggs had been released*: Dodd, Biological, 5; Dodd,
     Conquest; Simonsen; Walton, Reclaiming, 25-26.
215 ...*estimated that it takes about*: Walton, Reclaiming, 24.
215 ...*others protested the wholesale destruction*: Prickly Pear, Preparation as Fodder.

311

215 *Traditional mindsets*: Biologist and Poisoner.
216 *Several species of birds tear open*: Mann, Cacti, 85; QPPLC 5th Annual Report; Ryan.
216 *In another report*: Dodd, Biological, 7.
216 *The rapidity of the onslaught was astonishing*: Dodd, Progress.
216 *...and hear them eating*: Osmund.
216 *...mixture of bacteria and fungi that usually*: Mann, Cacti, 112-113.
216 *Likening it to the stench*: Eggleston; Ryan; Walton, audio; Walton, Reclaiming.
217 *...collapse of the prickly-pear menace was so fast*: Dodd, Biological, 6; Freeman.
217 *The soil was so rich that for 40 years*: Schroder.
217 *...Eric Geldard's property had originally*: Geldard.
217 *My brother Burt told me*: Ibid.
218 *In August 1930*: Dodd, Conquest; Parrington.
218 *Country that was absolutely impassable*: Four Years Care.
218 *...report of the prickly-pear warden*: QPPLC 7th Annual Report, Appendix 3, 26, 31.
218 *Arthur Hurse of Chinchilla remembers*: Green Invasion.
218 *...issued a statement declaring*: Prickly Pear Elimination.
219 *...a 16-minute-long black and white*: Cactoblastis Grub Now Screen Star; Conquest
     by Cactoblastis; How Prickly Pear Pest; Maplestone; Prickly Pear Story; Star.
219 *A tiny caterpillar is doing a big job that men*: Importing a Pest.
219 *They will have the consolation of the Glutton*: Dunbabin.
219 *...the last big area of primary prickly-pear*: Dodd, Biological, 6; Dodd, Conquest; Patterson.
219 *...had finally exhausted their food supply*: Dodd, Biological, 6; Dodd, Conquest; Freeman.
219 *...attacked nearby fields of green tomatoes*: Australia's Victory; Cactoblastis:
     Attack; Dodd, Biological, 59, 69; New Food; Queensland Triumph; Views.
220 *The regrowth grew extremely rapidly*: Argentine; Dodd, Biological, 141; Dodd,
     Present; Prickly Pear Menace Has Disappeared; Walton, Reclaiming, 27.
220 *...Cactoblastis population was far too small*: Dodd, Conquest.
220 *And it proved most palatable to Cactoblastis*: Dodd, Biological, 141.
220 *One of the strongest characteristics of this insect*: Dodd, Conquest.
221 *...during a meeting of the Historical Society*: Ibid.
221 *Queensland has been freed*: Ibid.
221 *Little remains to remind one*: Johnston, Day.
221 *It is astonishing to realize*: Delley; Mann, Cacti, vii; Prickly Pear Menace Has Disappeared.
222 *The miracle wrought by cactoblastis*: Freeman.
222 *Had Cactoblastis not come into the picture*: Dodd, Conquest; QPPLC 5th.
222 *A wave of the scientist's wand*: Samuel.
222 *...land available in two classes*: Dodd, Biological, 12.
222 *For surveyor John Meek*: Kitson, 128.
222 *Competition for these selections*: Fuller; Land Hunger; Samuel.
223 *...much like winning the lottery*: Land Settlement.
223 *...small factory produced 400,000 pounds*: Dodd, Biological, 12; Dodd, Conquest; Town.
223 *...unwanted trees have been killed*: Cactoblastis: A world first; Dodd, Biological, 12;
     Dodd, Conquest; Prickly Pear Menace Has Disappeared.
223 *...drawing of a single-story wooden building*: Ripley's.
224 *...permanently memorialize*: Argentine; Dodd, Conquest; Immortalising; Lake; Patterson.
224 *They built a bloody hall to commemorate*: Walton, audio.
224 *Esmé Davis, who grew up near Boonarga*: Davis, Esmé.
225 *...the hall has been extended by one-third*: Boonarga; Davis, Esmé.
225 *...eulogized the hall in a poem*: R.D. Dyke in Emmerson's, *From Cellars to Refrigerators*.
226 *...erected a large cairn*: Dalby; Rossmanith.
226 *...Hinwood's bronze statue*: Cactoblastis honoured in bronze.
226 *...erected near the site of the old*: Cameron, Margaret.

312

226 ...*estimated that the weight*: Osmund.
226 *There is a constant bout between the climate*: McFadyen, audio.
227 *There are places where*: Hosking, J.R., Sullivan, P.R., and Welsby,
    S.M.; Rolls, 356; Prickly Pear Pest.
227 *Alan Dodd recognized at least three*: Dodd, Biological, 6-7, 24, Low.
227 *The solution to the problem was secured*: Dodd, Biological, 6-7.
227 ...*new hormone-type weed killers*: Dedication Programme.
228 ...*it has reached an equilibrium*: Dodd, Present; Donnelly; Freeman; Tanner; Wolski.

Chapter 9 : The Good Bug Goes Bad

230 *As early as 1928*: Dodd, Conquest; Pear Eradication, Pest.
231 *Inquiries show that details*: Use Cactoblastis.
231 ...*Indian Government is considering*: Pear in India.
231 ...*dispatched to India*: Dodd, Biological, 35; Mann, Cacti, 96.
231 *As a result of this effort*: Dodd, Biological, 35.
231 ...*absent in both of these countries*: Dodd, Biological, 35; Invasive.
231 ...*returned to South Africa taking with him*: Brooks, Christopher; Dodd, Biological, 35;
    Mann, Cacti, 96; Simonsen; Use Cactoblastis; Zimmermann, Biology, 18.
231 *The first batch of eggs*: Use Cactoblastis.
232 ...*occupied more than 2.2 million acres*: Raghu; Zimmermann, Biology, 18.
232 ...*releasing some 580 million eggsticks*: Marsico; Raghu; Simonsen.
232 *Troops of free-ranging baboons*: Allies; Baboons Rush, 18; Monkey Tricks, 5.
232 ...*removing the conspicuous eggsticks*: Prickly Pear Control: South African
    Policy; Zimmermann, Renowned, 548.
233 ...*invaded some of that country's*: Raghu; Zimmermann, Biology, 20.
233 ...*similar attempts to establish*: European; Invasive; Iziko; Zimmermann, Biology, 21.
233 ...*supplied the Noumea Chamber of Commerce*: Dodd, Biological, 35.
233 ...*One early progress report*: Jacques.
233 ...*Mauritius received its Cactoblastis directly*: Iziko; Zimmermann, Biology, 21.
233 ...*then in 1950 or 1951, the Hawaiian Islands*: Mann, Cacti, 96.
233 ...*brought to the islands sometime before 1809*: Maui; Pratt.
233 ...*by 1910 several thousand acres*: Maui.
234 ...*two other species of introduced cactus*: Davis, Clifton.
234 *On the big island*: Ibid.
234 ...*by some of the ranchers*: Ibid.
234 *It took years of vociferous debate*: Ibid.
234 ...*cactus infestation on the Parker Ranch*: Davis, Clifton; Gardener.
235 *Nevis is a roughly cone-shaped island*: Nevis.
235 ...*much of Nevis's lowlands were deforested*: Johnston, Report, 94; Nevis; Raghu.
235 ...*Cactoblastis was sent by British entomologists*: Brooks, Christopher; Gilchrist;
    Marsico; Raghu; Simonsen; Zimmermann, Biology, 21.
236 ...*islands of Montserrat and Antigua*: Marsico; Simonsen; Zimmermann, Biology, 21.
236 ...*Grand Cayman Island also received a shipment*: Iziko; Zimmermann, Biology, 21.
236 ...*also made to Saint Helena Island*: Invasive; Iziko; Zimmermann, Insect Pest, 45.
236 ...*something might be going wrong*: Zimmermann, Insect Pest, 45.
236 *In Cuba, one of its native prickly-pear species*: Zimmermann, Renowned, 546.
236 ...*first instance of the cactus moth being*: Hernández; Zimmermann, Renowned, 546.
236 *Two more unverifiable reports*: Hernández; Simberloff, How risky is; Zimmermann,
    Renowned, 546.
236 ...*Cuban botanist Alberto Areces collected*: Hernández; Zimmermann, IAEA.
237 ...*in the Guantanamo region*: Zimmermann, IAEA; Zimmermann, Renowned, 546.

237 *Back in the autumn of 1961*: Guantanamo Bay; Opuntia: Wikipedia; Patrol. (The area immediately surrounding the perimeter fence at Guantamo Naval Base was once one of the heavily mined places in the world. At least 24 people have been killed by exploding mines there since 1962. The United States deactivated its minefield in the late 1990s, but the Cuban minefield is reported to still be active.)

237 *...restricted to a relatively small region*: Gilchrist; Zimmermann, Renowned, 546.

237 *...had never before been exposed to its predations*: Simonsen.

237 *In Texas, many ranchers*: Tyler.

238 *...formally considered in the 1960s*: Pemberton.

238 *...Cactoblastis in the States*: Habeck; Simonsen; Solis;Zimmermann, Biology, 22.

238 *Fearing that a devastating*: Bloem, K. A.; Simonsen; Zimmermann, Biology, 24-25.

238 *One early report suggested*: Stiling, Protecting; Majure; Zimmermann, Renowned, 547.

238 *...somewhere between 24 to 45 miles*: Ibid.

238 *In comparison*: Simonsen.

239 *...inspectors from the Florida Division of Plant Industry*: Ibid.

239 *Almost 90 species of prickly-pear cacti are found*: Stiling, Protecting; Zimmermann, Biology, 25; Zimmermann, Renowned, 548. (The total number of prickly-pear species (*Opuntia*) found in the USA and Mexico is still very much in debate. Estimates currently range from 87 to 127 distinct species. Genetical analysis will most likely lead to even more described species, not less.)

239 *Between the years 2000 and 2003*: Bloem, K. A.; Solis.

240 *...a delegation of Texas ranchers approached*: Pemberton.

240 *...even a Texas-based agricultural scientist*: Ibid.

240 *...based on the genetic analyses*: Marsico; Simonsen.

240 *...reported that during the 13-year period*: Ibid.

240 *Since only about 2% of each*: Ibid.

240 *...cactus plants at a Wal-Mart*: Stiling, Protecting; Zimmermann, Biology, 22.

241 *...intercepted at the Dallas International Airport*: Zimmermann, Biology, 22.

241 *By 2009, Cactoblastis had already chewed*: Hight, Expanding; Madsen, 25; Solis.

241 *...entire population of semaphore cactus*: CPC; IUCN; Low, 269-270; Possley; Stiling, Death; Stiling, Endangered; Stiling, Protecting; Status. (This cactus grow in hammocks on nearly bare rock with a minimum amount of soil cover, only a few feet above the high tide mark.)

242 *...sterile insect technique*: Madsen; Eradication, 9; Carpenter, 254-255.

244 *...halted Cactoblastis's westward advance*: Hight, personal.

244 *...program has subsequently been canceled*: Carpenter, August 18, 2014; Hight, personal.

244 *...as many as 210,000 farmers*: Arroyo; Bloem; Gilchrist.

244 *...now worth more*: Arroyo; Chiapas; Moreno, World; Nopal; Zimmermann, Biology, 25-26. (Estimated production and value of Mexico's *nopal* industry varies widely between sources of information and from year to year. The figures that are quoted in the text are probably the most accurate rendition of these various sources. The report by Arroyo, *et al*, listed in the bibliography is the most comprehensive discussion of Mexico's *nopal* industry that I've seen.)

244 *...curious reversal of foreign aid*: Carpenter, Oct. 5, 2011; Moreno, Rebeca. (These funds were reportedly provided through an intermediary organization called the North American Plant Protection Organization (NAPPO), whose members include Canada, Mexico, and the USA.)

245 *...on two islands near Cancun*: Arroyo; Carpenter, Aug. 29, 2011; Eradication, 3; Varone.

247 *To follow up on the whole issue*: Background; Carpenter, March 25, 2015.

250 *...has also founded several other overseas*: Briano; Stelljes; Vail.

251 *...wasp, called Apanteles opuntiarum*: Varone.

255 *Our program has evolved*: Carpenter, August 18, 2014.

256 ...*biological control has long been touted*: Simberloff, Risks; Walton, vi.
256 *Biological control practitioners have rebutted*: Simberloff, Risks, Walton, 85.
256 ...*are usually self-sustaining*: Walton, 5, 86.
257 ...*Myxoma virus to control rabbits*: Simberloff, How risky is.
257 ...*for control of musk thistle*: Huber; Van Driesche.
258 ...*species of biological control agents*: Walton, 2-3.
258 ...*But it is often difficult to explain*: McFadyen, Larval. (On the whole, disruption of
    ecosystem processes caused by biological control agents is very unlikely to be
    observed. Primarily, this is because even intensive research projects rarely
    monitor more than a small fraction of ecosystem processes and even those
    efforts are nearly always abandoned after a just few years, especially after
    funding for such monitoring is terminated.)
258 ...*laws aimed at regulating biological control*: Simberloff, Risks; Walton, 10-11.
258 ...*are still evolving*: Huber; Simberloff, How risky is.
258 ...*like the Australian gall wasp*: Simberloff, How risky is.
258 ...*can change its virulence quite suddenly*: Ibid.
259 ...*some of these new arrivals can become*: Hosking, audio; Ivanov; Ogle, 330; Prance, 377.
260 ...*yet it did not eliminate the pear*: Hosking, Biological; McFadyen, Feb. 26, 2012.
260 ...*on the tiny Caribbean island of Nevis*: Pemberton.

Chapter 10 : The Song of the Prickly-pear

263 ...*many practical uses were found*: Clarke; Newberry, 25; Tongs. (David Challinor
    writes that "those of my vintage will remember the wind-up gramophone,
    whose steel needle at the end of the arm converted into sound [music] the
    bumps in the grooves of the record. Actually, a steel needle was too hard for
    the record substrate; when a record was played too often, its grooves became so
    worn that it caused an audible hissing that interfered with the clarity of the
    music coming from the speaker. Various substitutes were tried to replace steel
    needles, including bamboo slivers. The most successful substitute, however,
    turned out to be prickly-pear spines which were shaped and chemically
    hardened. The discoverer of this substitute was a South African who formed
    the BCN Gramophone Needle Company in the 1920s. The spines had just the
    right degree of hardness to pick up the sound clearly, yet were not so hard as to
    distort the bumps in the record's groove, thereby producing a hiss-less
    reception and minimum wear on the record.")
264 *Prickly-pear jam was part of our*: Kerr.
264 *The basic recipe that most folks*: Genge, Prickly-pear.
264 ...*Swedish watchmaker named Max Fries*: Lived.
265 *In 1856, a commercial distillery*: Johnston, Report, 53.
265 ...*this time in Granada, Spain*: Alexander, Prickly, 22.
265 *Unfortunately for Johnston and Tryon*: Johnston, Report, 1.
265 ...*this time in South Africa*: Petrol.
266 ...*a practice used in Sweden on a large scale*: Porkobidni.
266 *This is the psychological moment to start*: Ibid.
266 ...*a staunch advocate for power alcohol*: Cotton, Prickly pear.
266 *Only about 10 or 11 gallons of alcohol*: Jones, Uses; Johnston, Report, 53-54.
267 ...*after witnessing a demonstration*: Power Alcohol.
267 ...*proposal of a reward of £5,000*: Prickly Pear (From Friday Speech by Moore).
267 *The South African venture offers little*: Invasion.
268 *In Mexico, the nopal, or prickly-pear, is a key feature*: Lacy.
268 ...*when his own urine*: Baker, Effects; Casas, 155; Gerard, Chap 128, pg 1330; Gerbi, 402.

268 ...*grown for their fruits*: DeFelice; Griffith, Origins; Jacobo; Mondragon-Jacobo; Wilson.
269 ...*very irritating to the mouth and throat*: Giguet; Grubb, 91.
269 *Lyman Benson noted in his book*: Benson, 22.
269 ...*Giguet describes this process*: Giguet.
270 ...*they are esteemed by some*: Castle, 81.
270 ...*Mexico City writer, Eugenio del Hoyo*: Hoyo.
270 *A chemical analysis of tunas from*: Russell. (Analysis of the fruits from a number of
    North American species of prickly-pear indicate that the sugar content in their
    juice normally ranges from 3% to 10%.)
271 ...*enriched levels of certain mineral micro-nutrients*: Feugang. (An analysis of *tunas*
    grown in Argentina indicated that most fruits contained an average of 63 mg of
    calcium [oranges 46 mg], 38 mg phosphorus [oranges 15 mg, peaches 27 mg],
    and 14 mg of magnesium.)
271 ...*inadequate concentrations of selenium*: Bañuelos.
271 ...*exhibits chemotherapeutic qualities*: Ibid.
271 ...*exceptionally salt-soil tolerant*: Ibid.
271 ...*contain an edible oil that can be extracted*: Ennouri; Feugang; Mulas; Ramadan; Sawaya.
271 ...*discovery of this oil is not new*: Smith, composition.
274 ...*inspiration for the cactus creole recipe*: Hurst.
275 ...*management techniques*: Losada; Sáenz-Hernándes, 212. (The fresh, young
    cladodes are harvested when they preferably around three to four weeks of age.)
275 ...*the older indigenous system*: Hernándes-Pérez; Jacobo, 143-144.
275 ...*nopalitos that have been processed*: Kunte, 8; Sáenz-Hernándes, 215, 218.
275 *The first herbal medical book*: Badianus; Aztec.
276 *Eventually the book was sent to Spain*: Aztec; Libellus.
276 ...*English language version of this book*: Aztec.
276 ...*what had most impressed the Aztec doctor*: Aztec; Badianus; Cho; Feugang.
276 ...*widespread practical use aboard sailing ships*: Griffith, origins.
276 ...*this custom also greatly contributed*: Ibid.
276 ...*used in the treatment of whooping cough*: Prickly Pear, Nagaphana.
276 ...*to treat over 100 different ailments*: Knishinsky; Lim; Wilson.
277 ...*as a cure for hangover*: Feugang;Vázquez-Ramirez; Wiese.
277 ...*study discovered that a flavonoid*: Dok-Go; Wiese.
277 ...*issued as early as 1937*: Felker.
277 ...*decrease some people's blood*: Frati; Knishinsky; Meckes-Lozoya; Pizzorno, 917.
277 ...*supplementing the diet with cactus seed oil*: Feugang.
277 ...*rats with experimentally induced diabetes*: Ennouri; Trejo-González.
278 ...*found a decrease in plasma total cholesterol*: Frati-Munari; Knishinsky;
    Meckes-Lozoya; Palumbo; Tesoriere.
278 *In a small study of 29 human patients*: Knishinsky; Pizzorno, 917.
278 ...*suffering from extremely high cholesterol levels*: Palumbo.
278 ...*whose blood cholesterol is actually too low*: Bond.
278 ...*dried prickly-pear flowers in powdered form*: Jonas; Palevitch; Pizzorno, 917.
278 ...*contained an anti-viral agent*: Ahmad.
278 ...*inhibits the proliferation of cervical*: Feugang; Hahm.
279 ...*are diuretic or contain a complex*: Bisson; Galati; Park; Prickly Pear, (e); Trombetta.
    (Daily consumption of prickly-pear leaves have also been shown to promote
    weight loss, according to a 3-month-long clinical investigation led by
    Dr. Ralf Uebelhack and published in the December 2014 issue of *Current
    Theraputic Research*. Apparently, cactus fiber binds to dietary fat and its use
    results in reduced fat absorption and ultimately reduction in body weight.)
279 ...*species have been found to contain*: Benattia; Keller; Schultes; Shulgin.

316

279 *...was granted a United States patent*: United.
279 *...small bottle of a cactus-juice-based ointment*: Cactus Juice.
279 *...soak chopped cactus pads in water*: Anderson, Cactus.
280 *...thick mucilage that can act as a water purifier*: Knight.
280 *...removing arsenic in drinking water*: Fox. (Another, more traditional use for prickly-pear mucilage, is its addition to strengthen adobe mud, where it acts as a kind of "breathing water barrier." This mix was used in the restoration of Arizona's historic San Xavier Mission in Tucson. The mucilage is also often mixed into ordinary plaster to make it more durable and water resistant. To extract cactus mucilage for use in plaster or adobe, simple fill a bucket with prickly-pear pads that have been chopped to pieces roughly the size of cookies. Fill the container with water so that the top pieces float a little. Cover the container and place it in a dark place for about two weeks. Strain the liquid from the cactus pieces and mix with your mortar or plaster. Often the plaster's "stickiness" is markedly improved, making it easier to apply.)
281 *...but a few of the numerous insults that can cause*: Many Uses, Wood.
281 *...Africa has lost more than*: Progression.
281 *...also occurring in Australia*: Desertification.
281 *...the vast Gobi Desert is now considered*: Gluckman, Haner.
281 *...is critical for the successful future*: Nefzaoui, Forage.
281 *...recognized as ideal crops for these arid climates*: Griffith, origins.
282 *...when the plants are around 12 years old*: Russell.
282 *...plants of choice in both Mexico and northern Africa*: Le Houérou.
282 *...large areas in Libya, Algeria, and Morocco*: Kaufmann, Prickly Pear; Le Houérou; Nefzaoui, Opuntia.
282 *...used to retard wind erosion*: Nefzaoui, Opuntia.
282 *In 1919, a report was published*: Alexander, Prickly pear.
283 *I do not now poison on land fit for*: Prickly Pear: Destruction and Utilisation.
283 *...inspiring story of Phil Badier*: Cotton, Phil Badier's.
283 *When he settled down to this work*: Ibid.
284 *...breaking of the recent drought*: Ibid.
284 *Former scoffers were wending their way*: Ibid.

Epilogue

285 *There are nearly two dozen species*: Australian Invasive Cacti Network; Australian Invasive Cactus Forum; Chuk, personal; Lloyd; Weeds of National Significance.
286 *Some of the worst Cylindropuntia invaders*: Ibid.
286 *A survey of invasive cacti*: Chuk, Invasive; Chuk, personal; Invasive cactus; Lloyd.
287 *A cristated plant is a genetic monster*: Cristated; Cristation; Graham; Moe.
287 *...that were impaled on the spines*: Clark.
288 *Hence the rather unique situation*: Chuk, Invasive; Chuk, personal.
288 *These can lay on the soil*: Ibid.
289 *We had it controlled pretty well up to about 1995*: McPherson.
289 *In South Africa, where coral cactus*: Karoo.
290 *...three biotypes of this cochineal*: Chuk, personal; Jones, host range.
290 *...controlled by two species*: Hosking, Opuntia; Prickly-Pear Pest in NSW; Weed.
290 *...Curtis Island, located along*: McCallie.
291 *Jim Carpenter retired after*: Hight, personal.
291 *A recently discovered trail-following pheromone*: Ibid.
291 *...walking in the footsteps of Alan Dodd*: Ibid.
291 *How fitting that this book*: Ibid.

317

Bibliography

"1901 to 1920: Combating Infestations of Prickly Pear," online at
http://www.derm.qld.gov.au/ museum/articles_complete/surveying/pests.html
(accessed Jan. 14, 2010)

"Acanthophis," https://en.wikipedia.org/wiki/Acanthophis (accessed Sept. 4, 2016).

"Agricultural Journal of the Cape of Good Hope," as quoted in the *Queensland Agricultural Journal* (Nov. 1907): 259.

Ahmad, A., J. Davies, S. Randall and G. R. Skinner, "Antiviral properties of extract of *Opuntia streptacantha*," *Antiviral Research* 30, no. 2-3 (1996): 75-85.

"Allies of Prickly Pear: African Baboons Eat Cactoblastis Grubs," *The Telegraph*, Brisbane, June 3, 1937.

Alastor, "Prickly Pear," *Brisbane Daily Mail*, March 29, 1927. "Alexander, Wilfred Backhouse (1885-1965)," National Library of Australia, http://trove.nla.gov.au/people/1476342?c=people (accessed Jan. 13, 2017).

Alexander, W.B., *The Prickly Pear in Australia*, Bulletin #12, Institute of Science and Industry, Commonwealth of Australia, 1919.

———. *Natural Enemies of Prickly Pear and Their Introduction into Australia*, Bulletin #29, Institute of Science and Industry, Commonwealth of Australia, 1925.

———. *Notes On Work Carried Out In South America - 1920-1921* (unpublished M/S), Commonwealth Prickly Pear Board, Brisbane, Australia.

———. "Variation of the Acclimatised Species of Prickly-pear (Opuntia)," *Proceedings of the Royal Society of Queensland* XXXVIII, no. 3 (1926): 47-54.

Allendorf, F.W, *et al,* "The problems with hybrids: setting conservation guidelines," *Trends in Ecology and Evolution* 16, no. 11 (2001): 613-622.

Anderson, Edward, *The Cactus Family*, Portland, Oregon: Timber Press, 2001.

Anderson, Neil O. and Richard T. Olsen, "A Vast Array of Beauty: The Accomplishments of the Father of American Ornamental Breeding, Luther Burbank," *HortScience* 50, no. 2 (2015): 161-188.

Andersohn, Gunter, *Cacti and Succulents*, London: A & C Black Publications, 1982.

Andrews, Evan, "Gandhi's Salt March, 85 Years Ago," http://www.history.com/news/gandhis-salt-march-85-years-ago (accessed Dec. 28, 2017).

"Annual Report 1986-87," Tamworth, NSW: Prickly Pear Destruction Commission, 1987.

"Argentine bug is killing cactus," *N.Q.R.* (Northern Queensland Review), Sept. 8, 1979.

"Army of Insects to Attack Prickly Pear: Scientists Getting Ready," *The Telegraph*, Brisbane, Feb. 14, 1923.

Arroyo, Hussein Sánchez, Juan Cibrián Tovar, Juliana Osorio Córdoba and Cristóbal Aldama Aguilera, "Impacto Económico Y Social En Caso De Introducción Y Establecimiento De La Palomilla Del Nopal (*Cactoblastis cactorum*) En México," (Publisher unknown, available online and through Mexican government sources), October 2011.

"Arsenic," Environmental Health Guidance Note, Queensland Government Department of Health, March 2002.

"Arsenic in Drinking Water," Environmental Fact Sheet No. 409, Northern Territory Government Department of Health, Aug. 2012.

"Australia Pacific LNG Project EIS," Heritage Consulting Australia, Pty. Ltd., Vol. 5: Attachments (March, 2010): 16.

"Australian Colonial Plants Search," http://collection.hht.net.au/firsthht/searchColonialPlants.jsp (accessed June 28, 2012).

"Australian Invasive Cactus Forum," Hahndorf, South Australia, May 24, 2013. http://www.cactuswarriors.org/2013/06/02/australian-invasive-cactus-forum-24th-may-hahndorf-sa/ (accessed Feb. 29, 2016)

Australian Invasive Cacti Network web page, http://www.aicn.org.au/ (accessed Nov. 25, 2017)

"Australia's Cactus Pest: Prickly Pear Is Invading 20,000 Acres Every Month," *The New York Times*, Aug. 2, 1922.

"*Australia's Opportunity: Luther Burbank and the Thornless Edible Cactus*," booklet of extracts and illustrations, circa 1909.

"Australia's Victory Over Prickly Pear," *Truth*, May 19, 1957.

An Aztec Herbal: The Classic Codex of 1552, translation and commentary by William gates, Mineola, New York: Dover Publications, 2000. (ISBN: 0-486-41130-3)

"Baboons Rush to Aid of the Prickly Pear," *Brownsville Valley Sunday Star* [Brownsville, Texas] (July 11, 1937): 18.

"Background and Synopsis," Cactus Moth (*Cactoblastis cactorum*) Planning Meeting, hosted and sponsored by USDA, APHIS and PPQ, Miami, Florida, Dec. 9-10, 2003.

Baker, H., "The Effects of the Opuntia, or Prickly Pear, and of the Indigo Plant, in Colouring the Juices of Living Animals," London: Proceedings of the Royal Society of London; Philosophical Transactions of the Royal Society (1683-1775) 50 (Jan. 1, 1757): 296-297.

Baker, J., "*Opuntia robusta* H.L. Wendl. ex Pfeiff. - wheel cactus," in *Biological Control of Weeds in Australia*. edited by Mic Julien, Rachel McFadyen, and Jim Cullen, Collingwood, Victoria, Australia: CSIRO Publishing (2012): 427-428.

Baldwin, Isobel and Anne Thorpe (audio recorded interview), Brisbane, April 23, 2013.

Baldwin, Robert (Personal correspondence), March 17, 2012.

Bañuelos, Gary S., Sirine C. Fakra, Spencer C. Walse, Matthew A. Marcus, Soo In Yang, Ingrid J. Pickering, Elizabeth A. H. Pilon-Smits, and John L. Freeman, "Selenium Accumulation, Distribution, and Speciation in Spineless Prickly Pear Cactus: A Drought - and Salt - Tolerant, Selenium Enriched Nutraceutical Fruit Crop for Biofortified Foods," *Plant Physiology* 155, no. 1 (Jan. 2011): 315-327.

Barry Sinclair (Recorded interview), March 6, 2012.

———. Personal correspondence, March 12, 2012.

———. Ancestry.com, http://wc.rootsweb.ancestry.com/cgi-bin/igm.cgi?op= GET&db=barrysinclair34&id=I387

Bateson, Charles, *The Convict Ships 1787-1868*, Sydney: Library of Australian History, 2004.

"Battle Against Pear: Outstanding Experiment," *The Brisbane Courier*, Feb. 7, 1929.

"Battle With Pear: The Insect's War, Cochineal at Dulacca," *The Brisbane Courier*," Sept. 11, 1923.

Becker, Herman F., "Reassignment of Eopuntia to Cyperacites," *New York Botanical Garden, Bulletin of the Torrey Botanical Club* 89, no. 5 (1962): 319-330.

Benattia, Farah Kenza, Zoheir Arrar and Youssef Khabbal, "Psychotropic Activity and GC-MS Analysis of Cactus Seeds Extracts (*Opuntia ficus-indica* L.)," *Der Pharma Chemica* 9, no. 5 (2017): 98-101.

Benson, Lyman, *The Cacti of the United States and Canada*, Stanford University Press, 1982.

Binggeli, Pierre, "Introduced and invasive plants," in *The Natural History of Madagascar*, edited by S. M. Goodman and J. P. Benstead, 257-268. Chicago: University of Chicago Press, 2003.

——. "Cactaceae, *Opuntia* spp., prickly pear, raiketa, rakaita, raketa," in *The Natural History of Madagascar*, edited by S. M. Goodman and J. P. Benstead, 335-339. Chicago: University of Chicago Press, 2003.

"Biniguy," *Moree/Gwydir Examiner*, July 5, 1923.

"Biologist and Poisoner," *The Rockhampton Bulletin*, Oct. 3, 1928.

Bisson, J. F., S. Daubié, S. Hidalgo, D. Guillemet and E. Linarés, "Diuretic and antioxidant effects of Cacti-Nea, a dehydrated water extract from prickly pear fruit in rats," *Phytotherapy Research* 24, no. 4 (2010): 587-494.

Bloem K. A., "Overview of the cactus moth problem," Presented at the Cactus Moth *Cactoblastis cactorum* Planning Meeting, hosted and sponsored by USDA, APHIS and PPQ, Miami, Florida, Dec. 9-10, 2003.

Bloem, K., S. Bloem, J. E. Carpenter, S. Hight. J. Floyd, J. Hernandez, H. Sanchez, A. Bello, G. Gonzalez, and H. Zimmermann, "Don't Let Cacto Blast Us: Development of a Bi-national Plan to Stop the Spread of the Cactus Moth, *Cactoblastis cactorum*, in North America," in *Book of Extended Synopses*, pgs. 84-85, FAO/IAEA International Conference on Area-wide Control of Insects, Vienna, Austria, May 9-13, 2005.

Bond, Annie, "Prickly Pear Cactus for Cholesterol Management," June 12, 2008. Available online at: http://www.care2.com/greenliving/prickly-pear-cactus-for-cholesterol.html (accessed Dec. 18, 2017).

"Boonarga Cactoblastis Memorial Hall," (information leaflet), undated.

Bradley, Richard, *The History of Succulent Plants*, Volumes I and IV, London, 1715.

Briano, J. A., "Biological control of weeds at the USDA-ARS-SABCL in Argentina: history and current program," *Proceedings of the XII International Symposium on Biological Control of Weeds*, La Grande Motte, France, April 22-27, 2007.

Brooks, C., "Some Notes on Prickly Pear," *Agricultural Gazette of New South Wales* (July 1, 1923): 496.

Brooks, Christopher P., Gary N. Ervin, Laura Varone, and Guillermo Logarzo, "Native ecotypic variation and the role of host identity in the spread of an invasive herbivore, *Cactoblastis cactorum*," *Ecology* 93, no. 2 (2012): 402-410.

Brown, Charles R., "Russett Burbank: No Ordinary Potato," *HortScience* 50, no. 2 (2015): 157-160.

Brown, Rowland W., "Some Paleobotanical Problematica," *Journal of Paleontology* 33, no. 1 (1959): 120-124.

Bunce, Daniel, *1836 Catalogue of Seeds and Plants, indigenous and exotic, cultivated and on sale at Denmark Hill Nursery, New Town Road, Hobart Town*," NSW State Library, Sydney.

Burbank, Luther, "The New Agricultural-Horticultural Opuntias," Santa Rosa, California, June 1, 1907.

——. "The Gold Metal Newest Agricultural-Horticultural Opuntias," Santa Rosa, California, June 1, 1911.

Burbank, Luther (continued)
——. *Luther Burbank: His methods and discoveries and practical application*,
    Volume VIII, Santa Rosa, California: Luther Burbank Press, 1914.
——. "Luther Burbank's Spineless Cactus," The Luther Burbank Co., Santa Rosa,
    California, 1912.
Bustamente, J.A., "Production, transformation and sales of cochineal products made in
    Chile," *Cactusnet Newsletter*, no. 7, Aug. 2002.
    http://www.cactusnet.org/pdf/issue7.pdf
"Byrnestown: Pear Eradication, Demonstration at Byrnestown," *The Maryborough
    Chronicle*, pg. 8, Sept. 23, 1915.
Cabot, John & Gaspar Corte Real, *The Journal of Christopher Columbus (During His
    First Voyage, 1492-1493)*, London: The Hakluyt Society, 1813.
"Cactoblastis - A World First," *South Burnett Times*, Sept. 21, 1988.
"The Cactoblastis: Attack on Tomatoes," *The Brisbane Courier*, May 7, 1930.
"Cactoblastis Grub Now Screen Star," *The Telegraph* (Sydney), Oct. 27, 1933.
"Cactoblastis honoured in bronze," *The Chronicle*, Sept. 17, 1985.
"Cactoblastis & Prickly Pear," *The Telegraph* (Brisbane), Jan. 14, 1929.
"The Cactus Invasion," *Australasian Post*, Oct. 23, 1975.
Cactus Juice, Available online at http://cactusjuicetm.com/6oz-eco-spray/
"Cactus seeds are orthodox, they'll store a long time," Online forum, comments
    posted by Joe Shaw, shawjoej@gmail.com.
    http://opuntiads.com/oblog/2010/cactus-seeds-are-orthodox-theyll-
    store-a-long-time   (Accessed June 2, 2012)
Cameron, H.C, *Sir Joseph Banks: The Autocrat of the Philosophers*, London:
    The Batchworth Press, 1952.
Cameron, Margaret, (audio recorded interview), Brisbane, Queensland, Australia,
    March 9, 2012.
"Campaign Against Prickly Pear," *The Brisbane Courier*, March 9, 1929.
Campbell, Neil A., *Biology*, 2nd Edition, San Francisco: The Benjamin/Cummings
    Publishing Company, 1990.
Candolle, Alphonse de, *Origin of Cultivated Plants*, New York: D. Appleton Pubs.,
    1885.
"Carlyle", William Bell (a), Australian Medical Pioneers Index
    http://www.medicalpioneers.com/cgi-bin/index.cgi?detail=1&id=1493
    (accessed Dec. 23, 2011).
"Carlyle", William Bell (b), http://genforum.genealogy.com/carlyle/messages/147.html
    (accessed May 2, 2012).
"Carlyle", William Bell (c), Colonial Secretary Index 1788-1825, State Records of New
    South Wales
    http://colsec.records.nsw.gov.au/indexes/colsec/c/F09ccab-car-14.htm
    (accessed May 2, 2012).
"Carlyle", William Bell (d),
    http://www.jenwilletts.com/william_carlylse.htm (accessed Dec. 15, 2015).
"Carlyle", William Bell (e), (Biographical information card held by Australian National
    Library, Canberra), undated.
"Carlyle", William Bell (f),
    http://www.hastings.nsw.gov.au/www/html/2186-hibbard-reserve.asp
    (accessed March 13, 2012).

"Carlyle", William Bell (g),
>http://boards.ancestery.com.au/localities.britisles.scotland.dfs.general/ 75.1.2/mb.ashx (accessed May 2, 2012).

Carn, K. G., *Control of Weeds*, New South Wales Dept. of Agriculture, 1939.

Carpenter, J. E., S. Hight, S. Bloem, K. A. Bloem, and C. Tate, "Developing the Sterile Insect Technique for Area-wide Management of the Invasive Cactus Moth, *Cactoblastis cactorum*," *Book of Extended Synopses*, pgs. 254-255, FAO/IAEA International Conference on Area-wide Control of Insects, Vienna, Austria, May 9-13, 2005.

Carpenter, James E., Recorded interview, August 29, 2011.

——. Recorded interview, October 5, 2011.

——. Personal correspondence, August 18, 2014.

——. Recorded interview. March 25, 2015.

Carter, Harold B., *Sir Joseph Banks: 1743-1820,* London: British Museum, 1988.

"Caryophyllids: Fossil Record"
>http://www.ucmp.berkeley.edu/anthophtya/caryos/carophyllidfr.html (accessed Feb. 19, 2016)

Casas, A. and Barbera, G., "Mesoamerican Domestication and Diffusion," in *Cacti Biology and Uses*, edited by Park Noble, University of California Press, 2002.

Castle, L., *Cactaceous Plants: Their History and Culture*, London: Horticultural Press, 1884.

Centenary 1881-1981: Warra State School, NBCAE Warra Centenary History Research Group, undated, but assume 1981.

Centenary of Progress: Dulacca, Jackson, Drillham and Districts, Eric Newberry, editor (souvenir history booklet) published by the Dulacca Sports Ground Committee, 1962.

Chaney, Ralph J., "A fossil cactus from the Eocene of Utah," *American Journal of Botany* 31, no. 8 (Oct. 1944): 507-528.

Charles, Graham, *Cacti and Succulents*, Wiltshire, England: The Crowood Press, 2003.

"Chiapas Studied for More Nopal Cultivation," *Mexico Daily News*,
>http://mexicodailynews.com/news/chiapas-studied-for-more-nopal-cultivation/ (accessed Aug. 10, 2017).

Chinchilla Historical Museum, (Display sign), Chinchilla, Queensland, Australia, 2013.

Cho, J. Y., S.C. Park, T. W. Kim, K. S. Kim, J. C. Song, S. K. Kim, H. M. Lee, H. J. Sung, H. J. Park, Y. B. Song, E. S. Yoo, C. H. Lee and M. H. Rhee, "Radical scavenging and anti-inflammatory activity of extracts from *Opuntia humifusa* Raf.," *Journal of Pharmacy and Pharmacology* 58, no. 1 (2006): 113-119.

Chuk, Mike, "Invasive Cacti - a threat to the rangelands of Australia," in *Proceedings of the 16th Biennial Conference of the Australia Rangeland Society*, Perth: Australian Rangeland Society, 2010.

——. (personal correspondence), May 17, 2014.

Clark, Peter and Liz Clark at Leander Station, Longreach, QLD (audio recording), May 2, 2014).

Clarke, B. P., "A Moth to the Rescue," *Sunday Mail*, published in Jan. 1979.

"Clearing of Pear: Recovery of Costs, Opposition Protest Ignored," *Brisbane Courier*, Sept. 16, 1926.

Clerk, Arthur Temple, "The Prickly Pear Problem in Queensland," self-published 42-page booklet, Brisbane, Australia, April 20, 1913.

——. "Prickly Pear Problem," (Letter to the Editor), *Brisbane Daily Mail*, July 20, 1923.

323

Clifford, H. Trevor, *Australian Dictionary of Biography*, Vol. 16, 2002. Online at http://adb.anu.edu.au/biography/white-haney-rose-ethel-janet-jean-12015/text21549 (accessed March 16, 2012)

Clifford, Mary, *Looking Through Our Window: A History of James Teare Wearne and His Descendants*, c. 1995.

"The Closer Settlement Act of 1906," Original material held in Miles Historical Village, Miles, Queensland (author not noted).

Coates, W. N., "Memories of the Prickly Pear and Death Adders," typewritten essay held by Miles and Region Historical Society, Miles, Queensland, undated.

"Cochineal and Pear: Compulsory Infection," *The Telegraph* (Brisbane), May 1, 1928.

"The Cochineal Insect: Interesting Interview With Mr. A. Temple Clerk," *Dalby Herald*, May 30, 1924.

"Cochineal is Near End," *L'Abelle de la Nouvell-Orleans*, Nov. 20, 1911.

"Common Death Adder," http://reptilepark.com.au/animals/reptiles/snakes/venomous/common-death-adder/ (accessed Sept. 4, 2016).

"Compulsory Pear Destruction Recommended for South Africa," *Agricultural Journal of the Cape of Good Hope*, Aug. 1907, (as quoted in the Queensland Agricultural Journal, pg. 258, Nov. 1907).

"Consumer Price Index," Federal Reserve Bank of Minneapolis, https://www.minneapolisfed.org/community/teaching-aids/cpi-calculator-information/consumer-price-index-1800 (accessed June 20, 2016).

"Conquering Prickly Pear: QLD has Gained New Province As Big As Ireland," *The Courier Mail*, June 10, 1939.

"Conquest by Cactoblastis," *The Sydney Morning Herald*, Oct. 27, 1933.

Cotton, Frank, "Prickly Pear and Power Alcohol," (Letter to the Editor), *Sydney Telegraph*, April 7, 1926.

———. "Phil Badier's Prickly Pear Farm," *The Australian Worker*, Jan. 22, 1936.

"CPC National Collection Plant Profile," Center for Plant Conservation, www.centerforplantconservation.org (accessed June 15, 2011).

"Cristated cactus," http://www.cactuscollection.com/info/succulents/crests_monstrose.html (accessed May 29, 2015).

"Cristation," http://www.cactus-art.biz/note-book/Dictionary/Dictionary_C/dictionary_cristation.htm (accessed May 29, 2015).

Cullen, William, *Is Arsenic an Aphrodisiac?: The Sociochemistry of an Element*, undated.

Cunningham, G.M., W.E. Mulham, P.L. Milthorpe, and J.H. Leigh, *Plants of Western New South Wales*, Clayton, Victoria, Australia: CSIRO Publishing, 2011.

"Dactylopius tomentosus," *The Morning Bulletin* (Rockhampton), May 27, 1924.

"Dairy: Valuable Fodder Plant: Spineless Cactus in Victoria," *The Melbourne Leader*, April 17, 1915.

Dalby Cactoblastis Memorial, http://www.hss.uts.edu.au/centres/public-history/index.htmlh (accessed Feb. 5, 2011).

"Dalucca," Unsigned, undated essay held by Miles and District Historical Society, Miles, Queensland.

Davis, Clifton J., Ernest Yoshioka and Dina Kageler, "Biological Control of Lantana, Prickly Pear and Hämäkua Pämakani in Hawaii: A Review and Update," University of Hawaii, 1992. www.hawaii.edu/ (accessed 9 Aug. 2017)

Davis, Esmé, (audio recorded interview), Chinchilla Museum, Chinchilla, Queensland, Australia, April 15, 2013.

"Dedication Programme: The Alan P. Dodd Tropical Weeds Research Centre" (Official opening), Charters Towers, Queensland, Australia, April 17, 1985.

DeFelice, M. "Prickly Pear Cactus, *Opuntia* spp. - A Spine-tingling Tale," *Weed Technology* 18 (2004): 869-877.

Delley, Russell, "Sharp reminder of pear's pillage," *Gold Coast Bulletin*, Sept. 13, 1988.

"Desertification," International Fund for Agricultural Development, August 2010. Downloadable pdf document available online at: https://www.ifad.org/documents (accessed Dec. 6, 2017).

"A Destroyer of prickly Pear," *Brisbane Courier*, Dec. 29, 1926.

Dixon, Robert (Surveyor), New South Wales Settlers Map, 1837, National Library of Australia, http://nla.gov.au/nla.obj-231316713/view (accessed Dec. 21, 2015).

Dodd, A. P., *A Diary of the World War, 1917-1918*, unpublished M/S, annotated by the author in 1941, held by the Queensland Museum, Brisbane.

———. "Report on Investigations in Argentine and Uruguay, November 27, 1924 to March 5, 1925. Commonwealth Prickly Pear Board, Brisbane.

———. (Letters from 1924 to 1925), Courtesy of Isobel Baldwin and Anne Thorpe, Brisbane, Australia. April 23, 2013.

———. "The Progress of Biological Control of Prickly Pear in Australia," Commonwealth Prickly Pear Board, 1929.

———. "The Present Position and Future Prospects in Relation to the Biological Control of Prickly Pear," Journal of the Council for Scientific and Industrial Research, Canberra, Australia. pgs. 10-11, 1933.

———. "The Control and Eradication of Prickly Pear in Australia," *Bulletin of Entomological Research*, 27, no. 3 (1936): 505-506.

———. *The Biological Campaign Against Prickly Pear*, Brisbane, Australia: Commonwealth Prickly Pear Board, 1940.

———. "The Conquest of Prickly Pear," Historical Society of Queensland, Feb. 25, 1941.

Dok-Go, H., K. H. Lee, H. J. Kim, E. H. Lee, J. Lee, Y. S. Song, Y. H. Lee, C. Jin, Y. S. Lee and J. Cho, "Neuroprotective effects of antioxidative flavonoids, quercetin, (+)-dihydroquercetin and quercetin 3-methyl ether, isolated from *Opuntia ficus-indica* var. *saboten*," *Brain Research*, 965, no. 1-2 (2003): 130-136.

Domico, Terry, "Native Cactus of the San Juan Islands," Friday Harbor, Washington, USA: Puget Sound Biosurvey, 1989.

———. *Kangaroos: The Marvelous Mob*," New York: Facts on File Publications, 1993.

Donkin, R. A., 'Spanish Red: An ethnographical study of cochineal and the Opuntia cactus," *Transactions of the American Philosophical Society*, 67, no. 5 (1977): 1-87.

Donnelly, Graham, (audio recorded interview), Nov. 21, 2012, Brisbane.

Dorrough, Bon, "Those Pear Days," undated typewritten essay held by Miles and District Historical Society, Miles, Queensland.

"Doubts Cast on Burbank Wizardy," *The New York Times*, Jan. 16, 1910.

Dreyer, Peter, *A Gardener Touched With Genius: The life of Luther Burbank*, Santa Rosa, California: Burbank Home & Gardens, 1993.

Dubielecka, B. and Wróblewski, A.K., "A history of cactus collecting in Poland," *Wiadomosci Botaniczne* 54, no. 1-2 (2010): 7-24.

Dunbabin, T., "Thirty Million Acres of Prickly Pear: Australia's lost province," *Sydney Sun*, June 5, 1926.

Dunnicliff, A. A., "Prickly Pear: A National Problem, Parliamentary Tour," *Sydney Daily Telegraph*, June 7, 1924.

Dutton, L.A., "Cochineal: A bright red animal dye," Master's Thesis, Baylor University, Waco, Texas, 1992.

325

Eggleston, John (Historian, Jondaryan Woolshed), personal communication, April 20, 2013.

Elverton, Peter, in discussion with author via telephone, April 6, 2012.

Emmerson, K., *From Cellars to Refrigerators*, Brisbane, Queensland, 1969.

"Enemy of Pear: Experiments With Caterpillars," *Daily Mail*, Dec. 22, 1926.

"The Enemy of Prickly Pear," *Brisbane Courier*, Dec. 20, 1926.

Ennouri, Monia, Bourret Evelyne, Mondolot Laurence and Attia Hamadi,
   "Fatty acid composition and rheological behavior of prickly pear seed oils,"
   Food Chemistry 93, no. 3 (2005): 431-437.

"Eradication of South American Cactus Moth, *Cactoblastis cactorum*, from 11 Parishes
   in Southeastern Louisiana," (Environmental Assessment), USDA, APHIS.
   Sept. 2009.

Essi, F. and Kobler, J., "Spiny Invaders: Patterns and determinants of cacti invasion in
   Europe," *Flora: Morphology, Distribution, Functional Ecology of Plants* 204,
   no. 7 (2009): 485-494.

European and Mediterranean Plant Protection Organization (Quarantine alert
   list) https:www.eppo.int/QUARANTINE/Alert_List/deletions.htm
   (accessed June 2, 2017)

"Experts of U.S. Pinheads, Says Plant Sage," *Los Angeles Examiner*, July 30, 1911.

Fara, Patricia, *Sex, Botany & Empire*, Cambridge, England: Icon Books, Ltd., 2004.

Felker, Peter and Paolo Inglese, "Short-Term and Long-Term Research Needs
   for *Opuntia ficus-indica* (L.) Mill. in Arid Areas," *Journal of the
   Professional Association for Cactus Development* 5 (2003).

Feugang, Jean Magloire, Patricia Konarski, Daming Zou, Florian Conrad
   Stintzing and Changping Zou, "Nutritional and medicinal use of Cactus
   pear (*Opuntia* spp.) cladodes and fruits," *Frontiers in Bioscience*
   11 (Sept. 1, 2006): 2574-2589.

"The Fight," unsigned, handwritten document held by Miles and District
   Historical Society, Miles, Queensland, undated.

"Fighting Pear: Cochineal at Work," *Brisbane Daily Mail*, June 9, 1924.

"Fighting Pear: Parasites on Way," *The Daily Mail* (Brisbane), Sept. 24, 1928.

"Fighting Prickly Pear in Northwestern NSW," *The Sydney Mail*, pg. 28, Sept. 1, 1924.

"Fighting Prickly Pear: Pest Losing Ground," *Brisbane Courier*, Feb. 5, 1927.

"Fighting Prickly Pear: The Work of the Prickly Pear Land Commission,"
   Brisbane Courier, Sept. 25, 1926.

"Fighting the Prickly Pear," *The Sydney Mail*, Aug. 8, 1928.

"Flowering Plants of the Sonoran Desert,"
   http://www.desertmuseum.org/books/nhsd_flowering.php
   (accessed Dec. 22, 2017).

Foster, Thomas, memoir and personal correspondence, April 17, 2012.

——. personal correspondence, Feb. 14, 2013.

——. personal correspondence, March 14, 2013.

"Four Years Care Needed: Western Prickly Pear Lands," *The Daily Mail* (Brisbane)
   Nov. 24, 1930.

Fox, Dawn I., Thomas Pichler, Daniel H. Yeh and Norma A. Alcantar, "Removing
   Heavy Metal in Water: The Interaction of Cactus Mucilage and Arsenate
   (As(V))," *Environmental Science and Technology* 48, no. 8 (2012): 4553-4559.

Frati-Munari, Alberto C., J. A. Fernández-Harp, M. B. Bañales-Ham and C. R.
   Ariza-Andraca, "Decreased blood glucose and insulin by nopal (*Opuntia* sp.),"
   Archivos de investigación médica (Mexico) 14, no. 4 (1983): 431-436.

Frawley, Jodi, "Containing Queensland Prickly Pear: buffer zones, closer settlement, whiteness," *Journal of Australian Studies* 38, no. 2 (2014): 139-156.

———. "Prickly Pear Land: Transnational Networks in Settler Australia," *Australian Historical Studies* 130 (2007): 323-338.

Freeman, Donald B., "Prickly Pear Menace in Eastern Australia 1880-1940," *Geographic Review* 82, no. 4 (1992).

Fuller, Harvey, "Memories of the Prickly Pear Days as Remembered by Harvey Fuller," unpublished, typed M/S, Chinchilla Historical Museum, Chinchilla, Queensland, Australia, undated.

Galati, E. M., M. M. Tripodo, A. Trovato, N. Miceli and M. T. Monforte, "Biological effect of *Opuntia ficus-indica* (L.) Mill. (Cactaceae) waste matter: Note 1: diuretic activity," *Journal of Ethnopharmacology* 79, no. 1 (2002): 17-21.

Gardener, Donald E. and Clifton J. Davis, "The Prospects for Biological Control of Non-native Plants in Hawaiian National Parks. Technical Report Number 45. University of Hawaii, 1982.

Geldard, Eric, (audio recording of interview), Miles Museum, Miles, Queensland, Australia, April 18, 2013.

Genge, Mrs. A. B., "Prickly-pear jelly," display sign at Miles Historical Village, Miles, Queensland, Australia, 2013.

Genge, Vera, "Lost in the Prickly Pear," *Milton House Newsletter*, June 2001. (Milton House is an aged-care facility located in Queensland.)

Gerarde, John, *The Herball or Historie of Plants*. London, 1597.

Gerbi, Antonello, *Nature in the New World: From Christopher Columbus to Gonzalo Fernandez de Oviedo*, University of Pittsburg Press, Pittsburg: USA, 1985.

Gibson, Arthur C., Kevin Spencer, Reni Bajaj and Jerry McLaughlin, "The Everchanging Landscape of Cactus Systematics," *Annals of the Missouri Botanical Gardens* 73 (1986): 532-555.

Giguet, Léon, *Les cactacées utiles du Mexique*, Paris: Au siége de la Société, publisher, 1928.

Gilchrist, Stuart, "The Cactoblastis Moth," (Transcript) ABC Radio, "The Science Show," Australian Broadcasting Corporation, April 7, 2007.

"Global Invasive Species Database," IUCN/SSC Invasive Species Specialist Group (accessed online 2013).

Gorelick, Root, "DNA sequences and cactus classification - a short review," *Bradleya* 20 (2002): 1-4.

Gluckman, Ron, "Beijing's Desert Storm," October 2000. Available online at: http://www.gluckman.com/ChinaDesert.html (accessed Dec. 6, 2017).

Graham, Arthur, "Memories of the Prickly Pear Days," unpublished M/S held by the Chinchilla Historical Museum, Chinchilla, Queensland, undated.

Graham, Charles, *Cacti and Succulents*, Wiltshire, England: The Crowood Press, 2003.

Graham, Mary, "Scone: Memories of Pioneers," *Sydney Morning Herald*, April 6, 1935.

"Granny Sutton" (a) (Mary Ann Gilder obituary), *Australian Town and Country Journal*, New South Wales, Australia, May 13, 1899.

"Granny Sutton" (b) (Mary Ann Gilder obituary), *The Bulletin*, May 13, 1899.

Gray, Arthur W., "John Matthew Rutland," *The Twenty-seventh Report of the Okanagan Historical Society*, Vernon, British Columbia, Canada, pgs. 20-30, 1966.

"The Green Invasion," *Chinchilla News*, pg. 7, Aug. 13, 2009.

"Green octopus almost wiped out Queensland agriculture," *Sunday Telegraph*, pg. 94, May 31, 1992.

Greenfield, Amy M., *A Perfect Red*. New York: HarperCollins Pubs, 2005.

Greensil, H., "A Plea For the Emu," (Letter to the editor), *Brisbane Courier*, Aug. 21, 1926.

Griffith, M.P., "The origins of an important cactus crop, *Opuntia ficus-indica* (Cactaceae): new molecular evidence," *American Journal of Botany* 91, no. 11 (2004): 1915-1921.

Griffith, M. P. and J. M. Porter, "Phylogeny of Opuntioideae (Cactaceae)," *International Journal of Plant Science* 170, no. 1 (2009): 107-116.

Griffiths, David, "The Spineless Prickly Pears," USDA, Bureau of Plant Industry, Bulletin #140, Washington D.C., Jan. 30, 1909.

——. "The Thornless Prickly Pears," USDA, Bureau of Plant Industry, Bulletin #483, Washington D.C., March 8, 1912.

——. "Prickly Pear as Stock Feed, USDA Farmer's Bulletin #1072, Washington D.C., March, 1920.

Groeneweg, D., "Save Our Soil," (Letters to the Editor), *The Maryborough Chronicle*, Feb. 22, 1927.

Grubb, A. and A. Raser-Rowland, *The Weed Forager's Handbook: a guide to edible and medical weeds in Australia*, Hyland House Publishing, Australia.

"Guantanamo Bay Naval Base and Ecological Crisis," Trade and Environmental Database. American University, undated. Google-search the following: http:///www.american.edu/TED/guantan.htm (accessed Aug. 9, 2017).

Guthrie, F. B., "Pear Pest: Government Steps," *Brisbane Daily Mail*, Aug. 14, 1923.

Habeck, D. H. and F. D. Bennett, "*Cactoblastis cactorum* Berg (Lepidoptera: Pyralidae) a Phycitine New to Florida," Entomology Circular Number 333, Florida Dept. Agric. & Consumer Serv., Division of Plant Industry, August 1990.

Hahm, S. W., J. Park and Y. S. Son, "*Opuntia humifusa* partitioned extracts inhibit the growth of U87MG human glioblastoma cells," *Plant Foods for Human Nutrition* 65, no. 3 (2010): 247-252.

Hale, Edward E., *The Life of Christopher Columbus: from his own letters and journals and other documents of his time*, Arc Manor, Rockville, Maryland (originally published in 1891), 2008.

Hale, Gordon, "Tribute to a Grub: The Eradication of Prickly-pear," *Toowoomba Chronicle*, February 20, 1976.

Haner, Josh, Edward Wong, Derek Watkins and Jeremy White, "Living in China's Expanding Deserts," *The New York Times*, Oct. 24, 2016. Online report available at: https://www.nytimes.com/interactive/2016/10/24/world/asia/living-in-chinas-expanding-deserts.html?_r=0 (accessed Dec. 6, 2017)

Harwood, W.S., *New Creations in Plant Life: An authoritative account of the life and work of Luther Burbank*, New York: The Macmillan Company, 1905.

Hecht, Hans, (English translation by Annette Englander) *Cacti and Succulents*, New York: Sterling Publishing, 1994.

Heinrich, Carl, "The Cactus-feeding Phycitinae: a contribution toward a revision of the American Pyralidoid moths of the family Phycitidae," *Smithsonian Institution*, vol. 86, 1939.

"Held In Check: Prickly Pear, Public Enthusiasm," *The Daily Mail* (Brisbane), Oct. 17, 1928.

Heilig, Herbert C., "Harsh Were Those Days of the Prickly Pear," *The Sunday Mail Color Magazine*, Oct. 17, 1971.

Hernández, Luis Roberto and Thomas C. Emmel, "*Cactoblastis cactorum* in Cuba," *Tropical Lepidoptera* 4, no. 1 (1993): 45-46.

328

Hernándes-Pérez, Ricardo, Juan Carlos Noa-Carrazana, Ricardo Gasper, Petro
Mata and Norma Flores-Estévez, "Detection of Phytoplasma on Indian
Fig (*Opuntia ficus-indica* Mill) in Mexico Central Region," *Online
Journal of Biological Sciences* 9, no. 3 (2009): 62-66.
"High Hopes for Reclaiming Prickly Pear Lands," *The Land*, June 20, 1930.
Hight, Stephen D., J. E. Carpenter, K. A. Bloem, S. Bloem, R. W. Pemberton, and
P. Stiling, "Expanding Geographical Range of *Cactoblastis cactorum*
(Lepidoptera: Pyralidae) in North America," *Florida Entomologist* 85, no. 3
(Sept. 2002).
Hight, Stephen, personal communication, August 7, 2017.
"History of Mining," Information sheet published by New South Wales Mineral
Resources, undated.
A History of Mungindi to 1988, Mungindi and District Historical Society Book
Committee, (ISBN: 07316-227-4), undated, but assume 1988.
"Honorary Life Membership, Mr. A. P. Dodd, O. B. E.," *Queensland Entomological
Society*, June 11, 1962.
Hornback, Bob, recorded interview at Luther Burbank Home and Gardens,
Santa Rosa, California, July 3, 2011.
Hosking, J.R., Sullivan, P.R., and Welsby, S.M., "Biological control of *Opuntia
stricta* (Haw) Haw var. *stricta* using *Dactylopius opuntiae* in an area of
New South Wales, Australia, where *Cactoblastis cactorum* (Berg) is
not a successful biological control agent," *Agriculture, Ecosystems and
Environment* 48 (1994): 241-255.
Hosking, John R., "*Opuntia* spp.," in *Biological Control of Weeds in Australia*,
edited by Mic Julien, Rachel McFadyen and Jim Cullen, Collingwood,
Victoria, Australia: CSIRO Publishing, 431-435, 2012.
———. (audio recording, Tamworth, NSW, Sept. 10, 2011)
Holtcamp, Royce H., *Cylindropuntia imbricata* (rope pear), *Cylindropuntia rosea*
(hudson pear), *CSIRO Publishing*, 2012. http://www.publish.csiro.au/
"How Prickly Pear Pest Is Fought: Film reveals value of scientific research,"
Daily Standard, Nov. 16, 1933.
Howard, L. O., *A History of Applied Entomology*, Smithsonian Miscellaneous
Collections, Washington D.C., vol. 84, 1930.
Howard, W. L., "Luther Burbank's Plant Contributions," Bulletin 691,
University of California, Berkeley, California, March 1945.
del Hoyo, Eugenio, *La Ciudad en Estampas* (The City in Sketches), Mexico City: Artes
de México, publisher, 1996.
Huber, D. M., *et al,* "Invasive Pest Species: Impacts on agricultural production,
natural resources, and the environment," *Council for Agricultural
Science and Technology* (Issue Paper #20), Ames, Iowa, USA, 2002.
Hurst, Joanadel, "How to Eat Cactus: Opuntia and Prickly Pears," *Mother Earth News*,
May/June 1984.
"Importing a Pest to Wipe Out a Pest," *The San Francisco Examiner*, Nov. 1, 1931.
"Immortalising the Cacto-blastis: Boonarga Hall, Official Opening Tomorrow
Night," *The Chinchilla News & Murilla Advertiser*, Feb. 21, 1936.
"In 10 to 15 Years," *Daily Mail* (Brisbane), Sept. 25, 1926.
"Information About Pear Poisons and Apparatus," Prickly Pear Land Commission,
Brisbane, undated.
"In Prickly Pear Land: How Pest Spreads, Difficulties of Eradication," *The Sydney Sun*,
June 8, 1924.

"Insects and Prickly Pear: Mr. Corser Hopeful of Good Results," *The Maryborough Chronicle*, Feb. 28, 1922.

"Interview With Creationist Biological Control Expert John Mann M.B.E.," *Creation Ex Nihilo* 5, no. 2 (1982): 20-21.

"Invasive cactus worries graziers," ABC News, Australia. Available online at http://www.abc.net.au/news/2011-08-02/wheel-cactus-spread-grazing/2820474 (accessed March 14, 2014)

"Invasive Species Compendium," Center for Agriculture and Bioscience International, www.cabi.org/isc/datasheet/10680 (accessed June 2, 2017).

"The Invasion of Australia: A Silent Terror That Has Captured 29,000,000 Acres of Our Inheritance," *The Sydney Mail*, Sydney, Australia, Feb. 28, 1923.

"Is the Pear Doomed?: Cochineal Gets Busy," *Brisbane Daily Mail*, April 29, 1924.

"Items," *The Sydney Morning Herald*, Dec. 10, 1910.

Ivanov, Boris, *et al*, "Invasive Alien Species," Roskilde University, Denmark, 2008. Available online at https://core.ac.uk/download/pdf/12516445.pdf (accessed Nov. 18, 2017).

The IUCN Red List of Threatened Species, www.iucnredlist.org/details/16329591/0 (accessed June 17, 2017).

Iziko Museums of South Africa, www.biodiversityexplorer.org/lepidoptera/pyralidae/cactoblastis_cactorum.htm (accessed Feb. 16, 2015).

Jacobo, C. M., "Cactus Pear Domestication and Breeding," in *Plant Breeding Reviews*, edited by J. Janick, John Wiley and Sons: New York, 2001.

Jacques, C., "Le *Cactoblastis cactorum*," Rev. agric. Nowvelle-Caledonie, 1085-1094, May 1933.

Janick, Jules, "Luther Burbank: Plant Breeding Artist, Horticulturalist and Legend," *HortScience* 50, no. 2 (2015): 153-156.

Ji Han, *Nanfang Caomu Zhuang*, (c. 304 CE), Published 1273.

"J. Mann Career Notes," (document courtesy Graham Donnelly, Brisbane) Nov. 20, 2012.

"Dr. John Mann MBE, 13-8-1905 - 27-6-1994," Obituary notice in an undated newspaper clipping, (publication unknown).

Johnson, Robert, "Cactus Man Praised: He bred a plague to wipe out a menace," *The Australian*, page. 2, July 2, 1970.

Johnston, Kathleen, "Day of the Cactus," *Toowoomba Chronicle*, Dec. 8, 1960.

Johnston, T. H. and Henry Tryon, *Report of the Prickly-pear Travelling Commission*, Queensland Government, Brisbane, Australia, 1914.

Jonas, A, G. Rosenblat, D. Krapf, W. Bitterman and I. Neeman, "Cactus flower extracts may prove beneficial in benign prostatic hyperplasia due to inhibition of 5-alpha reductase activity, aromatase activity and lipid peroxidation," *Urological Research* 26, no. 4 (1998): 265-270.

Jones, Daniel, "Uses of Prickly Pear," *Brisbane Courier*, Sept. 1, 1926.

Jones, Peter K., Royce H. Holtcamp, William A. Palmer, and Michael D. Day, "The host range of three biotypes of *Dactylopius tomentosus* (Lamarck) (Hemiptera: Dactylopiidae) and their potential as biological control agents of *Cylindropuntia* spp. (Cactaceae) in Australia," *Biocontrol Science and Technology* 25, no. 6 (2015): 613-628.

Kaufmann, Jeffery, "La Question des Raketa: Colonial Struggles with Prickly Pear Cactus in Southern Madagascar, 1900-1923," *Ethnohistory* 48, no. 1-2 (2001).

330

Kaufmann, Jeffery (continued)
———. "Prickly Pear Cactus and Pastoralism in Southwest Madagascar,"*Ethnology* 43, no. 4 (2004): 345-361.
"Karoo Invasion: is history being repeated?," *SAPIA News* (Southern African Plant Invaders Atlas), no. 35 (2015).
Keller, William J., "N-methyltryamine: Formation in *Opuntia clavata* and metabolism in *Coryphantha macromeris* var. *Runyonii*," *Phytochemistry* 19, no. 3 (1980): 413-414.
Kerr, Clarence, audio recorded interview, Chinchilla, Queensland, March 3, 2012.
"Killing Pear: Fine Progress, Rapid Destruction in Places," *Brisbane Courier*, Sept. 28, 1926.
Kitson, Bill and Judith McKay, *Surveying Queensland*, Queensland Dept. of Natural Resources and Water & the Queensland Museum, Brisbane, 2006.
Knight, Helen, "Cactus gum could make clean water cheap for millions," *New Scientist*, April 21, 2010.
Knishinsky, Ran, *Prickly Pear Cactus Medicine: Treatments for Diabetes, Cholesterol and the Immune System*, Healing Arts Press, Rochester, Vermont, USA. 2004.
Kunte, Libor and Rudolf Subik, *The Complete Encyclopedia of Cacti*, Netherlands: Rebo Intl., 2003.
La Casas, Fray Bartolomé, (Oliver Dunn & James E. Kelley, Jr., Eds.) *The Diario of Christopher Columbus's First Voyage to America 1492-1493*, University of Oklahoma Press, 1989.
Lacy, Alberto Ruy Sánchez, "Nopal: Cultivating and Worshipping Plants," *Artes de Mexico*, no. 59, Mexico City, 2002.
Laffey, P. J., "Letters to the Editor," *Brisbane Courier*, Oct. 22, 1923.
Lake, Bob, "Cactus Blaster: Our smallest hero battles on," *Queensland Country Life,* July 18, 1991.
The Land Acts 1897 & 1902 and The Land Regulations, 1903, edited by W. F. Wilson, Queensland Government, Brisbane, 1904.
"Land Hunger: Another record application for Chinchilla pear areas," *The Chinchilla News*, Oct. 28, 1932.
"Land Settlement: Continued big demand," *The Chinchilla News*, May 6, 1932.
Lanzendorfer, Joy, "10 Crazy Creations of "Plant Wizard" Luther Burbank," *Mental_Floss*, http://mentalfloss.com/article/57818/10-crazy-creations-of-plant-wizard-luther-burbank (accessed March 6, 2016)
"Lease of Prickly Pear Infested Selection Under the Land Act, 1897," Lessee: John George Bender, 14 Feb. 1910, Chinchilla District Land Records, (access courtesy Marie Gore).
Lee, Ida, *The Coming of the British to Australia*, London: Longmans, Green & Co., 1906.
Leese, Oliver, *Cacti*, London: Triune Books, 1973.
Le Houérou, H. N., "The role of browse in the management of natural grazing lands," *World Forest Congress*, Jakarta, Indonesia, October 16-18, 1978.
"Libellus de Medicinalibus Indorum Herbis," Online at http://en.wikipedia.org/wiki/Libellus_de_Medicinalibus_Indorum_Herbis (accessed Dec. 14, 2017)
"Links With the Past: The Saving of a Continent," *The Chinchilla News,* pg. 1, May 29, 1969.
Lim, T. K., *Edible Medicinal and Non-Medicinal Plants: Volume 1, Fruits*, Springer Dordrecht Heidelburg publishers, London/New York, 2012. (ISBN: 978-90-481-8661-7)
Linnaei, Caroli (Carl Linneaus), *Species Plantarum*, vol. 1, 1753.

Lithgow, Grace (audio recording), Chinchilla, Queensland, Australia, April 19, 2013.

"A Little Brown Moth 'Saved' the State," *Courier Mail* (Brisbane), pg. 13, Feb. 16, 1985.

"Lived on Pear for a Fortnight: Wandering Swede Located by Chinchilla Constable," *The Chinchilla News and Murilla Advertiser*, March 15, 1940.

Lloyd, Sandy and Andrew Reeves, "Situation Statement on Opuntioid Cacti (*Austrocylindopuntia* spp., *Cylindropuntia* spp. and *Opuntia* spp.) in Western Australia," Department of Agriculture and Food of Western Australia, 2014.

Logan, G. N., "Tryon, Henry (1856-1943)," *Australian Dictionary of Biography*, Australian National University, Vol. 12, 1990. http://adb.anu.edu.au/biography/tryon-henry-8864/text15561 (accessed April 2, 2012).

"Long-lived seeds of Opuntia," http://opuntiads.com/oblog/2010/cactus-seeds-are-orthodox-theyll-store-a-long-time (accessed June 2, 2012).

Losada, H., D. Grande, J. Vieyra, L. Arias, R. Pealing, J. Rangel and A. Fierro, "A sub-urban agro-ecosystem of nopal-vegetable production based on the intensive use of dairy cattle manure in the southeast hills of Mexico City," *Livestock Research for Rural Development* 8, no. 4 (1996).

Low, Tim, *Feral Future*, Penquin Books, 1999.

"Luther Burbank," *Encyclopedia of World Biography*, http://www.encyclopedia.com/topic/Luther_Burbank.aspx (accessed Dec. 24, 2010).

"Luther Burbank," Report Number 821, House of Representatives, 62nd Congress, 2nd Session, Washington D.C., June 1912.

"Luther Burbank," Calendar Number 827, Senate, 62nd Congress, 2nd Session, Washington D.C., July 1912.

"Luther Burbank," Western Sonoma County Historical Society, http://www.wschsgrf.org/articles/biographylutherburbank1849-1926 (accessed March 6, 2016).

"Luther Burbank," Wikipedia, https://en.wikipedia.org/wiki/Luther_Burbank (accessed March 6, 2016).

Lyders, E., "Letter to Luther Burbank dated Nov., 17, 1922." Copy held in library of Luther Burbank Home and Gardens, Santa Rosa, California.

Lyte, Charles, *Sir Joseph Banks: 18th Century Explorer, Botanist and Entrepreneur*, London: David and Charles, 1980.

Macarthur, William, *Catalogue of Plants Cultivated at Camden, New South Wales, 1843*, NSW State Library, Sydney.

——. *Catalogue of Plants Cultivated at Camden, New South Wales, 1850*, NSW State Library, Sydney.

Mackaness, George, *Sir Joseph Banks: His Relations With Australia*, Sydney: Angus and Robertson, 1936.

Madsen, J.D., R. Brown. G. Ervin, D. Shaw, C. Abbott, V. Maddox, R. Wersal, D. McBride, and N. Madsen, "Research to Support Integrated Management Systems of Aquatic and Terrestrial Invasive Species," (GRI Publication #5039) Geosystems Research Institute, Mississippi State University, Mississippi, USA, 2010.

Maiden, Joseph H., "Plan of an inquiry into the merits of prickly-pear as a forage plant," *The Agricultural Gazette of New South Wales*, Vol. VII, Part 10 (1896): 652-653.

——. *A Preliminary Study of the Prickly-Pear Naturalised in New South Wales*, Misc. Publication no. 253, Sydney: Dept. of Agriculture, 1898.

Maiden, Joseph H. (continued)

———. *Sir Joseph Banks: The "Father of Australia,"* Sydney: Govt. Printer, 1909.

———. "The Prickly Pears of Interest to Australians: No. 2," *Agricultural Gazette of New South Wales* 22, no. 8 (1911): 696-698.

———. "The So-called Indian Fig or Barbary Fig," in "The Prickly Pears of Interest to Australians: No. 6, *Agricultural Gazette of New South Wales*, Jan. 2, 1913.

———. "The Weeds of New South Wales," *Agricultural Gazette of New South Wales*, Vol. VI, Jan-Dec, 1895.

Majure, Lucas, "The Ecology and Morphological Variation of Cactaceae Species in the Mid-south United States," Mississippi State University, 2007.

"Man Who Helped Rid Australia of Prickly-pear," *The Sydney Morning Herald*, page 8, July 7, 1981.

Mandujano, M.C., J. Golubov, and C. Montana, "Dormancy and endozoochorous dispersal of *Opuntia rastrera* in the Southern Chihauhaun Desert, *Journal of Arid Environments* 36 (1997): 259-266.

Mann, John, "Cactus-feeding Insects and Mites," U.S. National Museum Bulletin 256, 1969.

———. *"Cacti Naturalised in Australia and Their Control,"* Department of Lands, Queensland, 1970.

———. Letter to acting curator, Australia National Museum, Canberra. 1986.

"The Many Uses of Prickly-pear Cactus," (radio transcript), *Farm Radio International*, Ottawa, Canada, 1979.

Maplestone, L. T. (letter to P. Murrell, CPPB, Brisbane), Oct. 8, 1935.

Marchant, Leslie R., "La Pérouse, Jean-François de Galaup (1741-1788)," *Australian Dictionary of Biography*, vol. 2, Canberra: Australian National University, 1967.

Marshall, W. Taylor and Thor M. Bock, *Cactaceae*, Pasadena, USA: Abbey Garden Press, 1941.

Marsico, Travis, Lisa Wallace, Gary Ervin, Christopher Brooks, Jessica McClure, Mark Welch, "Geographic patterns of genetic diversity from the native range of *Cactoblastis cactorum* (Berg) support the documented history of invasion and multiple introductions for invasive populations," *Biological Invasions* 13 (2011): 857-868.

Matthews, Tony, *Footsteps Through Time: A History of Chinchilla Shire*, Vol. 1, Chinchilla Shire Council, Chinchilla, Queensland, 2004.

"The Maui Plant Chronicles," http://mauimike6.wordpress.com (accessed June 8, 2010).

Maund, B. and J.S. Henslow, *The Botanist*, Vol. 1, 1836.

Mayne, Alan and Stephen Atkinson (Eds), *Outside Country: A History of Inland Australia*, undated.

McCallie, Kerensa, "Prickly Pear in Central Queensland." Available online at http://cactiguide.com/article/?article=article10.php (accessed Nov. 24, 2017)

McColl, Senator James H., "Prickly Pear: Report on the Plant Known as the Prickly Pear," Parliament of the Commonwealth of Australia, July 8, 1909.

McFadyen, Rachel E., "Larval characteristics of *Cactoblastis* spp. (Lepidoptera: Pyralidae) and the selection of species for biological control of prickly pears (*Opuntia* spp.)," *Bulletin of Entomological Research* 75, no. 1 (1985): 159-168.

333

McFadyen, Rachel E. (continued)

———. "Dodd, Alan Parkhurst (1896-1981)," *Australian Dictionary of Biography* 17, (2007): 322-323.

———. (audio recorded interview), Queensland, Australia, Feb. 26, 2012.

McGilp, J. Neil, "Birds and Prickly Pear," *Pastoral Review*, Jan. 6, 1926.

McPherson, Ross, at Bexley Station, Longreach, QLD (audio recording May 3, 2014).

Meckes-Lozyoa, M., and R. Roman-Ramos, "*Opuntia streptacantha*: a coajutor in the treatment of diabetes mellitus," *The American Journal of Chinese Medicine* 14, no. 3-4 (1986): 116-118.

"Menace in the North and Luxuriance in the South," *The Sydney Mail*, Jan. 22, 1919.

Miller, Philip, *The Gardener's Dictionary*, Vol. 2., London, 1735.

M'Mahon, Thos. J., "Reclaiming Dulacca: Cochineal Insects Destroying the Pear," *The Brisbane Courier*, Nov. 13, 1926.

Mondragon-Jacobo, C. and B. B. Bordelon, "Cactus Pear (*Opuntia* spp. Cactaceae) Breeding for Fruit Production," Department of Horticulture, Purdue University: West Lafayette, Virginia, 1996.

Moe, L. M., "Monstrose and Crested Plants," Available online at: https://mycotopia.net/topic/62972-what-causes-monstrose-and-cristate-growth/ (accessed May 29, 2015).

"Monkey Tricks on African Veldt," *Daily News* (Perth), pg. 5, June 3, 1937.

Monteith, Geoff, *The Butterfly Man of Kuranda: Frederick Parkhurst Dodd*, Brisbane: Queensland Museum, 1991.

———. (audio recorded interview), Queensland Museum, Brisbane, April 25, 2013.

Moreno, P. R., and C. F. Valdéz, "The World Cactus-pear Market," Universidad Autónoma Chapingo, Texoco de Mora, Mexico, 1996.

Moreno, Rebeca Adriana Gutiérrez, Depto. Campañas de Prioridad Nacional, Mexico. (personal correspondence), October 25, 2011.

Moss, Margaret, "The Life and Work of A. P. Dodd," unpublished M/S held by Queensland State Library, Brisbane, undated.

Moxham, Roy, *The Great Hedge of India*, New York: Carroll and Graf Pubs., 2001.

"Mr. Ley, M.P., Sued: Prickly Pear Poison," *The Sydney Morning Herald*, pg. 12, Sept. 25, 1928.

Mulas, M. & Mulas, G., "The Strategic Use of *Atriplexa* and *Opuntia* to Combat Desertification," University of Sassari, Desertification Research Group, Sassari, Italy, 2004.

Mulieri, *et al*, "The type specimens of Tachinidae (Diptera) housed in Museo Argentino de Ciencias Naturales 'Benardino Rivadavia', Buenos Aires," *Zootaxa* 3670, no. 2 (2013): 157-176.

Munro, Hector, "Pear Problem: What Can Be Done?," *The Brisbane Courier*, June 5, 1923.

———. "Prickly Pear: Why Selectors Fail, Faulty Administration," *The Brisbane Courier*, June 8, 1923.

Munro, John H., "The Medieval Scarlet and the Economics of Sartorical Splendor," In *Textiles, Towns, and Trade: Essays in the Economic History of Late-Medieval England and the Low Countries*, Part V: 13-70. (Variorum Collected Studies Series: CS 442), Brookfield, Vermont & Aldershot, Hampshire, England: Ashgate Publishing, 1994.

Munro, John H. (continued)

———. "Luxury and Ultra-luxury Consumption in Later Medieval and Early Modern European Dress: Relative values of woollen textiles in the Low Countries and England, 1330 - 1570." For Session #25 of the *14th International Economic History Congress* on "Production, Consumption and the Art Market in Early Modern Europe," Helsinki, Finland, Aug. 2006.

———. "The Anti-red Shift to the 'Dark Side': Colour changes in Flemish luxury woolens, 1300-1550." In *Medieval Clothing and Textiles*, Vol. 3, Edited by Netherton and Owen-Crocker, Suffolk, UK and Rochester, NY: Boydell Press, 2007.

———. "The Rise, Expansion, and Decline of the Italian Wool-based Textile Industries, ca. 1100-1730: a study in international competition, transaction costs, and comparative advantage," Dept. of Economics, University of Toronto, 2011.

Nassar, O. and Simcha Lev-Yadum, "How prickly is a prickly pear?," *Israel Journal of Plant Science* 57, no. 1 (2009):117-124.

Nefzaoui, Ali and Hichem Ben Salam, "Forage, Fodder and Animal Nutrition," in *Cacti: Biology and Uses*, edited by Park S. Nobel, chapter 12: 199-210, University of California Press, 2002.

———. "Opuntia spp. - A strategic fodder and efficient tool to combat desertification in the WANA region," Food and Agriculture Organization of the United Nations, 2002. Available online at: www.fao.org/docrep/005/Y2808E/y2808e0d.htm (accessed Dec. 18, 2017)

"Nevis," https://en.wikipedia.org/wiki/Nevis (accessed June 8, 2017).

Newberry, Eric (Ed.), *Centenary of Progress: Dulacca, Jackson, Drillham and Districts*, souvenir history booklet, published by Dulacca Sports Ground Committee, Dulacca, Queensland, Australia, 1962.

"The New Commission of Peace," *The Sydney Gazette and New South Wales Advertiser*, Sydney, Dec. 11, 1838.

"New Food for Cactoblastis, Now Attacking Tomatoes," *The Laidley Herald*, May 3, 1930.

"New Fruit Trees," *The Western Mail*, Perth, Australia, pg. 18, May 21, 1910.

Nicholes, John, *Sailor on the Track*, ISBN: 0975224107 (undated publication).

Noller, B. and G. Parker, "Arsenic, resulting from mineralisation in surface and ground waters," *Australian Chemistry Resource Book*, edited by C. L. Fogliani, vol. 17, 1998.

"Nopal Production in Mexico," Secretariat of Agriculture, Livestock, Rural Development, Fisheries and Food (SAGARPA), Mexico City, Mexico, 2011.

"Notes of the Week: Political and Otherwise," *The Catholic Press* (Sydney), pg. 27, June 12, 1924.

Ocampo, Gilberto and J. Travis Columbus, "Molecular phylogenetics of suborder of Cactineae (Caryophyllales), including insights into photosynthetic diversification and historical biogeography," American Journal of Botany 97, no. 11 (2010: 1827-1847.

"O. C. Roberts, Ltd.," *The Brisbane Courier*, pg. 12, April 25, 1929, http://nla.gov.au/nla.news-article21399471 (accessed Jan. 31, 2013).

"On The Land," *The Gundagai Independent*, June 23, 1924.

Ogle, H. J. and J. F. Brown, "Biocontrol of Weeds Using Plant Pathogens," *Plant Pathogens and Plant Diseases*, Chapter. 21, Rockvale Publications: Australia, 1997.

"On The Land: Pear Fighters, Problems of the North-west," *The Sydney Morning Herald*, pg. 5, June 9, 1924.

"Opuntia stricta," Centre for Agricultural and Biosciences International (CABI), Invasive Species Compendium, http://www.cabi.org/isc/datasheet/37728 (accessed March 17, 2016).

Opuntia: Wikipedia, https://en.wikipedia.org/wiki/Opuntia (accessed Aug. 9, 2017).

Osmond, B., Neales, T., and Stange G., "Curiosity and context revisited: Crassulacean acid metabolism in the Anthropocene," *Journal of Experimental Biology* 59, no. 7 (2008): 1489-1502.

Oviedo y Valdés, G.F. de, *Sumario de la Natural y General Historia de las Indias*. Toledo, Spain, 1526.

Pain, Stephanie, "The Ant and the Mandarin," *New Scientist*, pgs. 46-47, April 14, 2001.

Palevitch, Dan, Gideon Earon and Israel Levin, "Treatment of Benign Protstatic Hypertrophy with *Opuntia ficus-indica* (L.) Miller," *Journal of Herbs, Spices and Medicinal Plants* 2, no. 1 (1993).

Palumbo, Barbera, Yannis Efthimiou, Jorgos Stamatopoulos, Anthony Oguogho, Alexandra Budinsky, Renalto Palumbo and Helmut Sinzinger, "Prickly pear induces upregulation of liver LDL binding in familial heterozygous hypercholesterolemia," *Nuclear Medicine Review - Central and Eastern Europe* 6, no. 1 (2003): 35-39.

Park, E. H. and M. J. Chun, "Wound healing activity of *Opuntia ficus-indica*," *Fitoterapia* 72, no. 2 (2001): 165-167.

Parliamentary Debates, Public Statutes of the 1886 Session, New South Wales Parliament, pg. 14, 1886.

Parrington, Doug, "Little Grub Puts Bite on the Green Scourge," *The Chronicle: THIS WEEKEND* (magazine supplement), Queensland, Nov. 6, 2010.

Parsons, W. T. and E. G. Cuthbertson, *Noxious Weeds of Australia*, Collingwood, Victoria, Australia: CSIRO Publishing, 2001.

"Patrol Along a Cactus Curtain," *Life Magazine*, pgs. 2-3, April 27, 1962.

Patterson. Ewen K., "A Romance of Ages," *Walkabout Magazine*, Oct. 1941.

"Pear," *The Brisbane Courier*, June 6, 1927.

"Pear Commission: Wide Powers," *The Maryborough Chronicle*, pg. 5, March 14, 1924.

"Pear Destroyers," *The Rockhampton Bulletin*, April 13, 1927.

"Pear Destruction: Uses of Arsenic, State Mine Output," *The Brisbane Courier*, Feb. 20, 1923.

"Pear Destruction: Value of Cochineal Insects," *The Maryborough Chronicle*, Feb. 2, 1926.

"Pear Destruction: Vigorous Campaign, Commission's Work," *The Maryborough Chronicle*, pg. 4, May 15, 1924.

"Pear Destruction: Work of Cactoblastis," *The Brisbane Courier*, Aug. 1, 1927.

"Pear Destruction: Work of Commission," *The Telegraph* (Brisbane), June 20, 1929.

"Pear Eradication: Valuable Work Effected by Insects," *The Maryborough Chronicle*, Sept. 28, 1926.

"Pear Eradication: Pest Under Control," *The Maryborough Chronicle*, Oct. 17, 1928.

"Pear in India: Use of Cactoblastis," *The Brisbane Courier,* July 21, 1931.

"Pear Lands: Reduction of Rents, Commission's Decisions," *Daily Mail*, Sept. 22, 1926.

"Pear Pest: Dulacca Tests, Poison and Insects, the Flame Thrower," *Brisbane Daily Mail*, Aug. 16, 1923.

"Pear Poison: Contract for Supply," The *Brisbane Courier*, Sept. 18, 1925.

"Pear Poison: St. George," *The Brisbane Courier*, March 5, 1926.

"Pear Poison: State Arsenic Supplies, *The Telegraph*, Feb. 19, 1923.

336

"Pear Problem: Commission Busy, Poison Purchases, Concessions in Prices," *The Maryborough Chronicle*, pg. 5, July 3, 1924.

"Pear Scrub Cattle," unpublished document held by Miles and Region Historical Society, Miles, Queensland, undated.

Pemberton, Robert, and Hong Liu, "Control and persistence of native *Opuntia* on Nevis and St. Kitts 50 years after the introduction of *Cactoblastis cactorum*," *Biological Control* 41 (2007): 272-282.

Perry, Janice, audio recorded interview, (Chatswood, Sydney), May 27, 2013.

"Pest-pear in Chinchilla," Rachel McFadyen, personal correspondence, March 13, 2012.

Petherbridge, David, "The Man on the Land: Queensland Cactus Pest," *The Bulletin*, Sept. 4, 1957.

"Petrol Substitute Made From Prickly Pear," *The Maryborough Chronicle*, Jan. 19, 1923.

Phillip, Arthur, *(et al)*, *The Voyage of Governor Phillip to Botany Bay With an Account of the Establishment of the Colonies of Port Jackson and Norfolk Island*, London: John Stockdale, 1789.

"Physical and Chemical Characteristics - Arsenic, Australian Drinking Water Guidelines," *National Water Quality Management Strategy*, updated December 2013.

Pincushion, (Letter to the Editor), *The Western Champion*, Barcaldine, Queensland, pg. 19, undated.

Pinkava, Donald J., *Flora of North America*, Vol. 4, Available on-line at www.efloras.org/index.aspx (accessed Oct. 22, 2011).

Pizzetti, Mariella, *Simon and Schuster's Guide to Cacti and Succulents*, New York: Simon and Schuster, 1985.

Pizzorno, Joseph E., *Textbook of Natural Medicine*, New York: Elsevier, 2012.

"Plant Wizard Dies Quietly; Kin at Side," *San Francisco Examiner*, pgs. 1 & 3, Sunday, April 11, 1926.

"Poison Action: Imported Caterpillar Effective," *The Daily Mail*, Aug. 1, 1927.

Porkobidni, "Turning a Pest Into a Profit," *The World News*, March 1, 1924.

Portillo, L. & Viueras, A.L., "Mexico before the worldwide production of cochineal," *Cactusnet Newsletter*, no. 7, Aug. 2002, http://www.cactusnet.org/pdf/issue7.pdf

Possley, J. *et al*, "Conservation Action Plan, *Opuntia corallicola*, Research Department, Fairchild Tropical Botanic Garden, Coral Gables, Florida, 2004.

"Power Alcohol: Prickly Pear Tests," *Daily Mail*, March 26, 1926.

Prance, G. & Nesbitt, M. (Editors), *"The Cultural History of Plants,"* NY & London: Routledge, 2005.

Pratt, Linda W. and Lyman L. Abbott, "Distribution and Abundance of Alien and Native Plant Species in Kaloko-Honokohau National Historic Park," Technical Report 103. Hawaii National Parks and University of Hawaii, 1996.

Preece, John E. and Gale McGranaham, "Luther Burbank's Contributions to Walnuts," *HortScience*, Vol 50(2), Pgs. 201-204, Feb. 2015.

"Prickly Pair Offensive: Where We Are and What to Do," *Daily Standard* (Brisbane), Feb. 17, 1923.

"Prickly Pear," (a) *The Sydney Morning Herald*, pg. 8, June 10, 1924.

"Prickly Pear," (b) *Evening News*, (Sydney), June 9, 1924.

"Prickly Pear," (c) Fact Sheet # PP29, Queensland Government, Sept. 2009.

"Prickly Pear," (d) *Brisbane Courier*. (clipping), undated.

"Prickly Pear," (e) Drugs.com. Available online at https://www.drugs.com/npp/prickly-pear.html (accessed Dec. 18, 2017)

"Prickly Pear and Cochineal," *The Maryborough Chronicle*, June 24, 1924.

"Prickly Pear and Their Control in Queensland," Queensland Government, (undated fact sheet).

"Prickly Pear Battle: Victory Within Sight," *The Brisbane Courier*, July 2, 1927.

"Prickly Pear Being Cleaned Up: Commission's Report," *The Daily Standard* (Brisbane), Oct. 16, 1928.

"Prickly Pear: Board of Control, Mr. Wearne's Bill," *Evening News* (Sydney), pg. 7, June 9, 1924.

"Prickly Pear: Cochineal Campaign Proceeding," *Brisbane Courier*, Nov. 24, 1926.

"Prickly Pear Control: South African Policy," *The Brisbane Courier*, Aug. 20, 1934.

"Prickly Pear Controlled: Work of the Cactoblastis," *The Telegraph*, Nov. 4, 1930.

"Prickly Pear: Control Methods," *The Daily Mail*, Feb. 14, 1923.

"Prickly Pear: Control Methods, Bacteria and Insects, Prof. Johnston's Work," *The Daily Mail* (Brisbane), pg. 8, Feb. 14, 1923.

"Prickly Pear: Cost of Elimination; Long Leases Needed; Evidence Before Commission," *The Brisbane Courier*, June 14, 1923.

"Prickly Pear Country for Selection - Destruction of Prickly Pear," *Queensland Agricultural Journal*, July 1, 1903.

"Prickly Pear Destruction," *The Queenslander*, pg. 40, Aug. 9, 1913.

"Prickly Pear: Destruction and Utilisation," *The Brisbane Courier*, Aug. 31, 1926.

"Prickly Pear: Destruction By Gas, Experiments at Dalucca," *The Maryborough Chronicle*, Jan. 10, 1913.

"Prickly Pear Destruction: Successful Experiments," *The Sydney Morning Herald*, May 15, 1919.

"Prickly Pear Elimination: Good Work by the Cactoblastis," *[Daily] Telegraph*, July 30, 1934.

"Prickly Pear Eradication," *The Brisbane Courier*, Sept. 9, 1928.

"Prickly Pear Eradication: Closing of Dulacca Experimental Station," *The Maryborough Chronicle*, pg. 8, June 17, 1916.

"Prickly Pear: Experimental Work With Insect Enemies," *Rockhampton Morning Bulletin*, Aug. 17, 1923.

"Prickly Pear (From Friday Speech by Moore)," *Brisbane Telegraph*, April 9, 1926.

"Prickly Pear: Good Eradication Work," *The Maryborough Chronicle*, pg. 3, Dec. 20, 1918.

"Prickly Pear Insect Destroyers," *The Brisbane Courier*, Sept. 13, 1923.

"Prickly Pear: How It May Be Dealt With," (Interview with Joseph H. Maiden), *The Sydney Morning Herald*, Aug. 28, 1912.

The Prickly Pear in New South Wales, Prickly Pear Destruction Commission, New South Wales, 1954.

"Prickly Pear Land: Further Decisions," *Brisbane Telegraph*, June 25, 1926.

"Prickly Pear Lands: Parliamentarians' Visit," *Northern Daily Leader*, June 10, 1924.

"The Prickly Pear Menace," (a) *Sydney Daily Telegraph*, pg. 24, June 7, 1924.

"The Prickly Pear Menace," (b) Anonymous typed document held by Miles and Region Historical Society, Jan 26, 2000.

"Prickly Pear Menace: Factors in its Control," *The Telegraph* (Brisbane), May 2, 1928.

"Prickly Pear Menace: Methods of Combating Pest," *Toowoomba Chronicle & Darling Downs Gazette*, Sept. 14, 1926.

"Prickly Pear Menace Has Disappeared From State: Minister Tells of Cactoblastis's Great Work," *The Telegraph* (Brisbane), Sept. 7, 1936.

"Prickly Pear, Nagaphana, Indian Medicinal Plant," Online at
http://www.indianetzone.com/38/prickly_pear_plant.htm
(accessed Dec. 14, 2017)

"The Prickly Pear Pest: Eradication by the Cochineal Insect," *The Maryborough
Chronicle*, pg. 6, Nov. 6, 1915.

The Prickly-pear Pest in New South Wales, Handbook published by the New
South Wales Prickly Pear Destruction Commission, Sydney, 1980.

"The Prickly Pear Pest: Organising Huge Biological Armies," *The Telegraph*
(Brisbane), Jan. 23, 1929.

"Prickly Pear Pest: Official Poisoning Results," *The Maryborough Chronicle*,
May 23, 1919.

"The Prickly Pear Pest: Queensland Campaign," *Kalgoorlie Miner* (West
Australia), pg. 1, Feb. 9, 1923.

"Prickly Pear Poison: Reduction in Price, *The Sydney Morning Herald*, pg. 9,
Aug. 10, 1928.

"Prickly Pear: Preparation as Fodder, Results of Experiments," *The Telegraph*
(Brisbane), April 25, 1929.

"Prickly Pear Problem: Destruction by Gas Effectual, Mr. A.T. Clerk interviewed,"
The Maryborough Chronicle, pg. 3, Aug. 1, 1913.

"The Prickly Pear Story," (Fact Sheet), *Queensland Dept. of Primary Industries
& Fisheries*, 2007.

"Prickly Pear: Queensland's Chief Enemy, Some Astonishing Figures," *The
Maryborough Chronicle*, pg. 2, April 18, 1916.

"Prickly Pear: Queensland's Curse, Commission's Hard Task," *The
Maryborough Chronicle*, pg. 5, April 1, 1924.

"Prickly Pear: Queensland Party, Tour of the World," *The Sydney Morning
Herald*, pg. 9, Nov. 12, 1912.

"Prickly Pear: Rangers Appointed," *The Capicornian*, June 14, 1924.

"Prickly Pear Rangers: Campaign Against the Pest," *Western Star & Roma Advertiser*,
June 14, 1924.

"The Prickly Pear: Results of Experiments, *The Maryborough Chronicle*, pg. 3,
Oct. 6, 1913.

"The Prickly Pear Story," Biosecurity Queensland Fact Sheet, Sept. 2007.

"Prickly Pear: The New Commission, New Campaign to be Started," *The Brisbane
Courier*, April 1, 1924.

"The Prickly Pear: Who Introduced It?," *The Scone Advocate*, circa 1940.

"Prickly Pears and Their Biological Control," Weed Bulletin, Biological Branch,
Queensland Dept. of Lands, Brisbane, circa 1970.

"Prince Regent," (Ship's manifest), Feb. 19, 1833.

"Professor Dies," *The Courier Mail*, Aug. 31, 1951, pg. 3.

"La Progression Du Désert Du Sahara Augmente Chaque Année?" Feb. 12,
2010. Available online at http://www.savezvousque.fr/monde/
progression-desert-sahara-augmente-annee.html (accessed Dec. 6, 2017)

"Public Laws of the United States of America Passed by the Sixty-second
Congress 1911-1913," *The Statutes at Large of the United States of
America from March 1911 to March 1913*, Vol. XXXVII, Part 1,
pages 507-508, Govt. Printing Office, Washington D.C., 1913.

Queensland Agricultural Journal, Brisbane, Australia, Aug. 1898.

"Queensland Prickly Pear Land Commission 2nd Annual Report," *Queensland Prickly
Pear Land Commission*, 1926.

"Queensland Prickly Pear Land Commission 3rd Annual Report," *Queensland Prickly Pear Land Commission*, 1927.

"Queensland Prickly Pear Land Commission 4th Annual Report," *Queensland Prickly Pear Land Commission*, 1928.

"Queensland Prickly Pear Land Commission 5th Annual Report," *Queensland Prickly Pear Land Commission*, 1929.

"Queensland Prickly Pear Land Commission 7th Annual Report, Appendix 3: Extracts from Reports of Prickly-pear Wardens," *Queensland Prickly Pear Land Commission*, 1931.

"A Queensland Triumph: Eradication of Prickly-pear Menace by Cactoblastis Insect," (loose-leaf essay written by the Prickly Pear Land Commission for a visiting journalist from the *Melbourne Herald*), Feb. 27, 1936.

Raghu, S. and Walton, C., "Understanding the Ghost of *Cactoblastis* Past: Historical Clarifications on a Poster Child of Classical Biological Control, *BioScience* 57, no. 8 (2007): 699-705.

Ramadan, M. F. and Jörg-Thomas Mörsel, "Oil cactus pear (*Opuntia ficus-indica* L.)," *Food Chemistry* 82 (2003): 339-345.

Rebman, Jon P. and Donald J. Pinkava, "Opuntia Cacti of North America: An Overview," *The Florida Entomologist*. 84, no. 4 (2001: 474-483.

———. "What has happened to Opuntia?" *San Diego Natural History Museum Field Notes, 16: 15, 2001.*

"Regulation of Prickly-pear Destruction Act of 1886," document held by the New South Wales State Library, Sydney.

Reyes-Agüero, J. A., *et al,* "Reproductive biology of Opuntia: A Review," J*ournal of Arid Environments*, 64 (2006): 549-585.

Reynolds, S.G. and Arias, E., "Agro-ecology, cultivation and uses of cactus pear," *CACTUSNET*, 2000. http://www-data.fao.org/WAICENT/FAOINFO/ AGRICULT/ AGP/AGPC/doc/publicat/Cactusnet/cactus1.htm (accessed June 8, 2010).

"Reward for Prickly Pear Destruction," Queensland Agricultural Journal, pg. 258, Nov. 1907.

"Ripley's Believe it or Not," *Sunday Mail*, March 24, 1938.

Roach, John, "2000-Year-Old Seed Sprouts, Sapling is Thriving," *National Geographic News*, http://news.nationalgeographic.com/news/051122-old-plant-seed-food/ (accessed Feb. 29, 2016).

Rojas-Aréchiga, Mariana and Carlos Vázquez-Yanes, "Cactus seed germination: a review," *Journal of Arid Environments* 44 (2000): 85-104.

Rolls, Eric C., *They All Ran Wild*, Sydney: Angus and Robertson Publishers, 1969.

Rossmanith, Kate, (article mentioning Cactoblastis memorial cairn in Dalby), *The Monthly*, no. 31, Feb. 2008.

Russell, C.E. & Peter Felker, "The Prickly Pears (*Opuntia* spp., Cactaceae): A Source of Human and Animal Food in Semi-arid Regions," *Economic Botany* 41, no. 3 (1987): 433-445.

Ryan, Gary, audio recorded interview, Tamworth, NSW, March 31, 2011.

Sáenz-Hernándes, C., J. Corrales-Garcia and G. Aquino-Pérez, "Nopalitos, Mucilage, Fiber, and Cochineal" in *Cacti Biology and Uses*, edited by Park Nobel, University of California Press, 2002.

Sallon, Sarah, Elaine Solowey, Yuval Cohen, Raia Korchinsky, Markus Egli, Ivan Woodhatch, Orit Simchoni and Mordechai Kislev, "Germination, Genetics, and Growth of an Ancient Date Seed," *Science* 320, no. 5882 (June 13, 2008): 1464.

Samuel, Edward, "Fighting the Prickly Pear," *Walkabout Magazine*, Oct. 1, 1936.

Sandars, Dorthea, "Johnston, Thomas Harvey (1881-1951), "*Australian Dictionary of Biography*, Vol. 9, Australian National University, 1983. Available online at: http://abd.anu.edu.au/biography/johnston-thomas-harvey-6862/text11887 (accessed April 2, 2012).

Sawaya, W.N., J. K. Khalil and M. M. Al-Mohammad, "Nutritive value of prickly-pear seed, *Opuntia ficus-indica*," *Plant Foods for Human Nutrition* 33, no.1 (1983): 91-97.

Schroder, Walter C., (audio recorded interview), Chinchilla, Queensland, April 19, 2013.

Schultes, R. E., "Indole Alkaloids in Plant Hallucinogens," *Planta Medica* 29, no. 4 (1976): 330-342.

Schuster, Danny, *The World of Cacti*, Facts on File Publications, New York, 1990.

"Science to Rescue: Fighting the Pear," *The Daily Mail* (Brisbane), July 9, 1927.

Seabrook, Leonie and Clive McAlpine, *Queensland Historical Atlas*, Available online at: http://www.qhatlas.com.au/content/prickly-pear (accessed April 15, 2012).

Seagee, "The Rainbow Trail," *Rockhampton Morning Bulletin*, Aug. 7, 1924.

"Seed Longevity," pdf publication, Board of Trustees of the Royal Botanic Gardens, Kew, England, 38 pages, undated.

Shen-Miller, J., Mary Beth Mudgett, J. William Schopf, Steven Clarke and Rainer Berger, "Exceptional seed longevity and robust growth: Ancient Sacred Lotus from China," *American Journal of Botany* 82, no. 11 (1995): 1367-1380.

Shulgin, Alexander T., "Possible Implication of Myristicin as a Psychotropic Substance," *Nature* 210, no. 5034 (April 23, 1966): 380-384.

"The Silent Workers: Queensland's Fight With the Pear," *Dalby Herald*, June 6, 1924.

Simberloff, D. and Peter Stiling, "How risky is biological control?" *Ecology* 77, no. 7 (1996): 1965-1974.

——. "Risks of Species Introduced for Biological Control," *Biological Conservation* 78 (1996): 185-192.

Simonsen, *et al*, "Tracing an Invasion: Phylogeography of *Cactoblastis cactorum* (Lepidoptera: Pyralidae) in the United States Based on Mitochondrial DNA," *Annals of the Entomological Society of America* 101, no. 5 (2008): 899-905.

"The Singeing Move," *The Maryborough Chronicle*," pg. 3, Friday, Aug. 1, 1913.

Singh, S. P., "Some success stories in classical biological control of agricultural pests in India," *APAARI* publication: 2004/2, 72 pgs, 2004.

Sir Joseph Banks and the Royal Society, John W. Parker, Publisher, London, 1844.

Smith, Edward, *The Life of Sir Joseph Banks*, John Lane, Publisher, London & New York, 1911.

Smith, F. and L. A. Meston, "The composition of the oil of prickly-pear seed (*Opuntia* spp.)," *Proceeding of the Royal Society of Queensland*, Brisbane, Australia, Vol. XXVI, 1914.

Smith, Jane S., "Luther Burbank's Spineless Cactus: Boom times in the Californian desert," The Free Library, http://www.thefreelibrary.com/Luther+Burbank%27s+spineless +cactus%3a+boom+ times+in+the+california...-a0241514985. Published Sept. 1, 2010 (accessed July 10, 2011).

Socha, Aaron M., "From Areoles to Zygocactus: An Evolutionary Masterpiece," *New York Botanical Garden Webpage*, http://www.nybg.org/bsci/herb/ cactaceae1.html#Introduction#Introduction (accessed Jan. 20, 2011).

Solis, M. Alma, Stephen D. Hight, and Doria R. Gordon, "Tracking the Cactus Moth *Cactoblastis cactorum* Berg., as it flies and eats its way westward in the U.S.," *News of the Lepidopterist's Society* 46, no. 1 (Spring 2004).

"S. O. S.: Prickly Pear Eradication," *Brisbane Courier*, May 4, 1927.

"S. O. S. Prickly Pear Poison," *Brisbane Courier*, Feb. 3, 1927.

"S. O. S.: War on Prickly Pear," *Daily Standard*, April 31, 1927.

"Status of Semaphore Cactus on Swan Key," *The Nature Conservancy*, 2012.

"A Star: Mr. Cactoblastis," *Sydney Sun*, October 26, 1933.

Steele, B. D., *"Report of the Royal Commission appointed to inquire into certain matters relating to the prickly pear problem*, Brisbane, Australia: Govt. Printer, 1923.

Stelljes, Kathyrn B., "ARS foreign biological control laboratories: gateways to domestic weeds control," *Agricultural Research*, pg. 7, March 2000.

Stiling, Peter, "Death and Decline of a Rare Cactus in Florida," *Cactanea* (Southern Appalachian Botanical Society)75, no.2 (2010): 190-197.

Stiling, Peter and Moon, Daniel C., "Protecting Rare Florida Cacti From Attack by the Exotic Cactus Moth, *Cactoblastis cactorum* (Lepidoptera: Pyralidae), *Florida Entomologist* 84, no. 4, (Dec. 2001).

Stiling, Peter, Daniel Moon and G. Gordon, "Endangered Cactus Restoration: Mitigating the Non-target Effects of a Biological Control Agent (*Cactoblastis cactorum*) in Florida," *Restoration Ecology* 12, no. 4 (Nov. 30, 2004).

Tanner, Les, (audio recorded interview), Bingara, New South Wales, Feb. 21, 2013.

"The Taroom District: Prickly-pear Pest," by W. H. T., *Brisbane Courier*, March 9, 1923.

Teale, Ruth, "William Macarthur," *Australian Dictionary of Biography*, Vol. 5, 1974.

Tesoriere, L., D. Butera, A. M. Pintaudi, M. Allegra and M. A. Livrea, "Supplementation with cactus pear (*Opuntia ficus-indica*) fruit decreases oxidative stress in healthy humans: a comparitive study with vitamin C," *The American Journal of Clinical Nutrition* 80, no. 2 (2004): 391-395.

Theodori, D. Jacobi, *Book of Herbs*, 1588.

Thiery de Menonville, Nicolas-Joseph, "Travels to Guaxaca [1777]." In *Best and Most Interesting Voyages and Travels in all Parts of the World*," edited by John Pinkerton, chapter 13:753-876, London, 1812.

Thomas, Lowell, *Sir Hubert Wilkins: His World of Adventure*, McGraw-Hill: New York, 1961.

"The Thornless Cactus," *The Sydney Morning Herald*, pg. 4, Dec. 26, 1912.

"To Cost Less: Cactoblastis eggs," *The Daily Mail* (Brisbane), June 21, 1929.

Tongs, Val, "Pear Wars," *Australasian Post*, Feb. 19, 1987.

"Top Ten Amazing Facts About Cactus," http://cactus-guide.com/tag/cactus-species/ (accessed July 14, 2012).

"Town Progress: Buildings Being Erected, Faith in Chinchilla's Future," *The Chinchilla News*, May 5, 1933.

Trejo-González, A., G. Gabriel-Ortiz, A. M. Puebla-Pérez, M. D. Huízar-Contreras, M. R. Munquía-Mazariegos, S. Mejia-Arreguin and E. Calva, "A purified extract from prickly pear cactus (*Opuntia fuliginosa*) control experimentally induced diabetes in rats," *Journal of Ethnopharmacology* 55, no. 1 (1996): 27-33.

Trombetta, D., C. Puglia, D. Perri, A. Licata, S. Pergolizzi, E. R. Lauriano, A. De Pasquale, A. Saija and F. P. Bonina, "Effect of polysaccharides from *Opuntia ficus-indica* (L.) cladodes on the healing of dermal wounds in the rat," *Phytomedicine* 13, no. 5 (2006): 352-358.

Tyler, Laura, "Watch for the Cactus Moth," *The Cattleman*, pgs. 10-22, April 2006.

Uebergang, Tim, "Future Pollen," *Cactus and Succulent Journal*," 81, no. 6 (2009): 290-293.

Ueckert, Darrell N., "Pricklypear Ecology," *Texas Agrilife Research and Extension Center*, online paper. http: texnat.tamu.edu/library/symposia/brush-sculptors-innovations-for-tailoring-brushy-rangelands-to-enhance-wildlife-habitat-and-recreational-value/pricklypear-ecology/ (accessed Feb. 29, 2016).

Ulm, Clarence, (personal correspondence), Chinchilla, QLD, January 2013.
United States Patent 5736584, Available online at http://www.google.com/patents/US5736584 (accessed Dec. 15, 2017)

"Use Cactoblastis: Africa to Test on Pear," *The Daily Mail* (Brisbane), May 20 1929.

Vail, P. V., J. R. Coulson, W. C. Kauffmann, and M. E. Dix, "History of Biological Control Programs in the United States Department of Agriculture," *American Entomologist* 47, no. 1 (Spring 2001).

Van Driesche, J. and R. Van Driesche, "Weighing Urgency Against Uncertainty: The Conundrum of Biocontrol," *Conservation Magazine* 4, no. 2 (2003).

Varidel, Bill, "Memories of the Prickly Pear Days," unpublished M/S held by Chinchilla Historical Museum, Chinchilla, QLD, undated.

Varone, Laura, Guillermo Logarzo, Juan José Martínez, Fernando Navarro, James E. Carpenter, and Stephen D. Hight, "Field host range of *Apanteles opuntiarum* (Hymenoptera: Braconidae) in Argentina, a potential biocontrol agent of *Cactoblastis cactorum* (Lepidoptera: Pyralidae) in North America," *Florida Entomologist* 98, no. 2 (2015).

Vázquez-Ramirez, R., M. Olguin-Martinez, C. Kubli-Garfias and R. Hernádez-Muñoz, "Reversing gastric mucosal alterations during ethanol-induced chronic gastritis in rats by oral administration of Opuntia ficus-indica mucilage," *World Journal of Gastroenterology* 12, no. 27 (2006): 4318-4324.

"Views of the Authorities, A reported attack on tomatoes," *The Brisbane Courier*, May 6, 1930.

Wallace, Robert S. and Arthur C. Gibson, "Evolution and Systematics," in *Cacti: Biology and Uses*, edited by Park S. Nobel, Chapter 1: 1-21, University of California Press, 2002.

Walters, M., E. Figueiedo, N.R. Crouch, P.J.D. Winter, G.F. Smith, H.G. Zimmermann and B.K. Mashope, "Naturalised and invasive succulents of southern Africa," *ABC Taxa*, Belgium Development Corp. [www.abctaxa.be], Vol 11, 2011.

Walton, Craig, *Reclaiming Lost Provinces: a century of weed biological control in Queensland*, Brisbane, Australia: Queensland Dept. of Natural Resources and Mines, 2005.

———. (audio recorded interview), Brisbane, Queensland, Australia, April 24, 2013.

Wearne, John T., *Bingara 1827 - 1937*, Bingara Historical Society, undated.

"Weeds," *Australian Government Biodiversity Website*, http://www.environment.gov.au/biodiversity/invasive/weeds/weeds/why/index.html (accessed March 17, 2016).

"Weeds of National Significance: Strategic Plan: Opuntioid cacti," *Australian Weeds Committee*, Canberra, Australia, 2012.

Wickson, Edward J., "Luther Burbank: Man, Methods, and Achievements," Reprinted from *Sunset Magazine*, published by Southern Pacific Company, San Francisco, circa 1902.

"Wilkins, Sir George Hubert," http://adb.anu.edu.au/biography/wilkins-sir-george-hubert (accessed Sept. 11, 2016).

343

Wilson, Michael, "Medicinal Plant Fact Sheet: Opuntia: Prickly Pear Cactus,"
    IUCN and North American Pollinator Protection Campaign, Oct. 2007.
White, Charles, *Convict Life in New South Wales and Van Dieman's Land*,
    Bathhurst, NSW, Australia: Free Press, 1889.
White, Jean, "Prickly Pear Experimental Station, Dulacca: Reports up to 30th June,
    1913," Brisbane, Australia, 1913.
——. "Prickly Pear Experimental Station, Dulacca: Report from 1 July, 1913 to 30
    April, 1914," Brisbane, Australia, 1914.
White-Haney, Jean, "Prickly Pear Experimental Station, Dulacca: Report from 1 May,
    1915 to 30 June, 1916," Brisbane, Australia, 1916.
"Why Burbank Has Become Peevish About Government's Cactus Work," *Chico Record*,
    Chico California, July 22, 1911.
"Wilfred Backhouse Alexander," *Wikipedia*,
    https://en.wikipedia.org/wiki/Wilfred_Backhouse_Alexander
    (accessed April 13, 2017).
Wilson, Michael, "Medicinal Plant Fact Sheet: *Opuntia*: Prickly Pear Cactus," Published
    by IUCN and North American Pollinator Protection Campaign, Oct. 2007.
Wiese, J., S. McPherson, M. C. Odden and M. G. Shlipak, "Effect on Opuntia
    ficus-indica on symptoms of the alcohol hangover," *Archives of Internal
    Medicine* 164, no. 12 (2004): 1334-1340.
"With the Bug: Politician's Day, Paying Expenses!," *Evening News* (Sydney),
    pg. 6, June 7, 1924.
Wolski, Ian and Don, (audio recording of interview), Chinchilla district, Queensland,
    Australia, March 3, 2012.
"Wood Energy," Food and Agriculture Organization of the United Nations.
    Available online at: http:www.fao.org/forestry/energy/en/
    (accessed Dec. 6, 2017)
Yashina, Svetlana, Stanislav Gubin, Stanislav Maksimovich, Alexandra Yashina, Edith
    Gakhova, and David Gilichinsky, "Regeneration of whole fertile plants from
    30,000-y-old fruit tissue buried in Siberian permafrost," *Proceedings of the
    National Academy of Sciences USA* 109, no. 10 (March 6, 2012): 4008-4013.
Zehnyu, Li and Nigel P. Taylor, (Wu, Raven, & Hong, Eds) "Cactaceae," *Flora of
    China*, 13:209-212, Beijing: Science Press and St. Louis: Missouri
    Botanical Gardens, 2007.
Zimmermann, H. G., V. C. Moran and J. H. Hoffmann, "The Renowned Cactus Moth,
    Cactoblastis cactorum (Lepidoptera: Pyralidae): Its Natural History and
    Threat to Native *Opuntia* Floras in Mexico and the United States of America,"
    Florida Entomologist 84, no. 4 (Dec. 2001).
Zimmermann, H. and Granata, G. "Insect Pest and Diseases," in *Cacti Biology and
    Uses*, Park Nobel (Editor), University of California, 2002.
Zimmermann, H., S. Bloem and H. Klein, "Biology, History, Threat, Surveillance and
    Control of the Cactus Moth, *Cactoblastis cactorum*," (ISBN 92-0-108304-1)
    Vienna, Austria: International Atomic Energy Association, June 2004.

Index

345

346

348

Sri Lanka, 138, 169, 173, 231
Steele, Bertram, 136
sterile insect techinque, 241-243, 245
Stiling, Peter, 256
synthetic dye, 51-52
tall tales, 127, 128
Tetranychus opuntiae, 188-189
Texas ranchers, 237-238, 239-240
Thiery de Menonville, 22-31, 37, 38
Tiger pear, 74, 286, 290
Tongs, Val, 156
Traveling Commission, 136, 138, 168-171,
265
Trichilogaster acaciaelongifolia, 258
Tryon, Henry, 167-168, 169-170, 172, 175
Tucumania tapiacola, 290
tunas, 244, 269-271
Tunisia, 282
Ulm, Clarence, 214
Ulvalde, Texas, 184, 198-199, 202, 204
urine turning red-colored, 268
USDA Agriculture Research Service, 229,
244-245, 246, 247, 250
Varidel, Bill, 154
Varone, Laura, 250, 253, 254
Walton, Craig, 224
Wardian case, 184-185, 201
water purification, 279-280
Wearne, Walter "Ziff", 150, 157-158
weeds (definitions), II, 1, 75, 76, 77, 111,
114, 263, 284
Welsh, Charles, 96
Wheel cactus, 75, 109, 272, 278, 286
White-Haney, Dr. Jean, 137-138, 140, 141,
143-144, 145, 146, 169, 171
Wilkins, Sir Hubert, 125-126
World War I, 116, 141, 146, 156, 171, 173,
195, 197, 265

349